Charles Kingsley

BRENDA COLLOMS

Charles Kingsley

THE LION OF EVERSLEY

CONSTABLE *London*

BARNES & NOBLE *New York*

First published in Great Britain 1975
by Constable & Company Ltd
10 Orange Street London WC2H 7EG
Copyright © by Brenda Colloms 1975

ISBN 0 09 460020 1
ISBN 0 06 491269 8 (U.S.A.)

Set in Monotype Bembo
Printed in Great Britain by
Ebenezer Baylis and Son Ltd
The Trinity Press
Worcester and London

For my husband

LIONEL COLLOMS

Contents

Illustrations

Acknowledgements

A hundred years have passed since the death of Charles Kingsley, and it seems right to appraise the man after this interval of time. I have sought in this biography to clarify and assess the influence of his ideas, actions and writings upon the social and political movements of his day, and to pay tribute to what we also owe to him.

I have met with great assistance, interest and co-operation from more people than I can mention individually, but I would like to give thanks in particular to Mr. David Muspratt and Mr. Sidney Marks of the Working Men's College, London; to the Rt. Hon. Harold Macmillan; to Mr. E. G. Williams of Chester; to the Rector of Eversley, Hampshire; to the staffs of the Dr. Williams Library, London; University of London Library; the National Library of Scotland; Chester Public Library and Bideford Public Library; and finally, to my husband for the support and understanding he showed during the writing of this book.

1

Background Influences

Rebels and prophets often succeed in communicating their ideas
to their descendants whilst those who typify their own day are
usually rewarded in their lifetime but undervalued or misunderstood by succeeding generations. We look at the past through a
distorting mirror, and the more recent the past the more unreliable
our view. Many Victorian polymaths who created a furore in
their own society seem almost incredibly naïve and fulminating
to ours, and we are unjust to them. Such a victim has been Charles
Kingsley, one of the foremost of the Victorian 'forgotten
worthies'; a minor but none the less genuine poet; a major
reformer; a compulsive talker; and a thorn in the flesh of the
Establishment for a quarter of a century.

To most people, Kingsley is probably merely 'the *Water
Babies* man'. To the casual reader, he may be the Anglican
clergyman who got the worst of an argument with Dr. Newman.
To the student of Victorian literature he recalls the 'Muscular
Christian' who provided such malicious merriment for study-
bound agnostics. But to accept any of these facile judgments is
to be satisfied with a pasteboard effigy of a man who in life was
passionately flesh and blood, endowed with the gift of eloquence,
and strengthened by the trustful optimism of so many early
Victorians, although—again, like them—he alternated between
intense elation and tortured depression. Kingsley shared many
characteristics of middle-class Victorians. He believed in a stable
monarchy, a responsible aristocracy, a compassionate Established
Church, the English way of life and British Protestant virtues.
But he was ahead of his time in other respects, and earned profound hatred for his violently expressed views.

Although a fighter for social justice in the Puritan tradition, he was temperamentally more a Romantic than a Puritan, and a product of the Romantic revival. He was easily moved to impulsive gestures, thrilled equally by the beauties of nature and the discoveries of science; angry at the inhuman results of the agrarian and industrial revolutions, and sickened by the slothful callousness of people who should have known better. He could sympathise with the anxieties and satisfactions of ordinary folk and he won their devotion by his plain speaking on subjects close to their hearts. He had an especial charm and appeal for women, whilst men were drawn by his earnestness and generous nature.[1] In spite of a bad stammer, he was an amusing and lively conversationalist. Some of his close friends might occasionally grumble because he always worked himself up into a 'stringent excitement' over whatever affair claimed his attention at that moment, and he was certainly not always the easiest of men to get on with, but he had no personal enemies, and he corresponded with a vast circle of acquaintances.

Three people had an immeasurable effect on his thought and actions: his mother, his wife, and the Rev. F. D. Maurice. With their help and encouragement he was able to formulate a simple, even an oversimple, religious faith which saw him through bouts of wretchedness. Thus he was strengthened for what he considered a true mission—to change men's hearts so that the evils of capitalism and intolerance could be banished within the existing social structure of English society, for in this way Britain would come closer to the kingdom of God on earth.

The Kingsleys were of sound country stock, claiming descent from Anglo-Saxon England, a proud claim which slightly compensated for their subsequent impoverishment. The family could certainly be traced back to a Rannulph de Kingsley, a twelfth-century gentleman, and to the Kingsleys of Delamere Forest in Cheshire. A more illustrious family connection, by marriage of later date, was Archbishop Abbot in King James I's reign. Another Kingsley crossed the Atlantic to New England soon after the *Mayflower* Pilgrims, and a Kingsley fought on the Parliamentary side at Naseby and at Marston Moor. During the Seven Years'

War, a General William Kingsley fought the French at the battle of Minden.

Charles Kingsley's father (another Charles) was born at Battramsley House in the New Forest, Hampshire, in 1781, and was orphaned when a schoolboy. His modest inheritance was badly handled by guardians, so that when the young man came of age his money was almost totally gone. His education at Harrow and Oxford had given him merely the normal schooling of a country gentleman, and he had not even troubled to take a degree. He possessed the sporting tastes and cultivated mind of an eighteenth-century squire, none of which fitted him for any profession. In his mid-twenties he married Mary Lucas, a girl born in the West Indies but educated in England. Her father, Judge Nathaniel Lucas, came of a line of sugar plantation owners in Barbados, and when the West Indian sugar trade declined the judge retired to Norfolk, England. His lively young daughter had the run of his well-stocked library and was allowed to sharpen her wits in the company of their frequent guests. The Lucases enjoyed a full and interesting social life.[2] Mary Lucas was a suitable match for her cultivated and intelligent husband, and it was to be hoped that in due course she would inherit money from the Barbados interests.

The bridegroom's choice of career was severely limited. He was too old and impecunious to succeed as an army officer. He was unfitted for trade or business, and did not own sufficient land to support a family as a gentleman farmer. Only the Church remained, with the added argument in its favour that, since he knew several wealthy landowners who had livings to dispose of, it was not unreasonable to hope that once he had been ordained some friend or acquaintance would offer him a living. Accordingly, he went to Cambridge to read for holy orders.

At the beginning of the nineteenth century it was not considered essential for a man to have a religious vocation in order to become an Anglican clergyman. The performance of his parish duties could be practically as elastic as he wished. If he spent most of his time hunting and fishing, or devoted himself to some absorbing hobby, nobody thought much the less of him. Few

considered it seriously amiss if a parson held several livings at the
same time and attended adequately to none. This picture did not,
of course, hold good everywhere. The country had many representatives of respected and conscientious parish priests. On the
whole, however, the Anglican clergyman was considered by the
poorer classes in town and country to be a member of the upper
and governing classes, rather than a man with a calling.

In the event, Charles Kingsley senior did not receive much help
from his friends in the matter of clerical advancement. His first
appointment was as a curate at Holne, on the edge of Dartmoor,
in Devonshire, where Charles, the eldest child, was born.[3] Both
parents were already in their thirties: Mary Kingsley about
thirty-three, and her husband some five years older. The baby was
delicate, and his mother fussed and cosseted him. Born on June
12 1819 (the same year as Queen Victoria, George Eliot and John
Ruskin, and only a few months after Karl Marx), the child entered
a world where traditional values had been either overthrown or at
the very least seriously questioned as a result of the French
Revolution and the Napoleonic Wars. Britain was suffering
from unemployment and inflation, and there were vociferous
demands for parliamentary and social reform. Popular agitation
was unparalleled. In such a politically charged atmosphere,
William Cobbett deemed it safe to terminate his self-imposed
exile in the United States and accordingly returned, reverently
bearing with him the bones of Tom Paine, the radical democrat.
Parliament was compelled to pass legislation incorporating some
of Robert Owen's suggestions for regulations in cotton mills.
Significantly, too, 1819 was the year of the Peterloo Massacre in
Manchester, where a huge demonstration for parliamentary re-
form was broken up by a brutal charge of the Manchester
Yeomanry.

From an early age, the boy Charles Kingsley believed that he
was especially marked out as different from other children—a
belief that his mother seems to have fostered. Charles was always
convinced that the stresses of adolescence affected him more
poignantly than they did other boys. He regarded the dreams and
nightmares which beguiled or terrified him throughout life as

another sign of this difference, and similarly the strain of sadness and melancholy which was never far away. He could confess most of this to his mother, with whom he shared a close bond, but not to his father, who never seems to have had an intimate relationship with any of his children after they outgrew childhood.

He was to adopt his father's profession, although not for the same reason, and the Church which young Charles Kingsley joined in 1842 was far different from the institution his father had joined, for after a generation of apathy and decline the Church of England had been revitalised by controversial reappraisals. In the eighteenth century, the Church had been very much another arm of the State, but now, as post-Napoleonic Europe was gripped by a wave of Romanticism, spiritual values acquired fresh meaning in contrast to eighteenth-century rationalism. Religion became a subject of deep consideration and debate at Oxford, with repercussions which spread far outside the university. The Romantic revival was teaching people to trust their eyes and heart in reaction to the intellectual disengagement of the previous century, and it was no longer possible to disregard stupidity and degradation. Scott's novels imparted a glow to history, encouraging a new perspective which, when applied to religion, led to a desire for a purer, possibly a more scientific, view of man's place in the ultimate scheme of things. Samuel Taylor Coleridge, poet and philosopher, preached a reverence for life, proclaiming that only the man who loved all living creatures could truly pray to God. Orators, agitators, campaigners on social or political matters, authors, poets, preachers, all began to acquire one enviable ability: that of communicating directly with their audiences, either by the spoken or the written word.

Charles Kingsley grew up to be a man of action and a man of science as well as a clergyman. Like many public-spirited Victorians, he never spared himself, but engaged in so many activities simultaneously that his health often broke. He was frequently pained and surprised by the vehement criticism levelled at him, and in these moments of great tension found emotional release in poetry. His finest lyrics sprang from his worst experiences.

Kingsley never pretended to be an original theologian, taking his philosophy and ideas of God almost unaltered from F. D. Maurice.[4] He undoubtedly believed that one of his missions was to popularise Maurice's wisdom by paraphrasing it in comprehensible language. Maurice himself greatly appreciated the value of this undertaking, and often suggested points which he hoped Kingsley could explain more simply in his novels and sermons. When Maurice was attacked by the conservative wing of the Church of England on grounds of supposed heresy, Kingsley suffered by guilt through association. Similarly, when men of property who had been mortally offended by Kingsley's avowal of Chartist sympathies in 1848 classed him as a dangerous revolutionary, Maurice suffered because of his friendship with Kingsley. Both men maintained an antagonistic attitude to the Papacy. Maurice believed that the only real Catholic Church was the Protestant one wherein a people could 'come to nationhood under the laws and beliefs that stemmed naturally from recognition of the Righteousness of God'. Since the end of the Napoleonic Wars, Europe had been governed by repressive rulers, especially in countries where the Roman Catholic Church was dominant. In the 1840s German aspirations of nationhood still went unfulfilled; Italy was a 'geographical expression'. Maurice concluded that inasmuch as the Papacy sought to repress the natural aspirations of nationalism, and tried 'to impose a universal system on peoples in an unnatural way', so must the Roman Church have departed from God's true plan which unquestionably meant justice and rights for all. A Roman Catholic nation, thought Maurice, 'must be a God-denying nation, because the Pope *to* the nation is God'.[5]

Kingsley agreed ardently with this conclusion, no matter which century was under examination. He considered that the roots of English culture were to be found in the Elizabethan age and in the English Protestant victories against Catholic Spain in that age. In addition, and this was a vitally important addition, his intense preoccupation with the matter of celibacy made him oppose the Catholic Church, which he took to advocate celibacy as a higher form of life than marriage. An exceptionally happy married life made him a fervent apostle of what he called the 'delicious pleasures' of that state, and using his 'commonsense of the heart', Kingsley advanced the attractive theory that anything good must come from God; anything bad was not of God's making. Kingsley's tendency to harp on the theme of married love often irritated the more ascetic members of the English intelligentsia, as well as alarming those Victorians who were unaccustomed to outspoken remarks on the subject. Indeed, some highly placed Anglican officials found him suspect more on account of his supposed sensuality than for his supposed revolutionary opinions. It is ironical that a century after his death the belief that a married clergy is as fit or even better equipped to deal with pastoral matters than a celibate clergy is echoed by many priests today, even in the Roman Catholic Church.

Kingsley constantly adopted unconventional causes. He praised John Stuart Mill's book, *The Subjection of Women*, and in 1869 argued ably for the extension of the franchise to women. Loving the out-of-doors, he once scandalised a friend by saying that cathedrals copied the design of great forests and God was better worshipped in a forest than in a church. He followed eagerly the latest developments in geology and the natural sciences. He was keenly alive to the danger that urban man would pollute the world he lived in, and he frequently lectured on the subject. Indeed, his final great campaign was sanitary reform, which he declared would be more immediately beneficial to the population than parliamentary reform, or at least until the general population was sufficiently educated to make the right use of parliamentary reform.

By temperament and experience he was an old-fashioned Radical Tory. He criticised the Whig Party in its long years of office for protecting the capitalists who, as he saw them, cared only to increase their profits. On the other hand, a properly educated and responsible Tory aristocracy, he argued, would take its rightful place in a just scheme of society. He mistrusted democracy as a system of government, and thought that the failure of the Working Men's Associations, which he and the other Christian Socialists promoted, was due to the lack of education among working men, a lack which Kingsley reckoned would take two generations to overcome. For this reason he welcomed the foundation by the Christian Socialists of the Working Men's College in London in 1854, regretting that his duties in Eversley and the time taken by writing prevented his going regularly to London to teach there.

He was therefore a radical only in the sense that he wanted radical changes in men's hearts and actions. Socialism, as he and other Christian Socialists defined it, was not only compatible with the picture of society as Christ intended it, but was indeed the very essence of that society. Maurice and his followers wished to Christianise Socialism, to fight 'the unsocial Christians and the unchristian Socialists.' Failure would produce a society where relationships between people would be governed almost exclusively by the profit motive.[6] Nor did the middle classes offer greater hope, for many of their members were trying to apply scientific methods of proof to divinity, and were turning to humanism as a substitute for religion. Kingsley responded positively to the doctrine of evolution suggested by Charles Darwin, proclaiming that the new men of science could remain men of religion also. Indeed, he did not repudiate earnest agnostics who followed the moral teachings of Christ without being able to subscribe to a formal Christian faith.

It has been said of Kingsley, by way of criticism, that although he began his public life as a campaigner for the socialist cause he abandoned this in later years to become a pillar of the very Establishment which he had attacked so forcefully as a young man. This, however, is to miss the point through not understanding the kind of 'socialism' which he advocated. Also, like many successful campaigners, Kingsley was largely overtaken by the changes which he had laboured to produce, so that his criticisms became less outspoken as social conditions improved. Another frequent criticism, that of racism and prejudice against non-whites, is better founded, although in his defence it should be said that these were prejudices held by the vast majority of his countrymen at that time, and in his last years, under the enlightened tutelage of Arthur Gordon, his views became more liberal. In the matter of Ireland, in the controversies over Rajah

Brooke of Sarawak and Governor Eyre of Jamaica, he stood well to the right of the liberal groups. His loyalty and patriotism, rather threadbare concepts in our materialist and opportunist world, still had distinct appeal in the mid-nineteenth century.

Loyalty, one might ask, to whom and to what? Kingsley would never have been at a loss for an answer. Loyalty first and last to God's will—by which he meant to a good, loving and rational system of human relationships and government. Kingsley's great attraction for the thousands who followed his sermons, his lectures, and read his novels, was that he provided a practical and decent set of opinions and attitudes which would fit almost every possible contingency. Like a number of English reformers from the eighteenth century onwards, Kingsley stood both farther to the left and farther to the right than did similar figures in the reform movements of the Continent. These contradictory trends combined to form a powerful mental brake which prevented him from demanding the destruction of existing society, although at the same time they forced him to exert every effort to change it. Thus he was opposed by atheists like Holyoake, because Kingsley preached gradual change within society under God's law, and simultaneously he was vigorously opposed by the manufacturing class because of his constant attacks upon capitalism.

As a man of letters, Kingsley must stand in the forefront of propaganda writers. Immensely popular and widely read, both in his lifetime and afterwards during the era of cheap reprints, he opened the eyes of at least two generations to social problems and abuses. Had his financial circumstances been easier, it is probable that he would have devoted most of his time to poetry and science —if the warrior in him would have permitted it, for there is no doubt that his first instinct was to dash headlong into a battle. In spite of this belligerency, he was greatly loved. His friends ranged from Chartists to dukes, from monarchs to gypsies, from scientists to soldiers. At his death his widow was comforted by an immense number of sympathetic letters. He could have been buried in Westminster Abbey, but Fanny Kingsley, faithful to his wishes, saw that he was buried in Eversley churchyard, so that he died as he was proud to have lived, a country parson.

2

A Country Childhood

Two weeks after Kingsley's birth, his parents left Holne, and for the next five years moved from one temporary country curacy to another: an unsatisfactory and impecunious state of affairs. The close bond between mother and eldest son slackened when a second son, Herbert, was born at Burton-on-Trent in 1820, and then a third son, Gerald, in 1821 at North Clifton, near Nottingham. A daughter was also born at North Clifton, but she died in infancy. Young Charles accepted the birth of his brother Herbert philosophically, and they became close companions, but it was quite another matter when Gerald was born. Charles deeply resented the claims which the newest baby made upon his mother, and disliked having to play with him.

In 1824 the Rev. Charles Kingsley's meagre fortunes improved through the good offices of his former Cambridge professor, Dr. Marsh, then Bishop of Peterborough, in the Fen district of Lincolnshire. The bishop offered Mr. Kingsley the best living in his diocese—the rectorship of Barnack, near Stamford—on the express condition that when the bishop's schoolboy son had taken his degree and been ordained, Kingsley would vacate Barnack in favour of young Marsh. Although this was yet another temporary appointment, at least the family would be in comfortable circumstances for several years and Mr. Kingsley did not hesitate to accept it. Barnack Rectory, partly fourteenth century with a reputed ghost called 'Button Cap', was young Charles's home from his fifth to his eleventh year, and there the rest of the family was born: George Henry in 1826, Charlotte in 1828, Henry in 1830.

Charles was prone to sudden collapses from nervous excitement, called in those days 'brain fever'. He also had a weak chest and frequently developed croup in the winter. Mrs. Kingsley, though a loving mother, does not seem to have been very imaginative, for on at least one occasion when Charles was ill she isolated him from the other children by putting him to sleep in 'Button Cap's room', where the ghost was supposed to walk and where Charles awakened in the night, understandably tormented by nightmares and fantasies of ghosts.

All his life Charles Kingsley was a victim of dreams and nightmares, and he included accounts of them in his novels, even in the face of critical opposition, insisting that they had a true place in his books because they were experiences drawn from life.[1] Unquestionably, Kingsley's best 'dreamland' sequence is the passage in *Alton Locke* where the hero-narrator is delirious from cholera. The chapter is a series of hallucinatory pictures— quite remarkable coming from the pen of a young Victorian clergyman in the late eighteen-forties.

I was in a raging fever. And my fancy, long pent-up and crushed by circumstances, burst out in uncontrollable wildness, and swept my other faculties with it helpless away over all heaven and earth, presenting to me, as in a vast kaleidoscope, fantastic symbols of all I had ever thought, or read, or felt.

That fancy of the mountain returned; but I had climbed it now. I was wandering along the lower ridge of the Himalaya. . . . Above me was a Hindoo temple, cut out of the yellow sandstone. I climbed up to the higher tier of pillars, among monstrous shapes of gods and fiends, that mouthed and writhed and mocked at me, struggling to free themselves from their bed of rock. The bull Nundi rose and tried to gore me; hundred-handed gods brandished quoits and sabres round my head; and Kali dropped the skull from her gore-dripping jaws, to clutch me for her prey. Then my mother came, and seizing the pillars of the portico, bent them like reeds; an earthquake shook the hills—great sheets of woodland slid roaring and crashing into the valleys—a tornado swept through the temple halls, which rocked and tossed like a vessel

in a storm; a crash—a cloud of yellow dust which filled the air
—choked me—blinded me—buried me.

And Eleanor came by, and took my soul in the palm of her
hand, as the angels did Faust's, and carried it to a cavern by the
seaside, and dropped it in; and I fell and fell for ages ... and I
was in darkness, and turned again to my dust.

And I was at the lowest point of created life; a madrepore
rooted to the rock, fathoms below the tide-mark; and worst
of all, my individuality was gone. I was not one thing, but
many things—a crowd of innumerable polypi; and I grew and
grew, and the more I grew the more I divided, and multiplied
thousand and ten-thousand fold. If I could have thought, I
should have gone mad at it; but I could only feel.[2]

Whatever Charles Kingsley as a child may have believed about
Button Cap, as an adult he denied him. Writing in 1864 to his
niece, Mrs. Pelham, he commented drily: 'Everybody heard
him who chose. Nobody ever saw him.' As he remembered, the
ghost had been an unlovable rector, whose haunting was somehow connected with avarice and hoarded money. He was sure
the ghost would have departed by 1864, as 'ghosts only stay
where they are believed in!'

Family anecdotes from Barnack days reveal young Charles
as impatient and highly strung: qualities which he never outgrew.
From the age of four he composed poems and sermons, perhaps
not an outstanding feat when John Stuart Mill was learning Greek
at three. Charles enjoyed imitating his father, and the nursery
furniture was pushed back to represent a church and congregation, whilst the young preacher turned his pinafore back to front,
and gave 'little addresses of a rather severe tone of theology',
such as 'Religion is reading good books, doing good actions, and
not telling lies and speaking evil, and not calling their brother
Fool'.[3] His poems betrayed a childish preoccupation with death,
reminiscent of early Victorian religious homilies. Mrs. Kingsley
treasured these scraps to show to the bishop, who tactfully assured
her they were remarkable in so young a child.

Although Charles's emotions were very easily stirred, they

were not superficial. At six, he wrote sorrowfully to a Miss Dade, a friend of his parents, who had ended a visit, 'The house is completely changed since you went.' Much later, in 1855, when the lady was married, and reminded him of those days, he replied regretting that the family had not kept green its memories of the Barnack days. 'I remember every stone and brick of it, and you, too, as one of the first persons of whom I have a clear remembrance, though your face has faded, I am ashamed to say, from my memory.'

The Kingsley children were taught Latin, mathematics, botany, natural history and drawing by their father, who had a definite talent for landscape painting, both in water colour and in oils. Charles enjoyed drawing, whether the subjects were scientific or natural, and in adult life illustrated some of his books and letters, notably the first edition of *The Heroes*. He always considered sketching an excellent and educational hobby. These early lessons also gave him an enduring love of science. His parents used to tell how, at the age of six, during a Latin lesson, he stared fixedly at the fire and suddenly exclaimed, 'I do declare, papa, there is pyrites in the coal.'[4] At this age he had learned to write a clear copper-plate, but, inevitably, this deteriorated as he grew older.[5]

Of course, life was not all study at Barnack. Professor Hall described Charles's father as 'a type of the old English clergyman where the country gentleman forms the basis of the character which the minister of the gospel completes'. As soon as his eldest son was steady enough to sit on horseback without falling off, the rector allowed Charles to accompany the sportsmen on shooting days. The boy would sit in front of the keeper and share in the excitement of bringing back the bag. He was never to lose this pleasure and satisfaction in hard physical activity in the open air, although considerations of his clerical profession and limitations of his purse schooled him in adult life to confine his outdoor sport to fishing. In fine weather Charles went with his father to Peterborough when duty took him there. The child played in the palace garden, and in summertime he was allowed to feed strawberries to an ancient tortoise.[6]

The Fen country appealed strongly to the impressionable boy, as he later described in lectures and essays, and above all in *Hereward the Wake* and *Alton Locke*. Charles Kingsley the writer excelled in descriptions of land- and sea-scapes:

They have a beauty of their own, these great fens even now, when they are dyked and drained, tilled and fenced—a beauty as of the sea, of boundless expanse and freedom. Much more had they that beauty when they were still, for the most part, as God had made them, or rather was making them even then. The low rolling uplands were clothed in primeval forest; oak and ash, beech and elm, with here and there perhaps a group of ancient pines, ragged and decayed, and fast dying out in England even then; though lingering still in the forests of the Scottish highlands.

Between the forests were open wolds, dotted with white sheep and golden gorse; rolling plains of rich though ragged turf, whether cleared by the hand of man or by the wild fires which often swept over the hills. . . .

For always, from the foot of the wolds, the green flat stretched away, illimitable, to a horizon where, from the roundness of the earth, the distant trees and islands were hulled down like ships at sea. The firm horse-fen lay, bright green, along the foot of the wold; beyond it, the browner peat, or deep fen; and among that dark velvet alder beds, long lines of reed-rond, emerald in spring and golden under the autumn sun; shining 'eas' or river-reaches; broad meres dotted with a million fowl, while the cattle waded along their edges after the rich sedge-grass, or wallowed in the mere through the summer's day. Here and there, too, upon the far horizon, rose a tall line of ashen trees, marking some island of firm rich soil. In some of them, as at Ramsey and Crowland, the huge ashes had disappeared before the axes of the monks; and a minster tower rose over the fen, and orchards, cornfields, pastures, with here and there a tree left standing for shade.

Overhead the arch of heaven spread more ample than elsewhere, as over the open sea; and that vastness gave, and

still gives, such cloudlands, such sunrises, such sunsets, as can
be seen nowhere else within these isles. . . . that fair land, like
all things on earth, had its darker aspect. The foul exhalations
of autumn called up fever and ague, crippling and enervating,
and tempting, almost compelling, to that wild and desperate
drinking which was the Scandinavian's special sin. Dark and sad
were those short autumn days, when all the distances were shut
off, and the air choked with foul brown fog, and drenching rains
from the eastern sea; and pleasant the bursting forth of the keen
north-east wind, with all its whirling snowstorms. For though it
sent men hurrying out into the storm, to drive the cattle in from
the fen, and light the sheep out of the snow-wreaths, and now and
then never to return, lost in mist and mire, in ice and snow;—
yet all knew that after the snow would come the keen frost
and bright sun and cloudless blue sky, and the fenman's yearly
holiday when, work being impossible, all gave themselves up
to play, and swarmed upon the ice on skates and sledges, to
run races, township against township, or visit old friends full
forty miles away; and met everywhere faces as bright and ruddy
as their own, cheered by the keen wine of that dry and bracing
frost.

Such was the Fenland; hard, yet cheerful; rearing a race of
hard and cheerful men. . . .[7]

Kingsley drew freely on these Fenland memories, and in a
lecture which he gave to the Mechanics Institute, Cambridge, in
1867, he spoke with nostalgic affection of the Fens.

And yet the fancy may linger without blame, over the shining
meres, the golden reed-beds, the countless water-fowl, the
strange and gaudy insects, the wild nature, the mystery, the
majesty—for mystery and majesty there were—which haunted
the deep fens for many hundred years. Little thinks the Scots-
man, whirled down by the Great Northern Railway from
Peterborough to Huntingdon, what a grand place, even twenty
years ago, was that Holme and Whittlesea, which is now but a

black and unsightly steaming flat, from which the meres and
reed-beds of the old world are gone, while the corn and roots
of the new world have not as yet taken their place. But grand
enough it was, that black ugly place, when backed by Caistor
Hanglands and Holme Wood and the patches of the primeval
forest; while dark green alders, and pale green reeds, stretched
for miles round the broad lagoon, where the coot clanked, and
the bittern boomed, and the sedge-bird, not content with its
own sweet song, mocked the notes of all the birds around;
while high overhead hung motionless, hawk beyond hawk,
buzzard beyond buzzard, kite beyond kite, as far as eye could see.
Far off, upon the silver mere, would rise a puff of smoke from
a punt, invisible from its flatness and white paint. Then down
the wind came the boom of the great stanchion gun; and after
that sound, another sound, louder as it neared; a cry as of all
the bells of Cambridge and all the hounds of Cottesmere; and
overhead rushed and whirled the skein of terrified wild-fowl;
screaming, piping, clacking, croaking—filling the air with the
hoarse rattle of their wings, while clear above all sounded the
wild whistle of the curlew and the trumpet notes of the great
wild swan. They are all gone now. No longer do the ruffs
trample the sedge into a hard floor in their fighting rings, while
the sober reeves stand round, admiring the tournament of their
lovers, gay with ruffs and tippets, no two of them alike. Gone
are the ruffs and reeves, spoonbills, bitterns, avocets; the very
snipe, one hears, disdain to breed. Gone, too, not only from
the Fens, but from the whole world, is that most exquisite
of butterflies—*Lycaena dispar*—the great copper; and many a
curious insect more.[8]

Barnack was a rural backwater, but elsewhere, particularly in
the towns, the social struggles of the 1820s were finally resulting
in important changes. Trade unions were legalised, the penal
system was reformed, and restrictions were lifted on non-con-
forming religious beliefs, this last reform giving a new lease of
life to Catholic thought in England. However, the Rev. Charles
Kingsley and his wife were staunch Anglicans and Tories, main-

taining a rigid view of social, political and religious practices and taking no part in movements for social change.

When the family had to move in 1830 Mr. Kingsley was not altogether reluctant, for the bleak Fenland winters gave him the ague, and his doctor advised a milder climate. The family settled in Devonshire, where lodgings were found at Ilfracombe, chosen mainly because the local squire, Sir James Hamlyn-Williams, was a family friend, and had in his gift the living of the picturesque hill village of Clovelly, a few miles to the south on Bideford Bay. In 1831 Sir James was able to offer Mr. Kingsley the curacy of Clovelly, and when the aged rector died the following year Mr. Kingsley became the new incumbent, and at long last the family was financially secure. If he wished, Mr. Kingsley could remain in Clovelly until he died. For a man of his talents, intelligence and breeding, it was hardly the pinnacle of success, but it was an enchanting spot, and wonderful for the children. Charles Kingsley has a loving description of it in *Prose Idylls*:

I was crawling up the paved stairs inaccessible to cart or carriage, which are flatteringly denominated 'Clovelly-street', a landing-net full of shells in one hand, and a couple of mackerel lines, in the other; behind me a sheer descent, roof below roof, at an angle of 45°, to the pier and bay, 200 feet below, and in front, another hundred feet above, a green amphitheatre of oak, and ash, and larch, shutting out all but a narrow slip of sky, across which the low, soft, formless mist was crawling, opening every instant to show some gap of intense dark rainy blue, and send down a hot vaporous gleam of sunshine upon the white cottages, with their grey steaming roofs, and bright green railings, packed one above another upon the ledges of the cliff, and on the tall tree-fuchsias and gaudy dahlias in the little scraps of court-yard, calling the rich faint odour out of the verbenas and jessamines, and alas! out of the herring-heads and tails also, as they lay in the rivulet; and lighting up the wings of the gorgeous butterflies, almost unknown in our colder eastern climate, which fluttered from woodland down to garden, and from garden up to woodland, and seemed to form the connecting link between that swarming hive of human industry and the deep wild woods in which it was embosomed. So up I was crawling, to dine off gurnards of my own catching —excellent fish, despised by deluded Cockneys, who fancy that because its head is large and prickly, therefore its flesh is not as firm, and sweet, and white, as that of any cod who ever gobbled shell-fish. . . .[9]

The new rector immediately impressed his congregation of fishermen and farmers by proving he could fish, hunt and shoot with the best of them, and in time of storm and shipwreck he joined them on the beach, watching, hoping, praying. Charles called this district his 'dear old Paradise', in spite of the fierce Atlantic storms.

One morning I can remember well, how we watched from the Hartland Cliffs a great barque, which came drifting and rolling in before the western gale, while we followed her up the coast, parsons and sportsmen, farmers and Preventive men, with the Manby's mortar lumbering behind us in a cart, through stone gaps and track-ways, from headland to headland. The maddening excitement of expectation as she ran wildly towards the cliffs at our feet, and then sheered off again inexplicably;—her foremast and bowsprit, I recollect, were gone, shorn off by the deck; a few rags of sail fluttered from her main and mizen. But with all straining of eyes and glasses, we could discern no sign of man on board. Well I recollect the mingled disappointment and admiration of the Preventive men, as a fresh set of salvors appeared in view, in the form of a boat's crew of Clovelly fishermen; how we watched breathlessly the little black speck crawling and struggling up in the teeth of the gale, under the shelter of the land, till, when the ship had rounded a point into smoother water, she seized on her like some tiny spider on a huge unwieldy fly; and then how one still smaller black speck showed aloft on the main-yard, and another—and then the desperate efforts to get the topsail set— and how we saw it tear out of their hands again, and again, and again, and almost fancied we could hear the thunder of its flappings above the roars of the gale, and the mountains of surf which make the rocks ring beneath our feet;—and how we stood silent, shuddering, expecting every moment to see whirled into the sea from the plunging yards one of those same tiny specks, in each of which was a living human soul, with sad women praying for him at home!

. . . And well I remember the last act of that tragedy; for a ship has really, as sailors feel, a personality, almost a life and soul of her own; and as long as her timbers hold together, all is not over. . . .

The ship was breaking up; and we sat by her like hopeless physicians by a death-side, to watch the last struggle—and 'the effects of the deceased'. I recollect our literally warping ourselves down to the beach, holding on by rocks and posts. There was a saddened awe-struck silence, even upon the gentleman from Lloyd's with the pen behind his ear. A sudden turn of the clouds let in a wild gleam of moonshine upon the white leaping heads of the breakers, and on the pyramid of the Black-church Rock, which stands in summer with such calm grandeur gazing down on the smiling bay, with the white sand of Braunton and the red cliffs of Portledge shining through its two vast arches; and against a slab of rock on the right, for years afterwards discoloured with her paint, lay the ship, rising slowly on every surge, to drop again with a piteous crash as the wave fell back with it under the coming wall of foam. You have heard of ships at the last moment crying aloud like living things in agony? I heard it then, as the stumps of her masts rocked and reeled in her, and every plank and joint strained and screamed with the dreadful tension. . . . A dull, thunderous groan, as if a mountain had collapsed, rose above the roar of the tempest; and we all turned with an instinctive knowledge of what had happened, just in time to see the huge mass melt away into the boiling white, and vanish for evermore. And then the very raving of the wind seemed hushed with awe; the very breakers plunged more silently towards the shore, with something of a sullen compunction; and as we stood and strained our eyes into the gloom, one black plank after another crawled up out of the darkness upon the head of the coming surge, and threw itself at our feet like the corpse of a drowning man, too spent to struggle more.[10]

When Charles was twelve and Herbert eleven they were sent to a small preparatory school in Bristol kept by the Rev. William Knight.[11] It was an informal school as schools went in those days, but Charles disliked the change from family to institutional living. He much preferred the company of girls and adults to that of boys. He was shy, timid, and used to solitary occupations, like reading, or rambling over the countryside looking for botanical and natural history specimens. His home studies had put him ahead of his classmates in some respects but behind them in others, and this, coupled with the boy's extreme shyness, led the headmaster to give Charles the run of the school library and to allow him to attend some lessons with his daughters and their governess.

Bristol gave the Kingsley boys their first introduction to national politics. The previous year, 1830, had been one of general unrest throughout Europe, including England, where many agricultural labourers had seized the opportunity to protest against their abominable conditions. Mrs. Priscilla Maurice, writing to her son, F. D. Maurice (Kingsley's future mentor), from her home near Southampton, was exceptional in sympathising with the demonstrators: 'I cannot but think that this rising of the people, these midnight fires, have been very necessary to awaken us to a sense of the dreadful sin of poor labourers having been for many years obliged to work hard for scarcely wages enough to buy them potatoes. It was proved at one meeting that a *noble* lord's workmen were employed in hedging and ditching for *two shillings a week*, and the parish paid them three more! Five shillings a week to support himself, wife and children. Every demand that the poor creatures have made has been most reasonable.' Mrs. Maurice, however, was in a minority. In practically every town the mayor organised the gentry and tradespeople as Special Constables or members of night patrols. Nervous

The Bristol Riots, 30 October 1831

A 'Punch' cartoon pointed the moral
which Kingsley elaborated upon in 'Yeast'

householders packed their treasured possessions in readiness to abandon their homes if trouble threatened.

To some public-spirited men parliamentary reform appeared the panacea for all social ills, including low wages. The political revolts in Paris, Brussels and Warsaw in 1830 heightened the excitement in England. The Radical north, stronghold of the industrialists, hotly demanded an extension of the franchise, and when the Duke of Wellington, then prime minister, made a policy speech alleging that the existing political constitution needed no alteration, popular resentment against the duke and the Tory Party boiled over. The general election held in April 1831 centred round the issue of parliamentary reform, and in June Lord John Russell presented a reform bill which was passed by the Commons, only to be rejected by the House of Lords in the following October. This rejection sparked off instant and prolonged demonstrations throughout the country, leading in some cases to riots and acts of arson. London, Nottingham, Derby, Worcester and Bath were all affected, but the worst riots occurred in Bristol, partly because Sir Charles Wetherell, one of the best hated men in England, was in the city at that time in his capacity as Recorder. Wherever he appeared, crowds awaited him in the streets, booing, yelling, hissing. The interruptions were so outrageous that the business of the courts had to be stopped. On one occasion he had to run for his life from the Mansion House in disguise, and troops were sent to quell the riot. The mob went on to set fire to public buildings, including the Bishop's Palace, which was entirely destroyed, and the cathedral, which was badly damaged.[12]

A working man who witnessed the riots, writing in his autobiography in 1844, described them as 'hideous bacchanals where Gorgon ugliness, matured in the filth and squalor of Bristol's darkest dens, and slums of slime and excrement, were in strict keeping with the seething hell of riot and rapine around—the Saturnalia of robbery and license got up under the pretense of liberty and reform.'[13]

Charles Kingsley at the age of twelve was a fascinated, sickened and uncomprehending spectator of this episode, which instilled

2

into him a horror of mob violence and a conviction that uneducated workers must be controlled by an educated and responsible gentry. It was a dramatic initiation into the political scene.

Lecturing in Bristol over a quarter of a century later, he recalled
the incident, admitting that its effect then was to make him a true-
blue Tory, but adding that ten years later he became socially
conscious enough to derive a totally opposite lesson from it.

It was an afternoon of sullen autumn rain. The fog hung thick
over the docks and lowlands. Glaring through that fog I saw
a bright mass of flame—almost like a half-risen sun. That, I
was told, was the gate of the new gaol on fire—that the
prisoners had been set free; that—. But why speak of what too
many here recollect but too well? The fog rolled slowly up-
ward. Dark figures, even at that great distance, were flitting
to and fro across what seemed the mouth of the pit. The
flames increased—multiplied—at one point after another; till,
by ten o'clock that night, one seemed to be looking down upon
Dante's Inferno, and to hear the multitudinous moan and wail
of the lost spirits surging to and fro amid that sea of fire.

Right behind Brandon Hill—how can I ever forget it?—
rose the central mass of fire, till the little mound seemed converted into a volcano, from the peak of which the flame
streamed up, not red above, but delicately green and blue, pale
rose and pearly white, while crimson sparks leapt and fell
again in the midst of that rainbow, not of hope, but of despair;
and dull explosions down below mingled with the roar of the
mob, and the infernal hiss and crackle of the flame.

. . . It was on the Tuesday or Wednesday, after, if I recollect
right, that I saw another, and a still more awful sight. Along the
north side of Queen Square, in front of ruins which had been
three days before noble buildings, lay a ghastly row, not of
corpses, but of corpse fragments. I have no more wish than you
to dilate upon that sight. But there was one charred fragment—
with a scrap of old red petticoat adhering to it, which I never
forgot—which, I trust in God, I never shall forget. It is good for
a man to be brought once at least in his life, face to face with

fact, ultimate fact, however horrible it may be; and have to confess to himself, shuddering, what things are possible upon God's earth, when man has forgotten that his only welfare is in living after the likeness of God.[14]

On an earlier occasion, talking privately to his pupil, John Martineau, Charles Kingsley gave fuller details of that crucial experience. He had slipped away from school to look at the scene:

... the brave, patient soldiers sitting, hour after hour patient on their horses, the blood streaming from wounds on their heads and faces, waiting for the order which the miserable, terrified Mayor had not the courage to give; the savage, brutal, hideous mob of inhuman wretches plundering, destroying, burning; casks of spirits broken open and set flowing in the streets, the wretched creatures drinking it on their knees from the gutter, till the flame from a burning house caught the stream, ran down it with a horrible rushing sound, and, in one dreadful moment, the prostrate drunkards had become a row of blackened corpses. Lastly, he [Kingsley] spoke of the shamelessness and the impunity of the guilty; the persecution and suicide of the innocent.

When Martineau asked whose was the responsibility for such a scene of horror, his tutor answered solemnly, 'Mine—and yours,' a cryptic reply which Martineau was then too young to appreciate. Later, when the social conscience awakened by Kingsley led Martineau to work with F. D. Maurice and the Christian Socialists, the younger man understood what Kingsley had meant.[15]

By 1832 the Kingsley boys were ready for their next school, and there was even a possibility that Charles might go to Eton, for the headmaster of that celebrated school had heard he was a promising student. But the Kingsley parents wanted their sons nearer home; in addition, they had to worry about household finances, and Eton was expensive; and, finally, there was considerable doubt as to whether boarders in public schools were able to lead a decent Christian life. (One of Lord Shaftesbury's sons had died as a result of a ten-round fight with another boy at Eton in the 1820s.)

There was some reason for the Kingsleys to fear that the moral and physical welfare of their boys would not be safeguarded at a big public school. James Anthony Froude, later to become a friend and relative by marriage of Charles Kingsley, barely survived his experiences as a boarder at Westminster School about this time (1830). 'The fagging was excessively severe. The bullying was gross and unchecked. The sanitary accommodation was abominable. The language of the dormitory was indecent and profane. Froude (then aged 11), whose health prevented him from the effective use of nature's weapons, was woken by the hot points of cigars burning holes in his face, made drunk by being forced to swallow brandy-punch, and repeatedly thrashed. He was also more than half starved, because the big fellows had the pick of the joints at dinner, and left the small fellows little besides the bone.'[16]

In later life, Charles Kingsley often expressed regret that his parents did not send him to Rugby, where Dr. Arnold's reforming methods were just taking hold. He believed that public school would have given him the poise and confidence to conquer his stammer, but it seems at least as likely that it might have made it worse. Possibly his fondness for Tom Hughes and his admiration for *Tom Brown's Schooldays* coloured his faith in Rugby. In any case, since Mr. Kingsley did not approve of Dr. Arnold's political and religious principles, finding them too liberal, the matter never arose. Instead, the boys went to Helston Grammar School in Devonshire, where the headmaster was the Rev. Derwent Coleridge, son of the poet and philosopher, Samuel Taylor Coleridge. Derwent Coleridge was a German scholar, a fact which pleased Mr. Kingsley and was to awaken Charles's interest in German history and literature.

Derwent Coleridge also encouraged Charles to write poetry, and a junior master, the Rev. C. A. Johns, joined the boy in his passion for collecting and classifying botanical and geological specimens. Johns often accompanied Charles on these natural history outings, and the two of them remained friendly after Charles left school.[17] As at Bristol, Charles made few friends, an exception being Cowley Powles. They shared a study, and their friendship was to be lifelong. Cowley Powles described his first sight of Charles and Herbert Kingsley at Helston:

> I remember the long, low room, dimly lighted by a candle on a table at the further end, where the brothers were sitting, engaged at the moment of my entrance in a course of (not uncharacteristic) experiments with gunpowder.
>
> Almost from the time of our first introduction Charles and I became friends.
>
> For all his good qualities, Charles was not popular as a school-boy. He knew too much, and his mind was generally on a higher level than ours. He did not consciously snub those who knew less, but a good deal of unconscious snubbing went on; all the more resented, perhaps, because it was unconscious. Then, too, though strong and active, Charles was not expert at games. He never made 'a score' at cricket. In mere feats of agility and adventure he was among the foremost. . . . Our play-ground was separated by a lane, not very narrow, and very deep, from a field on the opposite side. To jump from the play-ground wall to the wall opposite, and to jump back, was a considerable trial of nerve and muscle. The walls, which were not quite on a level, were rounded at the top, and a fall into the deep lane must have involved broken bones. This jump was one of Charles's favourite performances. . . . It was wonderful how well he bore pain. On one occasion, having a sore finger, he determined to cure it by cautery. He heated the poker red-hot in the school-room fire, and calmly applied it two or three times till he was satisfied that his object was attained.
>
> His own endurance of pain did not, however, make him careless of suffering in others. He was very tender-hearted—often more so than his school-fellows could understand; and what they did not understand they were apt to ridicule. And

this leads me to notice what, after all, I should fix on as the moral quality that pre-eminently distinguished him as a boy, the generosity with which he forgave offence . . . . He had no place for vindictiveness in his heart.[18]

Charles Kingsley's home background helped him develop a harmonious view of nature which included all he learned from poetry, from classical studies, and from Samuel Taylor Coleridge's philosophy of reverence for all forms of life. His poetry reflected his scientific interests and his adolescent fantasies:

> Then strange and fearful thoughts flit o'er my brain
> By indistinctness made more terrible,
> And incubi mock at me with fierce eyes
> Upon my couch; and visions, crude and dire
> Of planets, suns, millions of miles, infinity
> Space, time, thought, being, blank nonentity,
> Things incorporeal, fancies of the brain,
> Seen, heard, as though they were material,
> All mixed in sickening mazes, trouble me,
> And lead my soul away from earth and heaven
> Until I doubt whether I be or not!

Charles did not keep these early poems, but the admiring Powles safeguarded some of them.

In a letter to his future wife, Fanny Grenfell, written when he was a student at Cambridge, Charles described this Helston period as 'the dreamy days of boyhood, when I knew and worshipped nothing but the physical . . . my enjoyment was drawn . . . from the semi-sensual delights of ear and eye, from sun and stars, from wood and wave. . . . Present enjoyment, present profit, brought always to me a recklessness of moral consequences which has been my bane.'[19]

Meanwhile, an event took place in London which had a direct bearing on the fortunes of the Kingsley family. This was the parliamentary bill to abolish slavery passed in 1833, compensation being paid to slave-owners. It led William Wilberforce, the

Evangelical campaigner for this cause, to say: 'Thank God, I have lived to witness the day in which England is willing to give £20,000,000 for the abolition of slavery.' The Kingsley family may have echoed these admirable sentiments, but they knew that they would suffer financially, since Mrs. Kingsley's inheritance was tied up in her family's West Indian plantation interests. It would mean that there would be no money to launch the Kingsley boys on their adult careers. Like their father, they would have to make their own way in the world.

In 1834 when at school Charles had an attack of 'English cholera' at the same time that Herbert fell ill with rheumatic fever. Charles quickly recovered, and Herbert also seemed to be making satisfactory progress when he had an unexpected relapse and died suddenly. Charles, entirely unsuspecting, was called into the sick room and confronted with his brother's corpse. The shock was almost unbearable. He and Herbert had always been the best of companions. A few months later, Charles collapsed, predictably, with 'brain fever'.

Summer holidays at Clovelly gave him opportunities for distraction, collecting and classifying sea creatures and examining them under a microscope (like his doctor-hero in *Two Years Ago*). He made friends with William Turton, a doctor living at Bideford—'poor dear old opium-eating Dr. Turton'. But he was lonely without Herbert, and in 1835 his science master, Johns, joined him for an enjoyable fortnight spent tramping round Devon, botanizing. Then in the spring of 1836 the Rev. Charles Kingsley announced that he had accepted a London living, and Charles would have to leave Helston School at the end of the summer term. Mr. Kingsley was distantly related to the well-known Cadogan family, whose influence procured for him the lucrative living of St. Luke's, Chelsea. Delightful though Clovelly was, it could never match St. Luke's financially, and the Kingsley boys would soon incur expenses for their education. The least their father could do was to see them through university.

Chelsea Rectory was a spacious house with one of the finest gardens in London. The church was a recent (1824) replacement for a much older building, and in spite of being only a half-hour's walk from the heart of the capital, Chelsea was still semi-rural, as Thomas and Jane Carlyle had recently discovered. Mr. Kingsley could now rest on his laurels, having in his mid-fifties ascended as high as he could expect in his clerical career, while his wife, a born organiser, would have scope at last for her energies and abilities.

Nothing, however, could persuade their eldest son that this change had anything to commend it. Country born and bred, he had no love for towns. All his knowledge and interests were rooted in the country. He was increasingly lonely and eyed the stream of visitors to the rectory with all the scorn of a lofty teenager, writing to Cowley Powles at Helston: 'I find a doleful difference in the society here and at Helston . . . for I am sickened and enraged to see "silly women blown about with every wind", falling in love with the preacher instead of his sermon, and with his sermon instead of the Bible. I could say volumes on this sub-ject that should raise both your contempt and indignation.' He confided to Powles that his father shared his strong dislike of this aspect of parochial work. Mr. Kingsley was happiest in his library composing his weekly sermon, or in the country visiting friends to enjoy the sporting life of a country gentleman. He was content to leave parish and family management to his capable wife ('a second Mrs. Fry, in spirit and act', as her son later des-cribed her),[20] and he withdrew gradually into a scholarly world of his own. Charles and the rest of the children accordingly looked towards their mother as the respected and much-loved centre of the household, and this affectionate devotion was freely given until her death.

Charles joined King's College, Strand, which had not long been established, and was entered for a general studies course in preparation for Cambridge. His subjects included classics and mathematics, languages and physical science. The boy used to walk the four miles from Chelsea to the Strand with his nose buried in a book. His father's extensive library was a joy to him, as it later became to his youngest brother, Henry. Among Charles's favourite books were Spenser's *Faerie Queene*, Malory's *Morte d'Arthur*, the Greek myths and legends, and the works of Rabelais, which he read and re-read at regular intervals through his life.

Reading, indeed, was almost the only recreation and companionship permitted to him because of his parents' disapproval of other
forms of entertainment, such as the theatre.

In the following year Cowley Powles joined Charles at King's
College, but afterwards the friends would be separated again,
since Powles was destined for Oxford. After studying in a sporadic
and unsystematic fashion, Charles unexpectedly applied himself
with a ferocious burst of study as the date of his university entrance examinations approached, and he passed them surprisingly
well. One of his tutors at King's College commented to Mrs.
Fanny Kingsley after her husband's death, 'I own his subsequent
career astonished me, for as a youth he was gentle and diffident
even to timidity.'[21]

3

The Cambridge Student

Queen Victoria had been on the throne for one year when Charles
Kingsley went up to Cambridge, and the moral earnestness which
was to mark so much of the Victorian age was far from evident
at the university. Life for young gentlemen at Cambridge, and
particularly for rich young noblemen, had hardly changed since
the eighteenth century. Their favourite pursuits were drinking,
gambling, hunting and womanising, and although daily chapel
attendance was obligatory it was often observed only in the flesh,
for many undergraduates were too drunk to know what was
going on. A sharp class division between Town and Gown revealed itself in frequent squabbles and skirmishes in the city.[1]

Charles Kingsley's family background, upbringing and financial circumstances kept him from gravitating to the fastest sets in
the university, although his college, Magdalene, was more notable
for its sportsmen and rakes than for its scholars, but mere freedom
was enough. Freed from the constraints of his parents, his personality expanded. At Cambridge he felt independent—a gentleman's son, living and studying with other gentlemen's sons.

Suddenly, and to his amazed delight, he became popular with
his contemporaries. His conversation, stammer and all, was
interesting and amusing, and he could ride, shoot, hunt and fish
with the best of them. He tramped through all weathers for a
night's fishing. He learned to drink beer, to gamble at cards
and to row for his college (in the second boat). It was at Cambridge
that he was introduced to the solace of pipe-smoking, and became a lifelong addict.

Kegan Paul, a friend of his later years, wrote: 'He always used
a long clean *churchwarden*, and these pipes used to be bought a

barrel-full at a time. They lurked in all sorts of unexpected places. A pipe would suddenly be extracted from a bush in the garden, filled and lighted as by magic, or one had even been drawn from a whin bush on the heath, some half mile from the house [Eversley Rectory, in Hampshire]. But none was ever smoked which was in any degree foul, and when there was a vast accumulation of old pipes, enough to fill the barrel, they were sent back again to the kiln to be rebaked, and returned fresh and new. This gave him a striking simile, which in *Alton Locke* he puts in the mouth of James Crossthwaite; "Katie here believes in purgatory, where souls are burnt clean again like 'bacca pipes".'[2]

Kingsley had no settled future in mind during his first year at Cambridge, apart from the negative one of being sure he did not want to become a clergyman. (In those days a large proportion of Cambridge students were sons of clergymen, destined for the Church, or at least for ordination.) Unfortunately, there were few careers open to him, and he certainly considered emigration, with its twin lure of fortune and adventure. He knew himself to be a sensual man. He wrote to Fanny Grenfell during their courtship: 'Had I been a Haroun Alraschild, with every sense "lapped in Elysium", I could have enjoyed it all. The man who cannot enjoy, cannot be healthy and cannot be self-denying. But had I been a prairie hunter, cold and nakedness and toil would have been no evils to me. I could have enjoyed that which was given to me, and never, I believe firmly, remembered that there were greater sensual pleasures in life.'[3]

He discovered that one of his fellow students at Magdalene was Frank Penrose, whom he had known as a child, when Penrose's father was Mr. Kingsley's curate at North Clifton. Penrose was one of the college's best oarsmen, rowing in the first boat, and he persuaded Charles to join the rowing club. Both men excelled at mathematics, and attended lectures together. They were also interested in art and painting, unusual for undergraduates in those days. Through Penrose, Charles Kingsley met Charles Blachford Mansfield, a student at Clare College. Mansfield was Kingsley's age, a clergyman's son also, and became a close friend. The Mansfield family was well-connected, and Mansfield, who

had tremendous charm, was completely at ease mixing with high
society. He had by will-power and exercise overcome certain
childhood diseases and trained his body until it was lithe and
active—'as graceful as an antelope', declared Charles admiringly.
For compassionate reasons he was a vegetarian. Science attracted
him strongly, especially chemistry, and he and Kingsley dabbled
in mesmerism, discussing health and personality in terms of
'animal magnetism' and being 'magnetised' or 'demagnetised'.
Both Penrose and Mansfield later became disciples of F. D. Maurice,
and (as did Kingsley) formed part of the Christian Socialist group
which developed after 1848.

Kingsley attended Professor Adam Sedgewick's Geological
Field Lectures, famous throughout the university because they
were given in the field on horseback. Some students joined the
class solely for the country gallops, but Kingsley had the added
incentive of being already a keen geologist, and he greatly admired
his professor. Adam Sedgewick was an important reforming
influence in the university, believing there were three branches
of study necessary if a university were to be truly 'a place of
sound learning and christian education'.[4] These branches were
the laws of nature, the laws of ancient literature, and the laws of
human creatures considered as social beings. Sedgewick was a
devout believer in God. 'Geology, like every other science when
well interpreted, lends its aid to natural religion. . . . It shows
intelligent power not only contriving means adapted to an
end, but at many successive times contriving a change of
mechanism adapted to a change of external conditions; and thus
affords a proof, peculiarly its own, that the first great cause
continues a provident and active intelligence.' He held that
languages and the classics, which stimulated the imagination,
should be learned before the student went on to the more rigorous
discipline of science, but he feared that during the previous half-
century at Cambridge the teaching of classics had been misguided,
for it valued 'the husk more than the fruit of ancient learning.'[5]

Sedgewick disliked the philosophy of utility, because he
insisted that every human being was born with a conscience, a
built-in moral principle by which later experiences could be

judged. Referring to a study of morals, he said, 'We may see that the foulest crimes have oftentimes been enacted under the fairest forms of government; and that in all conditions of a state (from its beginning to its end) corruption of manners is ever incompatible with true liberty.' These were reflections which Kingsley could subscribe to, but he was certainly disillusioned by the manners he observed at Cambridge, so different from the earnest and busy life at his father's rectories. In the first edition of *Alton Locke,* and speaking through his hero, an intelligent, priggish, poor, Dissenter-bred tailor, he declared:

I cannot say that my recollections of them [i.e. young university men] were pleasant. A few of them were very bigoted Tractarians—some of whom seemed to fancy that a dilletante admiration for crucifixes and Gothic architecture, was a form of religion which, by its extreme perfection, made the virtues of chastity and sobriety quite unnecessary—and the rest, of a more ascetic and moral turn, seemed as narrow, bitter, flippant and unearnest young men as I had ever met, dealing in second-hand party statements, gathered, as I could discover, entirely from periodicals of their own party—taking pride in reading nothing but what was made for them, indulging in the most violent nick-names and railing, and escaping from anything like severe argument by a sneer or an expression of theatrical horror at so 'painful' a notion. . . .

But the great majority of the young men whom I met were even of a lower stamp. I was utterly shocked and disappointed at the contempt and unbelief with which they seemed to regard everything beyond mere animal enjoyment, and here and there the selfish advantage of a good degree. They seemed, if one could judge from appearances, to despise and disbelieve everything generous, enthusiastic, enlarged. Thoughtfulness was a 'bore';—earnestness, 'romance'. Above all, they seemed to despise the university itself. The 'dons' were 'idle, fat old humbugs'; Chapel 'a humbug too'; tutors 'humbugs', too; who played into the tradesmen's hands, and charged men high fees for lectures not worth attending—so that any man who wanted to get on was forced to have a private tutor, besides his college one. The university-studies were 'a humbug'—no use to man in after-life. The masters of arts were 'humbugs' too, for 'they knew all the evils, and clamoured for reform till they became Dons themselves; and then, as soon as they found the old system pay, they settled down on their lees, and grew fat on port wine, like those before them.' They seemed to consider themselves in an atmosphere of humbug—living in a lie—out of which lie-element those who chose were very right in making the most, for the gaining of fame or money.[6]

Earlier, in the same novel, Kingsley had laboured this very point in a conversation between Alton Locke and his cousin, a rich man's son, who had decided for worldly reasons to go into the Church. Alton Locke had asked why the college authorities did not right such obvious wrongs, and received the following answer:

'Because, my dear fellow, they are afraid to alter anything, for fear of bringing the whole rotten old house down about their ears. They say themselves that the slightest innovation will be a precedent for destroying the whole system, bit by bit. Why should they be afraid of that, if they did not know that the whole system would not bear canvassing an instant. That's why they retain statutes that can't be observed, because they know, if they once began altering the statutes in the least, the world would find out how they themselves have been breaking the statutes. That's why they keep up the farce of swearing to the Thirty-Nine Articles, and all that; just because they know, if they attempted to alter the letter of the old forms, it would come out, that half the young men of the university don't believe three words of them at heart. They know the majority of us are at heart neither churchmen nor Christians, nor even decently moral; but the one thing they are afraid of is scandal. So they connive at the young men's ill-doings; they take no real steps to put down profligacy; and, in the meantime, they just keep up the forms of the Church of Englandism, and pray devoutly that the whole humbug may last out their time. There isn't one Don in a hundred who has any personal influence over the gownsmen. A man may live here from the time he's a fresh-man, to the time he's taken a degree, without ever being spoken to as if he had a soul to be saved.'[7]

The more Charles Kingsley saw of the plan of studies laid down by the university, and the poor teaching available, the less inclined he was to apply himself to any academic work. It was common knowledge that a student had to engage a private tutor in order to get a good degree. One of his tutors, Dr. Bateson, later Master of St. John's College, Cambridge, wrote afterwards: 'My own relations with Charles Kingsley in those early days were always agreeable, though I was unable to induce him to apply himself with any energy to his classical work, until quite the close of his undergraduate career.'

Kingsley's first year was fully occupied with social activities, but at a deeper level he was restless and unsatisfied. He had outgrown his adolescent raptures over nature, was cynical about religion in its institutional forms, and unsettled in every way. During his first summer vacation he went to a country rectory in Checkenden in Oxfordshire, his father having exchanged clerical duties with that rector as a cheap and convenient method of giving the Kingsley family two months' holiday in clean country air. Charles did not particularly look forward to his vacation, convinced he would be the odd man out. He had no inclination to study, and did not see himself expressing his doubts and disappointments to his parents. His brother, Gerald, never a close friend, had recently joined the Royal Navy, and would doubtless be full of his experiences. Still—to look on the bright side—he would at least be in the country instead of the city, and he could shoot, fish and ride.

And on one of his many canters through the country lanes he met Frances Grenfell—Fanny, to her friends—youngest of the large and prosperous Grenfell family, a comfortable, correct and bourgeois clan which was rising in the world, materially and socially. The Grenfells were of Cornish descent, and Fanny

Grenfell was dark and handsome in a buxom, Spanish style. When she encountered Charles she was already a mature, poised young woman of twenty-five years, although to her family she was still 'the baby'. Her father married twice, and the eldest son by the first marriage, Pascoe Grenfell, was now middle-aged. Fanny's mother died in 1837, and her father the following year: bereavements which Fanny took to heart. She was especially fond of two sisters, Charlotte and Georgina, both unmarried, but had no close friend of her own.

Like Charles Kingsley, Fanny Grenfell was particularly lonely in that summer of 1839, yearning for some companion with whom she could discuss ideas, philosophy, religion, books, life. There was surely more to life than merely learning how to order a well-managed household, take tea in the drawing-room or preside over a formal dinner. She knew that Pascoe Grenfell believed, like most men of his generation, that his first duty to Fanny was to find her a good husband—some banker, Member of Parliament, even a peer of the realm. The prospect bored Fanny. She was a clever, serious girl who might have enjoyed a career. Her conscience and imagination had been aroused by the elevated religious views of High Church writers like Dr. Pusey. Indeed, she had almost decided to enter an Anglican sisterhood in Park Village, Regent's Park, London, under the direction of Dr. Pusey, where she might find scope for her vague notions of devoting herself to social service.

Suddenly life exhibited a new dimension when she met Charles Kingsley. The discrepancy in their ages was unnoticed by them, though not by outsiders. They discussed every subject imaginable. Fanny saw him as a doubting Thomas whom it was her delectable task to lead back to the paths of righteousness. This, and not a celibate sisterhood, could be her religious duty. Charles, for his part, saw her as a beautiful damozel to be rescued before she was immured behind convent walls, where her lovely spirit would be perverted by unnatural spinsterhood. And beneath it all, although neither would have admitted it, was a strong sexual attraction.

They met on July 6, 1839, and in later life they pinpointed this date as their true wedding day. Charles coined the rather pedantic word 'eye-wedlock', which he used both for himself and for his semi-autobiographical hero, Lancelot Smith, in *Yeast*. Fanny Kingsley, primly but touchingly, gave her first impressions of him: 'He was then full of religious doubts; and his face, with its unsatisfied hungering look, bore witness to the state of his mind. It had a sad longing expression, too, as if he had all his life been looking for a sympathy he had never found—a rest which he never would attain in this world. His peculiar character had not been understood hitherto, and his heart had been half asleep. It woke up now, and never slept again. For the first time he could speak with perfect freedom, and be met with answering sympathy. . . . as new hopes dawned, the look of hard defiance gave way to a wonderful humility and tenderness, which were his characteristics, with those who understood him, to his dying day.

'He was just like his own Lancelot in *Yeast*, in that summer of 1839—a bold thinker, a bold rider, a most chivalrous gentleman—sad, shy, and serious habitually; in conversation at one moment brilliant and impassioned; the next reserved and unapproachable; by turns attracting and repelling, but pouring forth to the friend whom he could trust, stores of thought and feeling and information on every sort of unexpected subject which seemed boundless. It was a feast to the imagination and intellect to hold communion with Charles Kingsley even at the age of twenty.'[8]

What chance did Pascoe Grenfell's business friends have against such a one in competing for Fanny's favours?

Two months slipped by like a flash, and when Charles returned to college the friends continued their dialogue by correspondence. Fanny Grenfell begged him to read the Bible daily (as his mother had always entreated him), and he promised to do so although he had little hope that it would deepen his belief. Away from her physical presence he was overcome by intense depression which he could shake off only by plunging into active sports. He had no respect for the curriculum prescribed for his degree, despising its barren, outmoded ideas, completely removed from contemporary life. In any case, his final examinations were two years ahead. Also, even so unworldly a man as Charles Kingsley realised that the Grenfells would never approve of him as a friend for their adored Fanny—and from their standpoint, they would be quite right. He was too young for her, too odd, and much too poor.

He forgot his troubles when he went fishing, and a fellow student, E. Pitcairn Campbell, found his first experience of fishing with Charles enjoyable but daunting. 'I was to call him, and for this purpose I had to climb over the wall of Magdalene College. This I did at two a.m. and about three we were both climbing back into the stonemason's yard, and off through Trumpington, in pouring rain all the way, nine miles to Duxford.

'We reached about 6.30. The water was clouded by rain, and I in courtesy to your husband yielded my heavier rod in order that he might try the lower water with the minnow.

'He was, however, scarcely out of sight, before I spied, under the alders, some glorious trout rising to caterpillars dropping from the bushes. In ten minutes I had three of these fine fellows on the bank—one of them weighed three pounds, others two pounds each. We caught nothing after the rain had ceased.

'This performance set me up in your husband's opinion and he took me with him to Shelford. . . .'9

Charles tried conscientiously to follow Fanny's well-meant advice over religion, but found his scientific training a stumbling block, especially with regard to the Athanasian Creed.10 The story of Christianity, of the saints, of the Catholic Church and of the Bible, was at that time being subjected to close scrutiny by university scholars, especially those from Germany. A key book in religious debate was David Friedrich Strauss's *Das Leben Jesu*,11 wherein Christ was treated as an historical personage but not the Son of God. At Oxford the followers of Pusey and Newman tried to give deeper meaning to religion. Charles Kingsley was hard put to find one single steadfast doctrine which he could wholeheartedly embrace.

After another year at Cambridge he was able to assure Fanny, 'I begin to find that there is an object to be attained in morality beyond public esteem, and self-interest—namely, the love and esteem of the Good, and, consequently, of God himself.' He was not yet absolutely sure that this latter point followed logically, but he hoped so. He realised that a firm religious belief would calm his over-excitable temperament. He was attracted by the Oxford Movement and its High Church rituals, but was deterred by the sternly repressive attitude which most of the Oxford reformers took towards displays of emotion and towards the Greek love of beauty and landscape which was second nature to Kingsley, nor could he ever discipline himself to study in the meticulous fashion demanded by the Oxford scholars. Of course, he did his painful best to be honest. He was aware that the trite language used by many Anglican clergymen sounded shallow and hypo-critical. He tried to choose only phrases which his experience told him were valid. Yet, he brooded, 'Man does want something more than his reason,' and he remembered that even Socrates had spoken of some spiritual guide.

By the beginning of 1841 Charles and Fanny understood that their intense epistolary relationship had in reality been a courtship —they were deeply in love, now and for ever, and their future was in the hands of Providence. Charles Kingsley's animal vigour asserted itself as he reviewed the position. Marriage was a God-given relationship in all its aspects—celibacy was a mistaken ideal which warped the mind and soul. He could see this clearly: surely Fanny must also? Back at Cambridge after the vacation, he sternly renounced cards, hunting and driving, to the astonish-ment of his old friends, and to his own mortification. He tried to explain to Fanny the exhilaration of being a young man, so that she could appreciate his sacrifice.

You cannot understand the excitement of animal exercise from the mere act of cutting wood or playing cricket to the manias of hunting or shooting or fishing. On these things more or less young men live. Every moment which is taken from them for duty or for reading is felt to be lost—to be so much time sacrificed to hard circumstance. And even those who have calmed from age or from the necessity of attention to a pro-fession, which has become custom, have the same feelings flowing as an undercurrent in their minds; and, if they had not, they would neither think nor act like men. They might be pure and good and kind, but they would need that stern and determined activity, without which a man cannot act in an extended sphere either for his own good, or for that of his fellow-creatures. When I talk then, of excitement, I do not wish to destroy excitability, but to direct it into the proper channel, and to bring it under subjection. I have been reading Plato on this very subject, and you would be charmed with his ideas.[12]

That was Kingsley at the age of twenty-two, but it could stand for a later date. He did not change this view.

Greatly encouraged by this evidence that Charles was shaping himself into her ideal mould, Fanny Grenfell sent him books— Coleridge's *Aids to Reflection*, and the works of Thomas Carlyle. Both these authors helped Kingsley towards a belief in God, so that his mind was fertile for the unconventional and unexpected ideas set forth in Frederick Denison Maurice's *Kingdom of Christ*, which she sent him later. Maurice's views at last supplied the answers to Kingsley's questioning. He could now both believe in God and accept the Church of England intellectually and emotionally, and from the status of an Anglican try to lead a useful life as a member of society. From this it was but a short step to abandon the law as a future profession (his name had been put down tentatively at Lincoln's Inn) and to decide to take Holy Orders. As an Anglican parson he would have a job for life, together with an unassailable social position whence he could sally forth as a people's Sir Galahad. He agreed with Coleridge that the Christian religion was 'a process of living, proved in the act'.[13] He would be involved with human beings and have opportunities of helping them, whilst at the same time his impetuous instincts would be curbed in the best and most solemn way possible.

His circle of friends and acquaintances changed. Instead of the 'fast set', his rooms were filled with young men who intended to enter the Church. He began attending chapel more frequently than the regulations demanded, and he found that the atmosphere and rituals soothed him. He convinced himself that he was cut out to be a clergyman, and once he was sure, he began to study hard for a good degree, since this would count in his favour when he applied for a living. He grew reconciled even to the thought of the daily routine of parish life, in spite of having chafed at it in Chelsea, because he realised that the clerical profession would give him time to read and study and to get to know 'the minds of those under my charge—how a good clergyman must understand the human mind'.

The examinations of the winter of 1841 hung over his thoughts 'like a vast incubus', he wrote to his mother. Cowley Powles had been working hard at Oxford, and like Kingsley, dreaded the examinations. Kingsley tried to console his friend: 'As for your degree, leave it in God's hands.' All that a university education should do, added Kingsley, was make the student and those around him wiser, better, happier. Not that he did not sympathise with Powles, for he, too, had been overtaxing his strength for the past six months—'not because I felt distinction here an object, but because having a battle to fight with the world—a bride to win as a penniless adventurer from rich relations, I found it necessary to attack Mammon with weapons he could feel and appreciate; and the first weapon thrown in my way was the tangible proof of talent and application, and claim to attention, implied in a good degree.'[14]

His attempts to make up in six months the study which should have been spread over three years brought on violent headaches which were treated by an application of leeches, and a feeling of utter despondency about his future. He gained a first class degree in classics and a second class in mathematics: good, but not good enough for the coveted Fellowship, which might have impressed the Grenfells. But when he heard the result he was past caring; all he wanted was to leave Cambridge and rest his exhausted mind.

What had he gained from university? Certainly not the ability to discipline his thoughts, which was one of the alleged aims of university life. Perhaps in the case of Charles Kingsley it was best summed up in his first novel, *Yeast,* in the picture he drew of Lancelot Smith as a graduate:

. . . he had gone to college with a large stock of general information, and a particular mania for dried plants, fossils, butterflies, and sketching, and some such creed as this:

That he was very clever

That he ought to make his fortune

That a great many things were very pleasant—beautiful things among the rest

That it was a fine thing to be 'Superior', gentleman-like, generous, and courageous

That a man ought to be religious

And left college with a good smattering of classics and mathematics, picked up in the intervals of boat-racing and hunting, and much the same creed as he brought with him, except in regard to the last article.[15]

As for how outsiders regarded Lancelot Smith:

'Oh, I remember him well enough at Cambridge: He was one of a set who tried to look like blackguards, and really succeeded tolerably. They used to eschew gloves, and drink nothing but beer, and smoke disgusting short pipes, and when we established the Coverley Club in Trinity, they set up an opposition and called themselves the Navvies. And they used to make piratical expeditions down to Lynn in eight oars, to attack bargemen, and fen girls, and shoot ducks, and sleep under turf-stacks, and come home when they had drunk all the public-house taps dry. I remember the man perfectly.'

'Navvy or none,' said the colonel, 'he has just the longest head and the noblest heart of any man I ever met. If he does not distinguish himself before he dies, I know nothing of human nature.'

'Ah, yes. I believe he is clever enough:—took a good degree, a better one that I did—but horribly eclectic; full of mesmerism, and German metaphysics, and all that sort of thing. I heard of him one night last spring, on which he had been seen, if you will believe it, going successively into a Swedenborgian chapel, the Garrick's Head, and one of Elliotson's magnetic soirees.'[16]

In February, 1842, when Charles Kingsley left Cambridge, not even the most daring seer could have foretold that the next time he went there, nearly two decades later, he was to be Regius Professor of Modern History.

4

The Earnest Young Man

Although the decision to become a clergyman was final, doubts still nagged Charles as to whether by entering the Church of England he was not doing the right thing for the wrong reason, outwardly dedicating himself to God but inwardly doing so in the hope that it would persuade the sophisticated Grenfells to approve his marriage to Fanny. He wanted to be sincere but he also recognised the strength of his sexual desires and understood enough psychology to appreciate that these might make him rationalise his choice. He went into retreat at Holne to read theology for the coming ordeal, and was charmed by Devonshire. He wrote to Cowley Powles: 'I shall be most happy to have you as a temporary sharer in the frugalities of my farm house lodging. Whether you will despise hard beds and dimity curtains, morning bathes and even trout fishings, mountain mutton and Devonshire cream, I do not know. . . .'[1]

He did not expect to fail the examination but could not resist dramatising his situation as he spent the night before ordination in reflection and prayer. He felt like a squire of old, keeping vigil on the eve of knighthood, offering his life to the service of God— and, most especially, to the service of his lady. Fanny took this attitudinising as solemnly and romantically as he did, and they both prayed that Heaven would reward their devotion by softening the hearts of the Grenfells.

Charles was safely ordained, and his father bestirred himself to see that the young man was offered a curacy. Through the influence of the Rev. Gerald Wellesley[2] he was offered the choice of two Hampshire curacies. Charles picked Eversley, a parish which consisted of three scattered villages on the edge of Old

Windsor forest, not far from Reading, and moved there in 1842. Once committed to a clerical career, he felt nothing but enthusiasm for it, and bombarded Fanny with a constant stream of letters. He told her that an Anglican clergymen should make the most of all the gifts God gave him, physical as well as spiritual, for 'the body is the temple of the Living God', and therefore to allow it to deteriorate was actual blasphemy. People who neglected their bodies, pretending to do so from religious motives, were using this excuse as a disguise for laziness, said Kingsley sternly. He was glad he had a natural love of outdoor pursuits, because these gave him the physical stamina which a conscientious country clergyman needed to carry out his parish duties. (Countryman that he was, it apparently never occurred to him that the Lord might call him to serve in a town parish.)

At every tiff and turn his mind would wander off into fantasies of marriage. He forced himself to be calm, trying to involve himself in every aspect of his work. He composed sermons while chopping wood, held imaginary conversations with Fanny all the time, and wrote to her each night when work was done. The duty of a clergyman, he told her, was to be able to communicate with every individual in his parish, or outside it for that matter, and this was best done if he could demonstrate that he was strong enough to do a day's work alongside his parishioners, at the same time being able to talk to them man to man. Kingsley hoped to be able to impress the young men by proving that he could be their equal, even their superior, in physical prowess. He was bursting with plans, reading projects, writing ideas, parish visits, river fishing. He was fascinated to discover that Eversley Church, red brick and seventeenth-century, was actually built on a Saxon foundation, and thus was hallowed by centuries of Christian devotion.[3]

It is interesting to note that although he was deeply in love for the first time, he wrote no poetry. His best poems were composed either when he was solitary or else under some profound emotional stress.

He dearly wanted to convince Fanny that married bliss was a higher spiritual state than celibacy (which he could rarely resist coupling with the word 'torment'). It was not sufficient that Fanny should merely agree out of love for him: to satisfy Kingsley she had to be intellectually convinced as well. Towards this goal he began work on a prose biography of St. Elizabeth of Hungary, a married German saint of the Middle Ages, well known in Victorian Sunday Schools. Kingsley always enjoyed German studies, and this would be a labour of love. He had for a long time been irritated by the genteel descriptions of the Middle Ages given by contemporary Catholic and High Church writers, and Kingsley's book was to redress the balance and show the coarseness and miseries of the time. He was very serious about this project and to get a background of the religious outlook of the Middle Ages and of the nature of asceticism and mysticism he read 'Teersteegen, Jacob Behman, Madam Guyon, Alban Butler, Fenelon, some of Origen and Clemens Alexandrinus and Coleridge's *Aids to Reflection*, also some of Kant and a German history of mysticism'.[4] When he felt unable to make his point forcefully enough in words he drew sketches to illustrate them. He did not feel bound to hurry to finish the book, since it was to be a bridal gift, and in the face of Grenfell opposition to their marriage time was hardly of the essence.

His thoughts and actions showed that he tended to look for harmony in social groupings as well as in nature. In spite of plunging into controversies when he spoke and wrote as vehemently as he knew how, he harboured no grudges against his opponents, and this fairmindedness evoked a similar response from others in spite of his stormy life. Partisan writing distressed him. He wrote to Fanny: 'I hate party books. Men think wrongly when they suppose that in order to combat error, they must not allow their opponents to have the least right on their side; no opinion in the world hardly is *utterly* wrong.' He complained about Newman at this time, 'He does not put forward views which he does not believe, but that he does use arguments and statements which he knows to be false and illogical to support the principles he believes in.' Kingsley was forced to conclude that this was insincere, or 'Jesuitical', an adjective which encompassed enormous and emotional depths of disapproval. F. D. Maurice was soon to reinforce Kingsley's hatred of party strife and his innate conviction that truth and sincerity were the foundations of manly honour.[5] Thomas Carlyle and J. A. Froude would also later reinforce Kingsley's belief that the Protestant Church was the only true church wherein a people could achieve nationhood.

Unfortunately, the English Protestant Church at that time was no shining example of Christ's teaching, and it was not surprising that many people were perturbed about it. The universities began to study religion and Christianity as an academic discipline, especially on the Continent, and growing numbers of literary figures admitted to an atheist position. In the manufacturing towns and the poorer country villages, where the social welfare activities of a priest were most sorely needed, it was almost invariably the Dissenting ministers who bore the burden and received the respect and loyalty of the inhabitants. A significant proportion of labouring men either completely ignored religion and its institutions (except where it was in their self-interest to pay occasional lip service to them) or else were actively opposed. Yet the problems of the working class were so acute, and the greed and hypocrisy of many members of the employing class so blatant, that it should have been impossible for a sincere church to stand apart while the moral teachings of the Bible were so plainly flouted on every side.

Kingsley was still casting about for a strong, practical faith to serve as his personal bulwark. The Oxford Reformers were attractive in that they offered a strong faith, but Kingsley decided that their writings did not pass scientific examination. A letter to Fanny Grenfell on this subject is particularly interesting in view of the debate with John Henry Newman into which he was dragged two decades later: '... My idea about quotations is this. Communication is now made so easy and quick by the increase of civilisation, that no man of name or standing dare misquote another. And though it might be said that these quotations are only partial, and that we must read all to know what they really mean, I feel certain from experience that single sentences contain the pith of a man's opinions, more than pages of "talk", and I know enough of these men from my own reading, to know that to read all would rather endanger my opinions by mystifying me in the mass of words, and soothing me when I found opinions with which I did agree. But taking these single quotations, of whose genuineness it is easy to satisfy oneself, one can get at the great dogmatic truths which they hold, and one can ask them, "Either prove that this single sentence is right, or confess that as all your system hinges upon it, therefore all your system is wrong." Feeling this I waited, when I first interested myself upon the point . . . till something should come out which should make a "row", because in that I knew the pith of their opinions would lie. Out came Tract 90. I read it scientifically, and made up my opinion at once as to them and their opinions much more safely than if I had waded through a thousand pages of their previous cautious aesthetic verbiage.'[6]

He knew it was important for his thoughts to be clearly expressed, because the spoken or written word was the clergyman's most potent tool. 'Tell me if I am ever obscure in my expressions, and do not fancy that if I am obscure, I am therefore deep. If I were really deep, all the world would understand, though they might not appreciate. The perfectly popular style is the perfectly scientific one. Tell me then when I am obscure, for to me obscurity is a reason for suspecting a fallacy.'[7] Fanny responded by introducing him to more books and articles of F. D. Maurice, where Kingsley found not only the philosophy which solved his religious difficulties, but—extending as it did over every aspect of life, especially man's relationships with the family, with society and finally with God—also developed his social beliefs and activities.

Maurice's influence over more than a generation of students and clergymen was considerable. His personality was a singular compound of charm, sincerity and humility, and his thought processes were intuitive and paradoxical. Daniel Macmillan, the Scottish bookseller in Cambridge, later to go into publishing, telling a friend of the effect on him of reading Maurice's *The Kingdom of Christ*, wrote: 'I looked into this part, and then into that, and in a very short time found that he was no common man, that he dwelt in a higher, purer, clearer region than that of party.

I found it to be a book that I could not live without. I have learnt much from it, but don't expect to master it for many a day. It is a most extraordinary book. For calmness, for candour, for insight, I have never seen anything on the same subject equal to it. . . . I think it in every way an admirable book; and just suited to meet the wants of our strange distracted time.'[8]

The Macmillans were not alone in feeling that Maurice had some special quality. Gladstone, a fellow student at Oxford, where Maurice went to study for Holy Orders, recalled Maurice for an extreme 'fastidiousness of conscience'. Arthur Hallam, as a student of nineteen, writing to Gladstone in 1830 about Maurice's influence on his fellow university students, said, 'The effect . . . is far greater than I can dare to calculate, and will be felt, both directly and indirectly, in the age that is upon us.'

In a footnote to her life of her husband, Mrs. Kingsley briefly explains Maurice's theology, and this is worth examining in some detail as a reflection of Kingsley's interpretation at least of Maurice's views. F. D. Maurice, writing in the 1840s, insisted that the conscience of men was then in opposition to popular theology, whether Catholic or Protestant, as it prevailed throughout England and the Continent, because popular theology regarded men as existing in a fallen state of evil, with Jesus Christ being born to redeem solely those men and women who happened to believe in him. Maurice was more optimistic and compassionate. Basing his conclusions upon a close and individualistic reading of the Bible and of the history of the early Christian Church, he asserted that man was made in the image of God; that the Fall was the result of first man rebelling against the 'image of God' side of his nature and, indeed, denying its existence. From this initial denial there followed the entire series of denials from all men and women born thereafter, and the Old Testament was really a record of God's patient teaching of one particular people—the Jews—to accept the divine constitution of mankind, and to believe that if a man has faith in God he therefore has the capacity to live up to the divine side of his nature.

Maurice argued that Christ was the true representative of man, clearly revealing his divine origin, and thus with the advent of

Christ there had come the Kingdom of God on earth, intended for men. This was the substance of the teaching of the Apostles, and the baptised Church was a witness to it. God intended the Christian Church to educate the nations into living a life according to the teachings of Jesus Christ. All nations, therefore, had to recognise the overriding sovereignty of an invisible God; this, and only this, declared Maurice, could save a nation from godless absolutism.

His ideas, substantiated through scholarship, became well known by his sermons, lectures, books and articles, and his entire life testified to the sincerity of his belief. A handsome man, with sensitive, intellectual features, and dark eyes which held an audience with almost hypnotic fervour, Maurice inspired an astonishing number and variety of men and women. The deeper implication of his doctrine—and this was the feature which caused such opposition—was that a true Church could never dissociate itself from social and political issues. Followers of Maurice (amongst whom Kingsley was to be the most famous) made themselves consistently unpopular by proclaiming that it was the bounden duty of the Church of England to speak out against all social abuses.

Furthermore, Maurice preached a God of love, loving towards all men and women, so the concept of Hell as a geographical location where people were condemned to eternal physical torture was completely incongruous. Hell, said Maurice, was putting oneself outside communion with God—a common interpretation today, but a dangerously novel one in the mid-nineteenth century. It also, of course, removed that fear of some future Hell which had long been used by the Establishment as a bogeyman to keep rebellious spirits in order, and its abolition was resented. A long period of Whig rule was ending, and the succeeding Tory government was to be compelled by public demand to introduce a massive programme of social reform, because the 1840s were years of economic depression and hunger. The Chartists were organising the workers in an attempt to win a share of parliamentary power. In retrospect, one can see that the Chartist movement had little hope of success on its own terms, but the fiery oratory of its leaders was well calculated both to alarm the middle class and to arouse the workers. If the punitive concept of Hell were abolished, asked Maurice's opponents, who could foresee to what extremes the Chartists might not incite the workers? Nor did Maurice stop short of discussing Hell. He was even more infuriating when he insisted that normal capitalist competition could never be justified on spiritual grounds. Small wonder, then, that all his teaching was regarded as playing into the hands of the revolutionaries, and he and his followers were marked down by the ruling class as men to be suspected and watched.

These bitter controversies were, however, still a few years ahead when Kingsley was gaining experience as a young curate in 1842—and overwhelmed by a sudden Grenfell ukase that all correspondence between himself and Fanny must cease. The Grenfells packed Fanny off on a Continental tour, hoping this would break the relationship. Pollyanna-wise, Kingsley tried to put a brave face on it: 'There are two ways of looking at every occurrence—a bright and a dark side. Which is most worthy of a rational being, a Christian and a friend? It is inconsistent in a Christian to see God's wrath, rather than his mercy in everything. . . .'[9]

He sought to comfort himself by looking round his circle of friends to find other examples of star-crossed lovers. The early Victorians were not ashamed of emotion, and their courtships included many features which became clichés of sentimental fiction. Kingsley needed to look no farther than Cowley Powles and Charles Blachford Mansfield to find two men who were enduring agonies in their private relationships with the opposite sex. Mansfield's personal life and his potential as a brilliant inventive scientist were utterly wrecked by his unhappy involvements with unsuitable women. Kingsley understood very well how easy it was to swing from elation to depression, and he advised Cowley Powles, in a situation similar to his own, to adhere to a strict plan of work so as to avoid any possibility of morbid thoughts. Too much subtle thinking was bad; one should act directly, like a child, and having made a decision should then complete the action and refrain from analysing it. (Kingsley certainly practised what he preached.)

'I am studying it [medicine]. Make yourself thoroughly acquainted with the wages, wants and habits and prevalent diseases of the poor wherever you go. . . . See how much a day can do! I have since nine this morning; cut wood for an hour; spent an hour and more in prayer and humiliation and thereby established a chastened but happy tone, which lasts till now; written six or seven pages of a difficult part of my essay; taught in the school; thought over many things while walking; gone round two-thirds of the parish, visiting and doctoring; and written all this. Such days are lives—and happy ones. One has no time to be miserable and one is ashamed to invent little sorrows for one's self while one is trying to relieve such griefs in others as would kill us. . . .'[10]

He quickly became a familiar figure, striding through the lanes and fields of Eversley, with a few leisure moments to enjoy fishing and hunting (when a generous friend could lend him a mount). But he was appalled by what he saw of the general condition of the agricultural labourer and his family. Many of the Eversley inhabitants could be described in Friedrich Engels' phrase as 'the bold peasantry of England', for a number were descended from gypsies. During the Napoleonic Wars most of them had been engaged in smuggling goods from France—silks and laces and spirits—and the peacetime enforcement of anti-smuggling laws was a genuine hardship. With agricultural wages as low as six shillings a week (Kingsley told Powles that if he were paid only nine shillings a week to keep a wife and family he would turn revolutionary) the men were bound to look to poaching to augment their larder, even though England's game laws were possibly the most barbarous in Europe. Penalties were so severe that whenever there was an encounter between poachers and gamekeepers blood almost certainly flowed and fatalities were frequent.[11] Men who gained a bad reputation through coming before the local magistrates (these for the most part being the landowners and farmers of the district) discovered that knowledge of their misdemeanours preceded them from job to

'Work' by Ford Madox Brown. F. D. Maurice and Thomas Carlyle in right foreground

F. D. Maurice (1805–72), after Laurence

job. Any man protesting against low wages was branded as a malcontent and offered no work except at that low rate. One practical solution to the agricultural problem was suggested by the colonisation schemes propounded by Edward Gibbon Wakefield. In 1831 Wakefield had published a pamphlet on the causes of fire-raising in country districts, and the picture he drew then of the agricultural worker was still valid. Kingsley in 1842 would have recognised it instantly.

'What is that defective being, with calfless legs and stooping shoulders, weak in body and mind, inert, pusillanimous, and stupid, whose premature wrinkles and furtive glance tell of misery and degradation?

'. . . Too degraded to be desperate, he is thoroughly depraved. His miserable career will be short; rheumatism and asthma are conducting him to the workhouse, where he will breathe his last without one pleasant recollection, and so make room for another wretch who may live and die in the same way.'[12]

Compare this picture with Kingsley's account of country labourers in *Yeast*. It is the occasion when the middle-class hero, Lancelot Smith, is taken by the gamekeeper, Tregarva, to a village feast in the year 1847, but we may take it as typical of what Kingsley found in the country when he began work in Eversley. Lancelot has asked innocently why the English villagers cannot practise light and interesting handicrafts at home, like German peasants.

'Who'll teach 'em, sir? From the plough-tail to the reaping-hook, and back again, is all they know. Besides, sir, they are not like us Cornish; they are a stupid pig-headed generation at the best, these south countrymen. They're grown-up babies who want the parson and the squire to be leading them, and preaching to them, and spurring them on, and coaxing them up, every moment. And as for scholarship, sir, a boy leaves school at nine or ten to follow the horses; and between that time and his wedding-day he forgets every word he ever learnt, and becomes, for the most part, as thorough a heathen savage at heart as those wild Indians in the Brazils used to be.

'. . . But as for reading, sir, it's all very well for me, who have

3

been a keeper and dawdled about like a gentleman with a gun over my arm; but did you ever do a good day's farm-work in your life? If you had, man or boy, you wouldn't have been game for much reading when you got home,—tumble into bed at eight o'clock, hardly waiting to take your clothes off, knowing that you must turn up again at five o'clock the next morning to get a breakfast of bread, and perhaps a dab of the squire's dripping, and then back to work again; and so on, day after day, week after week, year after year, without a hope or a chance of being anything but what you are, and only too thankful if you can get work to break your back, and catch the rheumatism over.'

'But do you mean to say that their labour is so severe and incessant?'

'It's only God's blessing if it is incessant, sir, for if it stops, they starve, or go to the house [the Workhouse, set up by the Act of 1834] to be worse fed than the thieves in gaol. And as for its being severe, there's many a boy, as their mothers will tell you, comes home night after night, too tired to eat their suppers, and tumbles, fasting, to bed in the same foul shirt which they've been working in all the day, never changing their rag of calico from week's end to week's end, or washing the skin that's under it once in seven years.'

'No wonder,' said Lancelot, 'that such a life of drudgery makes them brutal and reckless.'

'No wonder, indeed, sir; they've no time to think; they're born to be machines and machines they must be; and I think, sir,' he added bitterly, 'it's God's mercy that they daren't think. It's God's mercy that they don't feel. Men that write books and talk at elections call this a free country, and say that the poorest and meanest has a free opening to rise and become prime minister, if he can. But you see, sir, the misfortune is, that in practice he can't; for one who gets into a gentleman's family, or into a little shop, and so saves a few pounds, fifty know that they've no chance before them, but day-labourer born, day-labourer live, from hand to mouth, scraping and pinching to get not meat and beer even, but bread and potatoes;

and then, at the end of it all, for a worthy reward, half a crown a week of parish pay—or the workhouse. That's a lively hopeful prospect for a Christian man!'

In the same chapter, Kingsley makes his hero reflect on the conversation of the villagers at the annual feast.

Sadder and sadder, Lancelot tried to listen to the conversation of the men round him. To his astonishment, he hardly understood a word of it. It was half articulate, nasal, guttural, made up almost entirely of vowels, like the speech of savages. He had never before been struck with the significant contrast between the sharp, clearly defined articulation, the vivid and varied tones of the gentleman, or even of the London street-boy, when compared with the coarse, half-formed growls, as of a company of seals, which he heard round him. That single fact struck him, perhaps, more deeply than any.[13]

Similar pictures of the countryside abounded in the contemporary press. Alexander Somerville, writing under the name of 'The Whistler at the Plough', recorded the resentment of farm labourers against parsons 'who were always begging', that is, for causes like the conversion of heathens to Christianity.[14]

Meanwhile, Kingsley had to force himself to endure life without any kind of communication with Fanny. Mrs. Kingsley visited Eversley and described her son's living conditions to Fanny Grenfell, so that she might visualise her lover in his new surroundings. The thatched cottage and flower-filled garden, the village green and duck pond, like a charming watercolour, sometimes drove the young curate to despair. 'Around me are the everlasting hills, and the everlasting bores of the country'—but this frankness was carefully reserved for his Cambridge friend, Peter Wood, also now in the Church. Kingsley met some of the staff of Sandhurst military college, not far away, and one of these officers described the lanky young man, bumping his head against the low ceilings and lintels of his cottage—'like a caged bird'—

and yearning for domestic bliss with Fanny in the snug but spacious rectory.

A year slowly passed and then unexpectedly, in September 1843, the situation was transformed. Fanny's steadfast devotion, her approaching thirtieth birthday, and her insistence that if she did not marry Charles Kingsley she would marry no one, gradually wore down most, if not all, family opposition. Mrs. Glyn, a Grenfell lady who had married into the banking family, continued to find Kingsley uncongenial. But, in welcome contrast, the Rev. S. G. Osborne, who had married a Grenfell, had every sympathy for Kingsley. Osborne was a socially-conscious man, of excellent family, who had been directed into the Church by his father, and as a clergyman was able to campaign publicly on behalf of various causes, chief among them being that of the impoverished country worker. Fanny Grenfell enlisted his support and he promised to use his influence to find Kingsley a curacy or living that would satisfy Fanny's relatives.

To the young man in Eversley it was a dream come true. Speech was altogether too commonplace. Despite a croaking voice, he simply had to burst into song. The impending marriage —marvellous in itself—was even more wonderful because it was proof, if proof were needed, of the efficacy of prayer. Before the year was out, Osborne was able to report that Kingsley would be offered a good curacy immediately, and thereafter the first vacant living in the gift of Lord Portman. A wedding date could now be set, and come the New Year, Charles and Fanny would be man and wife.

5

'Blissful Future'

A quiet marriage ceremony was conducted in Bath, Somerset, by the Rev. S. G. Osborne, most of the Grenfell relatives still disapproving. The newly-weds spent a rapturous honeymoon at Cheddar, lasting some two months, and composed themselves to await the promised Dorset living. In the meantime Kingsley was to be curate at Pimperne. Then, quite unexpectedly came the news that the rector of Eversley had fled to the Continent to escape prosecution by the Church authorities. Not only had he neglected his parish duties, but his relationships with local women had become so notorious that husbands finally complained. Mr. Stapleton, the indefatigable churchwarden, acted quickly, and suggested to the squire, Sir John Cope, that young Charles Kingsley had recently made an excellent curate and had the makings of an excellent rector. The turn of events thrilled Kingsley, who had enjoyed the hospitality of the Stapletons, and longed to return to Eversley.

Such matters took time to arrange, so he went alone to Pimperne, which allowed Fanny to stay with her sister, Mrs. Warre, whose husband was a Member of Parliament, and who could offer Fanny the kind of social life which would be impossible in Eversley. Pimperne was close to Durweston Rectory, where the Rev. S. G. Osborne lived, and the Osbornes insisted that Kingsley live with them rather than find lodgings in Pimperne. He enjoyed the three-mile walk from Durweston to Pimperne, through the grass and woodlands of Cranborne Chase. There were leisure moments when he could go fishing. He wrote almost daily to Fanny, a continuing diary of his existence. 'Conceive my pleasure at finding myself in Bemerton, George Herbert's parish, and seeing his house and church, and fishing in the very meadows where he, and Dr. Donne, and Izaac Walton, may have fished before me. I killed several trout and a brace of grayling, about three-quarters of a pound each—a fish quite new to me, smelling just like cucumbers. The dazzling chalk-wolds sleeping in the sun, the clear river rushing and boiling down in one ever-sliding sheet of transparent silver, the birds bursting into song, and mating and toying in every hedgerow—everything stirred with the gleam of God's eyes. . . .'[1]

He read poetry, including Wordsworth's *The Excursion* which left him with the conviction that the Lakeland poet was as much a preacher and prophet as his admired Coleridge. There seemed more poverty at Pimperne than he had noticed at Eversley, possibly because he had the energetic Osborne at his elbow to draw his attention to it. Kingsley told Fanny he thought that the Pimperne paupers had lost all hope in life, and had been trampled on so much that religion had no meaning for them. He blamed the irresponsible rich—'Those who lounge upon down beds, and throw away thousands at Crockford's and Almack's. . . . I have been very sad lately seeing this, and seeing, too, the horrid effects of that new Poor Law.'[2] This was the Poor Law Amendment Act, passed under the Whig government in 1834, and representing the first major overhaul of British poor law since 1601, an attempt to reform the entire system and to compel a distinction between poverty and pauperism. It set up workhouses (called Unions), which separated husband and wife (a crude birth control device), and it filled the poor with hatred and bitterness for the governing class which had such power to direct them to the dreaded Union. Although in the long run the Act succeeded in forcing employers to raise wages so that the burden on the parishes was correspondingly reduced, the decade immediately following 1834 was one of penury and misfortune for the great majority of the working class.

Kingsley's burgeoning social conscience made him an admiring and ready listener to his host's views on an entire range of social problems. S.G.O. (as he became known from 1844 onwards from the initials with which he signed letters to *The Times* newspaper on social and political questions) was exactly the man to justify and enlarge Kingsley's tentative opinions. He was an enthusiastic campaigner for the impoverished Dorset labourers,[3] although he received scant thanks from the labourers themselves, and was reviled by his social equals in the landowning class.[4] He was far in advance of his time on many subjects, several of which— education, hospitals, sanitation, cholera epidemics, women's rights—became favourite stamping grounds for Kingsley.

The young man particularly admired S.G.O.'s trenchant turn of phrase. It was a powerful weapon whereby the preacher-turned-reformer could attack targets like a bold horseman riding at fences.[5] In the pulpit, addressing a different kind of audience, S.G.O. was plain and direct—again, characteristics which Kingsley emulated. The rector was bored by the ordinary conventions of country life, and Durweston Rectory was rarely the scene of dinner parties, although the house was always open to S.G.O.'s friends, who inevitably shared his interests. He had a wide circle of acquaintances, and a still wider one of correspondents, and these more than compensated for his self-restricted social life.

S.G.O. declared that the health and happiness of a nation could be measured by the health and happiness of the domestic home, because the home was the unit of the nation. He believed that one fundamental way to improve family conditions was to educate the children, and therefore advocated education for all. 'To destroy privilege and to throw open to the people opportunities for decent life, harmless enjoyments, and intellectual training, was to Osborne the highest pleasure of his life.'[6] He certainly enjoyed combat and controversy, carried on through public and private correspondence. It added zest to the simplicity of his country existence. Like F. D. Maurice, S.G.O. remained aloof from party faction, preserving his independence and integrity. Charles Kingsley found plenty to respect in Fanny's kinsman by marriage. 'God grant that I may be half as useful in my generation as he is!' he wrote to his wife.

For S.G.O. demonstrated to Kingsley by daily example that within the Church of England a man might reconcile the military, religious and social aspects of his character. Under this influence, the 'militant Christian' in Kingsley pushed its way to the fore, where it remained, to a greater or lesser degree, until his death. 'Militant Christian', in fact, is a fairer and apter description of Kingsley than the 'muscular Christian' tag[7] which pursued him mercilessly, to his intense annoyance.

Meanwhile, at Eversley, Mr. Stapleton enlisted the powerful support of his Heckfield neighbour, Sir Henry Dukinfield. In addition to being a baronet, Sir Henry was vicar of St. Martin-in-the-Fields, London, and a prebendary of Salisbury Cathedral. These two men pleaded Kingsley's cause with the Bishop of Winchester, and since the time had expired during which the absent rector, John Toovey Hawley, should have written a letter of explanation, if not of expiation, the bishop announced that the living was vacant, and that Kingsley was an acceptable candidate. All now depended upon Sir John Cope's reaction to Kingsley, and thus ultimate success would hang entirely upon the interview with the squire.

Sir John Cope was a hard-drinking, hunting man who might have stepped right out of a Fielding novel.[8] He was prepared to invite his rector to dinner once in a while, and to say hello in the hunting field, but took no interest in spiritual responsibilities, and certainly had no intention of spending money on church, parish or rectory. Indeed, in Sir John's view Hawley's finest recommendation was the fact that he never approached the squire for money. Sir John lived at Bramshill Park, a magnificent mansion built in the reign of James I, only a short distance from the rectory, which Sir John never visited.[9]

Kingsley was extremely nervous about the interview. He spent the week-end with his parents at Chelsea, so that he was on the spot to meet Sir John at Arthur's Club in London the following Monday afternoon. He made a good impression. Sir John saw before him a country-bred, out-of-doors young man who could discuss fishing and horses with the familiarity of an expert. The squire was not percipient enough to realise that behind the painful stammer and the eagerness to please lurked an impulsive hot-head destined to disturb the peace of Sir John's declining years.

He was perfectly agreeable to accept Kingsley, so the matter was satisfactorily concluded. A minimum of furniture was sent down immediately to Eversley, followed very shortly by the jubilant new rector.

This time Kingsley surveyed the parish with the grave eyes of an incumbent, one moreover who had become alerted to reality, and soon got the measure of the problems he had inherited. The parish had been disgracefully neglected by Hawley, whose escapades had been fully known to the villagers, however much the gentry and his ecclesiastical superiors may have been either ignorant of them or deliberately blind. Kingsley never underestimated the clear-sightedness of village folk, as he once made clear in a piece of plain speaking delivered to the ladies of the Needlewomen's Institution in London. Speaking of ordinary people, he said:

> Fancy not that they know nothing about you. There is nothing secret which shall not be made manifest; and what you do in the closet is surely proclaimed (and often with exaggeration enough and to spare) on the house-top. These poor folk at your gate know well enough, through servants and trades-men, what you are, how you pay your bills, what sort of temper you have; and they form a shrewd, hard estimate of your character, in the light of which they view all that you do and say to them.[10]

Church attendance at Eversley was minimal—hardly surprising, since the church furnishings were in shocking disrepair, the churchyard was an open invitation to straying sheep, and ser-vices had been cancelled at short notice whenever the former rector felt disinclined to take them. Even more galling for Kings-ley was the discovery that although the Church was stagnant, Dissent was thriving. He disliked Dissenting preachers, whose ranting sermons he considered preyed upon the ignorance and superstition of their hearers. Kingsley's novels exhibit these prejudices, and to any criticisms about this he replied stubbornly that he portrayed Dissenters only as he had known them.

In *Alton Locke*, for example, the narrator-hero has a Baptist mother who 'gloried in her dissent':

My mother moved by rule and method; by God's law, as she considered, and that only. She seldom smiled. Her word was absolute. She never commanded twice without punishing. And yet there were abysses of unspoken tenderness in her, as well as clear, sound womanly sense and insight. But she thought herself as much bound to keep down all tenderness as if she had been some ascetic of the middle ages—so do extremes meet! It was 'carnal', she considered. She had as yet no right to have any 'spiritual affection' for us. We were still 'children of wrath and of the devil'—not yet 'convinced of sin', 'converted, born again'. She had no more spiritual bond with us, she thought, than she had with a heathen or a Papist. She dared not even pray for our conversion, earnestly though she prayed on every other subject. For although the majority of her sect would have done so, her clear logical sense would yield to no such tender inconsistency. Had it not been decided from all eternity? We were elect, or we were reprobate. Could her prayers alter that?[11]

In a later novel, *Two Years Ago*, Kingsley had another tilt at Nonconformism. The Cornish town of Aberalva is stricken with cholera, and the young doctor wishes to check the disease by improved sanitation. The Dissenting preacher, however, declares that the epidemic is God's punishment for mortal sins. Major Campbell, a sensible retired army officer, is deputed to attend the revivalist meeting in the town, in the hope that his common sense will counter the hysteria engendered by the preacher.

At six o'clock that evening, the meeting-house was filling with terrified women, and half-curious, half-sneering men; and among them the tall figure of Major Campbell, in his undress uniform (which he had put on, wisely, to give a certain dignity to his mission), stalked in, and took his seat in the back benches.

The sermon was what he expected. There is no need to transcribe it. Such discourses may be heard often enough in churches as well as chapels. The preacher's object seemed to be—for some purpose or other which we have no right to

judge—to excite in his hearers the utmost intensity of selfish
fear, by language which certainly, as Tom had said, came under
the law against profane cursing and swearing. He described the
next world in language which seemed a strange jumble of
Virgil's 'Aeneid', the Koran, the dreams of those rabbis who
crucified our Lord, and of those medieval inquisitors who tried
to convert sinners (and on their own ground, neither illogically
nor over-harshly) by making this world for a few hours as
like as possible to what, so they held, God was going to make
the world to come for ever.

At last he stopped suddenly, when he saw that the animal
excitement was at the very highest; and called on all who felt
'convinced' to come forward and confess their sins.

In another minute there would have been (as there have been
ere now) four or five young girls raving and tossing upon the
floor, in mad terror and excitement; or, possibly, half the
congregation might have rushed out (as a congregation
has rushed out ere now) headed by the preacher himself, and
run headlong down to the quay-pool, with shrieks and shouts,
declaring that they had cast the devil out of Betsy Pennington,
and were hunting him into the sea; but Campbell saw that the
madness must be stopped at once; and rising, he thundered, in a
voice which brought all to their senses in a moment—

'Stop!'[12]

Kingsley worried so much about the problem of Dissenters
in Eversley that he plucked up courage to write to F. D. Maurice
for advice, and also for suggestions on how best to study the
Bible. Kingsley was very much the respectful neophyte approaching 'the elder prophet'. Maurice, in a typically long letter, advised
a mild and conciliatory approach to Dissenters. He said that
Kingsley should adopt their opinions and language to demonstrate
how Dissenters could abandon their strict views on the elect
and non-elect in favour of a more compassionate belief. Maurice
insisted that God's plan to send Jesus Christ, the truly incarnated
God, to earth existed *before* the Fall of Man (i.e. before Adam and
Eve ate the apple from the Tree of Knowledge in the Garden of

Eden); therefore, it could not be logically true that Jesus was sent afterwards to *remedy* the consequences of that Fall. Anglicans— in the Maurician view—believed that God would choose, not by judging people on their previous life, but only as it seemed good to Him. As for Bible study, Maurice considered any system was good as long as it was applied methodically, and as long as the Bible was regarded as revealing a gradual knowledge of God.[13] For Kingsley, 'a very working man with 750 sheep in the wilder- ness, many of whom will not hear my voice', as he described himself to Cowley Powles, this was guidance gratefully followed.

In the matter of the more mundane details of day-to-day routine Kingsley had already elaborated a programme, subscrib- ing to that school of thought which says start as you mean to continue. He told Fanny of the timetable he would want to see followed long before they were installed in Eversley. 'Family prayers before breakfast; 8.30–10, household matters; 10–1, studying divinity, or settling parish accounts and business—our doors open for poor parish visitants; between 1 and 5, go out in all weathers, to visit sick and poor, and to teach in the school; in the evening we will draw, and feed the intellect and the fancy.... We must devote from 9 to 12 on Monday mornings to casting up our weekly bills and accounts, and make a rule never to men- tion them, if possible, at any other time; and never to talk of household matters, unless urgent, but between 9 and 10 in the morning; nor of parish business in the evening. I have seen the *gene* and misery which not following some such rule brings down! We must pray for a spirit of order and regularity and economy in the least things....'[14]

John Martineau, who became Kingsley's pupil in January 1840, described life at the rectory in his letters home, and the rector's original precepts were followed fairly closely. 'We have prayers at 8.45, but I intend in future to be down before that and get some work done,' planned the sixteen-year-old boy. 'Mr. Kingsley reads a chapter or half a one, and then we have a sub- stantial meat breakfast, and then we work till one o'clock, when we have lunch; and after lunch we go out walking till about five, when we dine; then work from seven till nine; at half-past nine prayers, Mr. Kingsley only reading three or four verses, then I go to bed.' The boy was mothered by Fanny Kingsley. 'Mrs. Kingsley is particularly kind and delicately attentive; she insists on my having my fire lighted when I get up every morning, and again to go to bed by. A broken brace-end that I happened to leave on my table the other day I found ready mended the next time I came into my room; I have a nice large room, writing materials, pens, bookshelves, and everything very complete, but I am not to work (as Mr. K. calls it, "grind") in my bedroom at all.'[15] (Martineau was treated as an adopted son by Charles and Fanny. She always addressed him in letters as 'My dearest John' or 'My dearest boy'. Martineau reciprocated, and his daughter's life of her father emphasises the point by its very title: *John Martineau, Pupil of Kingsley*.)

There was a warm, hospitable air about the rectory, due in large measure to Fanny's excellent household management. Her servants remained faithfully with her for years, leaving only to get married. Twenty years was not an exceptional time for a servant to stay. Guests frequently came to dinner, and after the meal would retire to Kingsley's study, which opened on the side of the house, to talk and smoke for as long as they wished. There were often house-guests, staying for a few days.

In material comfort, however, the rectory was sadly deficient, for it was badly sited in a dip, so that water ran off a hill opposite to collect in springs and channels under the foundations of the house. In wet weather the stables and ground-floor rooms were flooded, and Kingsley frequently joined the servants in staying up to all hours of the night bailing out the water with a chain of buckets. He continually expended almost superhuman effort digging irrigation ditches in the garden to divert the stream. Sir John Cope, when appealed to, refused either to finance repairs or to consent to a new rectory on a drier site. Kingsley had to use his own money to keep the damp at bay, and everyone suffered from persistent colds and influenza. (It was not until the 1960s that minimal central heating was installed to keep the rectory warm and dry in the winter, and in 1971 the Church authorities built a new rectory on a better site and Kingsley's house was sold by auction.)

Before the Kingsleys were properly settled in at Eversley news
came that Gerald Kingsley had died at sea. Fanny had barely
known him, for he was already in the navy when she and Charles
met. The young cadet had seen action at Acre in 1839, and in 1844,
promoted to a bigger ship, H.M.S. *Royalist*, he was on a routine
tour of the Gulf of Carpentaria when the whole ship's crew took
sick with fever. Gerald was one of the last officers to die. The
Kingsleys were an affectionate and united family, and Gerald's
sudden death, especially its manner, hit them all very hard. It was
worst for Gerald's father, who had the devastating experience of
learning about it casually by overhearing the conversation of two
strangers in Chelsea Public Library. The shock made him prematurely old. Charles hurried to Chelsea to comfort his parents,
and to try to explain the meaning of life and death to his young
brother, Henry.

Kingsley's depression caused by Gerald's death was cured by a
happy turn of events, of the kind that did not happen very
frequently to him. It came about through his Cambridge friend,
Peter Wood, whose father, Dean Wood, had the disposal of two
honorary canonries in the Collegiate Church of Middleham in
Yorkshire. The dean bestowed one canonry on his son, and
offered the second to Kingsley, who was both pleased and amused
to accept it. There were no duties—and no pay—attached to this
office, but the title of Canon was irresistible, and besides, here was
the chance of a free holiday. The canonry, incidentally, was
abolished not long afterwards.

It was Kingsley's first visit to Yorkshire, and he was almost
overwhelmed by the scale of local hospitality, since he and
Fanny lived a fairly abstemious life at Eversley. He kept careful
notes of everything, transcribing them in his daily letters to
Fanny, not forgetting the Kendal mail coach which took him on
the last lap of the journey, and made him sorry for the animals
which pulled the vehicle—'two tortured horses for which the
knacker's yard cries, indignant.'[16]

Middleham was a racing town, full of jockeys and stable-boys
and horses. Behind the town was the enchanting little river
Cover, where he could recover from the boundless hospitality.

'Today I go up the lovely Cover, to fish and dream of you,' he wrote sentimentally, but truly. He was to write up parts of his visit years later in an essay called *Chalk Stream Studies*, where he described

> ... the exquisite Cother brook, near Middleham in Yorkshire. In that delicious glen, while wading up beneath the ash-fringed crags of limestone, out of which the great ring ouzel (too wild, it seemed, to be afraid of man) hopped down fearlessly to feed upon the strand or past flower-banks where the golden globe-flower, and the great blue geranium, and the giant campanula, bloomed beneath the white tassels of the bird cherry. . . .'[17]

The break refreshed him, and when he returned to Eversley he was ready to share in the repair work of the rectory, as well as the organisation involved in building up a loyal congregation.

Early in 1846 their first child, Rose, was born. Fanny came through this confinement very well, in view of her age, and she and Kingsley were delighted to have started a family, but thereafter her health became delicate, and she had at least one miscarriage. Fanny Kingsley described rectory life at that time as 'uneventful in the routine of parish life and home happiness. Adult classes, a singing class on Hullah's plan[18] to improve the Church music (which had been entirely in the hands of three or four poor men, with a trombone and two clarinets) brought his people on several nights of the week up to the rectory where the long unfurnished dining-room served the purposes of school-room.'

In the spring of 1846 Fanny took the baby to Shanklin, on the Isle of Wight, to recover from influenza, and Charles joined her for a few days. He took his illustrated manuscript of the life of St. Elizabeth, for he now had the notion of turning it into a verse drama. His natural bent was towards poetry, most especially towards short lyrics of intense emotion. John Keble, when Professor of Poetry at Oxford, would have classified Kingsley as a 'primary poet', one of those who 'spontaneously moved by impulse, resort to composition for relief and solace'.[19] The proposed piece was to be a carefully disciplined work of blank verse.

While working on the St. Elizabeth play, Kingsley, like others of like mind, fretted about the 'condition of England'. Disraeli's fine novels, *Coningsby*, published in 1844, and *Sybil*, published in 1845, had described social conditions which Kingsley certainly did not ignore, for he wrote tartly to his friends that the upper classes really ought to solve the social problems of the country unless they were prepared to let the lower classes have a shot at it, as he confessed 'I would, if I were hovering between nine shillings a week and the workhouse as the sum of all attainabilities this side of heaven'.[20]

Unlike S.G.O., who had friends in high places, Kingsley could not expect to get published in the London *Times*, but neither could he keep silent. He believed that a new, serious periodical, circulating among the professional and upper middle class, would give him, and others like him, a suitable platform. Cowley Powles, now a Fellow at Exeter Hall, Oxford, was ideally placed to promote such a magazine, and Kingsley wrote to him, urging this. 'I am more and more painfully awake to the fact that the curse of our generation is that so few of us deeply believe in anything. Men dally with truth, and with lies. . . . My friend, we must pray to God to give us faith, faith in something—something that we can live for, and would die for.' He noted that the new element for spiritual good in Europe in 1846 was democracy, a trend which was establishing itself in Church as well as in State. Democracy seemed inevitable, so —with the pragmatic approach typical of the English—Kingsley added, '. . . we cannot stop it. Let us Christianise it instead.'[21]

Meanwhile, his homespun remedy for depression and pessimism was a happy married and family life, sexually and spiritually satisfying. ('Oh, teeming tropic sea of Eros!' as he put it to Cowley Powles, when his friend finally came safely through the shoals of an engagement to the harbour of marriage.) God and Fanny were equally essential to Kingsley's physical and emotional balance, although in his advice to others (to dear Charles Mansfield, for instance, agonising again between religion and disbelief) he was careful to keep God firmly in the forefront. Modern readers, accustomed to a cooler detachment towards morality, may feel that Kingsley protested his belief in God too much, but his contemporaries would have disagreed. Kingsley's sincerity was always manifest, just as his generous heart and wide interests charmed so many different characters. In spite of his gad-fly eloquence, he possessed the gift of healing, and his kindness was balm to many a wounded spirit.[22]

Fanny took an admiring interest in the St. Elizabeth play throughout and urged him to publish it. She had the business head in the family, and when Kingsley became better known she would sometimes send sermons and essays off to editors without telling him. Kingsley was diffident about the merits of the play, but finally submitted it to friends whose judgment he could trust: Cowley Powles, Derwent Coleridge, the Hon. and Rev. Gerald Wellesley, and, of course, F. D. Maurice, 'the prophet'. All congratulated him, and told him to seek a publisher. Maurice went over the manuscript with him at one of the former's famous breakfast sessions.[23] Maurice was a well-established author of books on morals and philosophy, and to aid his young friend he offered to write a preface, hoping that this would not only help him find a publisher but would also explain to a public unaccustomed to Kingsley's vigorous language that the purpose behind the theme was irreproachable. J. Parker, of 445, West Strand, London, a firm which published the popular *Fraser's Magazine*, agreed to take the book with a preface by Maurice. It was to be called *The Saint's Tragedy*, and Kingsley was well aware of his good fortune in being published.

A second child, a son, was born to the Kingsleys in 1847, and named Maurice, after one of his godfathers (Cowley Powles was the other). In the summer Charles took the services for a brief spell at Pennington, in the New Forest near Lymington, which gave the family a country holiday and the rector a much-appreciated rest from parish visiting. He relaxed by riding through the New Forest, composing ballads in his head, and planning an historical romance with a New Forest setting. The poems were put down on paper, but the romance was never completed.

Airly Beacon, his best poem of this period, is more in the tradition and spirit of Robert Burns' love poetry than the Anglican poetry of the nineteenth century.

> Airly Beacon, Airly Beacon;
> Oh the pleasant sight to see
> Shires and towns from Airly Beacon,
> While my love climbed up to me!
>
> Airly Beacon, Airly Beacon;
> Oh the happy hours we lay
> Deep in fern on Airly Beacon,
> Courting through the summer's day!
>
> Airly Beacon, Airly Beacon;
> Oh the weary haunt for me,
> All alone on Airly Beacon,
> With his baby on my knee!

All too soon it was time to return to Eversley, where the heavy commitment of work engulfed him once more. 'Every winter's evening,' wrote Fanny Kingsley, 'was occupied with either night-school at the rectory, about thirty men attending; or little services in the outlying cottages for the infirm and labouring men after their day's work. During spring and summer a writing class was held for girls in the empty coach-house; a cottage school for infants was also begun on the common—all preparing the way for the National School that was to be built some years later.'[24]

The Saint's Tragedy dealt with a story which was already familiar to Victorians through sentimental Sunday School tales and illustrated postcards. It came as a shock when Kingsley drew new, harsh lessons from it and supported his thesis by copious references to historical authorities, drawing in particular upon the biography of St. Elizabeth by Dietrich of Appold, who had been alive at her death and had spoken to people who knew her. Kingsley asserted that Elizabeth personified two of the great mental struggles of the Middle Ages: true innocence (i.e. that drawn from the Scriptures) versus prudery (i.e. false innocence dictated by the Catholic Church), and married love versus celibacy and ascetism. It was also his first joust against fanaticism, which he later expanded in *Hypatia*.

In his preface, Maurice declared that Kingsley did not approve of telling his readers what to believe; actions and characters should speak for themselves, and the readers must draw their own conclusions. The questions posed in the play were dangerous, warned Maurice, touching upon the spirit of the Middle Ages and the nature of self-sacrifice, and were particularly interesting to the English public in the mid-nineteenth century. As for the poetic form of drama, Maurice believed that all the great national poets of England—Chaucer, Shakespeare, Milton—had adopted that form, so he felt it must respond to some special element in the English cast of mind. Although written with the best of motives, Maurice's preface did Kingsley something of a disservice, with its warning of dangerous questions. It predisposed readers to categorise Kingsley as a dangerous writer, a label which his subsequent activities amply justified.

Kingsley's introduction was interesting because it hinted at his personal beliefs. Of Lewis, Elizabeth's handsome but weak husband, he wrote that he was 'possessed of all virtues but those of action', a Hamletesque thought recalling Kingsley's father, of whom Kingsley said in another context that he was possessed of all the talents except that of knowing how to use them. Conrad, spiritual director to Elizabeth and Lewis, is a powerful personality: 'a noble nature warped and blinded by its unnatural exclusions from those family ties through which we first discern or describe God and our relations to Him. . . .' Walter of Varila, a knight, is Kingsley's semi-fictional creation, meant to infuse balance and common sense into the story, a healthy-minded Teuton who in a later age might be a follower of Martin Luther.

Kingsley deliberately drew the background of castle and peasant life as 'gross, a coarse barbarous and profligate age', partly because it was true, and partly as a contrast to the purity and beauty of Elizabeth. In addition, it proved another point, which Kingsley thought important, that a wild and excessive age produced a peculiar reaction: ascetic saints who turned their back on such a world.

Kingsley displayed his facility with words from the early scenes, where Lewis and Walter are riding through Thuringia, in order that the young prince can survey his domain. He is gloomy, unimpressed by his estates.

'Possession's naught; a parchment ghost.'

His stalwart knight disagrees.

'Possession's naught? Possession's beef and ale—
Soft bed, fair wife, gay horse, good steel.—Are they naught?
Possession means to sit astride of the world
Instead of having it astride of you.'

Conrad the monk appeals to Lewis's mystical and romantic side, bidding him love the Virgin Mary, not a mortal woman.

'Why hath the rose its scent, the lily grace?
To mirror forth her loveliness, from whom,
Primeval font of grace, their livery came.'

It is a sentiment which does not appeal to bluff Walter, who mutters under his breath

'Ay, catch his fever, Sir, and learn to take
An indigestion for a troop of angels.'

Lewis and Elizabeth are married, but the happiness she finds in the marriage-bed troubles the bride, for the priests told her that 'love is of the flesh ... the adder in our bosoms'. So on their wedding-night she leaves their warm, luxurious bed to lie, conscience-stricken, on the cold floor, her body scarred with the lashes which she had ordered her maid-servants to inflict upon her. Lewis, waking up, is horrified and uncomprehending, but she calms him.

'Am I not as gay a lady-love
As ever clipt in arms a noble knight?
Am I not blithe as bird the live-long day?
It pleases me to bear what you call pain.'

It is then, at the crossroads of her life, torn between love of her husband and a desire to experience all the physical agonies of Christ so that she can feel herself close to God, that Elizabeth meets Conrad. Her beauty and queenliness make an immediate appeal to him. She surrenders the direction of her life and of Lewis's to him. Henceforth, Conrad devotes himself to training Elizabeth for sainthood, and driven by his insistence and by her natural sympathy for the poor, Elizabeth devotes herself entirely to charity and self-sacrifice. She is horrified by what she sees just outside the castle.

'I turned into an alley 'neath the wall—
And stepped from earth to hell.—The light of heaven,
The common air, was narrow, gross, and dun;
The tiles did drop from the eaves; the unhinged doors
Tottered o'er inky pools, where reeked and curdled
The offal of a life; the gaunt-haunched swine
Growled at their christened playmates o'er the scraps.
Shrill mothers cursed; wan children wailed; sharp coughs
Rang through the crazy chambers; hungry eyes
Glared dumb reproach, and old perplexity,
Too stale for words; o'er still and webless looms
The listless craftsmen through their elf-locks scowled;
These were my people! all I had, I gave—
They snatched it thankless (was it not their own?
Wrung from their veins, returning all too late?)'.

Lewis's religious fervour takes the form of departing on a Crusade. He dies of fever on the way. Elizabeth mourns him passionately, remembering their six happy years together. Her unsympathetic mother-in-law summons Lewis's younger brother, now the ruler of Thuringia, and Elizabeth is turned out of the castle. Nobody will help the young widow and risk the displeasure of the new ruler. Under Conrad's relentless command, Elizabeth becomes increasingly fanatical in her charities and penances, so thin that she is 'a bag of bones', and forced by him in the end to renounce even the act of giving because it gives her pleasure.

> '. . . do God's work
> In spite of loathing; that's the path of Saints',

says Conrad severely.

Soon the young woman is on her deathbed, where her last words are decidedly ambiguous:

> 'Now I must sleep, for ere the sun shall rise
> I must begone upon a long, long journey
> To him I love.'

Conrad:

> '. . . She means her heavenly Bridegroom
> The spouse of souls.'

Elizabeth:

> 'I said, to him I love.
> Let me sleep, sleep.
> You will not need to wake me—so—goodnight.'

Elizabeth's death is the signal for countless miraculous cures effected at her tomb, and before ten years are out she has been officially canonised by Rome, mainly as a result of Conrad's persistent urging. But, alone with his thoughts, he sometimes has doubts.

> 'The work is done. Diva Elizabeth!
> And I have trained one saint before I die!
> Yet now 'tis done, is't well done? On my lips
> Is triumph; but what echo in my heart?'

Meanwhile, heretical preachers are roaming through Germany, stirring up mob hatred against the Roman Catholic priests, and Conrad, a future martyr, dies at the hands of a fanatical mob, calling upon his St. Elizabeth to pray for him.

London and Cambridge circles did not pay much attention to *The Saint's Tragedy*, but in Oxford, the home of Tractarianism, the book made quite a stir, not so much for its literary merit as for its message that ascetism was not an essential ingredient of the religious attitude—a message which Kingsley never ceased to repeat. Baron Bunsen, Prussian ambassador in London and a cultivated patron of the arts, greatly admired the play. A 'prophet of the present' was how he described Kingsley later in a letter to Max Müller, the Oxford philologist.

Kingsley went to Oxford for a few days in March, to stay with Cowley Powles and to be exposed to some gentle 'lionising' as a new writer. He wrote to Fanny that it was 'very funny and very new'.[25] He and Fanny were gratified, though a little surprised, that the passage which people liked best was the lyric, 'Oh that we two were Maying', and when Hullah set it to music the song passed instantly into the repertoire of Victorian and afterwards Edwardian drawing-room music-makers.

However, fame was one thing, unpaid bills quite another, and now that he was a published author Kingsley hoped to get more work on a paid basis. He wrote to Parker, soliciting commissions, and in March 1848 an article entitled *Why should we fear the Romish priests?* enlarged some of his ideas in *The Saint's Tragedy*. Then, within weeks, events occurred in London which took Kingsley out of the literary scene and propelled him into the limelight of political controversy.

6

The Revolutionary Year

The revolutionary year of 1848 was probably more important than any other in the development and direction of Charles Kingsley. The success of *The Saint's Tragedy* had already suggested writing as a way of publicising his ideas, and also of earning extra money, sorely needed at this juncture because of urgent repairs to the rectory. Fanny Kingsley had a small income (most of her money was in trust) but her husband was deeply reluctant to touch any of it. Either Sir John should pay the bills, or he should apply to the appropriate Church funds for a grant. But the squire turned a deaf ear to his rector's complaints, and Kingsley prepared to shoulder the burden himself.

He visited London fairly frequently, drawn especially by the congenial and stimulating company to be found at Maurice's home in Queen's Square, Bloomsbury.[1] Maurice was Chaplain of Lincoln's Inn, and law students and barristers gathered round him. Foremost among these was Thomas Hughes, a barrister, and he and Kingsley became firm friends. Hughes was a product of Dr. Arnold's pioneering work at Rugby, a bluff, honest young man, who shared Kingsley's passion for fishing. Kingsley's relationship with Hughes was one of equality, in contrast to his friendship with Maurice, which had a strong father/son, teacher/pupil element.

It was at the Maurice home that Kingsley was dubbed 'Parson Lot' in the course of some argument in which he was a little upset to find himself in a minority of one. He remarked ruefully that he felt like Lot faced by his sons-in-law, an observation which provoked gales of laughter and led promptly to the nickname.

During that winter there were many indications in Britain of trouble to come. Thomas Hughes, in a preface to editions of *Alton Locke* published after Kingsley's death, described those months for the benefit of later generations. 'Through the winter of 1847–8, amidst widespread distress, the cloud of discontent of which Chartism was the most violent symptom, had been growing darker and more menacing, while Ireland was only held down by main force. In March there were riots in London, Glasgow, Edinburgh, Liverpool and other large towns.'

In France, trouble broke out in February 1848 where a revolt in Paris overthrew the régime of Louis Philippe. Kingsley, enormously excited, tried to explain to his isolated and uneducated country parishioners what was happening, and why. The English Chartists, aroused by the revolutionary activity on the Continent, organised a new petition, to be presented to Parliament, demanding that they be granted the six points of their Charter.[2] Kingsley agreed that the Chartists had legitimate grievances, but he was far from sure that the franchise was the perfect answer.

In a key passage in his Chartist novel, *Alton Locke*, Kingsley tries to identify with the Chartists and to show 'How Folk Turn Chartist'. Although written with the advantage of hindsight, and after he had made the personal acquaintance of highly articulate Chartists, the passage is worth quoting here, if only as an example of Kingsley as a teacher of politics and sociology through the medium of fiction.

Young Alton Locke, recently apprenticed to a tailor's sweat shop, is talking to Crossthwaite, a Chartist.

'I really do not understand political questions, Crossthwaite.'

'Does it want so very much wisdom to understand the rights and wrongs of all that? Are the people represented? Are you represented? Do you feel like a man that's got any one to fight your battle in Parliament, my young friend, eh?'

'I'm sure I don't know—'

'Why, what in the name of common sense—what interest or feeling of yours or mine, or any man's you ever spoke of, except the shopkeeper, do Alderman A— or Lord C—D— represent? They represent property—and we have none. They

represent rank—and we have none. Vested interests—we have
none. Large capitals—these are just what crush us. Irresponsi-
bility of employers, slavery of the employed, competition
among masters, competition among workmen, that is the
system they represent—they preach it, they glory in it. Why,
it is the very ogre that is eating us all up. They are chosen by
the few, they represent the few, and they make laws for the
many—and yet you don't know whether or not the people are
represented!'

We were passing by the door of the Victoria Theatre;
it was just half-price time—and the beggary and rascality of
London were pouring in to their low amusement, from the
neighbouring gin-palaces and thieves' cellars. A herd of
ragged boys, vomiting forth slang, filth and blasphemy,
pushed past us, compelling us to take good care of our
pockets.

'Look there! look at the amusements, the training, the civilisation, which the Government permits to the children of the
people!—these licensed pits of darkness, traps of temptation,
profligacy, and ruin, triumphantly yawn night after night—
and then tell me that the people who see their children thus
kidnapped into hell are represented by a Government who
licenses such things!'

'Would a change in the franchise cure that?'

'Household suffrage mightn't—but give us the Charter,
and we'll send workmen into Parliament that shall soon find
out whether something better can't be put in the way of the
ten thousand boys and girls in London who live by theft and
prostitution, than the tender mercies of the Victoria—a pretty
name! They say the Queen's a good woman—and I don't
doubt it. I wonder often if she knows what her precious
namesake here is like.'

'But really, I cannot see how a mere change in representation
can cure such things as that.'

'Why, didn't they tell us, before the Reform Bill, that
extension of the suffrage was to cure everything? And how can
you have too much of a good thing? We've only taken them

at their word, we Chartists. Haven't all politicians been preaching for years that England's national greatness was all owing to her political institutions—to Magna Carta, and the Bill of Rights, and representative parliaments, and all that?'

These arguments convince Alton:

From that night I was a Chartist, heart and soul—and so were a million and a half more of the best artisans in England—at least, I had no reason to be ashamed of my company. Yes; I, too, like Crossthwaite, took the upper classes at their word; bowed down to the idol of political institutions, and pinned my hopes of salvation on 'the possession of one ten-thousandth part of a talker in the national palaver'. True, I desired the Charter, at first (as I do, indeed, at this moment) as a means to glorious ends—not only because it would give a chance of elevation, a free sphere of action, to lowly worth and talent; but because it was the path to reforms—social, legal, sanitary, educational—to which the veriest Tory—certainly not the great and good Lord Ashley—would not object. But soon, with me, and I am afraid with many, many more, the means became, by the frailty of poor human nature, the end, an idol in itself. I had so made up my mind that it was the only method of getting what I wanted, that I neglected, alas! but too often, to try the methods which lay already by me. 'If we had but the Charter'—was the excuse for a thousand lazinesses, procrastinations. 'If we had but the Charter'—I should be good, and free, and happy.'[3]

Meanwhile, the Chartists announced they would hold a huge demonstration in London on Monday, April 10, for the purpose of presenting their new petition. The day was awaited with considerable unease, particularly among government circles, as it was feared that London would be swarming with marauding Chartist rioters and that mob rule would take over. People needed only to look across the Channel to get some idea of what could happen. John Parker junior, son of Kingsley's publisher, and a former fellow Cambridge student, was staying at the rectory the week-end preceding April 10, and naturally the subject of Chartism was discussed. Parker was only half joking when he said that the firm's premises in West Strand might be attacked by Chartists. It was like a trumpet call to Kingsley. He had to go to London that week in any case for an interview at King's College, where Maurice, who taught there, had put his name forward as a candidate for an assistant lectureship in divinity, and he now offered to accompany his friend to London first thing on Monday morning.

Accordingly, they caught an early train at Winchfield, and upon reaching London Kingsley went at once to Maurice for advice on how he could be most useful. Kingsley was afraid violence would break out, in which case the Chartists ('poor fellows, they mean well') would suffer. Maurice was confined to his home that day with a bad cough but scribbled a quick note of introduction for Kingsley to take to a barrister of Lincoln's Inn, John Malcolm Ludlow.[4]

Ludlow was a cautious, unemotional man, educated in France, which usually put him at a slight disadvantage with his English colleagues. However, the tension of that day, combined with Kingsley's natural warmth and disarming stammer, created a situation which allowed Kingsley to pierce Ludlow's habitual reserve, and these two dissimilar men were delighted to find they had so many aims and ideals in common. This encounter between Kingsley and Ludlow finally linked the quartet which formed the basis of the Christian Socialist group: four gifted, energetic and dedicated men, Maurice, Ludlow, Kingsley and Hughes, each contributing some individual quality which together created a formidable whole.

Ludlow was born in India, son of an Indian Army officer, but brought up in Paris by his widowed and impecunious mother. He was a devout Protestant, and greatly influenced by the French Socialists, especially Fourier. He took the English bar examinations but could not decide whether to be a barrister in England or a politician in France. Like Kingsley, he had worried over the events of the winter of 1847-8, and again like Kingsley, had turned to Maurice for guidance. It was indeed through Ludlow that Maurice's attention was drawn to social and political matters, and Maurice's growing preoccupation with these problems was an important factor in persuading Ludlow to remain in London. He wanted to promote some kind of political journal, either in Paris or in London, but his French friends told him he would have little success in Paris.

When the French government fell in February he hurried over to Paris to make sure his sisters were safe. He had long considered that Louis Philippe's government was so corrupt that any alternative was to be preferred, but he could not raise much enthusiasm for the new provisional government. He had more respect for the impromptu street-corner orators, and was pleased to see that they gave prominence to social issues, which Ludlow considered were more pressing than political changes. He was also relieved to find that these reformers were not hostile towards religion. He came to the conclusion that the challenge to Christianity posed by socialism was so serious that it had to be honestly met, otherwise Christianity 'would be shaken to its foundations, precisely because socialism appealed to the higher and not to the lower instincts of the working class.'[5]

Back in London, Ludlow did not take a great deal of notice of the Chartists, for he did not regard them as politically effective. On that April 10, 1848, therefore, he was one of the few professional men who remained calm, and was thus placidly at his office desk when Kingsley erupted into his chambers and his life. Kingsley persuaded Ludlow to accompany him to Kennington Common, and they walked briskly through the chilly spring rain whilst Kingsley poured into his companion's receptive ears all the ideas which had been incubating in Eversley. Ludlow reciprocated by confiding his own hopes, and by the time they neared the river, to discover that Feargus O'Connor had disbanded the meeting, the two men were already deep in agreement as to future plans. They were complementary: Ludlow supplied the organising ability, Kingsley the reckless verve.

They infected Maurice with their eagerness, and Kingsley stayed the night at Queen's Square, drafting a political poster addressed to the Chartists. It was signed 'A Working Parson' and marked the first time an Anglican clergyman had made direct contact with a working-class political group. Kingsley sent a reassuring note to Fanny on Tuesday morning: 'I was up till 4 this morning, writing posting placards under Maurice's auspices, one of which is to be got out tomorrow morning, the rest when we can get money. Could you not beg a few sovereigns somewhere, to help these poor wretches....'[6] Elsewhere he wrote to her, 'I am helping in a glorious work.'

He remained in London for the Wednesday, and spent the afternoon with Archdeacon Hare[7] and John Parker, senior, who was persuaded to publish the new periodical Maurice and the others were contemplating. He had been a working printer, and was emotionally touched by the atmosphere and events of that week. Kingsley emphasised one vital point in his poster: 'But will the Charter make you free? Will it free you from slavery to ten pound bribes? Slavery to beer and gin? Slavery to every spouter who flatters your self-conceit, and stirs up bitterness and headlong rage in you? That, I guess, is real slavery....'

Now it was Ludlow's turn to be welcomed into the warmth of the family circle at Eversley, and he spent the next week-end there, where he met Mansfield, falling under his spell like everyone else. The little 'band of brothers', as Ludlow liked to call them, in imitation of the French phrase, was fast forming, and all were enthusiastic about a socialist journal. Mansfield agreed to write nature articles under the pen-name of 'Will Willow-Wren' whilst Kingsley would sign himself 'Parson Lot'. Kingsley was overjoyed. At last he would have a platform, as S.G.O. had in *The Times*, and in the kind of journal he had once hoped men like Powles would promote at Oxford.

The rector plunged into all these activities with an ardour which dismayed his wife and irritated her relatives, with the exception of S.G.O. (who wrote Sam Gonze's Country Letters for the new journal). But Kingsley stood firm. Although deferring to Fanny's judgment in most moral and social affairs, he was convinced that he and his friends were doing God's work, and he did not respond to her pleas. 'My path is clear, and I will follow it. He who died for me, and who gave me you, shall I not trust Him, through whatsoever new and strange paths He may lead me?'[8] The band of brothers worked at such pressure that the first number of their paper—*Politics for the People*—appeared on May 6. At first Kingsley and Ludlow were joint editors, but Kingsley did not have enough time for this additional work, and thereafter Ludlow was sole editor. Parson Lot's open letters to the English working men returned constantly to one central theme: 'Be fit to be free, and God himself will set you free.' Kingsley was distressed at finding that Chartist literature was sold mainly in bookshops which specialised in horror stories, in 'dirty milksop French novels[9], and in propaganda material for the United Irishmen cause. Kingsley did not sympathise with Irish patriots, whom he considered to be rebels to the English crown, and he could not understand how any Englishman could support their cause since those particular Irish men and women prided themselves on hatred of the English nation and recommended 'schemes of murder which a North American Indian, trained to scalping from his youth, would account horrible'.[10]

The prospectus of *Politics for the People* stated its object very clearly: '. . . to consider the questions which are most occupying our countrymen at the present moment, such as the Extension of the Suffrage; the relation of the Capitalist to the Labourer; what a Government can, or cannot do, to find work or pay for the Poor. By *considering* these questions, we mean that it is not our purpose to put forth readymade theories upon them . . . politics have been separated from household ties and affections, from art, and science, and literature. . . . When they become POLITICS FOR THE PEOPLE they are found to take in a very large field; whatever concerns man as a social being must be included in them. . . . Politics have been separated from Christianity; religious men have supposed that their only business was with the world to come. But politics for the people cannot be separated from religion.'

Maurice found work for Kingsley as a visiting teacher of literature at the newly-formed Queens College for Women in Harley Street. Maurice had been the motive force behind this pioneering venture in education for girls. Kingsley enjoyed the lectures, and hoped that through literature and the particular examples he chose, the girls would learn something of history and human psychology as well. He described his teaching method to the Rev. Alfred Strettell who took over from him the following year. 'Go your own way; what do girls want with a "course of literature"? Your business and that of all teachers is: not to cram them with things, but to teach them how to read for themselves. A single half century known thoroughly, as you are teaching, will give them canons and inductive habits of thought, whereby to judge all future centuries. We want to train—not cupboards full of "information" (vile misnomer) but real informed women.'[11]

Kingsley now toiled like a man possessed, accomplishing in one day what most men would do in three. Ideas, scenes, dialogues, poems, 'seethed' in his mind, as he was convinced they were seething in the minds of most of his generation. These were the natural responses to the tensions of the times, which had not vanished overnight after April 10. Tom Hughes described it: 'For months afterwards the Chartist movement, though plainly subsiding, kept the Government in constant anxiety; and again in June 1848, the Bank, the Mint, the Custom House, and other public offices were filled with troops, and the Houses of Parliament were not only garrisoned but provisioned as if for a siege.' In Paris the month of June saw an outbreak of fighting between Left-wing extremists and Government troops, but in Britain the great cities escaped such disorders. Nonetheless, the English middle class had been badly frightened, and its raw nerves were further shaken by a series of muck-raking articles by Henry Mayhew in the *Morning Chronicle* on London labour and the London poor. These uncovered such disgusting conditions that the only surprise was that the Chartists had not been more violent in their demands and demonstrations.

Kingsley wondered whether his jumble of ideas could not be worked up in some fictional form—a novel perhaps—which would be an exposé of rural conditions, comparable to the Mayhew articles. He broached the notion to his friends, who all encouraged him—several of the Maurice circle had tried their hands at novel-writing—and accordingly he began work on a

series of sketches, which he hoped would be published in instalment form in *Fraser's Magazine* under the general title, *Yeast*.
Fraser's was popular among the country gentry, the precise class
which Kingsley wished to arouse to a sense of its responsibilities
towards the rural poor. At the same time, Kingsley continued his
contributions to *Politics for the People*. His fellow writers for that
journal, which ran for seventeen issues, from May to July 1848,
were mostly professional men: Anglican clergymen, barristers,
scientists, who gave their services free. Its columns were also open
to letters from working men, although very few availed themselves of this forum. One such signed himself sardonically, 'One
of the wicked Chartists of Kennington Common.'

During its brief life, *Politics for the People* gained an entirely
undeserved reputation for encouraging firebrands. The only
possible explanation of this opinion is that the opponents never
actually read the articles. *The Times*, in its obituary of Kingsley,
published on January 25, 1865, even repeated the myth that
Charles Kingsley, or rather Parson Lot, complained in 'burning
language' that the 'Charter did not go far enough'. What in fact
Kingsley said in his *Letter to Chartists No. 1* was, 'But my only
quarrel with the Charter is, *that it does not go far enough in reform.*
I want to see you free: but I do not see how what you ask for
will give you what you want.'

His first *Letter to the Chartists* indeed said that the French slogan
and aim of 'Organisation of Labour' was worth a thousand of the
Chartist demands for the vote because the Christian Socialists
foresaw the salvation of the contemporary social and economic
ills through organisation of working men in production associations or co-operatives. They followed the views of Louis Blanc
and the French National Workshops. In his second Letter, Kingsley insisted that the Bible was the true 'Reformer's Guide',
demanding for the poor as much, and more, than they demanded
for themselves. He declared that it was the fault of himself and
his fellow parsons that they had failed to make this point clear,
and that because of this failure working men had turned in other
directions. 'It is our fault, our great fault, that you should sneer,
sneer at the only news that ought to be your glory and your

strength. It is our fault. We have used the Bible as if it were the special constable's handbook—an opium dose for keeping beasts of burden patient while they were being overloaded—a mere book to keep the poor in order.' (The opium simile was later borrowed by Karl Marx.)

The first instalment of *Yeast* now appeared in *Fraser's*, winning instant approval from a readership which had no idea of what lay in store. Ludlow, a serious critic indeed, wrote to congratulate Kingsley and to prophesy that he might become the 'greatest novelist of the age'—a compliment which went some way towards compensating for the news in the same letter that King's College had turned him down for the lectureship. Maurice had been told this unofficially, and had asked Ludlow to inform Kingsley. The rejection was actually a blessing in disguise, for he was already seriously overworking, preaching two sermons every Sunday, doing all the parish visiting (he could not afford the assistance of a curate), 'grinding' to prepare his weekly litera-ture lecture at Queen's College, writing his articles for *Politics for the People* and keeping up with the *Yeast* instalments, as well as mulling over half a dozen additional literary projects. But naturally he felt slighted, although he merely commented to Ludlow that King's College had not behaved well towards Maurice in refusing the candidate whom Maurice recommended for his assistant. But he ended philosophically: 'Let us forward. God leads us, though blind.'[12]

At least he could open his heart to the public on a multitude of topics. His articles in *Politics for the People* on the British Museum and the National Gallery show his concern for the quality of life available for working people.

The British Museum is my glory and my joy; because it is almost the only place which is free to English citizens as such, where the poor and the rich may meet together, and before those works of God's spirit 'who is no respecter of persons' feel that 'the Lord is the maker of them all'. In the British Museum and the National Gallery alone the Englishman may say, 'Whatever my coat or my purse, I am an Englishman, and therefore I have a right here. I can glory in these noble halls as if they were my own place. . . .

The British Museum is a truly equalizing place, in the deepest and most spiritual sense; therefore I love it.

He was one of the first to make a plea for modern science museums.

What a noble, and righteous, and truly brotherly plan it would be if all classes would join to form a free National Gallery of Art and Science, which might combine the advantages of the present Polytechnic, Society of Arts, and British Institution, gratis. Manufacturers and men of science might send thither specimens of their new inventions. The rich might send, for a few months in the year—as they do now to the British Institution—ancient and modern pictures, and not only pictures, but all sorts of curious works of art and nature, which are now hidden in their drawing-rooms and libraries. There might be free liberty to copy any object, on the copyist's name and residence being registered. And surely artists and men of science might be found, with enough of the spirit of patriotism and love, to explain gratuitously to all comers, whatever their rank or class, the wonders of the Museum. I really believe that if once the spirit of brotherhood got abroad among us; if men once saw that here was a vast means of educating, and softening, and uniting those who have no leisure for study, and few means of enjoyment, except the gin-shop and Cremorne Gardens; if they could but once feel that here was a project, equally blessed for rich and poor, the money for it would be at once forthcoming from many a rich man, who is longing to do good, if he could only be shown the way; and from many a poor journeyman, who would gladly contribute his mite to a truly national museum, founded on the principles of spiritual liberty, equality, and fraternity. All that is wanted is the spirit of self-sacrifice, patriotism and brotherly love—which God alone can give—which I believe He is giving more and more in these very days.

This concept of professional men giving voluntary service to uneducated and illiterate workers, which was to become the mainspring of the Working Men's College, founded by the Christian Socialists in 1854, was always stressed by Kingsley. In 1852 he wrote to a young nobleman: 'I liked to hear that you were teaching a carpenter boat-building. Men ought to know how to do such things; and gentlemen and noblemen ought to find an honour in teaching them.'[13]

Finally, there is an article by Kingsley about art galleries:

Picture galleries should be the workman's paradise, a garden of pleasure to which he goes to refresh his eyes and heart with beautiful shapes and sweet colouring, when they are wearied with dull bricks and mortar, and the ugly, colourless things which fill the workshop and the factory. . . .

Of course, if he can get the real air, the real trees, even for an hour, let him take it, in God's name; but how many a man who cannot spare time for a daily country walk, may well slip into the National Gallery or any other collection of pictures, for ten minutes. *That* garden, at least, flowers as gaily in winter as in summer. Those noble faces on the wall are never disfigured by grief or passion.

It is significant that the first visit of Alton Locke, the tailor's apprentice, to the Dulwich Art Gallery is in the nature of an emotional experience. The painting of St. Sebastian by Guido has a dramatic effect on the sheltered boy, strictly reared by his Puritanical mother. 'My heart swelled within me, my eyes seemed bursting from my head with the intensity of my gaze, and tears, I know not why, rolled slowly down my face.'[14]

Kingsley enjoyed a few breaks in the headlong pace of 1848, notably some days spent with Maurice in Cambridge, during which visit they went to Crowland Abbey, near Peterborough. This was the Fen country of Kingsley's boyhood and the scene of his student days, but everything had more meaning with Maurice at his side to interpret: '. . . these days with Maurice have taught me more than I can tell.' A letter to his young daughter shows a different Kingsley from the one the Chartists knew, the man who had it in him to write *The Water Babies*.

My dear Miss Rose,
  I am writing in such a curious place. A mill where they grind corn and bones, and such a funny little room in it full of stuffed birds. And there is a flamingo, such a funny red bird, with long legs and a long neck, as big as Miss Rose, and sharks' jaws, and an armadillo all over great scales, and now I will tell you about the stork. He is called Peter, and here is a picture of him. See what long legs he has, and a white body and black wings, and he catches all the frogs and snails, and eats them, and when he is cross, he opens his long bill, and makes such a horrible clattering like a rattle. And he comes to the window at tea time, to eat bread and butter, and he is so greedy, and he gobbled down a great pinch of snuff out of Daddy's box, and he was so sick, and we all laughed at him, for being so greedy and foolish.[15]

Sometime that summer Kingsley came across a long poem, dedicated to Carlyle, called *The Purgatory of Suicides*, by Thomas Cooper, a well-known Chartist, who had written it while in Stafford Gaol, and was so impressed by the poem that he wrote to the author. Kingsley had been hurt by attacks made upon him throughout the year in the Chartist periodical, *Commonwealth*, particularly one passage which had accused him of 'medieval tyranny', and he dearly wanted to meet one or two Chartists in order to clear himself of what he resented as a calumny. Who could be better than a brother poet? He wrote to Cooper; 'My ancestors fought in Cromwell's army, and left all for the sake of God and liberty, among the pilgrim fathers, and here were men accusing me of "medieval tyranny". I would shed the last drop of my blood for the social and political emancipation of the people of England, as God is my witness; and here are the very men for whom I would die fancying me an "aristocrat". It is not enough for me that they are mistaken in me. I want to work with them. I want to realise my brotherhood with them. I want someone like yourself, intimately acquainted with the mind of the working classes, to give me such an insight into their life and thoughts, as may enable me to consecrate my powers effectually to their service. For them I have lived for several years. I come to you to ask you if you can tell me how to live more completely for them.'[16] The two men became friendly, and in fact Cooper turned to Christianity through Kingsley's influence, a conversion which alienated atheistic Chartists. When Cooper was penniless in his latter years, Kingsley organised a fund to keep him out of the poorhouse. There is no doubt that Cooper's experience was invaluable to him when writing *Alton Locke*.

To keep abreast of his *Yeast* instalments Kingsley had to work after the rest of the household went to bed. He would stride up and down his study, just as if he were in the garden, puffing away at his pipe, pausing just long enough at his desk to secure his thoughts on sheets of paper which fluttered to the floor as he filled one and passed on to the next. His desk was merely a broad shelf which protruded from the wall near the window. He was a rapid, impatient writer, with incidents which raced through his mind, crowding one after the other, and he could never write fast enough to keep up with his invention. He visualised scenes complete with characters and dialogue, interspersed with picturesque descriptive passages and—more rarely—little homilies.

He had caught the attention of *Fraser's* country-house readership from his second sentence, when he described a hunt starting off on a raw March day.

The edge of a great fox-cover; a flat wilderness of low leafless oaks fortified by a long, dreary, thorn-capped clay ditch, with sour red water oozing out at every yard; a broken gate leading into a straight wood-ride, ragged with dead grasses and black with fallen leaves, the centre, mashed into a quagmire by innumerable horse-hoofs; some forty red coats and some four black; a sprinkling of young farmers, resplendent in gold buttons and green; a pair of sleek drab stable-keepers, showing off horses for sale; the surgeon of the union, in mackintosh and antigropelos; two holiday schoolboys with trousers strapped down to bursting point, like a penny steamer's safety-valve; a midshipman, the only merry one in the field, bumping about on a fretting, sweating hack, with its nose a foot above its ears; and Lancelot Smith, who then kept two good horses, and 'rode forward', as a fine young fellow of three-and-twenty, who can afford it, and 'has nothing else to do' has a very good right to ride.[17]

Lancelot Smith, the hero, is a rich man's son, just down from Cambridge, conceited, self-indulgent, but decent enough if only something—or someone—will bring out the best in him. Just the kind of young man, indeed, with whom most young men from Cambridge or Oxford could readily identify. The heroine, Argemone Lavington, the squire's stately, serious daughter, meets Lancelot in a romantic encounter which we might consider pure fiction had not Mrs. Kingsley made it clear that it was a fairly accurate description of her first meeting with Kingsley.

On a sudden the chapel-door opened, and a figure timidly yet loftily stepped out without observing him, and, suddenly turning round, met him full, face to face, and stood fixed with surprise as completely as Lancelot himself.

That face and figure, and the spirit which spoke through them, entered his heart at once, never again to leave it.

We meet more key characters. Colonel Bracebridge, a likeable army officer who has marred his life through unfortunate sexual entanglements; Luke Smith, Lancelot's cousin, who leans towards Rome; and the squire's two gamekeepers, Tregarva, a strong, handsome Cornishman, with a social conscience, and Harry Verney, a squire's man, and a type whom Kingsley disliked, but could describe perfectly:

He was a short, wiry, bandy-legged, ferret-visaged old man, with grizzled hair and a wizened face tanned brown and purple by constant exposure. Between rheumatism and constant handling the rod and gun, his fingers were crooked like a hawk's claws. He kept his left eye always shut, apparently to save trouble in shooting and squinted and sniffed and peered, with a stooping back and protruded chin, as if he were perpetually on the watch for fish, flesh and fowl, vermin and Christian.[18]

Kingsley wrote poignantly of Verney's death later on:

'What's that thumping and roaring?' Alas, it was the failing pulsation of his own heart. 'It's the weir, the weir—a-washing me away—thundering over me.—Squire, I'm drowning—drowning and choking! Oh, Lord, how deep! Now it's running quieter—now I can breathe again—swift and oily—running on, running on, down to the sea. See how the grayling sparkle! There's a pike! 'Tain't my fault, squire, so help me—Don't swear now, squire; old men and dying maun't swear, squire. How steady the river runs down! Lower and slower—lower and slower—now it's quite still—still—still—'

His voice sank away—he was dead!

No! once more the light flashed up in the socket. He sprang upright in the bed, and held out his withered paw with a kind of wild majesty, as he shouted,—

'There ain't such a head of hares on any manor in the county. And them's the last words of Harry Verney!'

He fell back—shuddered—a rattle in his throat—another—and all was over.

Lancelot decides to make an investigation of rural poverty in order to be worthy of Argemone. Sanitary reform, he insists, is the great fact of the age. As for education—'If a man living in civilised society has one right which he can demand it is this, that the State which exists by his labour shall enable him to develop, or at least, not hinder his developing his whole faculties to their very utmost, however lofty that may be.'[19] The love story proceeds apace, again reflecting the true life of its author. When Argemone timidly suggests they part, Lancelot reacts manfully.

'I see—I see it all, Argemone! We love each other! You are mine, never to be parted!'

What was her womanhood, that it could stand against the energy of his manly will? The almost coarse simplicity of his words silenced her with a delicious violence. She could only bury her face in her hands and sob out—

'Oh, Lancelot, Lancelot, whither are you forcing me?'

By now, even the most obtuse reader was aware that this was no common country romance, but when in Chapter XI Kingsley made Tregarva compose a ballad on the plight of the agricultural poor, one of the bitterest social poems in the English language, country squires were maddened.

THE BAD SQUIRE

The merry brown hares came leaping
Over the crest of the hill,
Where the clover and corn lay sleeping
Under the moonlight still.

Leaping late and early,
Till under their bite and their tread
The swedes and the wheat and the barley
Lay cankered and trampled and dead.

A poacher's widow sat sighing
On the side of the white chalk bank,
Where under the gloomy fir-woods,
One spot in the ley throve rank.

She watched a long tuft of clover,
Where rabbit or hare never ran;
For its black sour haulm covered over
The blood of a murdered man.

She thought of the dark plantation,
And the hares, and her husband's blood,
And the voice of her indignation
Rose up to the throne of God.

'I am long past wailing and whining—
I have wept too much in my life:
I've had twenty years of pining
As an English labourer's wife.

'A labourer in Christian England,
Where they cant of a Saviour's name,
And yet waste men's lives like the vermin's
For a few more brace of game.

'There's blood on your new foreign shrubs, squire,
There's blood on your pointer's feet;
There's blood on the game you sell, squire,
And there's blood on the game you eat.

'You have sold the labouring-men, squire,
Body and soul to shame,
To pay for your seat in the House, squire,
And to pay for the feed of your game.

'You made him a poacher yourself, squire,
When you'd give neither work nor meat,
And your barley-fed hares robbed the garden
At our starving children's feet;

'When, packed in one reeking chamber,
Man, maid, mother, and little ones lay;
While the rain pattered in on the rotting bride-bed,
And the walls let in the day.

'When we lay in the burning fever
On the mud of the cold clay floor,

Till you parted us all for three months, squire,
At the dreary workhouse door.

'We quarrelled like brutes, and who wonders?
What self-respect could we keep,
Worse housed than your hacks and your pointers,
Worse fed than your hogs and your sheep?

Our daughters with base-born babies
Have wandered away in their shame,
If your misses had slept, squire, where they did,
Your misses might do the same.

'Can your lady patch hearts that are breaking
With handfuls of coals and rice,
Or by dealing out flannel and sheeting
A little below cost price?

'You may tire of the jail and the workhouse,
And take to allotments and schools,
But you've run up a debt that will never
Be paid us by penny-club rules.

'In the season of shame and sadness,
In the dark and dreary day,
When scrofula, gout, and madness
Are eating your race away;

'When to kennels and liveried varlets
You have cast your daughter's bread,
And, worn out with liquor and harlots,
Your heir at your feet lies dead;

'When your youngest, the mealy-mouthed rector,
Lets your soul rot asleep to the grave,
You will find in your God the protector
Of the freeman you fancied your slave.'

She looked at the tuft of clover,
And wept till her heart grew light;
And at last, when her passing was over,
Went wandering into the night.

But the merry brown hares came leaping
Over the uplands still,
Where the clover and corn lay sleeping
On the side of the white chalk hill.

The fictional Squire Lavington had a stroke, and Tregarva's excuse that 'The Bad Squire' was not meant to apply to him personally did not deceive him. 'If it don't, it applies to half the gentlemen in the vale, and that's just as bad,' he says shrewdly, and sacks his gamekeeper on the spot. Equally unpalatable to *Fraser's* readers was a ballad about rick-burning.

Lancelot's fortune is lost when his uncle's bank fails, but Lancelot does not care. 'I took money which I never earned, and cared as little how it was gained as how I spent it. Henceforth I shall touch no farthing which is the fruit of a system which I cannot approve.' This is what Argemone wants to hear, but her parents are appalled, and forbid all communication between the lovers.

By way of a sub-plot we have Lancelot trying to find consolation in the Catholic Church, where his cousin Luke has found comfort and peace. But after an interesting discussion with 'a certain remarkable man', and a recent convert to Rome (most of Kingsley's readers assumed this was Newman), the young man turns away from what he conceives to be Catholic attitudes. 'I want a live Christ, not a dead one. . . . That is noble . . . beautiful . . . it may be true, but it has no message for me.'

As *Yeast* unfolded throughout the year and into the next, successive chapters brought fresh complaints from indignant squires threatening to cancel their subscriptions. Doubtless the reaction would have been even sharper had the readers known that *Yeast's* anonymous author and the notorious Parson Lot were

one and the same. By the autumn of 1849 Kingsley was under
strong editorial pressure to wind up the story before *Fraser's*
went bankrupt. Kingsley was disappointed, for he had been
discussing with Ludlow the possibility of running *Yeast* as a two-
or even three-volume-length novel, in which Lancelot and
Argemone would marry and become model country landlords.
However, in the face of an editorial ultimatum Kingsley hastily
killed his heroine. With the disease-ridden conditions of Jacob's
Island in his mind, he chose typhus as his weapon of destruction.
The girl contracts the disease from some cottagers on the Lavington estate, but she does not blame them. 'Their neglect, cupidity,
oppression [i.e. of her Lavington forbears] are avenged on me!
Why not? Have I not wantoned in down and perfumes, while
they, by whose labour my luxuries were bought, were pining
among scents and sounds one day of which would have driven
me mad! And then they wonder why men turn Chartists!'[20] To
get rid of Lancelot, and to give hope for Tregarva, for whom
Kingsley had an especial affection, Kingsley introduced a 'mysterious stranger', who takes Lancelot and Tregarva on a mystical
journey to the East, where they will 'find themselves'. Lancelot
gladly agrees. He needs something, or someone, to give meaning
to his life. 'As I live, the height of my ambition, small though
it be, is only to find my place, though it were but as a sweeper of
chimneys. If I dare wish—if I dare choose, it would be only this—
to regenerate one little parish in the whole world.'

Thus Lancelot Smith, but surely thus also Charles Kingsley,
country parson?

Professor Conington, in a criticism of *Yeast*, took Kingsley to
task for copying Sidonia in Disraeli's *Coningsby*, to which Kingsley replied that at the time of writing *Yeast* he had not read
Disraeli's novel. However, the device of a mysterious, omniscient
stranger was quite popular in Victorian fiction. The book itself,
which appealed greatly to young men, was published early in 1851,
and attracted some unexpected reviews, particularly in the
Guardian, where the reviewer accused Kingsley of heresy and
of encouraging profligacy. Although extremely thin-skinned,
and deeply wounded by these aspersions on his moral principles,

Kingsley tried to forget them, and find satisfaction in the steady stream of correspondence from strangers who wrote to confide in him, to ask advice, or to thank him for putting into words thoughts and difficulties which had been perplexing them. Kingsley replied dutifully to each one, though throughout his life this mass of letters was an additional burden. Often, these correspondents made the journey to Eversley to attend a church service. Often, too, letters came from people overseas.

No man, least of all Kingsley, could have survived unscathed the exertions of 1848. One autumn Monday he awoke so tired that his wife at once sent for the doctor, who prescribed rest and a change of scenery. The family went to Bournemouth for a few weeks, and was joined by Charles's young brother, Henry. This boy had all the Kingsley liveliness, but he was a poor scholar, and had done badly at school. Fanny, considerably his senior, rather resented his schoolboy chatter, and assumed it was bound to be bad for her husband, although Charles never complained.

As soon as he found strength returning, he insisted upon re-turning to his duties at Eversley, although it meant leaving his family by the sea. But he was still tired, and since separation from Fanny was always a physical and emotional strain, his letters to her were full of an unconscious self-pity. He looked forward to death, he declared, as a time of everlasting bliss for him and for Fanny. 'There we shall be together for ever, without a sigh or a cross.'[21] Mansfield joined his friend at the rectory to shield him from unnecessary vexations so that he could finish *Yeast* and his other commitments. It was, both friends agreed, a matter of being 'demagnetised'. But Kingsley was far from well, and the doctor now spoke of a rest in terms of months, not weeks. Mansfield saw to all the arrangements. Charles's parents installed a curate in Chelsea, and moved to Eversley to deputise for their son. Kingsley and his family were sent to North Devon. They took lodgings first in Ilfracombe, then in Lynmouth, where they remained until the spring of 1849.

'*I am a Chartist*'

Mansfield's care and company, which included 'demagnetising sessions' when his friend felt feverish and debilitated,[1] and the Devon breezes restored Kingsley's strength sufficiently so that by the New Year he could begin planning his next novel, *Alton Locke*, although he was still writing *Yeast*. His second novel was intended to prove to the Chartists that in spite of the class barrier and his clerical profession his heart and intellect ranged him on their side. He would write only about what he actually knew, or had been told by others. He wrote to Ludlow: 'I have hope also of the book which I am writing, the Autobiography of a Cockney Poet, which has revealed itself to me so rapidly and methodically that I feel it comes down from above, and that only my folly can spoil it—which I pray against daily.'[2]

His relationship with Ludlow was very close and frank, and continued to be so until about 1852 or 1853. In view of their geographical separation, their discussions had to be carried on by correspondence, and their letters were frequent, long and detailed, covering the social problems which involved them, religious arguments, each other's literary work and the strategy and tactics best suited to accomplish the aims of the Christian Socialists. Their instinctive reactions were widely different. Kingsley was the thrusting warrior who had to be restrained; Ludlow was the evolutionist who trusted in development through legislation. Both found their friendship at this time of immense value in clarifying their thoughts.

Neither Ludlow nor Mansfield altogether approved of Kingsley writing another novel. Ludlow believed that Kingsley's God-given talent was for poetry, and that he should concentrate on refining his verse.[3] Mansfield took another view. He was going through one of his deeply religious phases and thought that Kingsley's vocation was to be a disciple and populariser of F. D. Maurice, so that anything which took him away from this task was to be regretted.

Alton Locke was not written for publication by instalments but as a complete story. At first Kingsley wrote it late at night, as he had done *Yeast*, when the rest of the household was in bed, but later the writing was changed to a morning stint. He would rise at 5 a.m., when he felt fresher. He wrote a first draft, revised it, and gave it to Fanny to make a fair copy for the printer. This is the only case of Kingsley revising a prose work, other than in his head, and the reasons seem fairly obvious. Ludlow's conscientious and detailed criticisms as he went along forced Kingsley to discipline himself. He was also eager to make a literary reputation, so that he could use writing as an additional source of future income. Finally, he was burning with indignation, and wanted to educate the world. *Alton Locke* was to do for the town workers, particularly in the tailoring trade, what *Yeast* had done for the agricultural workers: draw the attention of thinking people to the injustices of these workers.

It was while still in Devonshire that Kingsley became personally involved with James Anthony Froude, an Oxford don who had just written a novel, *The Nemesis of Faith*, which seemed about to destroy his career. Kingsley invited Froude into his household, a typical act of generosity which greatly alarmed Kingsley's parents, because the scandal which surrounded Froude inevitably extended also to Kingsley. Since Froude, however, was destined to become a permanent member of the Kingsley circle, and to influence Kingsley in his work and beliefs, it is useful to trace the course of events which led to their relationship. *The Nemesis of Faith* had been something in the nature of an act of exorcism. Froude said of it: 'There is something in the thing I know; for I cut a hole in my heart and wrote it with the blood. I wouldn't write such another at the cost of the same pain for anything short of direct promotion into heaven.' Its religious theme touched many doubting hearts, and was taken seriously. Unfortunately for Froude the novel was regarded as either atheist propaganda or an autobiographical confession of a man who had no place in decent religious society. Like *Yeast* and *Alton Locke*, *The Nemesis of Faith* was uncompromisingly contemporary, its hero made a 'shipwreck of his life in the shipwreck of his faith', and it arrived like a bombshell in circles whose members were likewise experiencing crises of faith. In spite of Froude's denials, many readers insisted upon seeing points of similarity between him and his hero, Markham Sutherland, and the officers of Exeter College, where Froude had been a Fellow since 1844, decided to remove his name from the rolls. He spared them the embarrassment by requesting them to do so.[4]

The novel was really the culmination of many doubts and difficulties which Froude had suffered since going to Oxford where he matriculated in 1835, and began studying for his degree. He had been warmly welcomed by John Henry Newman, whose rooms at Oriel College were below Anthony's, because of the close emotional ties between Newman and Froude's eldest brother, the strange and brilliant Hurrell Froude. Hurrell inherited the family weakness for tuberculosis, and was slowly dying at home in Dartington Rectory when Anthony arrived in Oxford. Hurrell Froude was a major theoretician among the Oxford Reformers, and had he not died in February 1836 would certainly have been as celebrated as Newman. So when, in the early 1840s, Newman invited Anthony to join him in some of the stories in the series *Lives of the Saints*, it did not occur to him that the young man, influenced by Thomas Carlyle, had become a firm supporter of the Protestant Church. Nor did Froude consider that this was any drawback to collaborating in a collection of edifying tales intended to create a vague religious sentiment. Froude accordingly wrote a *Life of St. Neot*, about which (by Froude's account) Newman advised him in general terms— 'Rationalise where the evidence is weak, and this will gain credibility for others, where you can show that the evidence is strong.'[5] It is reasonable to assume, in view of later developments, that Froude told Charles Kingsley about this, and that Kingsley would have considered it an unjustifiable extrapolation, since the phrase 'where the evidence is weak' is difficult to overlook. Literary myth, incidentally, has wrongly saddled Froude with the delightful concluding sentence to one of these Lives: 'This is all that is known, and perhaps more than all—yet nothing to what the angels know—of the life of a servant of God.'[6]

Froude's father, the squire-parson Archdeacon of Totnes, was so outraged by his son's novel, and the stir it caused, that he turned the young man out of the rectory, where he had rather naturally gone after leaving Oxford, and stopped his allowance. Homeless, penniless and jobless (the offer of a schoolmastering job in Tasmania was withdrawn as soon as word of the novel reached the Antipodes), Froude found a veritable refuge in Charles Kingsley's Devon lodgings. These afforded him not only sympathy and hospitality but also a totally unexpected future, for staying there was Charlotte Grenfell, Fanny's sister and her senior by two years. Charlotte was a handsome, intelligent woman, recently converted to Roman Catholicism, and with ruthless logic was planning to enter a nunnery. The Grenfell clan, greatly distressed, had persuaded her to delay this ultimate step for a few months in the hope that something would happen to change her mind.

What happened was James Anthony Froude. Like Fanny Kingsley before her, Charlotte was seduced by the spectacle of a vigorous, chivalrous and intellectual young man being persecuted by conventional society. As for Froude, he, like Kingsley, fell deeply in love with an older woman—'magnificent' was his word for her. In their case there was none of the family disapproval which had plagued Charles and Fanny. Charlotte, of course, was a mature woman, and Froude had in effect brought her back to the family, and Anglican, fold. Fanny was in two minds about the affair, as she disapproved of Froude's general religious attitude and was shocked by his total lack of interest in Maurice's theology. Kingsley regarded the entire business as simply another manifestation of the utter unsuitability of the Catholic Church and a celibate life for a healthily-sexed woman, and approved the impending marriage which took place about six months later.

It was now essential for Kingsley to return to Eversley and thus save the expense of a curate. He hoped to get book reviewing from *Fraser's*, and to take private pupils, fixing upon £250 as a reasonable sum for a student to live with the family for a year and be tutored. He outlined his aims as a teacher to Mrs. Scott:[7] 'In my eyes the question is not what to teach, but how to educate; how to train not scholars, but men; bold, energetic, methodic; liberal-minded, magnanimous.' Maurice wrote to Professor Thompson at Cambridge, soliciting a pupil for Kingsley. 'He is a good, accurate and enthusiastic scholar, full of knowledge of all things about him, and delight in them; and more likely to give a young man of the day a good direction in divinity, meeting his difficulties and dealing honestly with them, than any person I have fallen in with. His conversation is full of interest even when he is ill; when he is well he is the freshest, freest hearted man in England.' Nevertheless, Kingsley's reputation was too dangerously liberal for orthodox Anglicans to entrust their sons to him, and he had to wait until January 1850 before he had a pupil, and then it was a boy from a Unitarian family.

Kingsley's motive in looking for pupils was not merely financial. He enjoyed the pleasure and relaxation in concentrating upon academic and scientific subjects after the routine of parish work, and in communicating his knowledge and enthusiasms to a young man; there was the satisfaction of influencing a young person and setting him on the right road; finally, and most significantly of all, he confessed 'That by leaving the parish routine work in the hands of a devoted and methodical man I might find time to labour on those social questions to which I cannot but believe myself, by strange providence, especially called.'[8]

Leaving the family in Devonshire for a while longer, Kingsley prepared to return to Eversley, paying a short visit to London first to catch up with events during his absence. He stayed with his parents at Chelsea, a convenient centre for calling upon friends and acquaintances and hearing gossip generally. As he hurried from one person to another, he could not help feeling that there were more opportunities to do important work in

London than in Eversley. It reminded him of the exciting days of the previous year.

Ludlow had been disappointed with the progress made by the Christian Socialists, and decided it was essential to work more closely with the Chartists. It was a matter of overcoming the natural suspicion which working men had for the Established Church. The initiative had to come from the Maurice circle, and there were small personal contacts made in Maurice's house. Then the Christian Socialists arranged a series of public meetings in the spring of 1849, to be held at the Cranbourne Tavern. Kingsley was in the audience at one of these early meetings (probably the April 20 one), with Maurice in the chair. To his dismay, Kingsley could sense the palpable antagonism, and suspicion in the body of the hall. He foresaw all the delicate work which Maurice, Ludlow and the others had put into co-operation with the Chartists being destroyed at this one meeting. Kingsley sprang to his feet, and in a loud but stammering voice which made his statement of position all the more impressive, declared 'I am a Church of England parson . . . and a Chartist!'

It was an electrifying moment. Kingsley had nailed his flag quite deliberately. Nearly a year had passed since the April day on Kennington Common, so his avowal was a proof of his continuing sincerity, and the whole temper of the audience changed. There was agreement at maintaining at least a dialogue, perhaps something more substantial, with the Christian Socialists. Tom Hughes wrote, 'I had a singular proof that the effect did not pass away. The most violent speaker on that occasion was one of the staff of the leading Chartist newspaper. I lost sight of him entirely for more than twenty years, and saw him again, a little grey shrivelled man by Kingsley's side, at the grave of Mr. Maurice, in the cemetery at Hampstead.'[9] It was this incident, coupled with the notoriety he afterwards incurred through *Alton Locke*, and the republication of *Yeast* in 1851 in book form, which made Kingsley a national figure, criticised for being a Chartist as often as he was referred to as a Christian Socialist. R. B. Lichfield, when a student at Cambridge, in about 1854, proudly hung a portrait of Kingsley in his rooms. It was a reproduction which had been given away with one of the Christian Socialist journals. A fellow student, recognising the face, exclaimed disgustedly, 'Here's that damned Chartist!'

Kegan Paul points out that Kingsley's ideas met a wide public because he had three works in circulation at roughly the same time: *The Saint's Tragedy, Yeast*, and a collection entitled *Twenty Five Village Sermons*. 'Taken collectively, they were the notes of a chord which was echoed back from the hearts of many young men who wanted, and thought they had found, a leader.'[10]

In June, Kingsley paid another hasty visit to London. He made careful notes of all his activities, so that Fanny could read his letters and take vicarious pleasure in everything he did.

I could not write yesterday, being kept by a poor boy who had fallen off a truck at Croydon and smashed himself, whom I escorted to Guy's Hospital. I have spent the whole day running up and down London on business. I breakfasted with Bunsen, such a divine-looking man, and so kind. I have worlds to tell you. Met F. Newman[11] last night, and breakfast with him tomorrow. I had a long and interesting talk with Froude last night. . . .

Monday. I spent yesterday with Ludlow, and went with him to Dr. Thorpe's, and to Lincoln's Inn Chapel in the afternoon—a noble sight. Maurice's head looked like some great, awful Giorgione portrait in the pulpit, but oh, so worn, and the face worked so at certain passages of the sermon. It was very pleasant, so many kind greetings there from old friends, male and female, for some of the Co-operative friends were there. Tonight for the meeting. They expect to muster between one and two hundred. I am just going with my father and mother to Deptford to put Mary T.[12] on board an emigrant ship.

London is perfectly *horrible*. To you alone I look for help and advice—God and you,—else I think at times I should cry myself to death. There is a great Tailor's meeting on Friday. The women's shoe-makers are not set up yet. My sermons are being lent from man to man, among the South London Chartists, at such a pace that Cooper can't get them back again.

And the Manchester man stole his copy of *The Saint's Tragedy*.
I have just been to see Carlyle.

On Friday I dined at Maurice's. Met Mrs. Augustus Hare,
and a brother of the Archdeacon's, an officer in the Prussian
army, also Mr. and Mrs. Scott, who were very kind indeed.
I took George to a soiree at Parker's, and introduced him to all
the set there. On Saturday we dined at Ludlow's, met dear
Charles Mansfield and a Frenchman, now being tried in Paris
for the June Row, a complete Red Republican and Fourierist;
he says nothing but Christianity can save France or the world.
I had an intensely interesting talk with him. In the evening
the Campbells, Shorter the Chartist, and Dr. Walsh came in,
and we had a glorious evening. G. is quite in a new world. He
says he never saw 'live' men before and he sees a new 'avatar'
opening for him.[13]

Mayhew's articles exposing abuses in various London trades,
especially the slop system in the tailoring trade, confirmed the
Christian Socialists in their contention that working men would
improve their conditions better by forming associations on the
French model than by continuing to agitate for the vote. An
important meeting was held in order to promote the first association for production, and Kingsley described it in a letter to his
wife. 'Last night will never be forgotten by many many men.
Maurice was—I cannot describe it. Chartists told me this morning
that many were affected even to tears. The man was inspired,
gigantic. He stunned us.' Chartists and other working men rose
in applause as Maurice told them: 'Competition is put forth as
the law of the universe. That is a lie. The time is come for us to
declare that it is a lie. I see no way but associating for work instead of for strikes. I do not say or think we feel that the relation
of the employer and employed is not a true relation. I do not
determine that wages may not be a righteous mode of expressing
that relation. But at present it is clear that this relation is destroyed,
that the payment of wages is nothing but a deception. We may
restore the old state of things; we may bring in a new one. God
will decide that. . . . But it is no old condition we are contending

with, but an accursed new one, the product of a hateful devilish theory which must be fought with to the death.'[14]

The first Cooperative Association of Tailors was formed as a direct result of this meeting, with a capital of £300, enough to rent a house in Castle Street, W.1. Walter Cooper was the manager, from whom Kingsley obtained many details of tailors' sweat shops for incorporation in *Alton Locke*.

The summer of 1849 was unhealthy: there was a good deal of fever in Eversley, and the fear of a cholera epidemic on the way. Kingsley wore himself out visiting his sick parishioners, often three or four times a day. An hour's fishing, snatched between visits, helped him carry on. But he was still preoccupied with financial worries, and that year he gave back ten per cent of his tithes to help with village charities. In addition, he resigned the sinecure of a clerkship at Chelsea which had been pressed on him by his father when he and Fanny married, because he disapproved of sinecures. His total income that year was reduced to £400. The contrast between his financial circumstances and the soaring fortunes of Fanny's relatives was galling, but an unexpected loan of £500 helped him over the worst of his troubles. It was engineered secretly by Mansfield and Ludlow, alerted to the situation by an appeal from Fanny. Neither of the Kingsleys was aware who the real lenders were, although towards the end of the repayment the truth apparently dawned upon Fanny.

Kingsley was a man who could never rest. He could barely sit still through a meal. He composed most of his sermons, essays, chapters of books, poems, whilst tramping round his extensive parish, or pacing with nervous energy on his 'quarter deck'—the rectangular plot of grass which was blessed with afternoon sunshine, outside his study window on the west side of the rectory. Sometimes he polished his writings as he sat fishing, puffing away on his pipe. When Ludlow, who took a censorious view of human frailties, complained that the rector smoked too much, Kingsley replied plaintively that it was only the very cheapest tobacco. Smoking and fishing were essential tranquillisers.

As might be expected, he became listless and depressed again, and this time the doctor suggested a long trip, possibly to the United States with the faithful Mansfield as companion. Nothing came of it. The expense was prohibitive, and in any case Kingsley could not bear the thought of a long separation from his wife; but he agreed to return to Devonshire, leaving the family in Eversley. He believed in returning to one's roots, and liked to call his homeland the 'heimveh'. 'This is the place,' he wrote to his mother from Devonshire. 'The wounded bird goes to the nest and I firmly believe in the *magnetic* effect of the place where one has been bred.'

He became friendly with a Cornish ship-owner and fruit-vessel captain. 'The man is a thorough Cornishman; shrewd, witty, religious, well-informed; a great admirer of scenery; talks about light, and shadow, and colouring more like an artist than a brown-fisted merchant skipper, with a mass of brain that might have made anything had he taken to books.'[15] Tregarva, the secondary hero of *Yeast*, was a Cornishman of just this type.

Meanwhile, Kingsley roamed round the West Country—Appledore, Clovelly, Torridge Moors—fishing, butterfly-hunt-ing, sketching, talking, and recording everything in detailed letters which would serve as background material for books and essays. The Kingsley name was still a talisman in Clovelly, he was glad to find, 'and at every door there are daily inquiries, loving and hearty, after you and my father,' he wrote to his mother. To Fanny and Ludlow he confided that he was educating himself by re-reading Rabelais, and reading Pierre Leroux and Ruskin—'by way of a nice mixture'. Kingsley was a great admirer of Rabelais. In a lecture on Rondelet, the Huguenot naturalist, given at Cambridge in 1869, he spoke of 'one of the most remarkable men of that or of any age, François Rabelais himself. And what shall I say of him?—who stands alone, like Shakespeare, in his generation; possessed of colossal learning—of all science which could be gathered in his days—of practical and statesmanlike wisdom—of knowledge of languages, ancient and modern, beyond all his compeers—of eloquence, which when he speaks of pure and noble things becomes heroic, and, as it were, inspired—of scorn for meanness, hypocrisy, ignorance—of esteem, genuine

and earnest, for the Holy Scriptures, and for the more moderate
of the Reformers who were spreading the Scriptures in Europe—
and all this great light wilfully hidden, not under a bushel, but
under a dunghill.'

As strength slowly returned, Kingsley longed to work seriously
at his Chartist story. He also became aware of a new issue which
gradually obsessed him—sanitation. Cholera had, as predicted,
swept the country, causing superstitious people to declare it was
a direct and punitive intervention from Providence. Kingsley
attacked this ignorance in three sermons, explaining that the
epidemics were caused by man's own carelessness and selfishness
through disregard of the laws of sanitary reform. These sermons,
revised and 'peppered for London palates', were given to Ludlow
for printing in the *Christian Socialist* journal, and some years
later were reprinted in one volume, with a preface, under the
general title, *What causes Pestilence?*[16]

Press revelations about the disgraceful sanitary conditions in
the London slum district of Bermondsey brought that area to the
attention of the Christian Socialists, including Mansfield, Ludlow
and Dr. Walsh. Kingsley went to London especially to tour the
district with his friends. He was sickened. The practical side of
Kingsley's nature is nowhere more evident than in his suggestions
about dealing with these slums. He implored Fanny to get her
brother-in-law, George Warre, M.P. for Ripon, to find some
rich man willing to invest in low-priced housing. 'It is not a
question of alms. It is only to get some man to take the trouble of
making a profitable investment, and getting six per cent. for his
money.'[17]

The Christian Socialists saw the filthy sewers in Jacob's Island
(which Dickens had described as the scene of Bill Sikes's murder
in *Oliver Twist*) and watched, horrified, as the inhabitants drew
their drinking water from the same sewers. Kingsley begged his
friends to donate money to pay for a water cart which the
Christian Socialists would have pushed round Bermondsey with
clean water. He went to Oxford to enlist the support of Bishop
Wilberforce. He told Ludlow to discover the identity of the
chairman of the authority which actually owned the Bermondsey

sewers, so that Kingsley would have details to support his request
for interviews with Lord Carlisle and Lord John Russell. Finally,
he intended to win the support of the Bishop of Winchester.

Mansfield had the sensible idea of forming a Sanitary League,
and Kingsley at once backed him. He wrote to Ludlow from
Eversley, urging a public meeting to get it started, and insisting
that the most effective campaign would be to press for compulsory legislation to force landlords to provide sanitary housing.

Amid all this interchange of ideas and action a tiny rift appeared
between Kingsley and Ludlow, the forerunner of fundamental
disagreements over race and empire. Both men had family roots
overseas: Kingsley on his mother's side in the planters of the
West Indies, and Ludlow in India and in France. The effect on
Kingsley was to make him an idealistic imperialist, with a sense
of the white man's mission; on Ludlow it was to make him a
liberal, upholding a multi-racial commonwealth. The matter
which provoked dissension towards the end of 1849 concerned
the self-styled Rajah Brooke of Sarawak. In the interests of free-
ing the Borneo coast from pirates, and ensuring the safety of
traders, Brooke had used a gun-boat and taught the Dyak head-
hunters a lesson. It was said that he had taken 'head-money' from
the British in Singapore for those slain, but this allegation was
untrue, although the British maintained the practice. Questions
were asked in the House of Commons about the incident, and
Kingsley took one side and Ludlow the other. Indeed, Kingsley
flung himself impetuously on the side of the Rajah before knowing
the full details, following his instincts, which were soon enough
reinforced by partisan descriptions of the situation given him by
a new acquaintance who had worked with Brooke in Borneo.
He often behaved in this manner, yielding to a weakness which
dismayed his friends.

Like many other passionate Christians of his day, Kingsley
adhered to the view that pagan head-hunters barely qualified as
members of the human race, especially when they were not
advanced enough to understand the blessings of Christian civilisation. Kingsley tried to convince Ludlow that Brooke's actions
were in no sense contrary to God's will. 'The truest benevolence

is occasional severity. It *is* expedient that one man die to save a whole continent. One tribe exterminated, if need be to save a whole continent. . . . "Value of Life?" Oh, Ludlow, read history; look at the world, and see whether God values mere human existence.'[18] Similar sentiments appeared throughout Kingsley's argument in his articles on *Bible Politics*, which he wanted Ludlow to publish. Part of his thesis was that Old Testament history must be interpreted as the unfolding of God's will and plan for mankind, and therefore at certain points in time it was clearly God's will that the Canaanites had to be exterminated by the Israelites. Kingsley realised that this interpretation of Bible history was a trifle grisly for the taste of some Anglicans, but he was determined to hold to his beliefs in spite of Ludlow's editorial and personal disapproval. It was, after all, not difficult in 1849 to have faith in the white man's mission, and Kingsley certainly saw no incongruity between this position and his liberal views on domestic issues.

In January 1850 Kingsley obtained his first pupil, John Martineau, a shy boy of fifteen. Fanny mothered him, won his affections, as did the rector, and he repaid them both with the devotion and respect of an adopted son. The Martineaus were wealthy Unitarians, descended from Huguenots. John's second cousin was Harriet Martineau, the famous historian and writer of popular books on political economy. John's father was a partner in Whitbread's Brewery. The boy stayed at Eversley for a year and a half, and became Kingsley's 'constant companion, for during the greater part of that time he had no other pupil, and hardly any intimate friends within reach. He was then in his thirty-first year, in the fullness of his strength; I, a raw, receptive schoolboy of fifteen; so that his mind and character left their impression upon mine as a seal does upon wax.'[19]

Martineau wrote regular letters to his parents, who were not quite sure they had done the right thing in entrusting him to such a notorious man. His letters must have reassured them. 'A certain Mr. Charles Mansfield has been staying here. He is one of the first chemists in England, and a vegetarian, a great protégé of Faraday's, and altogether a very nice fellow indeed. He was at

Cambridge with Mr. Kingsley, and is very clever, but is not at all appreciated by his family.

'Mr. Maurice was to have come on Friday, but he wrote to say he could not. Mr. Kingsley has just finished a huge book which is to be published strictly anonymously, and which he has been working at very hard lately, getting up before five every morning, which he finds makes a wonderful difference in his health, for he has been immensely better since he took to that plan, and it is much better than sitting up late. When Mr. Smith[20] dines here he is very dormousish till we are just thinking about going to bed, when he becomes suddenly quite lively, and brings out his atrocious puns by dozens. The dog Dandie has become immensely fond of me; he coolly walked into the drawing-room yesterday, swinging his great tail and wriggling his body about, and as I was opening the pew door in church I happened to look round, and there was Dandie close to my heels, somewhat to my horror. Little John Parker, Mr. Kingsley's publisher, came on Saturday and went away this morning.'[21] Martineau was impressed by Froude. 'Mr. Froude is the handsomest and most fascinating man I ever saw. He has had a wretched life of it.'

Kingsley had another pupil for three months that summer, William Lees, a candidate for ordination, and these two were to be his only pupils. The days were certainly full. Kegan Paul recalled, '... his pupils—two in number, and treated as his own sons— were working in the dining-room; his guests perhaps lounging on the lawn, or reading in the study. And he had time for all, going from writing to lecturing on optics, or to a passage in Virgil, from this to a vehement conversation with a guest, or tender care for his wife, who was far from strong—or a romp with his children. He would work himself into a sort of white heat over his book, till, too excited to write more, he would calm himself down by a pipe, pacing his grass-plot in thought and with long strides.'

'One great element of success in his intercourse with his parishioners was his abounding humour and fun. What caused a hearty laugh was a real refreshment to him, and he had the strongest belief that laughter and humour were elements in the nature of God Himself.'[22] Finally, said Paul simply, '. . . to me he wasthenoblest,truest,kindestfriend I everhadorcanhopetohave.'

William Lees was old enough to take an interest in the work of the Christian Socialists. Kingsley wrote delightedly to Ludlow: 'When "God sends mouths, He sends meat". So Lees will lend us the £100 tomorrow. He is *engoué* with the thing; will do any-thing to help it—seems very much longing to buy up Jacob's Island, and build a model lodging house, etc. etc.

'Now—quick—present—fire. Can you and Walsh talk all over with the Master, and run down here for three or four hours, and let us organise this paper? Lees says that we shall have an enormous sale, that the young men are thirsting for something of the kind.'

Kingsley had a social topic very much to hand for the proposed new *Christian Socialist* journal. There had been a rash of burglaries in the south of England. The rector of Frimley, ten miles from Eversley, had been attacked and fatally injured. All big houses were vulnerable, and even the popular rector of Eversley had to take precautions. To young Martineau's great interest, an atmos-phere of tension and excitement pervaded the vicarage. Kingsley went to the unheard-of length of buying a metal shutter to pull over the glass door of his side study, and made sure the bolts were firmly fastened each night. There were two abortive attempts at house-breaking, once when Maurice was a guest, and Kingsley and Lees sat guard with pistols and a gun loaded with slugs. A few nights later there was another alarm, and prowlers were heard around the stables, so on the advice of Mr. Shaw Lefevre, Speaker of the House of Commons, who lived close by at Heck-field, Kingsley applied for the protection of a policeman, or bluebottle, as Martineau called him.

Unlike the property-owning gentry, who had scant sympathy with the rural thieves, Kingsley wrote about the causes of the disorders, the poverty and bad conditions of the agricultural areas. His comments were set forth in *Thoughts on the Frimley Murder*, for the *Christian Socialist*, which first appeared in Novem-ber 1850. Christian organisation of labour, he wrote, might have prevented it all, and increased numbers of police would not solve the problem but would merely drive the disease inwards and aggravate it. Ludlow edited the paper, and its title was the result of Maurice's insistence.

Alton Locke, completed in August, was published in November also, by Chapman and Hall, because Parker was afraid to publish Kingsley any more. Thomas Carlyle, with whom Kingsley was friendly, had read the manuscript and heartily approved it, and his lusty recommendation had helped Chapman decide to take the book. Carlyle admired Kingsley's sentiments, and approved particularly of the characterisation of Sandy Mackaye, whose Scottish dialect was, declared Carlyle, wonderfully lifelike. Although the hero was a Chartist poet, the final message was not revolutionary, since Kingsley, like Maurice, was a Tory at heart and valued order and stability. He believed that when working men struggled to rise above their station they usually succeeded only when they used the most brutish weapons of capitalism and industrialisation. Better, declared Kingsley, that they should improve themselves and their lives as far as they could according to God's law than that they should desert their class.

Order was what Kingsley admired—craved even. He had a profound need to be constantly assured that the true nature of the world revolved around the concepts of order, justice, compassion and imagination. He saw order in the laws of science, and thought that there were more miracles to be found in the laws of natural science than in the legends of the medieval saints. Inaction made him introspective, burdened by feelings of inadequacy. He needed the calm direction and encouragement which only a man like Maurice, the Master, the Prophet, could give him. And there was only one Maurice. 'I hear you are come home. If so, for God's sake come down and see me, if but for a day. I have more doubts, perplexities, hopes and fears to pour out to you than I could utter in a week, and to the rest of our friends I cannot open. You comprehend me; you are bigger than I.'[23] With children, and with younger men (who looked up to him almost as he looked up to Maurice) Kingsley was scrupulous in concealing this negative side.

With *Alton Locke* off his chest, he could not resist planning a third novel, although Fanny was not in favour of it, seeing how much the additional effort cost him. The story would be set in fifth-century Alexandria after the fall of Rome. He told Maurice: 'My idea in the romance is to set forth Christianity as the only really democratic creed, and philosophy, and above all, spiritualism, as the most exclusively aristocratic creed. Such has been my opinion for a long time, and what I have been reading lately confirms it more and more.'

Kingsley tried to take no notice of reviews of his books, since they either hurt or angered him. It seemed to him that critics only wrote long reviews when they disapproved of his novels, and in some cases the reviewers did not seem to have read the books properly—not even the title pages. Chapman and Hall printed two new editions of *Alton Locke* before the end of 1850, so from the financial point of view publisher and author were both satisfied. Nobody believed the novel was what it purported to be, i.e. by a genuine Chartist poet, but it was not immediately identified with either Parson Lot or Charles Kingsley.

Although *Alton Locke* does not exhibit the careful plot construction or the creative characterisation of great fiction, it is so packed with scenes, incidents and deeply-felt descriptions that most readers feel some degree of involvement, whatever their feelings about the book. By writing in the first person, and making the hero a man of the people, Kingsley neatly avoided the hint of patronage which clung to Lancelot Smith, gentleman, espousing the cause of the rural poor in *Yeast*. Alton Locke is a 'Cockney among Cockneys', only son and younger child of a poor widowed mother. A strict Calvinist, Mrs. Locke starves her children of affection and natural emotion. She apprentices Alton to a tailoring sweat-shop, through the introduction of her brother, a successful tradesman. In this way, Alton meets his cousin, George, who is destined for Cambridge and a worldly career as an Anglican clergyman. The lives and aspirations of these two young men form the dramatic contrast of the story.

Alton is moulded by two men—Crossthwaite, the Chartist tailor, a man of integrity and ideals; and Sandy Mackaye, Scottish bookseller and sage, a chip off the Carlylean block, who sympathises with Chartism but disapproves of physical force and violence. Mrs. Locke considers all books other than Holy Writ to be sinful, so Alton leaves home and lives with Mackaye. He has two interests, Chartism and poetry, and Mackaye solemnly advises him to make himself into a poet of the people.

Through cousin George, who takes a casual but friendly interest in his clever but prickly relative, Alton meets a beautiful but shallow girl, Lillian, with whom he falls instantly and chivalrously in love. Lillian's father, a rural Dean, and her serious, older cousin, Eleanor, compliment Alton on his poetic gifts and persuade him to tone down the political content of his poems in the interests of commercial success. Mackaye and Crossthwaite, however, feel that in so doing Alton has betrayed his class, so the young poet is stung into taking a more active part in Chartist agitation than he really wishes so that he can prove his working-class honour.

He is sent as a Chartist speaker to the area where Lillian lives. On his first visit there he had seen only the smiling aspect of the countryside with friendliness everywhere. On the second visit he sees only the grim features of a land where human beings are treated and housed worse than animals. The Chartist meeting turns into a riot, there are arrests, and Alton is sentenced to three years in prison. On release, he discovers that Lillian has married George, and, disillusioned, Alton returns to his true friends, Mackaye and Crossthwaite. The old bookseller dies on the eve of the 1848 Chartist meeting on Kennington Common. Crossthwaite is victimised and loses his job. Alton, who is able to support himself by journalism, tries to help a former fellow tailor, and in so doing becomes aware of the slums of Bermondsey and its fever-breeding sewers.

A terrible nemesis now overtakes the rich, careless customers of the old sweat-shop—the typhus germs of the tailors and their families infect the clothes, which give the customers the fatal disease, and George and Lillian both die. Alton realises that Eleanor, whose idyllic marriage to a rich, responsible and titled landlord has ended tragically through his sudden death, has always been a finer person than Lillian. There is no question of a romantic

attachment—for Alton is dying of tuberculosis. He is helped by
the dead Mackaye, who left a bequest to both Alton and Crossthwaite, to enable them to go to America and make a new start.
It is in line with Mackaye's later beliefs that emigration provides
a better solution to problems of poverty than revolutionary
violence. The dying poet writes his autobiography on board
ship, nursed by Eleanor, whose eloquence converts him to a trust
in Christianity as the only basis of justice for working people.

The opening of the story, 'I am a Cockney among Cockneys.
Italy and the Tropics, the Highlands and Devonshire, I know only
in dreams,' is as arresting in its poetic and pathetic way as the
bracing hunting scene in *Yeast*. It continues:

Even the Surrey Hills, of whose loveliness I have heard so
much, are to me a distant fairyland, whose gleaming ridges I
am worthy only to behold afar. With the exception of two
journeys, never to be forgotten, my knowledge of England is
bounded by the horizon which encircles Richmond Hill.

My earliest recollections are of a suburban street; of its
jumble of little shops and little terraces, each exhibiting some
fresh variety of capricious ugliness. The little scraps of garden
before the doors, with their dusty, stunted lilacs and balsam
poplars, were my only forests; my only wild animals, the
dingy, merry sparrows, who quarrelled fearlessly on my
window-sill, ignorant of trap or gun. From my earliest childhood, through long nights of sleepless pain, as the midnight
brightened into dawn, and the glaring lamps grew pale, I used
to listen, with pleasant awe, to the ceaseless roll of the market-
waggons, bringing up to the great city the treasures of the
gay green country, the land of fruit and flowers for which I
have yearned all my life in vain. They seemed to my boyish
fancy mysterious messengers from another world; the silent,
lonely night, in which they were the only moving things,
added to the wonder. I used to get out of bed to gaze at them,
and envy the coarse men and sluttish women who attended
them, their labour among verdant plants and rich brown
mould, under God's own clear sky.

5

In the course of the book, Kingsley described conditions of life and work which had rarely been so forthrightly presented to the reading public, except perhaps in the pages of Dickens. Unlike Dickens, however, Kingsley explicitly tried to give reasons for those conditions and to direct his readers to action to redress them. In later editions of the book he made some slight changes to the Cambridge sections. The first editions depict Cambridge much as Kingsley had known it in his student days. But in the mid-1860s, when Kingsley returned there as a professor, he discovered that the new generation of students was much improved in manners and its general attitude towards working men. Since he did not want his readers to assume that his 1840 Cambridge represented the 1860 town, he edited this section. The substance of the story was not changed, and as he believed, probably with justification, that many working people would read *Alton Locke* and identify with the narrator-hero, he considered it only fair to his university to present it in as accurate a light as possible.

It was both Kingsley's strength and his weakness as a literary man to be a preacher throughout his life. Consequently, his novels cannot fail to be extensions of his sermons. Only his poems stand apart as distillation of pure emotion. In his prose works Kingsley is for ever telling stories, explaining problems, describing nature, but from the pulpit as it were. Sometimes he leaves the narrative altogether to insert additional items of information, a practice which other Victorian novelists pursued, and which Kingsley stoutly defended on the grounds that many readers enjoyed these passages, especially intelligent women who were starved of opportunities for serious thought and discussions, in addition to readers who were so dull or ill-informed that they needed to be educated. In this respect Kingsley differed greatly from Dickens. Both men painted vivid word pictures of social conditions, but whereas Dickens never talked down to his working-class readers, Kingsley, through his moralising, sometimes gave the impression of so doing, although this was entirely unintentional. He used to call his parishioners 'my Hampshire clods', but this was not meant to be patronising, and Ludlow also used the word 'clods' in referring to country workers.

As for Kingsley's method of writing novels, he once told Tom Hughes that he could think of stories only in terms of characters holding conversations, and indeed his novels are almost entirely dialogue, divided by set-pieces of Victorian word painting. In the following extract Sandy Mackaye has taken Alton to visit a poor family which exists by doing piece-work for a rich tailor. The scene was intended to get under the reader's skin.

We went on through a back street or two, and then into a huge, miserable house, which, a hundred years ago, perhaps, had witnessed the luxury, and rung to the laughter of some one great fashionable family, alone there in their glory, Now every room of it held its family, or its group of families—a phalanstery of all the fiends;—its grand staircase, with the carved balustrades rotting and crumbling away piecemeal, converted into a common sewer for all its inmates. Up stair after stair we went, while wails of children, and curses of men, steamed out upon the hot stifling rush of air from every doorway, till, at the topmost story, we knocked at a garret door. We entered. Bare it was of furniture, comfortless, and freezing cold; but with the exception of the plaster dropping from the roof, and the broken windows, patched with rags and paper, there was a scrupulous neatness about the whole, which contrasted strangely with the filth and slovenliness outside. There was no bed in the room—no table. On a broken chair by the chimney sat a miserable old woman, fancying that she was warming her hands over embers which had long been cold, shaking her head, and muttering to herself, with palsied lips, about the guardians and the workhouse; while upon a few rags on the floor lay a girl, ugly, small-pox marked, hollow eyed, emaciated, her only bed clothes the skirt of a large handsome new riding-habit, at which two other girls, wan and tawdry, were stitching busily, as they sat right and left of her on the floor. The old woman took no notice of us as we entered; but one of the girls looked up, and, with a pleased gesture of recognition, put her finger up to her lips, and whispered, 'Ellen's asleep'.[24]

There was a brief visit to 'The sweater's den':

> As I had expected, a fetid, choking den, with just room enough in it for the seven or eight sallow, starved beings, who, coatless, shoeless and ragged, sat stitching, each on his truckle-bed.[25]

Kingsley made poor Jemmy Downes, his tailor friend, live in Jacob's Island. Downes becomes gin-sodden, crazy with delirium tremens, and his wife and children die of fever. He takes Alton home, and in drunken grief falls into the sewage ditch outside the balcony.

> We rushed out on the balcony. The light of the policeman's lantern glared over the ghastly scene—along the double row of miserable house-backs, which lined the sides of the open tidal ditch—over strange rambling jetties, and balconies, and sleeping-sheds, which hung on rotting piles over the black waters, with phosphorescent scraps of rotten fish gleaming and twinkling out of the dark hollows, like devilish gravelights—over bubbles of poisonous gas, and bloated carcasses of dogs, and lumps of offal, floating on the stagnant olive-green hell-broth—over the slow sullen rows of oily ripple which were dying away into the darkness far beyond, sending up, as they stirred, hot breaths of miasma—the only sign that a spark of humanity, after years of foul life, had quenched itself at last in that foul death. I almost fancied I could see the haggard face staring up at me through the slimy water; but no, it was as opaque as stone.
>
> I shuddered and went in again, to see slatternly gin-smelling women stripping off their clothes—true women even there—to cover the poor naked corpses; and pointing to cover the bruises which told a tale of long tyranny and cruelty; and mingling their lamentations with stories of shrieks and beating, and children locked up for hours to starve; and the men looked

on sullenly, as if they too were guilty, or rushed out to relieve themselves by helping to find the drowned body. Ugh! it was the very mouth of hell, that room. And in the midst of all the rout, the relieving officer stood impassive, jotting down scraps of information, and warning us to appear the next day, to state what we knew before the magistrates. Needless hypocrisy of law! Too careless to save the women and children from brutal tyranny, nakedness, starvation!—Too superstitious to offend its idol of vested interests, by protecting the poor man against his tyrants, the house-owning shopkeepers under whose greed the dwellings of the poor become nests of filth and pestilence, drunkenness and degradation.[26]

Not all of the novel is as bitter as this. Kingsley relieved the story here and there by poems—Alton's poems naturally, the most famous being *The Sands of Dee,* written by Alton in remembrance of a sketch of the Cheshire sands by, he thinks, Copley Fielding: '. . . a wild waste of tidal sands, with here and there a line of stake-nets fluttering in the wind—a grey shroud of rain sweeping up from the westward, through which low red cliffs glowed dimly in the rays of the setting sun—a train of horses and cattle splashing slowly through shallow desolate pools and creeks, their wet, red, and black hides glittering in one long line of level light.'

It was not long before in some circles it was an open secret that Kingsley was Parson Lot and also the author of *Yeast* and *Alton Locke.* Kingsley did not hide his views. Writing to the *Morning Chronicle* on January 28, 1851, he said '. . . We as Socialists believe the sanctity of family life to be the germ of all society', and the phrase which was remembered and held against him was 'We as Socialists'. Parker was reluctant to republish *Yeast,* bringing it out as a novel as Kingsley wished, and Kingsley wrote to Maurice and Ludlow, angry at Parker, and wanting to know if he had any legal redress or possession of copyright which could force Parker to publish. In 1851 *Yeast* appeared, and in book form reached a new and wider public. The two books established Kingsley firmly as a serious writer whom publishers would be pleased to have on their lists. The secret of his great appeal to young people especially was that his views, although advanced at the time when first expressed, were never innately minority views. A generation later they would coincide quite remarkably with majority public opinion. In a sense, therefore, he foreshadowed public sentiment on a variety of subjects, although one should be careful not to underestimate his part in shaping that public opinion.

Many of the reviews of *Yeast* and *Alton Locke* were hostile. Kingsley was stung by an anonymous review in the *Guardian*[27] which accused him of encouraging profligacy and heresy, and he departed from his usual practice of pretending these reviews did not exist and wrote a hot but dignified rebuttal. Kingsley was well aware that all the controversies around him were useful publicity. When Tom Hughes once congratulated him on his loyalty to the movement during 1848–1850, Kingsley retorted briskly: 'I lost nothing—I risked nothing. You fellows worked like bricks, spent money, and got mid-shipman's half-pay (nothing a day and find yourself) and monkey's allowance (more kicks than half-pence). I risked no money; 'cause why, I had none; but *made* money out of the movement, and fame too. I've often thought what a poor creature I was. I made £150 by *Alton Locke*, and never lost a farthing, and I got, not in spite of, but by the rows, a name and a standing with many a one who would never had heard of me otherwise, and I should have been a mendicant if I had holloaed when I got a facer, while I was winning by the cross, though I didn't mean to fight one. No. And if I'd had £100,000, I'd have, and should have, staked and lost it all in 1848–1850. I should, Tom, for my heart was and is in it, and you'll see it will beat yet. . . .'[28]

The national event of the spring of 1851 was the opening of the Great Exhibition in Hyde Park and Kingsley was deeply moved by the evidence of England's manufacturing greatness. Tears sprang to his eyes on his first visit and his admiration for the Prince Consort soared. He preached a sermon on behalf of a hospital at the fashionable church of St. Margaret's, Westminster, and referred to Albert as 'the representative of the highest and most sacred personage in these realms'. He declared that if a congregation of one thousand years earlier could have seen the Great Exhibition it would consider all those scientific inventions to be further proofs of the Kingdom of God. Yet, he continued dryly, apart from some official and quite perfunctory talk of God's blessing upon the Exhibition, there was no real belief that he could see that God was the fount and root of it. Indeed, Kingsley was convinced that most people hoped that God's blessing would consist in His leaving the Exhibition and its visitors severely alone.

Kingsley's irony could be as bitter as Dean Swift's. Speaking to another fashionable audience, he said:

Let us clear our minds of cant, gentlemen and ladies. What is the meaning of this word free? If it is profitable and right to make clothes by sweating, it is profitable and right to cultivate land by paupers, and still more profitable and right to cultivate it by slaves. I really do not see any reason upon economic grounds why you should care so much for the condition of those slaves; why you should not breed them for your own use as you do cattle and horses, and breed no more of them than you want—why you should not ascertain carefully the age at which their years of work begin to decline and then, instead of unprofitably supporting them in almshouses and unions, just make away with them painlessly by a few drops of strychnine, melt them down in the sulphuric acid tank, and drill them in your root crops.

Such a policy, he concluded, would lead to splendid profits without breaking a single law of what the experts called 'Political Economy'.

At about the same time he lectured to the Society for Promoting Working Men's Associations (one of the Christian Socialists' achievements) upon *The Application of Associative Principles and Methods to Agriculture*, a subject to which he had devoted considerable attention and upon which he could speak with immense practicality. Ludlow told Fanny Kingsley afterwards that the

two-and-a-half-hour lecture had been a 'triumph'. He had listened
to it with respect and admiration: 'it was the *manliest* thing I had
ever heard.'[29] 'Such a right bold honest way of turning from side
to side, looking everything straight in the face, and speaking out
all the good and all the ill that could be said of it, in the plainest
way.'[30] Ludlow later summarised the lecture for the *Christian
Socialist*. He was as aware as Kingsley that the rector's name was a
prime drawing-card for public lectures, and the Whit Tuesday
tea party organised by the Christian Socialists was advertised as
having the Rev. Charles Kingsley among its guests.

Ludlow had many other acquaintances besides the Christian
Socialist group, and one of these, the Rev. G. S. Drew, rector of
St. John's Church, Charlotte Street, London, decided in this year
of the Great Exhibition to hold a series of six sermons especially
directed towards a working-class congregation. Preachers whose
names would be familiar to such audiences were invited to parti-
cipate. Maurice promised to give two lectures; Drew himself
would give one. Kingsley, F. W. Robertson and Septimus
Hansard were to give the other three.

Kingsley's name was guaranteed to fill the church. To quote
the *English Churchman*, he was 'somewhat notorious as the author
of *Alton Locke, Tailor and Poet*, a book of doubtful principles, we
understand, but which we have never seen'.[31]

Kingsley took as text a passage from St. Luke which described
Jesus Christ quoting from Isaiah: 'The Spirit of the Lord hath
annointed me to proclaim the acceptable year of the Lord.'
Kingsley carefully spelled out what this meant: the practice,
instituted by Moses, of releasing debtors and bond-servants, and
returning land to its original possessors at the expiration of certain
given periods. 'If I wanted one proof above all others of the
inspired wisdom of Moses, I should choose this unparalleled
contrivance for preventing the accumulation of large estates, and
the reduction of the people into the state of serfs and day-
labourers.' From this, Kingsley went on to prove to his own
satisfaction (and indeed to that of most of his audience, who were
already in agreement with his views) that 'all systems of society
which favour the accumulation of capital in a few hands' were

'contrary to the Kingdom of God which Jesus proclaimed.'
Further, declared the preacher, could there be a greater sign of
equality than the Lord's supper? 'Wherever in the world there
may be inequality, it ceases there. One table, one reverential
posture, one bread, one wine, for high and low, for wise and
foolish. . . .'

The message of the Church of Christ, concluded Kingsley,
amid attentive and approving silence, was 'That the will of God
is good news to the poor, deliverance to the captives, healing to
the broken-hearted, light to the ignorant, liberty to the crushed,
and to the degraded masses the acceptable year of the Lord—a
share and a stake, for them and for their children after them, in
the soil, the wealth, the civilisation, and the government of this
English land.'

In fact, the sermon was very much what the congregation
expected from their 'Chartist parson'. Drew, however, unused
to Kingsley's style and message, was horrified, and rebuked
Kingsley on the spot for a sermon which he considered both
mistaken and dangerous. Drew's completely unexpected intervention was dynamite, for the audience was keenly partisan, and
any gesture of protest from Kingsley would have lit the fuse.
Kingsley was incapable of reply. He was hurt in his tenderest
spot, as a representative of the Church of England. He lowered his
head in silence, stepped down from the pulpit and groped his
way out of the church, pushing through groups of men who left
their pews and surged forward to greet and support him. His
friends took out of his unresisting hands a copy of the sermon he
had just delivered, and he was borne off to the security of the
Maurice home.

The affair blew up into an ecclesiastical storm in a teacup.
The Bishop of London, without having read the sermon, sum-
marily forbade Kingsley to preach in any London church. The
Daily News published an editorial suggesting that Kingsley was
unfit to preach anywhere. He thereupon wrote a quiet letter to
the Bishop, who read the sermon, realised that it contained no
subversive material and withdrew his ban on Kingsley and
London churches. The matter, which distressed Fanny Kingsley

considerably, was yet another example of the excitement and disturbance which Kingsley's words and deeds always aroused, and which added to his reputation as a firebrand and revolutionary.

There was one unexpected by-product of the St. John's Church incident. At Maurice's house afterwards, when the group were energetically discussing what steps to take to redeem its friend's reputation, Kingsley had seemed the calmest of them all. But when he reached Eversley late at night, he was too agitated to sleep, and spent the rest of the night pacing up and down the garden. He sublimated his own distress in the brief but touching poem, *The Three Fishers,* an almost perfect distillation of his own anguish transmuted into sympathy for others. When his wife came down for breakfast, Kingsley silently gave her the manuscript of the poem.

Three fishers went sailing away to the West,
Away to the West as the sun went down;
Each thought on the woman who loved him the best,
And the children stood watching them out of the town;
For men must work, and women must weep,
And there's little to earn, and many to keep,
    Though the harbour bar be moaning.

Three wives sat up in the lighthouse tower,
And they trimmed the lamps as the sun went down;
They looked at the squall, and they looked at the shower,
And the night-rack came rolling up ragged and brown.
But men must work, and women must weep,
Though storms be sudden, and waters deep,
    And the harbour bar be moaning.

Three corpses lay out on the shining sands
In the morning gleam as the tide went down,
And the women are weeping and wringing their hands
For those who will never come home to the town;
For men must work, and women must weep,

And the sooner it's over, the sooner to sleep;
And good-bye to the bar and its moaning.

His family worried in case Kingsley's health would give way again, and since Mr. and Mrs. Kingsley and Henry, then aged about twenty-one, were on the point of taking a holiday in Germany, Mrs. Kingsley suggested that Charles should accompany them. It would be an escape from the press, from irritating personal attacks, from more exhausting calls on his time and strength. Fanny fully agreed. Charles had a few days to buy some new clothes and arrange for a curate, and then the party set off.

8

Man of Letters

It was certainly more enjoyable for Henry to have Charles with him on the holidays, for their parents were in their late sixties and not strong enough for strenuous exertion. Besides, Henry rather hero-worshipped his famous, amusing, yet serious and well-informed elder brother. The gap of eleven years in their ages was no barrier. With Herbert and Gerald dead, there were only three Kingsley boys, and George, who was four years Henry's senior, was the odd man out in the family. He had taken up medicine, first in Paris, then in Edinburgh, and was at that time somewhere on the Continent.

Henry was a pleasant, athletic, rather ordinary young man. Since he was only six when the family left Clovelly, the move to London which Charles had so resented had been quite acceptable to him. Indeed, he loved Chelsea's picturesque riverside location, and the historic houses which surrounded Chelsea Rectory in the 1830s and 1840s. His favourite building was Essex House, an impressive pile in Church Place. Once the home of the Earls of Essex, it was pulled down in 1842. Henry had often explored the crumbling mansion, from whose windows he could peer down into his father's huge garden, with its long walk of pollarded lime-trees, the giant acacias bordering the smooth lawn, and its great mulberry tree, famous for miles around. The boy acquired a genuine feeling for history, which as an adult he put to good use in his novels.

The Chelsea parish was a demanding one, and Mr. Kingsley had neither the time nor with increasing years the will or the energy to tutor his youngest son with the zeal and attention he had given to Charles in the Barnack days. Henry was accordingly left rather to his own devices, and learned to be fairly self-reliant, with a liking for literature and adventure. When he was fourteen, Henry went to the junior section of King's College, and at sixteen he moved up into the senior department, where F. D. Maurice was then teaching English Literature and Modern History. Henry was a cheerful, harum-scarum boy, expecting to go to university in the ordinary way, but was a poor student and easily distracted. It was because he had done so badly at school that he had been packed off to Bournemouth to spend a month with Charles and Fanny in 1848. In 1851 he had managed to matriculate at Worcester College, Oxford,[1] and was therefore at the start of his student career. Like Charles, Henry greatly enjoyed the sporting side of college life, its companionship, its clubs, and the sudden freedom from the strictness of Chelsea Rectory. His way of kicking over the traces was to neglect his studies, to gamble, to hurl himself into sports and athletics, and to smoke.[2] Charles took an indulgent view of these high spirits, believing, as he had written in *Yeast*, that young men normally grow out of such behaviour.

The Kingsleys crossed the Channel on the same packet steamer as the Thackerays. The two families were acquainted. Charles and Henry greatly admired Thackeray, and Charles considered *Vanity Fair* one of the finest novels in the English language. Young Anne Thackeray, demure and bright-eyed, was impressed by the dashing Kingsley men with their new broad-brimmed hats. She lamented that her father looked very ordinary by comparison.

At Cologne, Charles wrote to Fanny of his admiration for the 'grand pictures in painted glass, with far distances which let the eye *out* of the building, instead of confining and crushing it inwards, as painted glass generally does'. He often felt uneasy in great cathedrals—once he wrote that Salisbury Cathedral, with its graceful spire, was 'crushing'—so it was indeed significant when he felt able to look outwards from the windows. The choir, the head of the Virgin in Koloff's triptych, all moved him to tears. Part of the attraction of the Continental trip for Charles was that he could visit some of the places Fanny saw when her relatives sent her away in the hope that she would forget him. The Kingsleys arranged a list of addresses for Fanny to write to, and Charles showered her with letters, sketches, poems, from every halting place.

The brothers exchanged views on university life as they tramped the German mountains, and discussed Henry's future. The likelihood was that Henry would not become an academic or professional man like his father and brothers. But Charles would probably not be dismayed. Before he met Fanny Grenfell he had considered going to the American West to seek his fortune. Emigration could easily be the answer for Henry now, and in America, certainly, the magnet was California, since the gold rush of 1849.

Kingsley had a wonderful capacity for extracting the utmost pleasure from existing circumstances, and the German trip was a splendid tonic. He picked and dried many small bouquets to be taken home, and climbed the rock face to the Lorelei's seat to pick flowers for Fanny. They reached Bonn and went to Ehrenbreitstein, which 'utterly disappointed me, except professionally. The lying painters paint it just three times as high as it is, and I was quite shocked to find it so small. But it is all beautiful—beautiful.' He made a special visit to the lofty castle of Rolandseck, and wrote to Fanny, 'Rolandseck and Nonnenwerth, *and that story*;—it seemed quite awful to find oneself in presence of it.'

'*That story*', underlined with so much emphasis, was a private bond between Charles and Fanny, a tale which had a personal meaning for them. It told of Roland, one of Charlemagne's knights, who fell in love with Hildegund, daughter of the Count of Drachenberg. Roland was called away to help Charlemagne fight the Saracens in the Pyrenees, and Hildegund, for safety's sake, took refuge in the nunnery at Nonnenwerth. After waiting patiently and in vain for her lover's return, she despaired of ever seeing him again, and took the veil, so that when Roland returned his bride was a nun. In his grief Roland built a castle, Rolandseck, high on the mountainside, so that he could look down on Nonnenwerth, where Hildegunde was encloistered. When the news was brought to him that she was dead he said nothing, but died in his turn, his face turned towards Nonnenwerth.[3]

Next the brothers reached the volcanic district of the Eifel, with its strange cones, its craters filled with ash and its stream of carbonic acid. Kingsley was 'stunned with wonders'. Trèves (Trier), where the dual influence of Roman civilisation and Christianity was particularly strong, made an indelible impression upon him. His strong sense of history worked powerfully in him as he wandered among the Roman ruins, doubly intrigued because his mind was already occupied with the historical novel about Alexandria. As he wrote to Fanny, '. . . the feeling that one is standing over the skeleton of the giant iniquity—Old Rome— is overpowering. And as I stood last night in that amphitheatre, amid the wild beasts' den, and thought of the Christian martyrdoms and the Frank prisoners, and all the hellish scenes of agony and cruelty that place had witnessed, I seemed to hear the very voice of the Archangel whom St. John heard in Patmos, crying, "Babylon the Great is fallen;" but no more like the sound of a trumpet, but only in the still whisper of the night breeze, and through the sleeping vineyards, and the great still smile of God out of the broad blue heaven. Ah! and you were not there to feel it with me! I am so longing to be home!'

His private letters to his wife were full of his longing for her. R. B. Martin quotes some of them from the Parrish collection at Princeton: 'You do not seem to recollect how dreadfully I long for you in *body*—as well as mind. I kiss those two locks of hair until I am ready to cry, & think of you *all day long*—I don't believe you are out of my mind for half an hour altogether by day—& I am always talking about you, & at night, unless I have walked myself tired, I cannot sleep for thinking of you, & if I wake I begin longing & thinking & picturing you to myself.'[4] No wonder that Kingsley, feeling so passionate after nearly ten years of marriage, should call people 'fools' who thought that love ceased at the altar.

He made good use of the tour a few years later in *Two Years Ago*, when one of his characters, Stangrave, goes to Germany, and in October 1854 walks along part of the route which Charles

and Henry had taken three years earlier. These descriptions must
have corresponded to Charles's own notes and recollections.

'He . . . was upon the hills between Ems and Coblentz. Walking
over a high tableland of stubbles, which would be grass in
England; and yet with all its tillage is perhaps not worth more
than English grass would be, thanks to that small-farm system
much be-praised by some who know not wheat from turnips.
Then along a road, which might be a Devon one, cut in the
hillside, through authentic "Devonian" slate, where deep
chocolate soil is lodged on the top of the upright strata, and a
thick coat of moss and wood sedge clusters about the oak-
scrub roots, round which the delicate and rare oak-fern mingles
its fronds with great blue campanulas; while the "white
admirals" and silver-washed "fritillaries" flit round every
bramble bed, and the great "purple emperors" come down to
drink in the road puddles, and sit fearlessly, flashing off their
velvet wings a blue as of that empyrean which is "dark by
excess of light."

Down again through cultivated lands, corn and clover,
flax and beet, and all the various crops with which the industrious Geoman yeoman ekes out his little patch of soil. Past
the thrifty husbandman himself, as he guides the two milch-
kine in his tiny plough, and stops at the furrow's end, to greet
you with the hearty German smile and bow; while the little
fair-haired maiden, walking beneath the shade of standard
cherries, walnuts, and pears, all grey with fruit, fills the cows'
mouths with chicory, and wild carnations, and pink sainfoin,
and many a fragrant weed which richer England wastes.

Down once more, into a glen; but such a glen as neither
England nor America has ever seen; or, please God, ever will
see, glorious as it is. Stangrave, who knew Europe well, had
walked that path before; but he stopped then, as he had done
the first time, in awe. On the right, slope up the bare slate
downs, up to the foot of cliffs; but only half of those cliffs
God has made. Above the gray slate ledges rise cliffs of man's
handiwork, pierced with a hundred square black embrasures;

and above them the long barrack-ranges of a soldiers' town; which a foeman stormed once, when it was young: but what foeman will ever storm it again? What conqueror's foot will ever tread again upon the "broad stone of honour", and call Ehrenbreitstein his?'[5]

Kingsley rapidly gained strength. 'Exceedingly well and strong; as lean as a lathe, as any one would be, who carried two stone of baggage daily increasing in weight from the minerals and fossils I find, on his back through broiling suns.' The brothers made it a rule that fifteen miles a day would be their maximum, with a sightseeing stroll in the evenings. 'Every night I dream of you and the children, and everywhere I go I pick you flowers *für denkmäler.*'

At Trèves, the rough clothing and foreign accents of the young men made them objects of suspicion. Charles turned it into a glorious joke.

Here we are at Trèves, having been brought here under arrest, with a gendarme from the Mayor of Bittsburg, and liberated next morning with much laughter and many curses from the police here. However, we had the pleasure of spending a night in prison, among fleas and felons, on the bare floor. It appears the barbarians took our fishing-rods for 'todt-instrumental'— deadly weapons—and our wide-awakes for Italian hats, and got into their addle pates that we were emissaries of Mazzini and Co. distributing political tracts, for not a word of politics had we talked. Luckily, the police-inspector here was a gentleman, and his wife and daughter ladies, and they did all they dare for us, and so about ten next morning we were set free with many apologies, and the gendarme (who, after all, poor fellow, was very civil) sent back to Bittsburg with a reprimand. We are the lions of Trèves at present, for the affair has made a considerable fuss.[6]

The brothers were not the only members of the family with stories to tell. Mrs. Kingsley, when out walking with an acquaintance at Dresden during that same holiday, had a fright when a gipsy-like young man ran up to her with shouts of delight. It was her other son, George, on one of his typically unconventional walking tours of Bohemia.

Wonderfully refreshed by the trip, Charles returned to Eversley, ready to work singlehanded in the parish, but depressed at finding that the press hostility had not abated. In September 1851 the *Quarterly Review,* a literary paper with Tory leanings, gathered together *Alton Locke, Yeast, The Message of the Church to Labouring Men, Politics for the People,* some sermons by Maurice, and some French historical and socialist books, and reviewed them all under the general title of 'Revolutionary Literature'. The reviewer did not mince his words, and was particularly censorious about two Anglican clergymen who went forth, he said, 'as the apostles of a doctrine fraught with such terrible consequences ... attempting to invest their miserable delusions with the authority of Christianity and the sanction of the Gospel'. This time Kingsley deliberately refused to answer the reviewers, consoling himself with the reflection that French and German critics thought highly of *Alton Locke.* The Prussian ambassador, Chevalier Bunsen, was a fervent admirer of Kingsley's writing, and he used his influence to see that Kingsley's books were translated by able and sympathetic linguists for their Tauschnitz editions. Charles and Fanny were also invited to receptions at the ambassador's house in Carlton Terrace. Such outings were a rare social and intellectual pleasure for Fanny especially.

The ideas of the Christian Socialists in general were taken more seriously in German circles than in English ones. This German link can be traced through Kingsley to Maurice, and farther back to Coleridge, whose writings and conversations introduced so many of the ideas of the Romantic movement from Germany. Maurice's first wife, Anna, had been an accomplished German scholar who first introduced her husband to German theology. Kingsley was also a fine German scholar, and both he and Maurice greatly admired Prussia, which they thought was a model Protestant state.

Kingsley was an early member of the Council of Promoters

of the Associations, one of the Christian Socialists' prime activities, though his Eversley commitments prevented him from being very actively involved. Ludlow and Hughes, however, were right in the forefront of the labour movement, particularly with a view to setting up associations for production. In January 1852 there was an industrial dispute in the North, in the iron workers' industry, and the employers locked out the men. Kingsley tried to put the men's case before the public by his articles in the Christian Socialist papers, but he thought the real answer lay not in a union, but in an iron workers co-operative producing association. In June a new bill became law. It legalised industrial associations, and was largely the work of Ludlow, who had been principal witness before a committee formed by an M.P., R. A. Slaney. Thomas Hughes had actually discovered the existence of this committee, and he and Ludlow swiftly realised how the Christian Socialists could use it to press legislation which would legalise co-operatives. They explained the situation to their readers in the columns of the *Christian Socialist*.

Kingsley welcomed this advance. He was losing the militant impulsiveness which had so characterised him in 1848. He was now completely in accord with Maurice's line of thinking which rejected any link with a particular party, and he anticipated improvement for the conditions of working men to be accomplished through education and legislation, not through the violent overthrow of institutions and the substitution of one political party for another. Reconciliation was now the keynote of Kingsley's hopes. In this vein he wrote to Hughes, in approval of Ludlow's bill, '. . . such a move will do more to carry out true Conservatism, and to reconcile the workmen with the real aristocracy, than any politician for the last twenty years has done'. He agreed with Maurice, who had said that political rule by the Manchester School of manufacturers and economists would be a 'horrible catastrophe'. 'Of course it would. To pretend to be the workmen's friends, by keeping down the price of bread, when all they want thereby is to keep down wages, and to increase profits, and in the meantime to widen the gulf between the working man and all that is time-honoured, refined, and chivalrous in English society, that they may make the men their divided slaves, that is—perhaps half unconsciously—for there are excellent men amongst them—the game of the Manchester School.

'I have never swerved from my one idea of the last seven years, that the real battle of the time is—if England is to be saved from anarchy and unbelief, and utter exhaustion caused by the competitive enslavement of the masses—not Radical or Whig against Peelite or Tory (let the dead bury their dead), but the Church, the gentleman, and the workman, against the shopkeepers and the Manchester School.'

With no more pupils at the rectory to keep his mind stretched, Kingsley was thrown back on letter-writing, and was in constant touch with Hughes and Ludlow. He and Ludlow wrote almost daily in connection with the Christian Socialist journals, or *Hypatia*, which Kingsley had now begun, or the poems he was writing. It was a period of great literary activity for Kingsley. Ludlow was also engaged in writing, for his career, like Kingsley's, had been jeopardised by his political work, and he used journalism to supplement his income. Over the years Ludlow trained himself to become a respected literary critic, a conscientious editor, a serious writer and a very minor poet. He did his best to criticise Kingsley's literary work constructively, but after a while it dawned on him that the rector was not as humble, or thick-skinned as he made out, and that Kingsley the writer really wanted only favourable criticism, so Ludlow gradually ceased to make suggestions. By contrast, Kingsley's letters to Ludlow were conversations in ink. 'Too tired, confused, and happy to work, I sit down for a chat with you,' he wrote in June 1852.

This was the month when Fanny came safely through another confinement, and their third child, Mary St. Leger, was born. In happiness and relief, Kingsley invited Ludlow down. 'In three weeks' time we shall be delighted to see you. My beloved roses will be just in glory, the fish will be just in season; thanks to the late spring. . . . Also we will talk of all matters in heaven and earth. . . . What you say about my "ergon" being poetry is quite true. . . . I do feel a different being when I get into metre—I feel like an otter in the water, instead of an otter ashore. He can run fast enough ashore, and keep the hounds at a tearing gallop, as my legs found this spring in Snowdonia,[7] but when he takes water, then indeed he becomes beautiful, full of divine grace and freedom, and exuberance of power. Go and look at him in the Zoological Gardens, and you'll see what I mean. When I have done *Hypatia*, I will write no more novels. I will write poetry— not as a profession—but I will keep myself for it, and I do think I shall do something that will live.'[8]

Ludlow apparently complained that the monks' conversation in *Hypatia* was very tedious. Kingsley agreed. 'As for the monks— 'pon my honour, they are slow fellows—but then they *were* so horribly slow in reality. And I can't see but that Pambo's palaver in my tale is just what I find in Rosweyde's *Vitae Patrum* and Athanases' *Life of Anthony*. Almost every expression of Pambo's is a crib from some one, word for word.' Kingsley researched historical sources available to him very thoroughly for the background of *Hypatia*. 'Ten years' grubbing in monk-Latin', he insisted. Part of Ludlow's criticisms arose because Ludlow thought that Kingsley should devote himself to poetry, especially as Ludlow, a pacifist at heart, found many of Kingsley's incidents too bloodthirsty for his liking. Kingsley, a born fighting man, as Thomas Hughes points out, managed to rationalise his intemperateness by asserting that the violence in his books was needed in order to arouse the public to an awareness of social wrongs and help to produce a climate of opinion which would force changes. Maurice once called Kingsley the Thalaba of the Christian Socialists, a reference to Southey's poem about the epic Arabian hero.

There were other visitors to Eversley, in addition to the Christian Socialists who were still his closest friends. There was Alfred Tennyson, a disciple of Maurice,[9] and a poet whose brilliant promise Kingsley had been one of the first to perceive. Tennyson contemplated buying a house in Eversley, but Kingsley, although loath to lose the company of a congenial spirit, felt bound to point out the disadvantages of the site Tennyson had chosen. (Anyone living at Eversley Rectory was pathologically aware of the importance of a warm, dry, sheltered site for a house.) The poet finally bought a house on the Isle of Wight. Another honoured guest was the Norwegian writer, Frederika Bremer, greatly honoured in her own country, less known in Britain. She admired the social content of Kingsley's novels, and recognised a Viking strain in him, the 'wolf vein' of the Goths.

Meanwhile, what the co-operators liked to call their Magna Carta had become law in June, and on July 26 and 27, 1852, a co-operative conference was held in the Hall of Association. Ludlow was one of the chief organisers and Kingsley made it his business to attend. He was 'warmly cheered on entering'. Delegates from twenty-eight societies were there and a representative of the Liverpool Tailors' Institute took the chair. The conference had to face the problem of whether there was a moral obligation upon co-operators to describe articles for sale truthfully. The resolution which finally embodied their decision to do so was drafted by Kingsley: 'That this Conference entreats all co-operative establishments, for the sake of the general good, to sell all articles exactly for what they know them to be, and to abstain, as much as possible, from the sale of all articles publicly known to be adulterated, even if demanded by their customers.' Later on he suggested that co-operatives should include welfare activities because the 'principle of the benefit society, that of mutual help, was not adjunct to co-operation, but lay at the very root of it.'

William Allen, one of the leaders of the engineers, speaking at another point in the proceedings, raised a laugh in which Kingsley joined when he described how on two occasions the members of a Mechanics' Institute had voted to buy *Alton Locke*, but each time they were prevented because the president of the Institute threatened to resign if they did buy it.

Meanwhile the first instalments of *Hypatia* opened in *Fraser's*, after some discussion as to whether Kingsley was morally bound to offer it first to Chapman, as he had published *Alton Locke* when Parker was afraid. George Henry Lewes, literary editor of the *Leader*, thought the first chapters were dull and uninteresting, and made the further criticism that the author mingled modern with ancient colouring. Lewes wrote another review, when the novel was farther advanced, but still insisted it was 'the failure of a remarkable writer'. The High Church periodical, *Guardian*, was pleased to damn the book as immoral: a view which Dr. Pusey later endorsed. Kingsley had rather invited this jibe in a preface, where, from the most chivalrous motives, he suggested there might be some strong passages in the book which his male readers might want to protect their wives and daughters from. 'A picture of life in the fifth century must needs contain much which will be painful to any reader, and which the young and innocent will do well to leave altogether unread,' Kingsley began the long, rambling preface, in which he described the historical background as if he were delivering a history lecture, complete with most of his historical sources. In conclusion he said, 'And so I send forth this little sketch,[10] ready to give my hearty thanks to any reviewer who, by exposing my mistakes, shall teach me and the public somewhat more about the last struggle between the Young Church and the Old World.' Kingsley was a trifle nettled by Lewes's disapproval of mingling modern with old, and cited Ben Jonson as a dramatist who had used the same technique.

In spite of being an historical novel, *Hypatia* was intended to include topics or comments touching on contemporary problems. Kingsley wrote primarily to instruct and to influence, not to create human characters and thus illuminate human nature. 'People are too stupid and in too great a hurry,' he insisted, 'to interpret the most puzzling facts for themselves, and the author must act as showman and do it for them. . . . Art ought to mean the art of pleasing and instructing, and, believe me, the passages in which the author speaks in his own person do so.'

Chapter I of *Hypatia* opens in strong Kingsley style by introducing the young monk, Philammon, living in a peaceful monastery called the Laura, some 300 miles south of Alexandria. It is the year 413 A.D. Rome has just fallen to the barbarian, the entire civilised world is in turmoil, and Africa, with Alexandria as the main city, is a key area. Philammon, however, has been brought up in seclusion, although he is now old enough to be curious about the secular world. One day he ventures into forbidden territory: a deserted ruin, once an Egyptian temple.

And dimly, through the gloom he could descry, on every wall
and column, gorgeous arabesques, long lines of pictured story;
triumphs and labours; rows of captives in foreign and fantastic
dresses, leading strange animals, bearing the tributes of unknown lands; rows of ladies at feasts, their heads crowned with
garlands, the fragrant lotus-flower in every hand, while slaves
brought wine and perfumes and children sat upon their knees
and husbands by their sides; and dancing girls in transparent
robes and golden girdles, tossed their tawny limbs wildly
among the throng. . . . What was the meaning of it all? Why
had it all been? . . . And they were all in hell . . . every one of
them. Every one of these ladies who sat there, with her bushy
locks, and garlands, and jewelled collars, and lotus-flowers,
and gauzy dress, displaying all her slender limbs—who,
perhaps, when she was alive, smiled so sweetly, and went so
fairly, and had children, and friends, and never once thought of
what was going to happen to her—what must happen to her.
. . . She was in hell. . . . Burning for ever, and ever, and ever,
there below his feet. He stared down on the rocky floors. If he
could but see through them . . . he should behold her writhing
and twisting among the flickering flame, scorched, glowing . . .
in everlasting agony, such as the thought of enduring for a
moment made him shudder.

Thus in the first half of Chapter I the reader understands that
the hero is unsophisticated but virile, and is reminded of the
naïveté of the old Catholic tradition of literal hell-fire. In Chapter
II, Philammon has been given permission to see Alexandria for
himself, and there the reader meets the rest of the cast. Hypatia,
the Greek blonde beauty, a pagan intellectual and aristocrat with
principles, the scholar virgin; Orestes, the mediocre politician,
whose guide-word is expediency; Raphael Aben-Ezra, the
Lancelot Smith of his day, a cultured, urbane Jew, who is true at
heart and therefore destined to be redeemed by the love of a good
woman—a Christian Roman, who brings Raphael into the
Christian Church. (Kingsley had a theory that the good Jew who
converted to Christianity was the highest type of Christian,

since he encompassed the noblest moral views of both great faiths.) Next we meet Pelagia, the beautiful courtesan (with a heart of gold, inevitably), and the Goths, ancestors of the coarse, fighting Teutons—'who, in spite of an occasional inclination to robbery and murder, were thoroughly good-natured, honest fellows.' Finally, we meet Cyril, head of the Alexandrian Church, an impressive, ambitious man 'who in reality, though not in name, sat on the throne of the Pharaohs'.

These characters, with a host of minor ones, are set against the backcloth of a great port, with all its luxury and its slums. Philammon, sent by Cyril to help the parabolani ('a sort of organised guild of district visitors'), is well placed to see Alexandria as it really is:

> And in their company he saw that afternoon the dark side of that world, whereof the harbour panorama had been the bright one. In squalid misery, filth, profligacy, ignorance, ferocity, discontent, neglected in body, house and soul, by the civil authorities, proving their existence only in aimless and sanguinary riots, there they starved and rotted, heap on heap, the masses of the old Greek population, close to the great food-exporting harbour of the world. Among these, fiercely perhaps, and fanatically, but still among them and for them, laboured those district visitors night and day. And so Philammon toiled away with them, carrying food and clothing, helping sick to hospital, and dead to the burial; cleaning out the infected houses—for the fever was all but perennial in those quarters—and comforting the dying with the good news of forgiveness from above. . . .

(Kingsley's readers might be forgiven for thinking that so far Alexandria barely differed from Victorian England.)

Worse is in store for the young monk. Under the leadership of some fanatical monks, the Christians are incited to riot, to loot and massacre in the Jewish quarters. The young man's ideas of right and wrong are jolted. 'Till then all Christians, monks above all, had been infallible in his eyes; all Jews and heathens insane and accursed. Moreover, meekness under insult, fortitude in calamity, the contempt of worldly comfort, the worship of poverty as a noble estate, were virtues which the Church Catholic boasted as her peculiar heritage; on which side had the balance of those qualities inclined that morning?'

Philammon finds a ready answer: it is all owing to the evil influence of Hypatia, the pagan philosopher, who hopes that Orestes will forbid the Christian Church and return Alexandria to the stoic virtues and worship of the Greek gods. Philammon attends her lectures, expecting these to confirm his preconceived notions of her, but he soon finds out that she is as sincere in her beliefs as he is in his. Indeed, there seems no insurmountable gulf between his Christianity and her paganism, and he decides it is his mission to convert her to Christianity. The first meeting between the pair resembles the fateful encounters of other Kingsley couples. Hypatia follows a well-worn path in being older than her lover. Philammon is, like all Kingsley heroes, awe-struck by her beauty. 'There she was! looking more glorious than ever; more than when glowing with the enthusiasm of her own eloquence; more than when transfigured last night in golden tresses and glittering moonbeams.'

A race apart, and in sharp contrast to the cultivated Alexandrians, are the Goths, wasting their time in drinking bouts after their battles, softened by luxury, fretting for action, looking back nostalgically to their heroic traditions. Kingsley here tried his hand at the saga form, taking advice from Max Müller.

> Over the camp fires
> Drank I with heroes,
> Under the Donau bank
> Warm in the snow-trench,
> Sagamen hear I there,
> Men of the Longbeards,
> Cunning and ancient,
> Honey-sweet-voiced,
> Scaring the wolf-cub,
> Scaring the horn-owl out,

Shaking the snow-wreaths,
Down from the pine-boughs,
Up to the star-roof
Rang out their song.
Singing how Winil men
Over the ice-floes
Sledging from Scotland on
Came unto Scoring;
Singing of Gambara
Freya's beloved.

The long novel contained Kingsley's most complicated plot to date. The Roman governor makes a bargain with Hypatia to try to suppress the Christians, whilst Cyril uses this opportunity to manifest his personal power by inciting a Christian riot. Hypatia becomes the target of the most fanatical Christians, who regard her as the symbol of their most dangerous antagonist. She is kidnapped, taken to Cyril's church, and quite literally torn to pieces inside by the blood-maddened mob.

She shook herself free from her tormentors, and springing back, rose for one moment to her full height, naked, snow-white against the dusky mass around—shame and indignation in those wide, clear eyes, but not a stain of fear. With one hand she clasped her golden locks around her; the other long white arm was stretched upwards towards the great still Christ appealing—and who dare say in vain?—from man to God. Her lips were opened to speak; but the words that should have come from them reached God's ear alone; for in an instant Peter struck her down, the dark mass closed over her again . . . and then wail on wail, one, wild, ear-piercing, rang along the vaulted roofs, and thrilled like the trumpet of avenging angels through Philammon's ears.

Crushed against a pillar, unable to move in the dense mass, he pressed his hands over his ears. He could not shut out those shrieks! When would they end? What in the name of the God of mercy were they doing? Tearing her piecemeal? Yes, and

worse than that. And still the shrieks rang on, and still the great
Christ looked down on Philammon with that calm intolerable
eye, and would not turn away.

That night the Goths sally out into the streets of the city,
armed and ruthless, with murder in their hearts, not caring whether
they kill Christian, Greek or Roman.

And so, by men and purposes which reeked not of her, as is
the wont of Providence, was the blood of Hypatia avenged in
part that night.

Kingsley intended by this stirring novel to show that Christianity was the religion of the poor, the under-privileged, and the
people—in short, it was the democratic religion. Paganism, even
in the pure form personified by Hypatia, was the exclusive,
aristocratic religion. But he warned his readers that even as his
sub-title was *New Foes under an Old Face*, 'The same devil who
tempted these old Egyptians tempts you. The same God who
would have saved these old Egyptians if they had willed, will
save you, if you will.' Judged by the canons of the day, *Hypatia*
was fierce, even crude. Lewis Carroll found it too powerful.
Tennyson disliked the bold word 'naked' in Hypatia's death
scene. Most readers, in fact, found Hypatia's end too barbarous
for comfort. Literary critics who acknowledged Kingsley's
prodigal talents wished he could discipline himself more, and
curb some of his didacticism. Nevertheless, these three novels,
Yeast, Alton Locke and *Hypatia*, established him as an important
contemporary novelist. The general reading public, which increasingly included university students and professional men,
found that Kingsley was saying things about society which they
wanted said. These people remained his faithful reading public,
no matter what the journalists and critics said about him.

Along with his *Hypatia* instalments, Kingsley experimented
with hexameters, a verse form which he and Ludlow knew well
from their Greek studies. Kingsley chose the Andromeda myth,
a great favourite of his, for he could not help seeing it as the

theme of the damsel in distress rescued by her knight. He meant in his poem to show the girl as the victim of a dark, unsympathetic religion, rescued by a gallant, handsome young man who symbolised the new, sunnier Greek religion. The poem is typical Kingsley in its striking nature similes and accurate details of wild life.

He discussed with Ludlow the splendid 'osprey simile' which he used to describe Perseus waiting to fall upon the Gorgon.

> As when an osprey aloft, dark-eyebrowed, royally
> crested,
> Flags on by creek and by cove, and in scorn of the
> anger of Nereus
> Ranges, the king of the shore; if he see on a
> glittering shallow,
> Chasing the bass and the mullet, the fin of a
> wallowing dolphin,
> Halting, he wheels round slowly, in doubt at
> the weight of his quarry,
> Whether to clutch it alive, or to fall on the
> wretch like a plummet,
> Stunning with terrible talon the life of the
> brain in the hindhead;
> Then rushes up with a scream, and stooping the
> wrath of his eyebrows
> Falls from the sky, like a star, while the wind
> rattles hoarse in his pinions.
> Over him closes the foam for a moment; and then
> from the sand-bed
> Rolls up the great fish, dead, and his side gleams
> white in the sunshine.
> Thus fell the boy on the beast, unveiling the
> head of the Gorgon;
> Thus fell the boy on the beast; thus rolled
> up the beast in his horror.

The poem was well sustained, and Ludlow admired it, using the opportunity to press once more the idea that Kingsley should abandon novel-writing for poetry. Perhaps Ludlow was sympathetic also to the early nineteenth-century view that novels were rather below the dignity of a serious literary man.

Kingsley finished another long poem, *St. Maura, A.D. 304*, which he called 'the concentrated outcome of all my martyrology reading. I felt always I should have a thing to say about them, though I read them simply for pleasure.' *St. Maura* was written at remarkable speed. A narrative poem, given in the first person, it has a strong Browning flavour. The story, being the crucifixion of an early Christian deacon and his bride of three months (the girl is talking to her husband during the night when they are alone, nailed to their crosses, the crowds having left them), is inescapably painful, but Kingsley did not dwell on the physical aspects of the martyrdom, and the shame inflicted upon the girl, but stressed the strength she gained through love for her husband and love for God. 'Pain is no evil Unless it conquers us,' she declares. Running through this poem, as in the verse drama, *The Saint's Tragedy*, is the secondary theme of married love. *St. Maura* is in some ways a poetic counterpart to *Hypatia*.

> 'Ah! Your lips are dry!
> Tomorrow, when they come, we must entreat,
> And they will give you water. One to-day,
> A soldier, gave me water in a sponge
> Upon a reed, and said, "Too fair! Too young!
> She might have been a gallant soldier's wife!"
> And then I cried, "I am a soldier's wife!
> A Hero's!" And he smiled, but let me drink.
> God bless him for it!'

Later, the girl says to her husband,

> 'Do I feel much pain?
> Not much. Not maddening. None I cannot bear.
> It has become like part of my own life,
> Or part of God's life in me—honour—bliss!
> I dreaded madness, and instead comes rest;
> Rest deep and smiling, like a summer's night.'

St. Maura did not receive such broad acclaim as *Andromeda*. It was too outspoken, and not everyone was as interested as Kingsley in the theme. He himself, however, was psychologically relieved after writing it, for once an idea gripped him, he was not easy until he had worked it out of his system.

A National School was now opened in Eversley and took a good deal of work and responsibility off Kingsley's shoulders, as up to this point the burden of providing classes for children and adults had been largely assumed by him. It was at this time that the last numbers of the Christian Socialist periodicals appeared and to a great extent it marks the end of the Parson Lot episode in Kingsley's life. Later critics have blamed him for starting to desert the political cause of his 1848 friends from this date, but his closest associates do not make this reproach. The need for his particular kind of writing was passing, and the Christian Socialists themselves were taking up new activities which Kingsley, based in Eversley, was unable to share. He hardly ever went to London, except for some special reason—such as when he lectured for the Needlewomen's Association, where he had at least one admiring listener in young Octavia Hill.

Kingsley was naturally depressed and angered by the action of King's College in dismissing Maurice in 1853. The disgrace was not entirely unexpected, being the culmination of five years of suspicion and complaints from the College Council. Maurice's views on eternal punishment, already quite well-known, were expressed very clearly in a new book, *Theological Essays,* whose publication made the break with Anglican orthodoxy inevitable. Earlier that year Maurice had resigned from Queen's College, a step which he found painful but entirely necessary, because the council of that college had publicly disapproved of *Alton Locke* to such an extent that Kingsley had resigned from the college rather than risk damaging its reputation. Maurice, no less scrupulous than Kingsley, had felt in honour bound to stand by his friend and resign also.

Maurice sent Kingsley an advance copy of *Theological Essays,* which the younger man read eagerly and respectfully, finding them one more example of Maurice's towering intellectual and spiritual superiority. 'I was utterly astonished in finding in page after page things which I had thought, and hardly dared to confess to myself, much less to preach. However, you have said them now: and I, gaining courage, have begun to speak more and more boldly, thanks to your blessed example, in a set of sermons on the Catechism, accompanying your angels' trumpet on my penny whistle. . . .'[11]

Many people besides the rector thought that Kingsley's most important mission in life was to blow that penny whistle loud and clear, as he simplified Maurice's involved, paradoxical, elliptical thought. Maurice's latest book was less obscure than the others, and he knew that his interpretation of 'life eternal' and 'eternity' would lead to accusations of unorthodoxy, although the antagonism he would arouse would be much more because of his position as a liberator of thought, and his insistence that the Church had a duty to assume social and political responsibilities as well as spiritual ones. Most of all, of course, his plain assertion that hell was no frightful place in a hereafter where people were punished, but was the state of wretchedness caused by living outside communion with God, was the reason for King's College taking the unusual step of dismissing him.

Kingsley was enraged by the action, and hoped that Maurice would make a fight of it. His friends were certainly willing to start a campaign to reinstate the professor. But this was not Maurice's way. He accepted the situation, and began to consider other fields of teaching. The Christian Socialists had indeed started night-classes in a slum quarter of Bloomsbury, teaching illiterate working men the basic skills of reading, writing and arithmetic, with Bible study. Tom Hughes was an instant success, and when the Hall of Association was erected, designed by Frank Penrose, and put up by a builders' association, these classes and lectures were given there in the evening, while by day the hall housed the tailors' association. A series of lectures started in 1852 had been so successful that a second series was given in 1853. Two of the lecturers, prominently advertised, were Kingsley, 'author of *Alton Locke*', and the Rev. F. McDougall, head of the Borneo mission. McDougall knew a number of people in the Christian

Socialist group, and as a medical missionary was interested in sanitation and education. He had worked with Rajah Brooke in Sarawak, and believed that he had been much maligned—a viewpoint that found a ready listener in Charles Kingsley.

McDougall had been in Borneo since 1847, two years before the punitive expedition led by Brooke, in conjunction with some units of the British fleet from Singapore. This expedition against the Malay pirates and their Dyak crews was intended to be harsh, and great slaughter was deliberately inflicted. It was this incident that had led to the first division between Kingsley and Ludlow, for Kingsley had supported Brooke from the start—not the least because of the intense press attacks, which led Kingsley to feel that if the press was against him there must be some justice in his position.

In 1851 Joseph Hume and Richard Cobden in the House of Commons charged Brooke with undue severity in his 1849 expedition. The Whig government, led by Lord John Russell, refused to set up a board of inquiry, but a political skirmish between Palmerston and Russell led to the fall of the Whigs and a short-lived Tory government under Lord Aberdeen, who consented to an inquiry. Accordingly, this was set up in Singapore and, as might be expected, the evidence so long after the event was conflicting and inconclusive, and a verdict of 'Non proven' was returned. To Kingsley, this was vindication. To Ludlow, it meant that the charges were still unrefuted. The British government did not let Brooke go completely unscathed, and deprived him of the governorship of Labuan, and abolished the practice of paying 'head money'. Brooke remained Rajah of Sarawak, for this title was bestowed upon him by the Sultan of Malaya, who was the nominal ruler of Sarawak.

In 1853 McDougall came to London on financial business for the Borneo mission, and he and Kingsley became friends. McDougall's exciting and amusing stories about the mission, and about Brooke's problems and administration, were 'cold water to a thirsty soul', as Kingsley enthusiastically described it to Tom Hughes.[12] It was certainly in 1853 (by 1854 McDougall was back in Sarawak) that Kingsley, Hughes and McDougall had

dinner together at Chelsea Rectory. Hughes has left a vivid
and appealing account of this evening in his preface to *Alton
Locke.*

He begins by explaining that much of the work of the Council
of the Society for Promoting Working Men's Associations, for
which he and Ludlow worked so hard, consisted of mediating and
arbitrating in the disputes between the members and managers
of the various associations. Hughes in particular spent considerable
time smoothing over such difficulties. On this day in question
Hughes was at his desk, working on a typical dispute, and had
just begun to write out his legal opinion. Some unfinished lines
were on his desk—'The Trustees of the Mile End Association of
Engineers, seeing that the quarrels between the associates have
not ceased . . .'—when he was called away. During his short
absence he discovered that Kingsley had called, read over his
opinion, added an impromptu comic verse invitation to dinner,
and departed. Using Hughes' words as his first line, Kingsley had
continued:

> And that every man is too much inclined to behave himself
>   like a beast,
> In spite of our glorious humanity, which requires neither
>   God nor priest,
> Yet is daily praised and plastered by ten thousand
>   fools at least—
> Request Mr. Hughes's presence at their jawshop in the
>   East,
> Which don't they wish they may get it, for he goes out
>   tonight to feast
> At the Rev. C. Kingsley's rectory, Chelsea, where he'll
>   get his gullet greased
> With the best of Barto Valle's port, and will have his
>   joys increased
> By meeting his old college chum, McDougall the Borneo
>   priest—
> So come you thief, and drop your brief.
> At six o'clock without relief;

And if you won't may you come to grief,
Says Parson Lot the Socialist Chief,
Who signs his mark at the foot of the leaf—thus.

Parson Lot's mark was a clenched fist, with 'Parson Lot, his mark' underneath it.

Hughes, amused and delighted, finished his afternoon's work and, correctly guessing where Kingsley would be, went to the offices of Parker, the publisher, where the rector was haranguing the junior partner, 'Little John', on politics. Kingsley and Hughes said goodbye and started off for Chelsea.

Hughes wrote: 'We started to walk down to Chelsea, and a dense fog came on before we had reached Hyde Park Corner. Both of us knew the way well; but we lost it half a dozen times, and his spirit seemed to rise as the fog thickened. "Isn't this like life," he said, after one of our blunders; "a deep yellow fog all round, with a dim light here and there shining through. You grope your way on from one lamp to another, and you go up wrong streets and back again; but you get home at last—there's always light enough for that." After a short pause he said, quite abruptly, "Tom, do you want to live to be old?" I said I had never thought on the subject, and he went on, "I dread it more than I can say. To feel one's powers going, and to end in snuff and stink. Look at the last days of Scott and Wordsworth, and Southey." I suggested St. John. "Yes," he said, "that's the right thing, and will do for Bunsen, and great, tranquil men like him. The longer they live the better for all. But for an eager, fiery nature like mine, with fierce passions eating one's life out, it won't do. If I live twenty years, I know what will happen to me. The back of my brain will soften, and I shall most likely go blind."

'The Bishop[13] got down somehow by six. The dinner did not last long, for the family were away, and afterwards we adjourned to the study, and Parson Lot rose to his best. He stood before the fire, while the Bishop and I took the two fireside arm chairs, and poured himself out, on subject after subject, sometimes when much moved taking a tramp up and down the room, a long clay pipe in his right hand (at which he gave an occasional suck; it was generally out, but he scarcely noticed it), and his left hand passed behind his back, clasping the right elbow. It was a favourite attitude with him, when he was at ease with his company.

'We were both bent on drawing him out; and the first topic, I think, raised by the Bishop was Froude's history, then recently published. He took up the cudgels for Henry VIII, whom we accused of arbitrariness. Henry was not arbitrary; arbitrary men are the most obstinate of men. Why? Because they are weak. The strongest men are always ready to hear reason and change their opinions, because the strong man knows that if he loses an opinion today he can get just as good a one to-morrow in its place. But the weak man holds on to his opinion, because he can't get another, and he knows it.

'Soon afterwards he got upon trout fishing, which was a strong bond of union between him and me, and discoursed on the proper methods of fishing chalk streams. "Your flies can't be too big, but they must be on small gut, not on base viol fiddle strings like those you brought down to Farnham last year. I tell you gut is the thing that does it. Trout know that flies don't go about with a ring and a hand pole through their noses, like so many prize bulls of Lord Ducie's." '

The conversation then turned to industrialisation, and the effect of art for art's sake on the genius of a nation, and anecdotes about Borneo, and back to Kingsley and his writing, ending with fishing once more. Hughes asked why Kingsley was so keen on fishing.

' "Ah" he said, "that's all owing to my blessed habit of intensity, which has been my greatest help in life. I go at what I am about as if there was nothing else in the world for the time being. That's the secret of all hard-working men; but most of them can't carry it into their amusements. Luckily for me I can stop from all work, at short notice, and turn head over heels in the sight of all creation, and say, I won't be good or bad, or wise, or anything, till two o'clock to-morrow."

'At last the Bishop would go, so we groped our way with him into the King's Road, and left him in charge of a link-boy. When we got back, I said something laughingly about his gift of talk, which had struck me more that evening than ever before.

' "Yes," he said, "I have it all in me. I could be as great a talker as any man in England, but for my stammering. I know it well; but it's a blessed thing for me. You must know, by this time, that I'm a very shy man, and shyness and vanity also go together. And so I think of what every fool will say of me, and can't help it. When a man's first thought is not whether a thing is right or wrong, but what will Lady A. or Mr. B. say about it, depend upon it, he wants a thorn in the flesh, like my stammer. When I am speaking for God, in the pulpit, or praying by bedsides, I never stammer. My stammer is a blessed thing for me. It keeps me from talking in company, and from going out as much as I should do but for it."

'It was two o'clock before we thought of moving, and then, the fog being as bad as ever, he insisted on making me up a bed on the floor. While we were engaged in this process, he confided to me that he had heard of a doctor who was very successful in curing stammering, and was going to try him. I laughed, and reminded him of his thorn in the flesh, to which he replied, with a quaint twinkle of his eye, "Well, that's true enough. But a man has no right to be a nuisance, if he can help it, and no more right to go about his fellows stammering, than he has to go about stinking." '[14] Kegan Paul wrote in similar terms about the social side of Kingsley's life at Eversley: 'Many a one has cause to remember that Study, its lattice window (in later years altered to a bay), its great heavy door, studded with large projecting nails, opening upon the garden; its brick floor covered with matting; its shelves of heavy old folios, with a fishing rod, or landing net, or insect-net leaning against them; on the table, books, writing materials, sermons, manuscript, proofs, letters, reels, feathers, fishing flies, clay-pipes, tobacco. On the mat, perhaps—the brown eyes, set in thick yellow hair, and gently-agitated tail, asking indulgence for the intrusion—a long-bodied, short-legged Dandy Dinmont Scotch terrier, wisest, handsomest, most faithful, most memorable of its race. When the rest of the household went to bed, he would ask his guest in, ostensibly to smoke. The wing-door would be flung open and slam heavily after him, as it always did, for he would never stop to catch and close it. And then in the quiet of the night, when no fresh face could come, no interruption occur to distract him, he would give himself wholly to his guest, taking up whatever topic the latter might suggest, whatever question he might ask, and pouring out from the full stores of his knowledge, his quick intuitive sagacity, his ready sympathy. Then it was, far more than in the excitement and distraction of many voices and many faces, that he was himself, that the true man appeared; and it was at times such as these that he came to be known and trusted and loved, as few men ever have been, as no man has been whom I ever knew. . . .

'Except during sleep—and even that was characteristic, so profound was it,—repose seemed impossible to him for body or mind. So that he seemed to live three days, as it were, while other men were living one, and already foresaw that there would be for him no great length of years.

'Connected with this rapid living was a certain impatience of trifles, an inaccuracy about details, a haste in drawing conclusions, a forgetfulness of times and seasons, and of words lightly spoken or written, and withal an impulsive and almost reckless generosity, and fear of giving pain, which sometimes placed him at an unfair disadvantage and put him formally in the wrong when substantially he was in the right. It led him, too, to take too hastily a favourable estimate of almost every one with whom he came personally into contact, so that he was liable to suffer from misplaced confidence; while in the petty matters of daily life it made him a bad guardian of his own interests, and but for the wise and tender assistance that was ever at his side would almost have overwhelmed him with anxieties.'[15]

The 'favourable estimate' which Kegan Paul mentioned was certainly applied by Kingsley to Rajah Brooke, for the rector canvassed his friend for money to buy a small steamer, which could be shipped out in parts to Borneo, and there assembled. To make it further clear where he stood, Kingsley dedicated his next book, *Westward Ho!*, truly a bloodthirsty yarn, to the rajah, jointly one must notice with Bishop Selwyn of New Zealand. 'This book is dedicated by one who (unknown to them) has no other method of expressing his admiration and reverence for their characters.

'That type of English virtue, at once manful and Godly, practical and enthusiastic, prudent and self-sacrificing, which he has tried to depict in these pages, they have exhibited in a form even purer and more heroic than that in which he has drest it, and than that in which it was exhibited by the worthies whom Elizabeth, without distinction of rank or age, gathered round her in the ever glorious wars of her great reign.'

In 1853 the whole Kingsley family was surprised by money coming their way. A cousin of Charles's father died, and old Mr. Kingsley received a legacy of £1,500, and his three sons £500 each. This windfall enabled Charles to clear off most of his debts, including the one secretly engineered by Hughes and Ludlow. Dr. George Kingsley, a cheerful rolling stone, could always find a good use for money, but it was Henry who benefited most from the timing of the gift. His career at Oxford was at a critically low point. He had completely neglected study in favour of a pleasant social and athletic life. He had Charles's love for physical activities, but was a better athlete. He was a fine oarsman, and won the Diamond Sculls at Henley. For a wager, he once ran a mile, rowed a mile and trotted a mile within fifteen minutes. Again like Charles, he smoked heavily, and once won a smoking match with another student, in which both young men smoked continuously for many hours. He ran up bills, and, without quite realising it, fell deeply in debt, a state of affairs he could not bring himself to confess to his parents. In fact, he had little to show for three years at Oxford except a reputation for being a good-hearted, hearty, impulsive character: not quite enough for the high standards of his earnest parents. The unforeseen legacy gave him a chance to throw everything up and go out to the colonies —to Australia, in fact.

Two years previously gold had been discovered, first at Bathurst in New South Wales, and then in richer veins at Ballarat in Victoria, attracting a hundred thousand immigrants by the end of 1852. So, with the blessing of his loyal and affectionate family, Henry set sail for Australia, travelling in some style, and with letters of introduction from no less a personage than Captain Charles Sturt, whose nephew was his travelling companion. Captain Sturt, with Major Thomas Mitchell, was one of the important explorers and map-makers of South Australia, and his investigations had been responsible for drawing the attention of prospective settlers to the possibilities of South Australia.

Certainly Charles Kingsley would have wished his young brother well in all sincerity that September 1853, for he, together with the redoubtable S.G.O., had for many years considered that emigration was a sensible, perhaps even the best, solution to the problems of a clever, impatient and vigorous young man with no discernible prospects in England. When Charles's own son, Maurice, who resembled his uncle Henry in many ways, decided to seek his fortune in one of the Americas, he had his father's unqualified approval.

It has been suggested that there may have been an additional, unformulated thought at the back of Charles Kingsley's mind as he bade farewell to Henry: a fear that Henry's eagerness to leave Oxford abruptly was connected with some homosexual relationship or activities there. One of Henry's minor achievements had been to found, with some friends, an association called the Fez Club, whose members, some fifty in number, 'declared themselves to be haters of women-kind, vowed to celibate freedom, pledged to diffuse the great principles of misogamy and misogyny in all realms and grades of society'.[16] The young men held meetings in Dickenson's Coffee Shop in the Turl, wore fezzes, and smoked oriental tobacco in ornate Eastern pipes. Whatever the professed tenets of the club, the general belief in the university was that the club was merely a cover for free love. Edwin Arnold, one of the founders, married the year he left Oxford, and indeed married twice subsequently. Henry Kingsley did not marry until after his return to England in 1864, but in his case the reasons appear to have been mainly economic. There is no history of emotional ties with young men that might have inhibited relationships with women of a type and class he might marry. The merest hint of this would undoubtedly have alarmed the fiercely heterosexual Charles Kingsley.

It is true that there is literary evidence that Henry Kingsley, like so many other Victorian figures, including even Charles Kingsley, enjoyed the sexual magnetism of a handsome, athletic young man. In 1871 a short story appeared, entitled *Jackson's of Paul's*, which is a tale about Oxford, and deals with the strong love between Jackson and his school friend, Lord Deverest: 'the two boys had that boy-love for one another; there is no love except the love of a good woman which surpasses it in purity and in the incitement to noble deeds.' This is the theme of *In Memoriam.* In 1871, when the story first appeared, it was published in the same short-lived magazine which published the poems of Algernon Charles Swinburne.

There is now no evidence to suggest, if indeed any existed at all, that Charles at any time feared that Henry was in sexual danger. Some of Charles's biographers, possibly irritated by his widow's lack of communicativeness regarding other members of his family, have hinted that his excessive hatred of the Roman Catholic doctrine of celibacy stemmed from a belief that celibacy might lead to homosexuality, and he feared this the more deeply because Henry Kingsley was inclined in that direction. It is surely, however, just as reasonable to regard his feeling about celibacy as the result of his personal conviction that marriage and family life was the natural pattern for men and women.

The year 1853 was full of shocks, changes and disappointments for Charles Kingsley. Old Sir John Cope died in 1852, and the line would have died out had not Charles quite fortuitously met an Irish Anglican clergyman called Cope. Charles was naturally interested in his family background. Upon investigation the Irishman was found to be a direct descendent of the first Cope baronet, and accordingly he succeeded to the title. To the disappointment of all at the rectory, Sir William Cope, although a very different man from Sir John, was no more willing than his predecessor to spend money on the damp rectory or the insanitary village cottages. Further, Sir William inclined to High Church and the Ritualistic School, was a friend of John Henry Newman, and rather disapproved of Charles's activities outside the parish.

In the same year Fanny had a bad miscarriage, which left her enfeebled, with an irritating cough. The doctor advised Charles to take her away for the coming winter, and the Froudes (who were then living at Babbacombe, south Devon) were asked to find comfortable and respectable lodgings for Fanny and the family in Torquay. Charles planned to join them whenever he could.

His links with the Christian Socialists in London became yearly more tenuous. The kind of explosive propaganda which he had made his speciality was not needed at this juncture. Maurice was uncertain of his next move, but, whatever he decided, he would be careful to embarrass neither King's College nor the Church by further scandals. Ludlow and Hughes were either working on legislation to strengthen the working men's associations or they were visiting the industrial Northern towns to promote more associations. Mansfield was preparing to make a naturalist's journey to South America as a desperate move to free himself from impossible personal entanglements.

Charles felt at a loose end, and without his wife's company became miserable and depressed, needing little persuasion to join the family. Torquay was growing quickly into a fashionable watering-place, newly accessible by railway. Its mild winter climate rivalled that of the south of France, and rich families built grand villas and kept yachts there. It may also have been in his mind—it certainly was in his wife's—that among the fashionable congregations of Torquay he might make some useful contacts which would advance him in his career.

The Naturalist and Soldier

It was very soon evident that Kingsley's reputation as a dangerous thinker had preceded him to the West Country. 'The attacks of the religious press, perhaps happily for him, had so alarmed the clergy of Torquay, High Church and Evangelical, that all pulpit doors were closed against the author of *Alton Locke, Yeast* and *Hypatia*,' wrote his wife sadly.[1] They were, of course, even more firmly closed to 'that d—d Chartist', and the man Dr. Jelf of King's College associated with Holyoake, the notorious atheist. It would have needed far more stamina and ambition than either of the Kingsleys possessed at that moment to press for the true recognition in Torquay of the Rev. Charles Kingsley.

Ambition and future prospects apart, Torquay could have provided additional immediate income for Kingsley, and certainly financial worries did not leave him. Fanny blamed herself for her delicate health, which compelled Charles to pay for two households, and a curate for Eversley. He did not react against the money difficulties in the way that Fanny did. He tried to calm her down, writing from Eversley in February 1854, 'Have we ever been in debt by our own sin? Have we ever really *wanted* anything we needed? Have we not had friends, credit, windfalls— in all things, with the temptation, a way to escape? Have they not been God's sending? ... I have thought, I have written, I have won for us a name which, please God, may last among the names of English writers. Would you give up the books I have written that we might never have been in difficulties? So out of evil God brings good; or rather, out of necessity He brings strength —and, believe me, the highest spiritual training is contained in the most paltry physical accidents. ... If we cannot be happy

now with ten times the blessings which nine-tenths of God's
creatures have, we shall never be happy though we lived a
thousand years. Let us lay this solemnly to heart, and take no
thought for the morrow.'

Nevertheless, Kingsley did begin to make cautious inquiries
about a rather more lucrative living. After all, the Church of
England had always kept established livings for literary parsons.
Unfortunately, Kingsley had nobody to speak up strongly for
him in the places where it really counted. Fanny's relatives were
either unable, or unwilling, to pull strings, and the Christian
Socialists were too far from the charmed circle of power, especially
with Maurice's dismissal still fresh in people's memories. The
rector accepted this lack of success as a sign that he was meant to
remain in Eversley, and he put hopes of preferment out of his
mind.

He was glad to know that Maurice was moving into new
spheres, and had not allowed the King's College affair to upset
him. The Master had remained in education, but education
with a difference. In December 1853 a meeting of working men
in the Builders' Hall, expressing support for Maurice, hoped that
he 'might not find it a fall to cease to be a Professor of King's
College and to become the Principal of a Working Men's College'.[2]
It was an obvious extension of those adult classes and lectures
which the Christian Socialists had been holding for some time.
In January 1854 Maurice was sufficiently sure that the project
would go forward to write to Kingsley about 'my College' and
the need to keep 'bigwigs' excluded from it. At a meeting of the
Council of Promoters of Working Men's Associations in London,
held on January 11, 1854, Tom Hughes moved, with Lloyd
Jones seconding, a proposal to set up a 'People's College in connection with the Metropolitan Associations'. Maurice accordingly
drew up a scheme for such a college, whose teaching practice
should begin with acceptance of the working man, with all his
limitations as an uneducated adult, but also recognising him as an
adult with experience of life. Maurice saw the college as an instrument whose teaching would bring freedom and order.
Students would learn principles, not merely acquire scraps of

information. They would learn that they were 'Persons, and not Things'. Maurice told his friends that such a college would exist first for the benefit of the teachers, secondly for the benefit of those taught: a typically Maurician and paradoxical statement which still holds good in the Working Men's College.

Kingsley's own teaching and lectures had always followed Maurician principles, and he was greatly in favour of the proposed college. 'As to your people's college, it is a noble plan. I wish I could help in it. It is certainly *the* thing which is wanted, and you are the man to get it done.' Kingsley was not a Founder of what became the most lasting contribution to English working-class life made by the Christian Socialists. The Founders were restricted to men who both attended Council meetings prior to the formation of the college and who subsequently taught there. Kingsley's parish duties in Eversley were the main obstacle to his teaching regularly at the College, and in 1854, when the College opened, he was either in Hampshire or in Devonshire.

He was, however, active in the sanitary reform movement, since this was possible at long range from Eversley. He supported the Anti-Cholera Fund, writing begging letters for it to all his rich acquaintances. He lobbied, again by letter, anybody he thought could be useful in the cause of sanitary reform, and went to London to give evidence on the subject as part of a delegation to Lord Palmerston. The delegation had high hopes of Lord Palmerston's sympathy, because he was father-in-law to Lord Shaftesbury, the delegation's most influential member. As a result, the Sewers Commission was abolished, and extra powers given to the new General Board of Health, whose President was to be an M.P., and thus open to questions in the House of Commons. 'God grant that they may use their victory well, and not spoil it by pedantry and idealism. Baines (capital man that he is!) brings in three clauses, which will reform the whole poor-law, and strike at the root of cottage-destruction. The squires intend to show fight,' wrote Kingsley with some satisfaction.

But in Torquay Kingsley had nothing to do except rejoice that his wife was daily growing better, and potter about the sea-shore teaching his children to be naturalists. Writing to his Chartist poet, Thomas Cooper, Kingsley said, 'I am now very busy at two things. Working at the sea animals of Torbay for my friend, Mr. Gosse, the naturalist[3] and thundering in behalf of sanitary reform.' He continued that he was coming increasingly to believe that 'the peculiar doctrines of Christianity (as they are in the Bible, not as some preachers represent them from the pulpit) coincide with the loftiest and severest science. This blessed relief did not come to me at once, and therefore I complain of no man who arrives at it slowly, either from the scientific or religious side; nor have I yet spoken out all that is in me, much less all that I see coming, but feel that I am on a right path, and, please God, I will hold it to the end.' This letter, written five years before the publication of Charles Darwin's *On the Origin of the Species*, indicates the tenor of Kingsley's mind, and why it was to be so receptive to Darwin's theories.

Although the sanitary reform campaign might seem, on the face of it, to be less controversial than Chartism or Christian Socialism, and would thus be less socially disadvantageous to Kingsley, it led to constant denunciations of landlords, whether these were private individuals or public corporations, and of members of his own class who begrudged the extra rates to pay for clean drinking-water and sensible sewage systems. These public protests, couched in Kingsley's customary biting terms, rankled with the individuals concerned, and it was noticeable that the Tory party, whether in or out of office, never risked showing him approbation. As Kingsley grew older it seemed to him that sanitary reform, especially if coupled with education (for girls as well as for boys), was of far more practical use in improving the material and cultural lot of the working class than the vote or the kind of political democracy which he saw in the United States, and which both he and Maurice considered to be a system which sacrificed all moral values to the business of material profit.

So while Fanny spent the afternoons dozing on her couch, her husband took the children on to the beach, collecting sea-creatures. He made friends with local naturalists, and specimens considered interesting enough he carefully packed in a hamper and sent to Gosse. The sea-shore provided a host of new interests and discoveries, all to be carefully sorted, classified, sketched, described, and written for the family diary. The Kingsleys stayed at a comfortable, airy house right on the beach, away from the fashionable part of Torquay, half-way to Paignton. The red rocks of Livermead and Corbyn's Head provided countless pools to be explored. All who visited the Kingsleys—the Froudes, Max Müller, Mansfield, Dr. George Kingsley—were invited to join in the fun and admire the beauties and ingenuities of nature. Kingsley became friendly with William Pengelly, a schoolmaster and amateur geologist, who was one of the first to explore Kent's Cavern, and to sort out the prehistoric bones found there. Geology was always one of Kingsley's interests, and his friendship with Pengelly continued long after the Kingsleys left Livermead House. Pengelly became an important member of the Devonshire Scientific Association, and in 1870 wrote to Kingsley, as a member of the council, inviting him to be president of the association for the coming year. The Torquay interlude allowed Kingsley to enjoy himself with a new outlet for his scientific curiosity.

In the autumn of 1854 all this was crystallised in a long article, entitled *The Wonders of the sea shore,* written for the *North British Review*. It was ostensibly a review of several of Philip Gosse's books, but as the author's enthusiasm grew so did the article. On the advice of friends, he expanded it into a book, *Glaucus*, the 'wise soothsayer' of Spenser's *Faerie Queene*, and the fisherman who became a sea god in Greek legend: a neat encapsulation which combined two of Kingsley's favourite literary sources. It was intended as a child's introduction to natural history, and was the first Kingsley book published by Macmillan. It was widely successful, and went into a number of editions, enlarged, corrected, and illustrated in colour as well as in black and white.

Kingsley solemnly described his ideal naturalist, a model for children to aspire to:

... always reverent, yet never superstitious, wondering at the commonest, yet not surprised by the most strange; free from the idols of size and sensuous loveliness ... holding every phenomenon worth the noting down; believing that every pebble holds a treasure, every bud a revelation; making it a point of conscience to pass over nothing through laziness or hastiness, lest the vision once offered and despised should be withdrawn, and looking at every object as if he were never to behold it more.

He must have that solemn and scrupulous reverence for truth, the habit of mind which regards each fact and discovery not as our possession, but as the possession of its Creator independent of us, our needs, our tastes—it is the very essence of a naturalist's faculty, the very tenure of his existence; and, without truthfulness, science would be as impossible now as chivalry was of old. . . .

As for the physical requirements, these were hardly less strenuous:

... our perfect naturalist should be strong in body; able to haul a dredge, climb a rock, turn a boulder, walk all day, uncertain where he shall eat or rest; ready to face sun and rain, wind and frost, and to eat or drink thankfully anything, however coarse or meagre; he should know how to swim for his life, to pull an oar, sail a boat, and ride the first horse which comes to hand; and, finally, he should be a thoroughly good shot, and a skilful fisherman; and if he go far abroad, be able on occasion to fight for his life.

Reading Kingsley's descriptions of nature, as later his descriptions and explanations of simple geology and physical geography, one is struck by his ability to talk directly to his audience. His explanations are always at the level of the knowledge and experience of his readers or listeners. His scientific writings were alive, dramatic and enjoyable, and in numerous cases opened new horizons for their readers.

Fanny Kingsley chose one of his best descriptions to reprint in her biography, 'in the hope of inducing those who do not know *Glaucus* to read a book which has been a blessing and an inspiration to so many':

At all events, whether we were intruding or not in turning this stone, we must pay a fine for having done so; for there lies an animal as foul and monstrous to the eye as 'Hydra, gorgon, or chimaera dire', and yet so wondrously fitted to its work, that we must needs endure for our own instruction to handle, and to look at it. Its name we know not (though here it lurks under every stone), and should be glad to know. It seems some very 'low' Ascarid or Planarian worm. You see it? That black, shiny, knotted lump among the gravel, small enough to be taken up in a dessert-spoon. Look now, as it is raised, and its coils drawn out! Three feet—six—nine, at least; with a capability of seemingly endless expansions; a slimy tape of living caoutchoc some eighth of an inch in diameter, a dark chocolate-black, with paler longitudinal lines. Is it alive? It hangs helpless and motionless—a mere velvet string across the hand. Ask the neighbouring Annelids, and the fry of the rock fishes, or put it into a vase, at home, and see. It lies motionless, trailing itself along the gravel; you cannot tell where it begins or ends; it may be a dead strip of sea-weed, 'Himanthalia Iorea' or 'Chorda filum'; or even a tarred string. So thinks the little fish, who plays over and over it, till he touches at last what is too surely a head. In an instant a bell-shaped sucker has fastened to its side. In another instant, from one lip, a concave double proboscis, just like a tapir's (another instance of the repetition of forms), has clasped him like a finger; and now begins the struggle, but in vain. He is being 'played' with such a fishing line as the skill of a Wilson or a Stoddart never could invent; a living line, with an elasticity beyond that of the most delicate fly-rod, which follows every lunge, shortening and lengthening, slipping and turning round every piece of gravel and stem of sea-weed, with a tiring drag, such as no highland wrist or step could ever bring to bear on salmon or trout. The victim is tired now; and slowly, yet dextrously, his blind assailant is feeling and shifting along his side, till he reaches one end of him; and then the black lips expand, and slowly and surely the curved finger begins packing him end foremost down into his gullet, where he sinks, inch by inch, till the swelling, which marks his place, is lost among the coils, and he is probably macerated to a pulp long before he has reached the opposite extremity of his cave of doom. Once safe down, the black murderer slowly contracts into a knotted heap, and lies, like a boa with a stag inside him, motionless and blest.

It was easy for readers to see Torquay through Kingsley's eyes:

Follow us, then, reader, in imagination, out of the gay watering-place, with its London shops and London equipages, along the broad road beneath the sunny limestone cliffs, tufted with golden furze; past the huge oaks and green slopes of Tor Abbey; and past the fantastic rocks of Livermead, scooped by the waves into a labyrinth of double and triple caves, like Hindoo temples, upborne on pillars banded with yellow and white and red, a week's study, in form and colour and chiaro-oscuro, for any artist; and a mile or so further along a pleasant road, with land-locked glimpses of the bay, to the broad sheet of sand which lies between the village of Paignton and the sea—sands trodden a hundred times by Montagu and Turton, perhaps, by Dillwyn and Gaertner, and many another pioneer of science. And once there, before we look at anything else, come down straight to the sea marge; for yonder lies, just left by the retiring tide, a mass of life such as you will seldom see again. It is somewhat ugly, perhaps, at first sight; for ankle-deep are spread, for some ten yards long by five broad, huge dirty bivalve shells, as large as the hand, each with its loathly grey and black siphons hanging out, a confused mass of slimy death. Let us walk on to some cleaner heap, and leave these, the great Lutraria Elliptica, which have been lying buried by thousands in the sandy mud, each with the point of its long siphon above the surface, sucking in and driving out again the salt water on which it feeds, till last night's ground-swell shifted the sea-bottom, and drove them up hither to perish helpless, but not useless, on the beach.

See, close by is another shell bed, quite as large, but comely enough to please any eye. What a variety of forms and colours are there, amid the purple and olive wreaths of wrack, and bladder-weed, and tangle (ore-weed, as they call it in the south), and the delicate green ribbons of the Zostera (the only English flowering plant which grows beneath the sea). What are they all? What are the long white razors? What are the tapering brown spires? What the tufts of delicate yellow plants like squirrels' tails, and lobsters' horns, and tamarisks, and fir-trees, and all other finely cut animal and vegetable forms? What are the groups of grey bladders, with something like a little bud at the tip? What are the hundreds of little pink-striped pears? What those tiny babies' heads, covered with grey prickles instead of hair? The great red star-fish, which Ulster children call "the bad man's hands"; and the great whelks, which the youth of Musselburgh know as roaring buckies, these we have seen before; but what, oh what, are the red capsicums?—

Yes, what are the red capsicums? and why are they poking, snapping, starting, crawling, tumbling wildly over each other, rattling about the huge mahogany cockles, big as a child's two fists, out of which they are protruded?

A hint here, surely, of the charm and fantasy of *The Water Babies* to come. Even in a book of this nature, Kingsley could not forbear to include his sanitary reform hobby-horse, bringing it up at a point when the reader might have been lulled into security by a description of Clovelly:

... finding an old coast-guard starting for his lobster-pots, I determined to save the old man's arms, by rowing him up the shore; and then paddled homeward again, under the high green northern wall, five hundred feet of cliff furred to the water's edge with rich oak woods, against whose base the smooth Atlantic swell died whispering, as if curling itself up to sleep at last within that sheltered nook, tired with its weary wanderings. The sun sank lower and lower behind the deer-park point; the white stair of houses up the glen was wrapped every moment deeper and deeper in hazy smoke and shade, as the light faded; the evening fires were lighted one by one; the soft murmur of the waterfall, and the pleasant laugh of children, and the splash of homeward oars, came clearer and clearer to the ear at every stroke; and as we rowed on, arose the recollection of many a brave and wise friend, whose lot was cast in no such western paradise, but rather in the infernos of this sinful earth, toiling even then amid the festering alleys of Bermondsey and Bethnal Green, to palliate death and misery which they had vainly laboured to prevent, watching the strides of that very cholera which they had been striving for years to ward off, now re-admitted in spite of all their warnings, by the carelessness, and laziness, and greed of sinful man. And as I thought over the whole hapless question of sanitary reform, proved long since a moral duty to God and man, possible, easy, even pecuniarily profitable, and yet left undone, there seemed a sublime irony, most humbling to man, in some of Nature's processes, and in the silent and unobtrusive perfection with which she has been taught to anticipate, since the foundation of the world, some of the loftiest discoveries of modern science, of which we are too apt to boast as if we had created the method by discovering its possibility. Created it? Alas for the pride of human genius, and the autotheism which would make man the measure of all things, and the centre of the universe! All the invaluable laws and methods of sanitary reform at best are but clumsy imitations of the unseen wonders which every animalcule and leaf have been working since the world's foundation; with this slight difference between them and us, that they fulfil their appointed task, and we do not.

Kingsley was not the only literary man to enjoy putting together a book devoted to sea-shore life. George Henry Lewes and George Eliot had also explored the beaches and rock pools of the west, and in 1858 Lewes published his *Sea-Side Studies at Ilfracombe, Tenby, The Scilly Isles and Jersey*, a book of which he wrote in 1876 that it was 'the book of all my books which was to me the most unalloyed delight'.

When George Kingsley visited Charles and his family at Torquay he was roped in to assist. He had the same love of nature, and his medical studies had made him an expert with the microscope. In his novel, *Two Years Ago*, Charles describes his doctor-hero, Tom Thurnall (who bears a close resemblance to Dr. George Kingsley, although one literary critic thought the model was Edwin Chadwick), on the sea-shore with 'that sturdy step and jolly whistle which burst in on you from the other end of the chasm, and Tom Thurnall, with an old smock frock over his coat and a large basket on his arm, comes stumbling and hopping towards you, dropping every now and then on hands and knees, and turning over on his back, to squeeze his head into some muddy crack and then withdraw it with the salt water dripping down his nose.'[4] A stormy night would be the signal for intense anticipation by the Kingsleys, for they had learned that the heavy seas washed up an abundance of new treasures, and they could not wait to rush to the shore. This simple and active existence was excellent for Kingsley's health. He was tanned and fit, the winter sunshine and salt air bringing a glow of health to his cheeks. A patient and sympathetic teacher always to small children, he was especially tender towards his own, and these weeks in south Devon were particularly happy ones.

The interest aroused by *Hypatia* led to an invitation to deliver four lectures before the members of the Philosophical Institute in Edinburgh. The subject matter was the theme of the novel, the decline of the aristocratic philosophy of neo-Platonism compared with the democratic philosophy of Christianity. He travelled to Edinburgh alone, to put up at Gibb's Hotel and suffer agonies of shyness and loneliness. The purpose of the Institution was to provide courses of popular lectures on science, literature and art. It ran classes for students, and had a news-room, reading-room and library. Its chief claim to fame was its annual course of lectures, given by invitation by the most distinguished men and women of their day. Maurice lectured there in April 1854, and Dickens in 1858. Ruskin lectured during the same session as Kingsley, giving great offence to many of his hearers because he favoured the Gothic style in architecture, and Edinburgh's New

Town had been recently constructed in the classical tradition. The Institute, at 4 Queen Street, just behind Prince's Street, was far from Gothic.

Kingsley's photograph shares pride of place with Dickens, Emerson, Thackeray, Huxley and Froude in the Institution's Jubilee Year Book, and his lectures are described there. 'Then came the perfervid picturesque genius of Charles Kingsley, discoursing on the congenial subject of the Alexandrian Schools. ... It was noteworthy that in lecturing, as in preaching, the deep earnest emotion of Kingsley carried him over the painful difficulties of stammering and hesitation that characterised his private conversation.'[5]

Kingsley was relieved that the lectures went down so well. He wrote to Fanny before the first lecture that he was so nervous he 'actually cried with fear up in my own room beforehand; but after praying I recovered myself, and got through it very well, being much cheered and clapped'. He was treated to Scots hospitality, and invited into the best Edinburgh circles, social and intellectual, which made a pleasant change after the miserable press attacks he had endured for years and the virtual ostracism he had experienced in Torquay. As in Devonshire, he made contact with scientific men during this visit to Scotland, and although in the future these connections tended necessarily to be confined to correspondence they were nonetheless real and important to him, and to his growing involvement in scientific subjects.

Then Kingsley's whole mind and heart was suddenly turned in a completely different direction, as Britain was gripped by a war hysteria arising out of the dispute over the guardianship of the Christian shrines in the Holy Land. In the ensuing months this dispute led to the Crimean War, in which Roman Catholic France and Protestant Britain supported Muslim Turkey against Orthodox Catholic Russia. Britain's traditionally anti-Russian policy, strongly backed by Palmerston, was at this time also supported to a considerable extent by liberal and radical groups, whose members recalled with indignation the reactionary policies of the Tsar in 1848 and the important assistance he had rendered the Austrian emperor. When in November 1853 the Russian fleet annihilated a Turkish squadron in the Bay of Sinope, the British cabinet decided it was in the interests of British security for British and French fleets to enter the Black Sea. Troops were placed on the alert to be sent to the Eastern Mediterranean, and in February 1854 the British government presented Russia with an ultimatum: either evacuate the Turkish principalities of Moldavia and Wallachia by the end of April, or be prepared for war.

On the very day that the ultimatum was presented Kingsley wrote to Fanny from Eversley, 'The Guards march to-morrow! How it makes one's blood boil! We send 10,000 picked men to Malta, *en route* for Constantinople, and the French 60,000.' By the end of March Britain and France were in fact at war with Russia, and Kingsley was agog with martial fervour. It was the first time in his life that Britain had been at war, and the spirit of his soldier ancestors seized possession of him. Even his sanitary reform campaign was of secondary importance now; it was useful only because it would help produce men strong enough to hold muskets. Some of his circle had explained the selfishness and cupidity of landlords and employers in the 1840s and early 1850s as a consequence of years of peace, when all that people could aspire to was increased profits. Tennyson had expanded this sentiment in his poem, *Maud*. The war, thought Kingsley, should shake people out of their complacency and make them understand real values.

It came as no surprise to him to learn that Dr. Pusey and the High Church supporters did not take up the patriotic cause with the same fervour. Dr. Pusey's loud complaint that *Hypatia* was an immoral book had greatly irritated Kingsley, but he had judged it more dignified to remain silent. Now, however, he had a chance to snap back at the Puseyites on a higher level than that of an aggrieved author. He accused them of hankering after the Russian Orthodox Church, for lack of an alliance with Rome, and of having a superstitious distaste of supporting the Muslim Turks —the Crescent, in fact, instead of the Cross.

Whilst Kingsley was in this bellicose mood, Froude casually mentioned one day in Devonshire that he was reviewing a new edition of Hakluyt's *Voyages*, a book first published in Queen Elizabeth's reign, in 1582. The first edition was very rare, and a limited annotated edition published in 1811 was also scarce, and extremely dull. The *Voyages*, in short, was an example of a famous book which everybody knew and nobody read. Kingsley borrowed a volume of the new edition, and sampled the epic descriptions for the first time. The more he read the more it came to life in his brain as material for his next novel, and he sketched out the opening ideas in February 1854, when the family left Torquay for Babbacombe, staying briefly at the Coombe Court Hotel.

About this time, too, he was asked by Bunsen to write a preface to an English translation of a book on German theology. Kingsley was dubious about agreeing, in case by putting his name to a preface he might appear to be in full sympathy with every word in the book, and so was reluctant to commit himself. He had been the victim of too many press attacks not to become a little wary. However, he did not wish to offend an important patron of the arts like the Prussian ambassador. As so often when in a quandary, he wrote to Maurice, whose advice was straightforward and sensible: 'I think your objections have great force, but I do not see that they need prevent you from stating your conviction that, as a practical work on Ethics, the book fully deserves to be translated and read.' Bunsen supported Maurice, whom he knew well and admired: 'My *practical* proposal coincides with that of Maurice. Keep to the ethic point, and refer as to the metaphysical terminology to Luther.' Kingsley accordingly wrote his preface and sent it to the translator, Susanna Winkworth, with instructions to show it to Maurice and to Bunsen, and to anyone else interested, to ask for suggestions and improvements. That task done, he put it out of his mind, and returned with a clear conscience to his Elizabethan project.

Although fighting in the Crimea did not begin until September 1854, war has been declared in March and the country was in a patriotic ferment. Kingsley had to commute between Eversley and Devonshire. In June he wrote to his brother George from Eversley, 'I am feeling homesick for the old country and the old Home. I shall endeavour to run down to Bideford for a few weeks as soon as I can hear of a clergyman who will act as "Locum Tenens" for me, if only for a short time. Dearest Brother, I am engaged in writing another book and that is mostly why I want to get away—to get rest and quiet, and also to be on the *spot* to enable me to get some "local colour" for I intend to name my next work—when completed—"Westward Ho". Does not the sound appeal to you—my dear brother?'[6] We do not know the inspiration for the title, although Dr. Brushfield, editor of Hakluyt thought it came from Dekker & Webster's comedy, *Westward Hoe*, or from Shakespeare's *Twelfth Night*, 'Then Westward Hoe', Act. III, Scene. I.

He found time for a quick visit to London, where he called upon Philip Gosse, who gave him a copy of his latest book. This was interesting because one whole chapter was devoted to the specimens sent by the Kingsleys from Torquay. Kingsley also went to a meeting of the Linnaean Society, one of his favourite pastimes, and met Charles Darwin.

On doctor's advice he decided to prolong his family's Devon visit, and took a year's lease on Northdown House, Bideford, north Devon. Fanny was still remorseful about the extra expenses which her frail health forced upon her hard-working husband. Charles replied serenely to all her laments: 'We have never really wanted yet; all we have had to do has been—best of all trainings—to live by faith, and to exert ourselves. Let us be content. We do not know what is good for us, and God does.' By July the Kingsleys were happily settled in Bideford. The house[7] was a large, graceful eighteenth-century mansion, facing east across the river, at the far end of the Strand. In those days it was on the outskirts of the town, just where the village of Northam began. There was a big, sheltered garden, and Kingsley appropriated a room on the first floor overlooking the garden at the back for a study, and sat there day after day, writing an action-filled, bloodthirsty book which sprang from the very fields and cobbled streets of the West Country. The rector was back near his beloved Clovelly, and boyhood memories of the Devon countryside speeded his pen. The river port of Bideford had been an historic centre for the Elizabethan seadogs, and there were plenty of seventeenth-century writers to provide detail. Kingsley had read some of these early books in his father's library. Froude, then engaged on the volumes of his massive and partisan survey of Tudor England, was always ready to give advice and suggestions.

Westward Ho! was almost a quarter of a million words long, and Kingsley wrote it in longhand in about seven months. The stress of his intense preoccupation with the war—how he longed to be on the heights of Alma, he told Maurice, taking his chances alongside those brave English lads, instead of fighting with his pen and hoping that the new book would stir others to fight— coupled with the mental and physical exertion of writing, ended with a familiar bout of listlessness and depression. He wrote to Maurice, his father confessor, as well as Master and Prophet, that a period of collapse was assailing him: that he looked back to the years 1844 to 1848 as years of lost innocence, since which time his vanity, haste and self-conceit had taken hold of him, and even his hatred of evil in all its forms had weakened. The historical researches he had undertaken for *Hypatia* and *Westward Ho!* and his personal experience of town and country life in the England of the nineteenth century made him confused and doubtful. 'Do I not hate history because it is the record of brutality, stupidity, cruelty, murder—to bring us *thus* far, to a nineteenth century in which one can look with complacency on no nation, no form of belief, from pole to pole.' Such reflections were part of a whole series of letters to Maurice. In such a gloomy state of 'dark nameless dissatisfaction', Kingsley found it hard to maintain his belief in Christ, the ideal and perfect man, who died to deliver the world from sin—'Oh, my God, is the world delivered from sin?' he wrote despairingly in August 1855.[8]

But whilst he was writing the book he had no time for gloomy thoughts. He made a few friends in Bideford, notably young Dr. W. H. Ackland, who reminded Kingsley of his brother, George. Ackland and he were in accord about the need for sanitary reform. Cholera swept the town that summer, and he volunteered to help Ackland in the vital tasks of house-to-house visitation. Cholera attacked suddenly, with frightening stomach cramps, vomiting and diarrhoea. The victim quickly collapsed, became short of breath, deathly cold, with a fading pulse. Sometimes he would linger for a few days, often only a few hours. The disease had first struck England about twenty years earlier, and its cause and treatment baffled the medical profession, although it was presumed that cholera had been introduced by soldiers returning from India, where it was endemic.

In the following years it was seen that cholera often followed outbreaks of typhoid fever, and some medical men deduced that closed sewage systems and clean water supplies would probably help to control the disease. At the time that Bideford was hit by cholera it was considered that the most effective method of limiting the spread of infection was house-to-house inspection by people trained to look at the sanitary and water supplies. Where these utilities were infected people were temporarily moved, often to open-air camps just out of town.

Occasionally Kingsley did parish duty at Northam, Hartland and Abbotsham. He began a drawing class for young men, held in the house of Edward Capern, postman (who was also a local poet), at 28 Mill Street. He gave some lectures on the Fine Arts, and tried to get a Government School of Art founded. As illustrations and models Kingsley would take fresh flowers from the conservatory of Northdown House, and as the students grew more adept he gave lectures on anatomy, with blackboard illustrations. (Today the Kingsley statue stands on the quay, not very far from Northdown House, and opposite the very flourishing School of Art, although it is doubtful whether many students pause to reflect that he was probably the first to press for their school.)

Kingsley could illustrate with chalk, pen and pencil almost as fluently as he spoke or wrote. He was an inveterate doodler, always drew in the margins of his books and letters, and would dash off thumbnail sketches when describing or explaining points to children or friends. 'And even when writing his sermons,' his wife notes, 'his mind seemed to find relief in sketching on the blotting paper before him, or on the black spaces in his sermon-book, characteristic heads, and types of faces, among the different schools of thought from the medieval monk to the modern fanatic.'

. Late in the year came the first news of battles in the Crimea. Mr. Russell's despatches to *The Times* were eagerly read. S.G.O. had the great good fortune to go out to the Crimea for six weeks as a chaplain, and he sent reports home to *The Times*. Kingsley's excitement mounted with a connection by marriage actually at the front, and he identified himself with the young soldiers on the battlefield. When Tom Hughes, who supported the war as much as Kingsley did, wrote asking for a ballad—had not Tennyson, and even Ludlow, written a poem about the Light Brigade?— Kingsley brushed him off impatiently, saying what he had told Maurice, that whilst the war was on he could think of nothing but the war, and God save the Queen and her brave soldiers. Rhyming would have to await quieter times.

Westward Ho! was finished by Christmas 1854 and in the hands of the Macmillans ready for publication early in 1855. Kingsley's former pupil, John Martineau, was now at Trinity Hall, Cambridge (Kingsley's father's old college), and Kingsley wrote to the Macmillans recommending the young man. To Martineau, Kingsley said simply, 'Cultivate those Macmillans, they are noble and wise men, and in their shop you will meet Hort, Brimley, and all the Trinity men who hold with Maurice, and who are not merely customers, but private friends of the Macs.'9 In this way Martineau, who was a shy young man, made important friends who drew him closer to the Maurice circle, to which in any case he had an inclination because of Kingsley's influence.

It is interesting to see how martial Kingsley's mind had become as a result of the war and his obsession with it. Advising Martineau on his university courses, he wrote: 'After all, try Classics and stick to the University routine. It is the right plan, the soldier-like plan, to do like the rest of the regiment, so get all the good out of the goose-step and musquet practice that you can.'

With the long novel off his hands, and his mind ticking over at half-pace, Kingsley was spurred by a chance letter from an acquaintance to write a religious pamphlet for the men in the Crimea, in which he would assure them that they were fighting for a righteous cause. It was called *Brave Words for Brave Soldiers and Sailors*, dashed off in one day at Kingsley's usual break-neck speed, and was printed anonymously by the Macmillans to avoid the notoriety of Kingsley's name. It sold well, was quickly reprinted, and was one of the few tracts which seemed to speak directly to the fighting man. Kingsley's postbag was sensibly increased as a result of it.

For his theme Kingsley took the vision of Christ seen by St. John in the Book of Revelations. He quoted: 'And I saw heaven opened, and behold a white horse; and He that sat upon him is called Faithful and True, and in righteousness He doth judge and make war. And His eyes were as a flame of fire; and He was clothed in a garment dipped in blood; and His name is called the Word of God. And the armies in heaven followed Him, riding upon white horses, clothed in fine linen, white and clean.' Commenting upon the passage, Kingsley asked his readers, 'Are not these brave words, my friends? Are not these soldier-like words? Is not this a general worth following? Then believe that that general, the Lord Jesus Christ, is your general. Believe that you are sharing in that everlasting charge, to which the glorious charge of Balaclava was as nothing; the everlasting war which the Lord Jesus wages against all sin, and cruelty, and wrong—'

The anonymity did not deceive those who were acquainted with Kingsley's style. Vernon Lushington, a follower of Maurice and friend of Martineau, wrote to Martineau in February 1855 that he was sure Kingsley was the author, especially since the text used was one applied by Maurice in a sermon called *The Doctrine of Sacrifice*. 'No disparagement this to the author of *Brave Words*, whoever he may be; he has made the right use of his teacher; he has *believed*, taken the thought given to his heart, and made it his own. Truth knows no monopoly. But it is blessed to see how a great man's work does tell, directly or indirectly. Some day the world will own its gratitude to Maurice.'[10]

But now, just before the publication of the novel which would make his reputation, and give him that financial security which had eluded him for so long, Kingsley was hurt by a personal bereavement as unexpected as it was painful. Charles Mansfield died as a result of a scientific accident.

The two men had been the same age and exceedingly close friends since Cambridge days. Mansfield was more one of the family than just a friend. As Fanny Kingsley put it, 'one who was so entwined with his Cambridge days, with the Rectory life at Eversley, with the winter at Devonshire, and at times when the presence of any other third person would have been interruption.' The death was a devastating blow to Kingsley, and no less tragic for Ludlow, whose habitual reserve had been conquered by Mansfield's quite outstanding charm and goodness. Kingsley's warmth had once affected Ludlow, in the Chartist days, but circumstances and gradual changes in political outlook had set these two men drifting farther apart. Indeed, for Ludlow the loss of Mansfield's companionship was worse even than for Kingsley, who had his wife and children to comfort him.

Ludlow was still a bachelor, because the woman he loved had family ties which were to prevent her from marrying him for thirteen years. At the time of Mansfield's death, Ludlow and his mother lived in a house in Wimbledon, 'The Firs', designed by Frank Penrose for Ludlow and for Tom Hughes, and built by the builders' co-operative. Ludlow, making one of his rare jokes, called it 'their Communistic experiment'. The two halves of the building were linked by a common library, where the two families joined in prayers, since the nearest church was some distance away, and in any case neither Ludlow or Hughes cared for the preacher there. The companionship of the boisterous Hughes family, with children, pets and farm animals, and a constant flow of visitors, kept Ludlow in touch with a social circle, but all of this was superficial compared with the sensitive understanding he found in Mansfield.

Mansfield was a professional scientist. In 1849 he published a paper, *Benzol: its Nature and Utility*, and patented a process to extract benzol from coal tar. Had he lived, he would certainly have become a very wealthy man, since the application of his process was to form the basis of the aniline industry. Mansfield had been invited to send specimens of benzol extracted according to his process to the Paris Exhibition of 1855, and in February was preparing his samples in rooms rented for the purpose in St. John's Wood. In Kingsley's words, 'One day he was at work on some experiments connected with his patent. By a mistake of the lad who assisted him, the apparatus got out of order, the naphtha boiled over, and was already on fire. To save the premises from the effect of an explosion, Mr. Mansfield caught up the still in his arms and attempted to carry it out; the door was fast; he tried to hurl it through the window, but too late. The still dropped from his hands, half flayed with liquid fire. He scrambled out, rolled in the snow and so extinguished the flame. Fearfully burnt and bruised, he had yet to walk a mile to reach a cab, and was taken to Middlesex Hospital, where after nine days of agony, he died like a Christian man.'[11]

Ludlow instinctively turned to Kingsley to put into words his sense of desolation. 'He came to me at a time when I never expected to have another intimate friend and surpassed all conceivableness of intimacy. He was to me almost what a wife should be, a better and more delicate conscience.'[12] In 1856 Kingsley wrote a brief sketch of his friend, as a foreword to the book based on Mansfield's South American travels in 1852, *Brazil, Buenos Ayres, and Paraguay*. Kingsley described how he had first been attracted to Mansfield by the combination of athletic grace, protection for the weak and a mistrust of authority; a brilliant intellect coupled with an earnest quest for truth. Mansfield's conventional Anglican family did not try to understand his complex, fascinating personality, and they disapproved of his friends, his social causes, and his vegetarianism. Kingsley recounted a strange story about Mansfield and a seal, which has a hint of Coleridge's Ancient Mariner and the Albatross. 'There was a seal-skin, too, hanging in his room, a mottled two-year-old skin, about five feet long, of a seal which was shot by him down on the Cornish coast. The seal came up to the boat side and stared at him, and he knocked it over. That thing haunted him much in after life. He deplored it as all but a sin; after he had adopted the notion that it was wrong to take away animal life; and he used to scold me in his sweet charitable way, for my fishing and entomologizing. He has often told me that the ghost of the seal appeared to him in his dreams, and stood by his bed, bleeding, and making him wretched.'

What Kingsley remembered with particular affection about his friend is as revealing about Kingsley as it is about Mansfield: 'He was always thinking how to please others in the most trivial matters; and that, not to make them think well of him (which breeds only affection), but just to make them comfortable; and that was why he left a trail of light wherever he went.

'It was wonderful, utterly wonderful to me in after life, knowing all that lay on his heart, to see the way he *flashed* down over the glebe at Eversley, with his knapsack at his back, like a shining star appearing with peace on earth and good-will to men, and bringing an involuntary smile into the faces of everyone who met him—the compelled reflection of his own smile. And his voice was like the singing of a bird in its wonderful cheerfulness, and tenderness and gaiety.'

The death of Mansfield (which Fanny Kingsley felt almost as acutely as her husband, for he had been her favourite among the Christian Socialists) snapped an important link with the 1848 days. Kingsley could now feel in his conscience to concentrate upon writing and on his campaigns for sanitary reform and education. This change in direction was given a decided push by the immense popular and critical success of *Westward Ho!* which appeared just after Mansfield's death and elevated Kingsley to the leading rank of popular novelists. It also set him squarely on the path of future respectability. His name might still be anathema in certain quarters—to Dr. Pusey, for instance—and his outspoken social and religious views might still provoke dissension, but from this date onwards he could count on the approbation of many thinking people, from the Prince Consort downwards, on at least some of the many subjects with which he concerned himself. It was balm to his inbred sense of social status. For Fanny the relief was immense: like an explorer seeing a broad path to the ocean after years of being trapped in the pack ice.

The reviews of *Westward Ho!* dealt with its literary merits, and were not, as in the past, full of vituperative complaints about

Kingsley's politics, or what the reviewers conceived to be his politics. For the first time he was measured against the literary giants in the field of historical writing—Scott and Thackeray—and found to be a worthy addition, if not yet up to their standard. The martial atmosphere of the novel neatly coincided with the military mood of the nation, and the Elizabethan battlescenes were strangely appropriate. The novel was really as much propaganda as any of his earlier novels, with the difference that on this occasion Kingsley was in tune with most of his countrymen, so that nobody complained about his recruiting propaganda tone. George Brimley, reviewing the book in the *Spectator*, spoke approvingly of its 'spirit-stirring trumpet tone'.[13] The *Leader* liked its 'manly earnestness and glowing vivacity'. *The Times* went so far as to use the adjective 'accomplished', whilst *Fraser's*, as might be expected, compared it happily with *Kenilworth*, and the *Guardian*, also predictably, insisted that it might have some immoral influence on its readers. George Eliot, writing a Belles Lettres article for the *Westminster Review* in July 1855, remarked on Kingsley's 'perpetual hortatory tendency. . . . Until he shakes off this parsonic habit, he will not be able to create truly human characters, or to write a genuine historical romance.'

The novel was a success for the Macmillan brothers as well as for Kingsley, and helped establish the fortunes of the newly-formed publishing company. Kingsley was an old family friend. In 1850 he had stood as godfather to Alexander Macmillan's son, Malcolm Kingsley Macmillan. The brothers had encouraged him from the start, when he sent them a draft of his ideas. 'We are greatly taken with all you tell us about the plan and characters of your novel. Of course you will not adopt that pseudo-antique manner in which *Edmond*, *Mary Powell*, etc. etc. are written. That style is now getting a bore. The free march of your own style will be much more Elizabethan in manner and tone than any you can assume,' Daniel Macmillan wrote in June 1854.[14]

There was one discordant sound in the reviews of 1855. *Blackwood's*, in their June number, saw fit to comment once more on *Yeast*, this time objecting to the secondary love affair of Argemone's younger sister, Honoria, with the gamekeeper,

7

Tregarva. 'If we consider it rightly, it implies an entire departure from the modesty of women, not to say a depraved instinct. Such things, doubtless, have taken place, but they are not to be mentioned with honour, or judged with leniency; and we cannot help thinking that the writer who unnecessarily brings forward such aberrations, and who treats them as if society were at fault in not recognising unions of that kind, ought to be treated with severest censure.'

Sales of *Westward Ho!* were steady. In March 1855 Kingsley received £300 for the first edition, which came out in three volumes at a guinea and a half, in an edition of 1,250 copies. In May the publishers brought out a second edition of 750 copies, and sent Kingsley a cheque for a further £250. In 1857 the novel was issued in one volume, in an edition of 6,000 copies, and Kingsley received another £300. By 1873 new arrangements were made for a ten per cent royalty on future editions, Kingsley having by that time received a total of £1,750. The really big sales of the book, as with all Kingsley's works, came with Macmillan's cheap reprints after Kingsley's death. Daniel Macmillan was the brother who had seen the possibilities in *Westward Ho!* and he was pleased to learn that two years after publication second-hand copies were selling for fifteen shillings, whilst Thackeray's *Esmond* could be had second-hand for only nine shillings.

Although primarily an adventure story, the novel had its quota of the word-pictures which the Victorians enjoyed and which Kingsley provided so ably. The opening introduces Bideford Bay, from Clovelly Court, through the eyes of Amyas Leigh, a schoolboy. Here was Kingsley's 'dear old Paradise':

So he goes up between the rich lane-banks, heavy with drooping fern and honeysuckle; out upon the windy down toward the old Court, nestled amid its ring of wind-clipt oaks; through the gray gateway into the homeclose; and then he pauses a moment to look around; first at the wide bay to the westward, with its southern wall of purple cliffs; then at the dim Isle of Lundy far away at sea; then at the cliffs and downs of Morte

and Braunton, right in front of him; then at the vast yellow
sheet of rolling sand-hill, and green alluvial plain dotted with
red cattle, at his feet, through which the silver estuary winds
onward towards the sea. Beneath him, on his right, the Torridge
like a land-locked lake, sleeps broad and bright between the old
park of Tapeley and the charmed rock of the Hubbastone,
where, seven hundred years ago, the Norse rovers landed to lay
siege to Kenwith Castle, a mile away on his left hand; and not
three fields away, are the old stones of 'The Bloody Corner',
where the retreating Danes, cut off from their ships, made
their last fruitless stand against the Saxon sheriff and the valiant
men of Devon. Within that charmed rock, so Torridge boatmen
tell, sleeps now the old Norse Viking in his leaden coffin,
with all his fairy treasure and his crown of gold; and as the boy
looks at the spot, he fancies, and almost hopes, that the day may
come when he shall have to do his duty against the invader as
boldly as the men of Devon did then. And past him, far below,
upon the soft south-eastern breeze, the stately ships go sliding
out to sea.

It is the voice of the countryman, in love with the country,
and was doubly appealing to readers in an age before cheap travel
brought such scenes within the experience of almost everyone.

Amyas's dead father is described in terms that suggest strongly
Kingsley's own father.

He had been often peevish, often melancholy; for he was a
disappointed man with an estate impoverished by his father's
folly, and his own youthful ambition, which had led him up
to Court, and made him waste his heart and his purse in following a vain shadow. He was one of those men, moreover, who
possess almost every gift except the gift of the power to use
them, and though a scholar, a courtier, and a soldier, he had
found himself, when he was past forty, without settled employment or aim in life, by reason of a certain shyness, pride,
a delicate honour (call it which you will), which had always
kept him from playing a winning game in that very world

after whose prizes he hankered to the last, and on which he revenged himself by continual grumbling.[15]

The hero of *Westward Ho!*, Amyas Leigh, is far less complex a character than the heroes of Kingsley's earlier novels. The author said he modelled him on his old friend, Frank Penrose. A young giant, unintellectual but honest, brave and loyal, Amyas is the kind of young man needed in the restless Elizabethan age, and the kind of young man needed also in the Crimean crisis. Sir Walter Raleigh teases him—he should be re-christened 'Sir Monoculus, or the Legend of Common Sense'—monoculus, or single-eye.[16] Don Guzman, the charming Spaniard, is a representative of treacherous, foreign Catholicism, and honest Amyas has a suspicion that the man is not to be trusted. 'In spite of his beauty, and his carriage, Amyas shrank from him instinctively.'

Amyas's first experiences of fighting and colonial administration occur in Ireland, under Sir Walter Raleigh. The Spaniards have been defeated in their attempt to use Ireland as a base against England, and a decision has to be taken about the Irish prisoners. Raleigh decides to make an example of them. He defends this butchering by referring to 'the West Indian cruelties of the Spaniards . . . "by which great tracts and fair countries are now utterly stripped of inhabitants by heavy bondage and torments unspeakable".' Raleigh has a straightforward method of eliminating the prisoners, distasteful to him, but in his view necessary. 'March one company in, and drive them forth, and let the other cut them down as they come out.—Pah.'

It was done. Right or wrong, it was done. The shrieks and curses had died away, and the Fort del Oro was a red shambles, which the soldiers were trying to cover from the sight of heaven and earth, by dragging the bodies into the ditch, and covering them with the ruins of the rampart; while the Irish, who had beheld from the woods that awful warning, fled trembling into the deepest recesses of the forest. It was done; and it never needed to be done again. The hint was severe, but it was sufficient. Many years passed before a Spaniard set foot again in Ireland.

Don Guzman, captured by Sir Richard Grenville, is invited
to stay in Bideford until his ransom is paid, but Amyas has to
remain in Ireland. The Spaniard meets the cream of Bideford
society, including the mayor, and his lovely daughter, Rose
Salterne, the 'Rose of Torridge', idol of Amyas, his elder brother,
Frank, their cousin, Eustace, and half the gallants of the West
Country. It was for Rose to sing at a Bideford banquet that
Kingsley wrote the dashing ballad, *It was Earl Haldan's daughter*.
This dinner is a farewell occasion, since Don Guzman's ransom
has arrived, and he will soon sail for Spain, to become governor
of La Guayra, in the Spanish Indies. Will Cary, a Devon boy who
loves Rose, suspects the truth about Rose and Don Guzman, that
they are secretly in love, and challenges Don Guzman to a duel.
Sir Richard Grenville stops it, but Don Guzman is advised to
leave England quickly, and he has to leave Rose behind. When
Amyas at last comes home, having been on the ill-fated New-
foundland expedition, he is amazed to learn that Rose has run
away to join her lover.

Rose's admirers, with financial help from her father, fit out an
adventure ship to sail to the Indies to rescue Rose, if they find she
needs rescuing. They reach La Guayra without incident, and
Amyas and Frank land and steal into the governor's grounds,
where, by one of the wild coincidences of Victorian fiction, they
happen to overhear Rose talking to Eustace, who has in the
meantime beome a Catholic and an assistant to Don Guzman.
The brothers hear their cousin say:

'Can you wonder if such strange conduct should cause at
least sorrow to your admirable and faithful husband?'
    'Husband!' whispered Frank faintly to Amyas. 'Thank God,
thank God! I am content. Let us go.'[17]

But circumstances rule otherwise. The brothers are discovered,
Rose is endangered, the English ship is attacked, and although
Amyas is rescued by his shipmates, Frank is captured. The next
day Amyas, in a vain bid to rescue his brother, attacks, in a
chapter most aptly entitled 'Spanish Bloodhounds and English

Mastiffs'. It was written with relish, as Kingsley tried to dissipate the guilt he felt at not fighting in the Crimea.

They were now within musket-shot, and opened fire from their bow-guns; but, owing to the chopping sea, their aim was wild. Amyas, as usual, withheld his fire.

The men stood at quarters with compressed lips, not knowing what was to come next. Amyas, towering motionless on the quarter-deck, gave his orders calmly and decisively. The men saw that he trusted himself, and trusted him accordingly.

The Spaniards, seeing him wait for them, gave a shout of joy—was the Englishman mad? And the two galleys converged rapidly, intending to strike him full, one on each bow.

They were within forty yards,—another minute, and the shock would come. The Englishman's helm went up, his yards creaked round, and gathering way, he plunged upon the larboard galley.

'A dozen gold nobles to him who brings down the steersman!' shouted Cary, who had his cue.

And a flight of arrows from the forecastle rattled upon the galley's quarter-deck.

Hit or not hit, the steersman lost his nerve, and shrank from the coming shock. The galley's helm went up to port, and her beak slid all but harmless along Amyas's bow; a long dull grind, and then loud crack on crack, as the "Rose" sawed slowly through the bank of oars from stem to stern, hurling the wretched slaves in heaps upon each other; and ere her mate on the other side could swing round, to strike him in his new position, Amyas's whole broadside, great and small, had been poured into her at pistol-shot, answered by a yell which rent their ears and hearts.

'Spare the slaves! Fire at the soldiers!' cried Amyas; but the work was too hot for much discrimination; for the larboard galley, crippled but not undaunted, swung across his stern, and hooked herself venomously on to him.

It was a move more brave than wise; for it prevented the other galley from returning to the attack without exposing

herself a second time to the English broadside; and a desperate
attempt of the Spaniards to board at once through the stern-
ports and up the quarter was met with such a demurrer of shot
and steel, that they found themselves in three minutes again
upon the galley's poop, accompanied, to their intense disgust,
by Amyas Leigh and twenty English swords.

Five minutes' hard cutting, hand to hand, and the poop
was clear. The soldiers in the forecastle had been able to give
them no assistance, open as they lay to the arrows and musketry
from the "Rose's" lofty stern. Amyas rushed along the central
gangway, shouting in Spanish, 'Freedom to the slaves! death
to the masters!', clambered into the forecastle, followed close
by his swarm of wasps, and set them so good an example of
how to use their stings, that in three minutes there was not a
Spaniard on board who was not dead or dying.[18]

The Bideford company remains in the Indies, treasure-hunt-
ing. Amyas is helped by a beautiful Indian girl, Ayacanora, who
follows him on board ship. The company captures a Spanish
galleon, and amongst their new prisoners the Devon men are
surprised to recognise Lucy Passmore, the white witch who had
accompanied Rose on her flight to join Don Guzman. Lucy
reveals that Rose and Frank were burned at the stake by the
Inquisition. They

did not feel it more than twenty minutes. They were both
very bold and steadfast, and held each other's hand (that she
would swear to) to the very last.

And so ended Lucy Passmore's story. And if Amyas Leigh,
after he had heard it, vowed afresh to give no quarter to the
Spaniards, wherever he should find them, who can wonder,
even if they blame?[19]

In the midst of all this carnage Kingsley provides the relief
of a potential love interest, for the 'Indian' maid is actually the
daughter of honest Devon seaman, John Oxenham, although—
alas for Amyas's peace of mind—her mother was a well-born
Spanish lady.

After a voyage of three years, Amyas and company return on the auspicious day of February 15, 1587.

But this evening Northam is in a stir. The pebble-ridge is thundering far below, as it thundered years ago; but Northam is noisy enough without the rolling of the surge. The tower is rocking with the peal of bells; the people are all in the streets shouting and singing round bonfires. They are burning the pope in effigy, drinking to the Queen's health, and 'So perish all her enemies!' The hills are red with bonfires in every village; and far away, the bells of Bideford are answering the bells of Northam, as they answered them seven years ago, when Amyas returned from sailing round the world. For this day has come the news that Mary, Queen of Scot is beheaded in Fotheringay: and all England, like a dreamer who shakes off some hideous nightmare, has leapt up in one tremendous shout of jubilation as the terror and the danger of seventeen anxious years is lifted from its heart for ever.[20]

(Kingsley had a particular dislike of Mary Queen of Scots. In 1845, when at Middleham, he had visited Bolton Castle, one of her prisons, and wrote to his wife that he had picked a rare flower from a rock where 'that evil woman' had been recaptured after one of her attempts at escape.)

England is now awaiting the inevitable open clash with Spain. Old Mr. Salterne bequeathes money to Amyas, on condition that he renames his ship the 'Vengeance' and sets sail against the Spanish within three years. Meanwhile, Amyas yields to his mother's entreaties and remains at home for a year, with Ayacanora living with them as an adopted daughter. He is restless, expecting news of an invasion, and obsessed with revenge. The situation

made him, for the first time in his life, moody, peevish, and restless, at the thought that others were fighting Spaniards, while he was sitting idle at home. For his whole soul was filling fast with sullen malice against Don Guzman. He was losing the 'single eye', and his whole body was no longer full of light. He had entered into darkness in which every man walks who hates his brother, and it lay upon him like a black shadow day and night. No company, too, could be more fit to darken that shadow than Salvation Yeo's. The old man grew more stern in his fanaticism day by day, and found a too willing listener in his master. . . .

Amyas's virulent and unbalanced hatred of all Spaniards extends even to Ayacanora. When Mrs. Leigh pleads with him to return the girl's love, he replies that she is half Spanish. 'I cannot bear the thought that my children should have in their veins one drop of that poison.' At this point the personal interest is overshadowed by the immensity of the battle with the Armada, and Kingsley apologises to his readers for his inadequacies as an author. 'And now began that great sea-fight which was to determine whether Popery and despotism, or Protestantism, and freedom, were the law which God had appointed for the half of Europe, and the whole of future America. It is a twelve days' epic, worthy, as I said in the beginning of this book, not of dull prose, but of the thunder-roll of Homer's verse; but having to tell it, I must do my best, rather using, where I can, the words of contemporary authors than my own.'

The highlight of the battle in *Westward Ho!* is the last encounter between Amyas, now dubbed a knight, in command of the 'Vengeance', and Don Guzman, commanding the 'Sta. Catherina'. After the battles in the English Channel, the Spanish ship has escaped and is seeking to reach Spain by sailing round the north of Scotland. For sixteen days the 'Vengeance' has chased and attacked the 'Sta. Catherina' along this route, and the last encounter is during a storm off Lundy Island, close by Bideford Bay. The Spanish ship runs on the rocks and founders.

Another minute. The galleon gave a sudden jar, and stopped. Then one long heave and bound, as if to free herself. And then her bows lighted clean upon the shutter.

An awful silence fell on every English soul. They heard not

the roaring of wind and surge; they saw not the blinding flashes of the lightning; but they heard one long ear-piercing wail to every saint in heaven rise from five hundred human throats; they saw the mighty ship heel over from the wind, and sweep headlong down the cataract of the race, plunging her yards into the foam, and showing her whole black side even to her keel, till she rolled clean over, and vanished for ever.

'Shame!' cried Amyas, hurling his sword far into the sea, 'to lose my right, my right! When it was in my very grasp! Unmerciful!'

It is then the turn of the English ship to be struck by lightning. Salvation Yeo is killed. Amyas is blinded.

With the battles over, Kingsley can afford to let the sensitive, feminine side of his nature dictate the end of the story, and he handles it with a genuine sense of tragedy. The disaster which has physically blinded Amyas has psychologically opened his eyes. The bitterness melts. He is compelled to realise that Rose and Don Guzman truly loved each other. Amyas has a dream fantasy in which he sees and talks to the dead Spaniard. The Don says that Rose and Frank have forgiven him; it is time that he and Amyas were friends, and in his dream Amyas shakes hands again with the Spaniard. With the emotional poison out of his system, the blind Samson recovers his health, and within days his devoted shipmates take him ashore to Appledore.

In the final scene, where Ayacanora claims him at last, Kingsley achieves delicate pathos. Amyas is alone in his old home.

And Amyas was sitting all alone. His mother had gone out for a few minutes to speak to the seamen who had brought up Amyas's luggage, and set them down to eat and drink; and Amyas sat in the old bay-window, where he had sat when he was a little tiny boy, and read *King Arthur*, and Foxe's *Martyrs*, and *The Cruelties of the Spaniards*. He put out his hand and felt for them; there they lay side by side, just as they had lain twenty years before. The window was open; and a cool air brought in as of old the scents of the four-season roses, and rosemary, and autumn gilliflowers. And there was a dish of apples on the table: he knew it by their smell; the very same old apples which he used to gather as a boy. He put out his hand, and took them, and felt them over, and played with them, just as if the twenty years had never been; and as he fingered them, the whole of his past life rose up before him, as in that strange dream which is said to flash across the imagination of a drowning man; and he saw all the places which he had ever seen, and heard all the words which had ever been spoken to him—till he came to that fairy island on the Meta; and he heard the roar of the cataract once more, and saw the green tops of the palm-trees sleeping in the sunlight far above the spray, and stept amid the smooth palm-trees across the flower-fringed boulders, and leaped down to the gravel beach beside the pool; and then again rose from the fern-grown rocks the beautiful vision of Ayacanora—Where was she? He had not thought of her till now. How he had wronged her! Let be; he had been punished and the account was squared. Perhaps she did not care for him any longer. Who would care for a great blind ox like him, who must be fed and tended like a baby for the rest of his lazy life? Tut! How long his mother was away! And he began playing again with his apples, and thought about nothing but them, and his climbs with Frank in the orchard years ago.

At last one of them slipt through his fingers, and fell on the floor. He stooped and felt for it; but he could not find it. Vexatious! He turned hastily to search in another direction, and struck his head sharply against the table.

Amyas, overwrought, breaks into tears. Ayacanora comes into the room, puts the apple into his hands, and comforts him. Now that he can never go to sea again she feels he is safely hers. As for Amyas, chastened and remorseful, he can only feel that he does not deserve the blessing of her love. So the story ends, with Ayacanora once again singing with happiness, and Amyas at peace with himself.

And so was Charles Kingsley, at least for the time being. He had written a good deal of the Crimean War fighting out of his system, and his Protestant hero was the kind of honest, overgrown public schoolboy Kingsley felt was the salt of the earth. It was his hearty tribute to the Amyas Leighs who were fighting in the Crimea.[21]

New Directions

The Kingsleys returned to Eversley in the summer of 1855, but with Fanny still delicate and the rectory still damp Kingsley rented Farley Court, situated on high ground in the next parish, Swallowfield. It was a pleasant house, convenient for entertaining, and the family never lacked for visitors who were always welcome to spend a night or more there. Kingsley was good company, a racy conversationalist who talked on practically every subject. His wife was charming to everyone and an excellent hostess and household manager, whose servants never left except to get married. The children were well-mannered but uninhibited. Kingsley used to romp with them in a most unparsonic fashion. His friend Peter Wood recounted a story that when Kingsley was visiting the Woods he found the boisterous Wood children waiting expectantly behind the front door. Kingsley promptly dropped down on the floor, like a father playing bears, and allowed the delighted youngsters to crawl over him.

The rector enjoyed telling stories to his children, and deplored the poor standard of available children's books, filled with moralising that was so dull it defeated its own purpose. Following the success of *Glaucus*, he hit on the notion of re-telling the old Greek myths, stories for which he had a special fondness. He had recently read Nathaniel Hawthorne's version of these stories, *Tanglewood Tales*, and as a Cambridge classics scholar he could not resist trying to improve upon the American writer. He wrote the stories quickly, the poet uppermost, and the collection, entitled *The Heroes*, appeared in Christmas 1855, dedicated to 'My children, Rose, Maurice and Mary. A little present of old Greek fairy tales.' In the short foreword to adult readers he apologised to 'the few scholars who may happen to read this hasty *jeu d'esprit*' for inconsistencies in spelling. He had kept the Greek where possible, but used the Latin where common sense dictated it.[1]

His preface was addressed to the children for whom he was writing, and gave an historical outline of the ancient Greeks at the time the myths arose. 'The stories are not all true, of course, nor half of them; you are not simple enough to fancy that; but the meaning of them is true, and true for ever, and that is—"Do right, and God will help you".'

Ludlow read many of the tales in manuscript, offering his usual conscientious comments, which Kingsley made use of where he thought good. When Ludlow complained that some of the expressions sounded too modern Kingsley defended himself: 'you must remember as to modernism, that we Cambridge men are *taught* to translate Greek by its modern equivalent even to *slang*.' (Ludlow had been educated in France.) Kingsley deliberately adopted a half-metrical form, believing it would help the children remember the stories more easily. He had just read Longfellow's *Hiawatha*, and was immensely taken with it. He strongly advised Ludlow to read it, and to persuade Tom Hughes to read it as well: 'never mind a few defects, old hole-picker; but read a set of myths as new as delightful.'

Hawthorne's *Tanglewood Tales* and Kingsley's *The Heroes* were the first books written for children without Victorian moralising. Kingsley allowed his dramatic and poetic gifts full rein—as in the account of the Argonauts finding the Golden Fleece:

Then Medeia brought them to a thicket beside the War-god's gate; and there she bade Jason dig a ditch, and kill the lamb, and leave it there, and strew on it magic herbs and honey from the honeycomb.

Then sprang up through the earth, with the red fire flashing before her, Brimo the wild witch-huntress, while her mad hounds howled around. She had one head like a horse's, and another like a ravening hound's, and another like a hissing snake's and a sword in either hand. And she leapt into the ditch with her hounds, and they ate and drank their fill, while Jason and Orpheus trembled, and Medeia hid her eyes. And at last the witch-queen vanished, and fled with her hounds into the woods; and the bars of the gates fell down, and the brazen doors flew wide, and Medeia and the heroes ran forward and hurried through the poison wood, among the dark stems of the mighty beeches, guided by the gleam of the golden fleece, until they saw it hanging on one vast tree in the midst. And Jason would have sprung to seize it; but Medeia held him back, and pointed, shuddering, to the tree-foot, where the mighty serpent lay, coiled in and out among the roots, with a body like a mountain pine. His coils stretched many a fathom, spangled with bronze and gold; and half of him they could see, but no more, for the rest lay in the darkness far beyond.

And when he saw them coming he lifted up his head, and watched them with his small bright eyes, and flashed his forked tongue, and roared like the fire among the woodlands, till the forest tossed and groaned. For his cries shook the trees from leaf to root, and swept over the long reaches of the river, and over Aietes' hall, and woke the sleepers in the city, till mothers clasped their children in their fear.

But Medeia called gently to him, and he stretched out his long spotted neck, and licked her hand, and looked up in her face, as if to ask for food. Then she made a sign to Orpheus, and he began his magic song.

And as he sang, the forest grew calm again, and the leaves on every tree hung still; and the serpent's head sank down, and his brazen coils grew limp, and his glittering eyes closed lazily, till he breathed as gently as a child, while Orpheus called to pleasant Slumber, who gives peace to men, and beasts, and waves.

Then Jason leapt forward warily, and stept across that mighty snake, and tore the fleece from off the tree-trunk; and the four rushed down the garden, to the bank where the *Argo* lay.

Kingsley's use of the 'half-metrical form' was very successful

in his description of the song of the Sirens. Here he was indeed
the poet-translator:

> And all things stayed around and listened; the gulls sat in
> white lines along the rocks, on the beach great seals lay basking
> and kept time with lazy heads; while silver shoals of fish came
> up to hearken, and whispered as they broke the shining calm.
> The Wind overhead hushed his whistling, as he shepherded
> his clouds toward the west; and the clouds stood in mid blue,
> and listened dreaming, like a flock of golden sheep.
>
> And as the heroes listened, the oars fell from their hands,
> and their heads drooped on their breasts, and they closed their
> heavy eyes; and they dreamed of bright still gardens, and of
> slumbers under murmuring pines, till all their toil seemed
> foolishness, and they thought of their renown no more.

The book became a children's classic, introducing countless
readers to the Greek legends, and it has been reprinted by so
many publishers that it would be impossible to estimate the
number of copies sold. In children's literature it stands in much the
same relation to Greek classics as Charles and Mary Lamb's
Tales do to Shakespeare.

Kingsley went up to London several times. He gave a sermon
in Bethnal Green, attended a sermon of Maurice's in Lincoln's
Inn, gave a lecture to the Working Men's College, and a lecture
to ladies, one of a series begun by Maurice. Kingsley's title was,
appropriately, *The Work of Ladies in the Country Parish*, and given
at the Needlewomen's Institution. Like all his compositions,
whether sermons, reviews, or novels, it came swiftly to the
point: 'It seems so much easier to women to do something for the
poor, than for their own ladies' maids, and housemaids, and
cooks. And why? Because they can treat the poor as *things*; but
they *must* treat their servants as persons.' This was Kingsley
echoing Maurice.

By August, back in Eversley, Kingsley had many loose threads
of parish work to gather up, and he was understandably tired
after the immense labour of *Westward Ho!* and the deep grief of

Mansfield's death. Alexander Macmillan, rejoicing in the success of the novel, urged Kingsley to embark at once on another historical work, but Fanny, far wiser, insisted that her husband needed a period of mental recuperation. Maurice, too, had been alarmed by Kingsley's haggard look, and tried to instil into him fresh hope and courage.

Ludlow felt depressed and dissatisfied at this time. He also missed Mansfield's bright presence, and was disappointed that Maurice had abandoned working-class activity. A Working Men's College was not sufficiently militant for Ludlow. Reluctantly he understood that Maurice could never be propelled in any direction save the one which he believed right, and that he would always suffer from 'system-phobia'. Maurice's philosophy was firm and fixed: the way to change society was to change men's hearts, not to trust to a new but man-made system. Gloomily, Ludlow opened his heart to Kingsley, who in turn confessed to the unexpected dangers which lurked for any man who achieved fame, since an honest man had to admit that fame and praise were pleasant things. Looking back to 1848, Kingsley realised that he 'took a pride in shocking, and startling, and defying, and hitting as hard as I could, and fancied, blasphemously as I think, that the word of God had come to me only, and went out from me only.'[2] In this view, he had certainly been encouraged by Maurice, who once said that Kingsley was the 'Thalaba with a commission to slay magicians and put the Eblis band which possesses our land to rout. I am jealous of anything which is likely to turn him out of his predestined course and may make him waste the God-given strength.'[3] Kingsley knew that he above all men needed to remain receptive to the ideas of others for fear that if he listened to his own voice alone he would end by hearing and believing nothing but that. With a typically Kingsleyan rough-and-ready measure, he concluded that if a man had 'the esteem of good men, and the blessings of the poor', it was a good sign that he had the blessing of God as well.

The continuing reviews of *Westward Ho!* brought wider fame than Kingsley had expected. William Rathbone Greg, an old opponent of the Christian Socialists, who had attacked *Alton*

Locke viciously in the *Edinburgh Review* in 1851, continued to snipe at its author, stressing, and not without justice, the 'red Indian' in him, and comparing him to a war-horse panting for battle. George Eliot reviewed the novel for the *Westminster Review*, praising its word-pictures whilst deprecating Kingsley's 'illogical theorising'.

As his literary reputation became more soundly based Kingsley tried once more to seek a way of moving from unhealthy Eversley Rectory. Tom Hughes suggested he should apply for the 'Golden Lectureship', awarded annually by the Haberdasher's Company, entailing a sermon to be given every Tuesday in a London church, which could easily be combined with Eversley duties. The lectureship carried fees of £400 a year. Attractive though the financial side was, Kingsley realised there was a comic aspect in the spectacle of the author of *Alton Locke* and *Cheap Clothes and Nasty* applying for money to a city company whose members were in the tailoring trade. 'No—give me again my hollow tree; my crust of bread and liberty,' he replied with wry humour. Now if only he could become a literary Dean attached to some cathedral—Westminster preferably. For such preferment he would need the support of the government, at that time Whig, and unfortunately he was not in good odour there, having so often belaboured the great Whig manufacturers of the North for their inhumanity towards their workers. The fact that he personally did not approve of trade union members who went on strike— 'the only advice I can give is, emigrate; but never *strike*'[4]—did not prevent him from observing those situations which led to strikes. He discussed the subject with Tom Hughes, and did not shrink from discussing it equally freely with perfect strangers. Such a one was a Mr. J. Nicholls, of Manchester, who sent him a copy of a lecture he had given on union strikes. Kingsley, without knowing anything about Nicholls, replied just as he would have done had his correspondent been a visitor to the rectory, talking after the household had gone to bed in one of what Kegan Paul called the 'tobacco parliaments':[5] 'But I cannot, in justice to the working men, forget the temper of the *nouveaux riches* of Manchester, during the forty years ending, say 1848—who were not even free-traders, till they found that cheap corn meant cheap wages, and of whom, certainly, the hardest masters and the most profligate men were to be found among those who had risen from the working classes. I fear that, some twenty years ago, the relations between the average of young masters and the girls of the factory, would not bear a close investigation; and were the unspoken cause, among brothers and sweethearts, of fearful indignation, which only found vent in political agitation, and rendered them easy dupes to those who told them that their masters' interests were as much opposed to theirs, as their luxury certainly was to the morality of their female relations. Let us honestly call a spade a spade, and recollect this fact, and the other fact that these millowners had been, for the last forty years, collecting vast heaps of people from every quarter (even bringing labourers from Ireland to degrade the civilised labour-wage to the level of what the Irish-men would take), without the least care as to their housing, education, Christianising or anything else, till the manufacturing towns became sinks of unhealthiness, profligacy, ignorance, and drunkenness. The mere fact that life in Manchester was shortened seventeen years, in comparison with life in the country, is very awful. Then agree with me, that though the repentance and amendment of the present generation may (and I trust in God, from what I see, will) cure and atone for all; yet that there is an arrear of moral debt, of which the workmen cannot but be aware, and that this does rankle, and will rankle for a few years to come. God grant that it may be a few; and, meanwhile, owe no grudge to those who have stoutly declared (as I have) that such careless heaping together of human beings is a sin in the sight of God and man.'[6] To Kingsley's surprise and slight embarrassment, Mr. Nicholls replied instantly, disclosing that he was a manufacturer.'

With apparently no preferment in sight, Kingsley resigned himself to remaining in Eversley, but promised his wife he would relax more. She suggested he go fishing with some friends. A trip to Ireland with Froude (as keen a fisherman as Kingsley) was mooted, but fell through, and North Wales was considered instead. Tom Hughes was invited to join them, and then, when

Froude backed out, Tom Taylor, editor of *Punch*, a playwright of some standing in his day, and one of the Christian Socialist group, was asked to take Froude's place. Kingsley had a great respect for Taylor, who also supported the cause of sanitary reform. In 1852 he had been secretary of the General Board of Health.

Kingsley knew Snowdonia well, for Anthony and Charlotte Froude lived in a secluded cottage near the foot of Snowdon. The Froudes, although poor, for their source of income was mainly Froude's freelance writing, were extremely hospitable. Froude would have lived in London, close to journalist contacts and libraries, but Charlotte Froude hated cities, so they remained in the country. They kept practically open house. The Kingsleys were invited more often than they were free to accept. So the rector posted one of his jesting invitations to Tom Hughes (of all his friends, the one most likely to appreciate it), inviting him to spend the following week-end at Eversley: 'Consider, behold, and perpend; then send 'em on to me, in the coat pocket of one Hughes, Esq., from a Saturday night to a Monday morning, and we will talk it out. My plan would be this. . . .

'There is no inn in Snowdon which is not awful dear
Excepting Pen-y-gwrydd (you can't pronounce it, dear)
Which standeth in the meeting of noble valleys three,
One is the vale of Gynant, so well beloved by me,
Once goes to Capel-Curig, and I can't mind its name,
And one it is Llanberis Pass, which all men knows the same.
Between which radiations vast mountains does arise.
As full of tarns as sieves of holes, in which big fish will rise,
That is, just one day in the year, if you be there, my boy,
About ten o'clock at night, and then I wish you joy.'

Hughes duly arrived at the rectory, the trip was mapped out, and just before the date of departure Kingsley sent Hughes and Taylor another invitation, one of his best comic inventions, and one of the gayest poems in the language. It is extremely personal, full of references to people, places and opinions which they would all readily appreciate, and shows Kingsley in an irrepressible, puppyish mood.

> 'Come away with me, Tom,
> Term and talk is done;
> My poor lads are reaping,
> Busy every one.
> Curates mind the parish,
> Sweepers mind the Court,
> We'll away to Snowdon
> For our ten days' sport,
> Fish the August evening
> Till the eve is past,
> Whoop like boys at pounders
> Fairly played and grassed.
> When they cease to dimple,
> Lunge, and swerve, and leap,
> Then up over Siabod,
> Choose our nest and sleep.
> Up a thousand feet, Tom,
> Round the lion's head,
> Find soft stones to leeward
> And make up our bed.
> Eat our bread and bacon,
> Smoke the pipe of peace,
> And, ere we be drowsy,
> Give our boots a grease.
> Homer's heroes did so,
> Why not such as we?
> What are sheets and servants?
> Superfluity.
> Pray for wives and children
> Safe in slumber curled,
> Then to chat till midnight
> O'er this babbling world.
> Of the workmen's college,
> Of the price of grain,

Of the tree of knowledge,
Of the chance of rain;
If Sir A. goes Romeward,
If Miss B. sings true,
If the fleet comes homeward,
If the mare will do,—
Anything and everything,
Up there in the sky
Angels understand us,
And no "saints" are by.
Down, and bathe at day-dawn,
Tramp from lake to lake,
Washing brain and heart clean
Every step we take.
Leave to Robert Browning
Beggars, fleas and vines;
Leave to mournful Ruskin
Popish Apennines,
Dirty Stones of Venice
and his Gas-lamps Seven;
We've the stones of Snowdon
And the lamps of heaven.
Where's the mighty credit
In admiring Alps?
Any goose sees "glory"
In their "snowy scalps".
Leave such signs and wonders
For the dullard brain,
As aesthetic brandy,
Opium and cayenne;
Give me Bramshill common
(St. John's harriers by),
Or the vale of Windsor,
England's golden eye.
Show me life and progress,
Beauty, health, and man;
Houses fair, trim gardens,

Turn where'e're I can.
Or, if bored with "High Art",
And such popish stuff,
One's poor ear need airing,
Snowdon's high enough.
While we find God's signet
Fresh on English ground,
Why go gallivanting
With the nations round?
Though we try no ventures
Desperate or strange;
Feed on common-places
In a narrow range;
Never sought for Franklin
Round the frozen Capes;
Even, with MacDougall,
Bagged our brace of apes;
Never had our chance, Tom,
In that black Redan;
Can't avenge poor Brereton
Out in Sakarran;
Tho' we earn our bread, Tom,
By the dirty pen,
What we can we will be,
Honest Englishmen.
Do the work that's nearest,
Though it's dull at whiles,
Helping, when we meet them,
Lame dogs over stiles;
See in every hedgerow
Marks of angels' feet,
Epics in each pebble
Underneath our feet;
Once a year, like schoolboys,
Robin-Hooding go,
Leaving fogs and fogies
A thousand feet below.

The friends were not blessed by good weather. The rain was torrential, the rivers were in flood, and the fishermen were soaked through day after day. Mrs. Owen, at the inn where they stayed, was always ready to dry out their clothes, 'socks, boots, and never-mention-'ems', as Tom Taylor wrote in the rhyming 'Thank You' which the trio contributed to the visitors' book. Kingsley did not object to the wind and rain. He enjoyed blustery weather, and wrote an ode to the wild north-easter. In his next novel he described the inn, and its pleasant family, including even their real names. One of the minor characters, the poet Vavasour, almost lost on Snowdon, comes down and

... found himself at the little inn of Pen-y-gwrydd, at the meeting of the three great valleys, the central heart of the mountains.

And a genial, jovial little heart it is, kindly little heart too, with warm life-blood within. So it looked that night, with every window red with comfortable light, and a long stream of glare pouring across the road from the open door, gilding the fir-tree tops in front ... through the open door came some sweet Welsh air, so sweet, that even he paused to listen. Men were singing in three parts, in that rich metallic temper of voice, and that perfect time and tune, which is the one gift still left to that strange Cymry race, worn out with the long burden of so many thousand years. He knew the air; it was "The Rising of the Lark". . . . He strode hastily in, and down the little passage to the kitchen.

It was a low room, ceiled with dark beams, from which hung bacon and fishing-rods, harness and drying stockings, and all the miscellanea of a fishing-inn kept by a farmer, and beneath it the usual happy, hearty, honest group. There was Harry Owen, bland and stalwart, his baby in his arms, smiling upon the world in general; and Mrs. Pritchard, bending over the fire, putting the last touch to one of those miraculous soufflets, compact of clouds and nectar, which transport alike palate and fancy, at the first mouthful, from Snowdon to Belgrave Square.[7]

The new novel was a return to the contemporary scene, and its title, *Two Years Ago*, was significant. 'Two Years Ago, while pestilence was hovering over us and ours; while the battle-roar was ringing in our ears; who had time to think, to ask what all that meant; to seek for the deep lesson which we knew must lie beneath? Two years ago was the time for work; for men to do with all their might whatsoever their hands found to do.' This novel, then, resembled the last in being at least partly inspired by the same spirit of national unity and duty which had engrossed him during the war. The 'pestilence' included cholera and typhoid fever—the 'battle-roar' was the Crimean War. Rather as an afterthought, Kingsley introduced the cause of the abolition of slavery. His interest had been aroused by two Americans, Mrs. Harriet Beecher Stowe, and a journalist named W. H. Hurlbert.

The Beecher Stowes were travelling in Britain in 1856 as propagandists for the abolitionists. Mrs. Beecher Stowe was thrilled to meet Kingsley, and her visit of three days to Eversley was one of the highlights of her English trip. 'How we did talk and go on for three days! I guess he is tired. I'm sure we were. He is a nervous, excitable being, and talks with head, shoulders, arms, and hands, while his hesitance makes it harder.'[8]

Hurlbert was a freelance journalist who had made the acquaintance of Tom Hughes and others in the Christian Socialist group in London. Hughes gave him an introduction to Kingsley, who in part modelled the American banker, Stangrave, on him. Hurlbert remained in Europe for some time. John Martineau met him in Vevey in 1858, where Hurlbert was organising the travel of Hughes and his wife, and Lord and Lady Goderich.[9]

Two Years Ago marks a public change in Kingsley's social teaching and a falling away from the vigour of his earlier fiction. Three important subjects share pride of place. He displayed his opposition to 'the Tartarus doctrine', belief in a Greek-like hell reserved for punishment, which he hoped would be dispelled for ever by the Maurician interpretation. He insisted on the need for sanitary reform, so as to prevent future epidemics, and gave a glancing blow at the practitioners of art for art's sake. It is no accident that the two most sympathetic male portraits are a

doctor and an army officer. In other contexts, Kingsley talks
of the officer's profession as being one which is ideally suited to
a man with a taste for botanising and natural history, and that
military training can develop the naturalist's 'seeing eye'.

The novel was set in countryside which Kingsley knew,
for he recognised his limitations as a writer, and preferred to
confine himself to things and places familiar to him. The scenes
range from the pleasant town of Whitbury, in chalk downland
country, with an ancient trout stream; the West Country fishing
port of Aberalva; the mountains of North Wales; the Rhine
valley of Germany. As in all Kingsley's novels, the chief characters
are introduced promptly: Stangrave, American banker and an
abolitionist; Tom Thurnall, a rolling-stone young doctor, the
hero who is destined to be redeemed by the beautiful Dissenter,
Grace Harvey; John Briggs, who changes his name to Vavasour
and becomes a 'Spasmodic' poet; Frank Headley, the shy Anglican curate with a love of Romish ritual; Marie, the beautiful
American quadroon who passes herself off as an Italian actress;
and Major Campbell, retired army officer, brave, tender-hearted
and a scientist at heart. Kingsley had a soft spot for Major Campbell, giving him a verse which was to be copied in many a Victorian and Edwardian birthday book and autograph book—the
verse beginning, 'Be good, sweet maid, and let who will be clever.'[10]

The plot was more carefully constructed than Kingsley's
previous stories. Grace Harvey is, like Alton Locke, born into a
Dissenting sect—the Brianites. Unlike Locke, Grace believes in
election and damnation, and constantly torments herself with
regret for the young lads who—especially in wartime—are
snatched by death, and doomed before they have had time even
to consider their sins, let alone repent them. Her beauty, sincerity
and utter goodness make her an object of interest, not to say awe
and reverence, in Aberalva. She rescues Tom Thurnall from
certain drowning when his ship is wrecked off Aberalva, but his
money belt, containing his gains from the Australian goldfields,
is lost. Rather naturally in the circumstances, though quite mis-
takenly, Tom believes Grace has stolen it, but in spite of this he
falls in love with her. Much later, Grace discovers that her un-

fortunate widowed mother stole it. Finally, after many twists of
the plot, including the cholera set-piece, Grace clears her name,
and returns the money to Tom, whose love she returns. Her
selfless devotion cures Tom of his cynical materialism, and his
warm humanity saves her from the neurotic bigotry of the dissenting creed. Frank Headley, a minor hero, is made more virile
by his love for the well-born Valencia, an unconscious echo,
perhaps, of young Kingsley, strengthened by the admiration of
Fanny Grenfell, coming of a higher social class than he.

Macmillans paid him an advance of £1,000, the most he had
yet received from writing, and he was able to clear off his debts
and feel financially secure for the first time in his married life.
He had turned thirty-five when he wrote *Two Years Ago*, but
felt older than his years. The novel may be considered Kingsley's
calmest and most mature. It hints at personal experiences, often
depicted with a mocking touch which, though a trifle heavy-
handed, is fairly sophisticated for Kingsley. The reflections of
Elsley Vavasour, finding that he prefers the company of society
hostesses in grand drawing-rooms, to that of the formidable
literary ladies whom he has met at the house of his publisher,
Hatchgoose, may not be very far removed from those of Charles
Kingsley, sadly aware that he had a weakness for 'high society'.

There is a house or two in town where you may meet, on
certain evenings, everybody; where duchesses and unfledged
poets, bishops and red republican refugees, fox-hunting
noblemen and briefless barristers who have taken to politics,
are jumbled together for a couple of hours, to make what they
can out of each other, to the exceeding benefit of them all. For
each and every one of them finds his neighbour a pleasanter
person than he expected; and none need leave those rooms
without knowing something more than he did when he came
in, and taking an interest in some human being who may need
that interest. To one of these houses, no matter which, Elsley
was invited on the strength of the "Soul's Agonies"; found
himself, for the first time, face to face with high-bred English-
women; and fancied—small blame to him—that he was come

to the mountains of the Peris, and to Fairyland itself. He had been flattered already, but never with such grace, such sympathy, or such seeming understanding; for there are few high-bred women who cannot seem to understand, and delude a hapless genius into a belief in their own surpassing brilliance and penetration, while they are cunningly retailing again to him the thoughts which they have caught up from the man to whom they spoke last; perhaps—for this is the very triumph of their art—from the very man to whom they are speaking. Small blame to bashful, clumsy John Briggs, if he did not know his own children; and could not recognise his own stammered and fragmentary fancies, when they were re-echoed to him the next minute, in the prettiest shape, and with the most delicate articulation, from lips which (like those in the fairy tale) never opened without dropping pearls and diamonds.

Oh, what a contrast, in the eyes of a man whose sense of beauty and grace, whether physical or intellectual, was true and deep, to that ghastly ring of prophetesses in the Hatch-goose drawing-room, strong-minded and emancipated women, who prided themselves on having cast off conventionalities, and on being rude, and awkward, and dogmatic, and irreverent, and sometimes slightly improper; women who had missions to mend everything in heaven and earth except themselves; who had quarrelled with their husbands, and had therefore felt a mission to assert women's rights, and reform marriage in general; or who had never been able to get married at all, and therefore were especially competent to promulgate a model method of educating the children whom they never had; women who write poetry about Lady Blanches whom they never had met, and novels about male and female blackguards whom (one hopes) they never had met, or about whom (if they had) decent women would have held their peace; and every one of whom had, in obedience to Emerson, 'followed her impulses', and despised fashion, and was accordingly clothed and bedizened as was right in the sight of her own eyes, and probably in those of no one else.[11]

In the same, rather cynical mood, Kingsley quotes Becky Sharp (he thought *Vanity Fair* one of the finest novels in the English language) to the effect that it is must be more difficult

to be good when one is poor than when one is rich. It is (and all rich people should consider the fact) much more easy, if not to go to heaven, at least to think one is going thither, on three thousand a year, than on three hundred. Not only is respectability more easy as is proved by the broad fact that it is the poor people who fill the gaols, and not the rich ones; but virtue, and religion—of the popular sort. It is undeniably more easy to be resigned to the will of Heaven, when that will seems tending just as we would have it; much more easy to have faith in the goodness of Providence, when that goodness seems safe in one's pocket in the form of bank notes; and to believe that one's children are under the protection of Omnipotence, when one can hire for them in half an hour the best medical advice in London. One need only look into one's own heart to understand the disciples' astonishment at the news, that 'How hardly shall they that have riches enter into the kingdom of heaven.'

Finally, we have another revealing passage in this same Chapter XI, when Elsley, after making a love-match with a nobleman's daughter, her family disapproving strongly, accepts the offer of free accommodation in a relative's house in the West Country. Kingsley identifies strongly with Elsley—and why not, since there, but for the grace of God, went he himself.

... but it is a question whether the change made Elsley a better man.

In the first place, he became a more idle man. The rich enervating climate began to tell upon his mind, as it did upon Lucia's health. He missed that perpetual spur of nervous excitement, change of society, influx of ever-fresh objects, which makes London, after all, the best place in the world for hardworking; and which makes even a walk along the streets an intellectual tonic. In the soft and luxurious West-country, Nature invited him to look at her, and dream; and dream he did, more and more, day by day. He was tired, too—as who would not be?—of the drudgery of writing for his daily bread; and relieved from the importunities of publishers and printers' devils, he sent up fewer and fewer contributions to the magazines. He would keep his energies for a great work; poetry was, after all, his forte; he would not fritter himself away on prose and periodicals, he would win for himself, etc. etc. If he made a mistake, it was at least a pardonable one.

The portrayal of Vavasour made a considerable impression on many readers, especially the scene in which the poet, literally out of his mind with jealousy, loses himself on Snowdon during a violent storm. One instance vouched for by Kingsley's friends concerned George Brimley, Librarian of Trinity College, Cambridge, who was a well-known literary reviewer. He was a close friend of Maurice, but had become, like many of his age and background at Cambridge, a virtual agnostic, whilst remaining nominally a Christian. At the time of the publication of *Two Years Ago* Brimley was dying of an incurable disease. The sense of sin evoked by the Snowdon scene brought Brimley back to a conviction of God which, so said his friends, brought him peace during the last years of his life.

An unfortunate misunderstanding occurred when somebody hinted to Alfred Tennyson that Vavasour was modelled on him, an idea which disturbed him enormously, largely on account of Vavasour's addiction to opium, which might have been construed as a reflection on his brother, who was a known addict. Maurice, as a friend of both Kingsley and Tennyson, was deeply shocked at the mere possibility that Kingsley might have committed such a wounding indiscretion. It was not, however, in Kingsley's nature to write anything which could be taken as an affront to a friend, especially since he considered Tennyson the best living poet, and as both families continued to be on the best of terms it is evident that the matter was cleared up to Tennyson's satisfaction.

The novel did not have such an intense effect upon all its readers. George Meredith (who as a young man had written to Kingsley telling him he had learned a lot from *Yeast*), reviewed *Two Years Ago* in the *Westminster Review* in April 1857. His own theory of novels was that they should reveal 'the natural history of man'. Like George Eliot, he could not approve of the narrowly didactic novel. Of Kingsley's book, he wrote: 'It will be seen that he has a purpose, and has consequently given us melodrama instead of life. The characters are in a hopeless subjection to purpose. . . . The novel is . . . not artistic, because Mr. Kingsley is always in the pulpit.'

The sanitary reform campaigns brought Kingsley new friends, mostly by correspondence. One such was John Bullar, a noted philanthropist, who served on sanitary committees and had been closely associated with Edwin Chadwick and Lord Shaftesbury in the anti-cholera campaigns. He and Kingsley differed on points of religion, but Kingsley found no difficulty in working with him. '. . . then let us not try to hold any more counsel together concerning the deep things of God. It will be honest on neither side, if both our theology and our anthropology differ by one enormous and all-important postulate. Let us talk of sanitary and social reform, and of birds and flowers, of the little pleasures of the sunshine and the spring. . . .' On this sensible basis the two men worked to advantage.

Nor did Kingsley ever feel officiously bound to convert others. A letter written some three years after the above letter to Bullar, but very similar in tone, was written to the editor of an atheist journal, a man with whom Kingsley had carried on a lengthy correspondence over the years. 'I hope that you and your friends will not always remain Atheists. . . . It is a barren, heartless, hopeless creed, as a creed—though a man may live long in it without being heartless and hopeless himself. . . . But what I want to say to you is this, and I do want to say it. Whatever doubt or doctrinal Atheism you and your friends may have, don't fall into moral Atheism. Don't forget the Eternal Goodness, whatever name you may call it. I call it God. . . . If you will keep that moral sense— that sense of the beauty of goodness, and of man's absolute duty to be good, then all will be as God wills, and all will come right at last.'[12]

He undertook very little extra work outside his parish duties. There was a preface for a translation by Miss Winkworth of another German book, Tauler's *Life and Sermons*, which Charles and Fanny admired greatly. He gave lectures to Mechanics Institutes and various societies. The halls were always full. His lectures on sanitary reform were addressed to middle-class women who had the education and leisure to devote to such a cause. Kingsley alone was a tremendous draw. One lady, attending his lecture at Bristol on *Great Cities, their Influence for Good and Evil*, confessed that she had forgotten the purpose of the meeting in her excitement at going to hear Kingsley. He went to Wimbledon one day when the entire Working Men's College was invited to the Ludlow-Hughes house for a midsummer afternoon. R. B. Lichfield had a vivid recollection of the occasion. 'It was on that day that many of us made our first acquaintance with Charles Kingsley, who was a prominent man in the Maurice group, though, being a country parson in Hampshire, he had then little to do with the College and their London activities. I remember the look of him, as he stood a decidedly unparsonical figure, the centre of a group of men collected on the edge of a weedy little pond, to whom he was expounding, with the help of a pocket miscroscope, the nature of various little creatures picked out of the water.'[13]

None the less, his familiar depression was stealing over him, accompanied by lassitude, a disinclination to make social contacts apart from his close family circle, and burning sensations in his head. He seemed to await some national disaster. The episode of the China War, resulting from a sordid squabble over a small boat called the 'Arrow' (an incident which did little credit to Lord Palmerston and the British government), stirred him to a pitch of jingoist patriotism again, as he plunged into the controversy, choosing his side before the full facts were known. Mr. Stapleton, Kingsley's friend in Eversley of many years, was saddened to find the rector so intemperate in his view that this was a war of the Christian white man against the heathen yellow man. The two men became more distant, in much the same way as Kingsley and Ludlow were becoming distant, and as Kingsley and Hughes were later to do—for much the same reasons.

Kingsley's martial ardour was rekindled every Sunday as officers from nearby Sandhurst College, attracted by the unusual personality of this parson who could speak their language, marched solemnly into the little church, swords jangling, uniforms immaculate. The war was over, peace had been signed in Paris, but Kingsley seemed almost disappointed—would the peace last a year, he asked a friend; did it deserve to last a year? Then, suddenly, the 'national disaster' which Kingsley had anticipated so feverishly struck the country in the shape of the Indian Mutiny.

He became obsessed with nightmarish fantasies about the mutiny, as details reached Britain, and he dwelt upon them with unholy fascination. To Maurice he wrote, 'I can hardly bear to look at a woman or child—even at my own beloved ones sometimes. It raises such horrible images, from which I can't escape.' And to John Bullar continuing this theme: '. . . my brain is filled with images fresh out of hell and the shambles. Show me what security I have that my wife, my children, should not suffer, from some unexpected outbreak of devils, what other wives and children have suffered, and then I shall sleep quiet, without longing that they were safe out of a world where such things are possible. . . .

'I have been in hell many times in my life; therefore, perhaps, have I had some small power of influencing human hearts. But I have never looked hell so close in the face as I have been doing of late.'

Now such a phrase as 'I have been in hell many times in my life' seems an unlikely exaggeration in normal terms when we examine Kingsley's life, unless it is to be taken as referring to his recurrent depressions. The 'brain fevers' which were such a feature of his boyhood obviously did not depart altogether, although there seems to have been a long period when he was free from any severe attacks. We know that although he showed a brave front to the world he was ultra-sensitive. Tom Hughes, in a

8

preface written in 1892 to a published lecture on Kingsley given
at Chester by J. A. Marriott, said: 'Now I don't think anyone
can appreciate Charles Kingsley rightly who is not aware of or
does not take into account this almost painful sensitiveness, and I
am glad to be able to make this addition to Mr. Marriott's excellent lecture. . . .' Hughes recalled the time of Kingsley's sermon,
The Message of the Church to the Labouring Man, given in 1851,
and then a scene at 'a crowded exhibition some weeks later, in the
summer of 1851, when I saw several persons deliberately pass him
without the least token of recognition, though they had known
him quite well.'[14] In the same way, the jibe 'Muscular Christian'
grated painfully upon a delicate nerve. Anthony Froude called
him 'self-conscious'. So probably 'I have been in hell' was an
informal hyperbole.

Still, Kingsley was always ready to apply his own remedies,
and he took his advice to 'do the work that's nearest though
it's dull awhiles.' He promised an article on sanitary reform for
John Parker, junior (who edited *Fraser's*): 'I will throw my whole
soul into it, please God, and forget India in Cholera.' To Bullar,
at about the same time, he wrote: 'I see one work to be done ere I
die, in which (men are beginning to discover) Nature must be
counteracted, lest she prove a curse and a destroyer, not a blessing
and a mother; and that is Sanitary Reform. Politics and political
economy may go their way for me. If I can help to save the lives
of a few thousand working people and their children, I may earn
the blessing of God.'

The subject of India was of immense interest to Ludlow as well
as to Kingsley, and Ludlow expanded a course of lectures given
at the Working Men's College into a colourful account of India's
religions and traditions, which Macmillan published under the
title *British India and its Races*. Ludlow had been staying at Eversley in September 1857, not long after the Mutiny broke out, and
as he and Kingsley argued about it he saw that Kingsley's limited
knowledge of Indian affairs seemed to make him more prejudiced.
He sent Kingsley a copy of his book, which the rector read, but
its effect on him was to make him feel that although Ludlow
might well be right in all he said, their attitudes on many subjects

were so at variance that it would be best if they could leave alone these topics, and work together only on matters which both considered important.

When the Mutiny ended, and the British policies for a new India, ending the old East India Company, were published, with an emphasis upon 'clemency', Kingsley could not entirely disapprove, but he lamented that there was not a more thundering and vengeful preamble to the legal documents. In this he tended to reflect the majority opinion in the country. Queen Victoria took a loftier view. She told her ministers that the new India Act 'should breathe feelings of generosity, benevolence, and religious feeling.' In the Act itself, her strong religious views were expressed: 'Firmly relying on the truth of Christianity, and acknowledging with gratitude the solace of religion, we disclaim alike the right and the desire to impose our convictions on any of our subjects.'

Without question, it was now Tom Hughes, of those old friends of 1848, that Kingsley felt closest to, leaving aside Maurice, who stood in a very special relationship. On his visit to London Kingsley was constantly in the Hughes/Ludlow house in Wimbledon—'a brown house with a brown cow in the field, and a brown dog in the kennel,' as John Martineau described it to his young sister, and later in the Hughes house when the family moved closer to town in Park Street.

Tom Hughes's daughter, Mary, recalled Kingsley in the Wimbledon days: 'Oh, he was in and out of the house so much that we'd scarcely call him a visitor. He just arrived without writing first and when there wasn't a bed for him, he'd sleep in the bath. One day he noticed some interesting looking papers on Father's desk. It was the story he was writing secretly to give my brother before he left home for boarding school, shewing him the sort of life, its temptations and its joys, that he must expect and prepare for. "Shew me, Tom," said Charles Kingsley. "Oh, no, it's nothing but a story. It's only for Tom," and he began to stuff the papers into a drawer. But later in the evening Charles Kingsley returned to the study and took the MS upstairs to read and was fascinated. At the big breakfast table next morning he said, "Why, Tom! I didn't know you were an author. That's good stuff. That must be published." "Nonsense, Charles!" said Father very embarrassed, almost ashamed. But Mother, pouring out numerous cups of coffee, pricked up her ears. Publication meant "royalties"; with such a family as ours a little extra income would be an unmixed blessing. She and Charles Kingsley eventually prevailed on Tom Hughes to send it to a publisher's. He was relieved when it was rejected. But she insisted on its going the rounds.'[15]

The manuscript in a more finished state was shown to Ludlow. In September 1856 Hughes wrote to Alexander Macmillan that he had partly finished a novel for boys, and completed it in his mind: 'to wit Rugby in Arnold's time.'[16] The book began to appear serially and anonymously in *Macmillan's Magazine* in November 1856. In April 1857 it was published in book form. Kingsley was enthusiastic, partly through loyal friendship, partly through genuine admiration for the merit and message of the book.

'It will be a very great hit. It is an extraordinary book. I should have been proud to have written that book, word for word as it stands.'[17] He promoted the book vigorously among his friends. He wrote to John Martineau, then at Cambridge, in February 1857, 'My first grey hairs are coming and I am on the wrong side of six and thirty. But if you will come down to see me you will find my heart as young as ever—to you at least. Buy, oh Buy, and Puff, oh Puff, *Tom Brown's School Life*, (by an Old Boy) the moment it comes out. Author, Tom Hughes. The wholesomest book I have read for many a day.'[18]

Kingsley's poems were now published as a collection by Parker, and were generally well received. Ludlow wrote an excellent review in the *Leeds Express*, pleased that in this respect at least he could say some unreservedly kind words about his old friend. Kingsley wrote to Ludlow that he knew he was only a minor poet, because the 'instinctive vision of a connexion between all things in heaven and earth which Poets *must* have, is very weak in me: and therefore I shall never be a great poet. And what matter? I will do what I can: but I believe you are

quite right in saying that my poetry is all of me which will last.'
In a letter to Professor Blackie, of Aberdeen, Kingsley said
'. . . poetry always comes to me first as music without words—
to think a thought in prose and then look about for a tune to set
it to is what I can't do.'

Ludlow always admired Kingsley as a poet. Writing in the
Edinburgh Review about twenty years after Kingsley's death, he
reflected: 'I believe God intended Kingsley to be above all, a poet.
I believe that in some of his poetry he rises higher than in all his
prose, ay, to the level of his greatest contemporaries. I believe
that since Shakespeare, there has been no such Shakespearian
promise as that of *The Saint's Tragedy*.'[19]

The collected poems did not represent any advance in Kingsley's creative work. Time and again he had promised himself
and Fanny that he would stop novel-writing, which was such a
strain on them both. When he felt driven by some tremendous
moral passion, as had been the case with *Yeast* and *Alton Locke*,
the book could hardly be denied, but the effort of finishing *Two
Years Ago* was tremendous. Now he had written himself out.
His imaginative muse, never strong, wilted. Daniel Macmillan
pressed him for another contemporary novel, but Kingsley had
now said his piece on nearly all the topics which he considered
important. Hesitantly, he began to draft a new historical novel,
to be set in the North Country, and to deal with the Pilgrimage
of Grace, a Catholic revolt against Henry VIII's Protestant policy
of closing down the monasteries. Here he apparently intended to
treat the Catholics sympathetically by way of amends. But the
project was more of a burden than a joy. His household expenses
had risen, and he economised by dispensing with a curate. He
joined the Hants. and Wilts. Education Society, but could not
afford the annual subscription, so paid his way by undertaking
an annual course of free lectures, which, since he was such a
nervous lecturer, had to be well researched and took considerable
time.

Fanny Kingsley, no doubt for the best of reasons, says that
what cheered him most at this juncture was letters from complete
strangers praising *St. Maura*, the poem which the general public

had liked least. These unsolicited communications helped heal the smarts caused by professional reviewers. Furthermore, Kingsley had been making new friends, such as the Rev. Arthur Penrhyn Stanley, who was liberal and reforming in spirit and extremely well connected, and might in the future help Kingsley in his career. Charles was comparatively young, and still hoped he might do better than live and die a country rector.

He made friends with the army officers from Sandhurst. It had long been one of Kingsley's minor hobbies to follow the course of past battles, and he had surveyed and mapped the Eversley area on the pretence that it might be needed in battle or for battle practice. He considered the Volunteer movement, which was formed about this time as a result of the bad feeling against Napoleon III over the Orsini bomb affair, with its motto, 'Defence, not Defiance,' to be a thoroughly democratic movement which, by drawing together all classes, would promote equality.

With the birth of Grenville Arthur, his youngest child, Kingsley had more than ever to put family and financial considerations first, and his function as social catalyst second. He did not, after all, regard himself as primarily a novelist. His prose works are extremely varied in form, although in each case he used them as vehicles for his religious and social opinions. He was a professional clergyman who used the literary form to say things which he believed to be important, much as Disraeli was a professional politician who wrote novels.

Poetry was quite another matter. Although some of the poems, notably the *Ballad of the Bad Squire*, and the rick-burning poem, are deeply social, most of his poems are brief outbursts of lyrical emotion. He and Fanny were always interested to hear the musical settings to his poems. He preferred John Hullah's arrangements—could it be because Hullah taught singing at the Working Men's College?—particularly his arrangement of *The Three Fishers*, of which he said it was 'the only setting which I have heard which at all rendered what I wanted to say, and entered into the real feeling of the words.' In a slightly earlier letter to Hullah, he commented: 'You are perfectly welcome, my dear Hullah, to set any of my songs you choose. Those that have been set by others hitherto have quite dissatisfied me.... I have not been at a concert this ten years; seldom in London, and then always over-busy, and getting no "amusement" there. My amusement is green fields and clear trout streams, and the gallop through the winter fir-woods; and perhaps this free healthy life make my little lark's pipe all the fresher and clearer when it tries a song.'[20]

He took some days off to stay with friends in Yorkshire. Most of the time he stayed with the Forsters, a Quaker family, interested in social reform and genealogies.[21] Kingsley was unprepared for the life of Yorkshire manufacturing villages, so bustling compared with the repose of rural Eversley. 'I am in a state of bewilderment,' he wrote home, with his customary family exaggeration. '—such machinery as no tongue can describe, about three acres of mills and a whole village of people, looking healthy, rosy, and happy; such a charming half-time school for the children, library for the men, etc.' He fished, of course; climbed the limestone crags; filled his mind with land-scape notes for the Pilgrimage of Grace story. On his return to Eversley he continued, rather slowly and dutifully, to research the background for the new story, but the entire business dragged.

Then, without warning, his brother Henry returned from Australia, to bring fresh life and interest to the Kingsley family, and to fill his mind with far more interesting and lively material than any Tudor chronicle. Henry had not made his fortune in Australia, indeed was returning to England a poorer man than he left it. He had been too embarrassed to write to his parents describing his situation, and when he disembarked in September 1858 he went to Chelsea Rectory, expecting to find them still there. He learned that his father was semi-retired, and living in Eversley with Mrs. Kingsley, whilst Chelsea was being looked after by a curate. Off went Henry to Eversley, to be warmly welcomed as the prodigal son, and in a short space of time he rented a cottage in the village.

Charles Kingsley was one of his brother's most eager listeners, for Henry's travels were wonderfully adventurous, and Charles had never been abroad except for the walking-trip in Germany. One day Henry showed the family a bulky parcel of manuscript.

It was unfinished, but had all the signs of a fine novel, the first to come out of Australia. It had vigour, colour, conviction—everything that Charles's Pilgrimage of Grace story was lacking so far. He pushed his draft story on one side, and quickly prepared another volume of sermons instead—*Good News of God*.

The weeks sped by. The Kingsleys had a big family celebration and spent 'a most blessed Christmas', as Charles wrote to Maurice. The New Year came, and the Pilgrimage of Grace notes still lay untouched. As it happened, the events of 1859 made novel-writing even less important to him.

Regius Professor

The winter and spring of 1859 saw Kingsley at a low ebb. He had 'spun his silk,' he told Bullar. It was much more interesting to forget writing, and to listen to Henry talk about the Caledonian Gold Fields and the prospectors. Henry J. Campbell, a friend of Henry Kingsley's, described those days. 'I slept in his tent, helped with the rough cooking, and we "toiled and moiled" and met with nothing but disappointment, for it was a very poor "diggings". . . . There was one thing that varied the monotony of digging for gold in hope and finding always Hope Deferred, and that was our Sunday's work, which was what is called Prospecting—poking about the gullies in the Denenong Ranges. This always tempted Harry Kingsley, for he was always keeping his eyes open for "Colour" in describing Bushrangers' haunts for the book he was even then writing, viz., *Geoffry Hamlyn*. When that book came out, I recognised some of the places he described.'[1] When the gold fields became less lucrative, Henry Kingsley drifted into the life of a 'sun-downer'—a man who rode about the countryside alone or in company, timing his travels so as to reach lonely farms around sundown, relying on the good nature of the station-owner to give him free supper and a bed.

Whilst Charles Kingsley was day-dreaming about his young brother's Australian experiences, wondering why he was for some inscrutable reason doomed to remain in Eversley, an intervention from the highest social quarter made him at one instant an acceptable, if still unusual, cleric. It came from the Prince Consort, who had long been an admirer of Kingsley's books, and was a fellow worker in the sanitary reform campaigns. The prince had read *The Saint's Tragedy*; he had enjoyed *Glaucus*;

he approved of the earnest sentiments in *Two Years Ago*. Baron Bunsen's stalwart respect for Kingsley did not escape the prince's notice. Hence, the rector of Eversley was invited to preach to the Royal Family at Buckingham Palace on Palm Sunday, 1859. The Palace, being above party politics, could afford to show favour to Charles Kingsley, a political decision which the Conservative and Whig governments shrank from taking.

Kingsley, thrilled but apprehensive, inquired discreetly as to the kind of sermons Queen Victoria preferred, and was relieved to learn she liked them direct and short. He passed his test triumphantly, and was appointed a royal chaplain. He had to preach once a year in London for a fee of £30 a year. Later in 1859 he was invited to preach before the Royal Family in their private chapel at Windsor, and was formally presented to the Queen, Prince Albert, and their daughter, the Princess of Prussia, who was staying at Windsor with her husband. Kingsley's appointment began a relationship between Kingsley and the Royal Family, marked by personal interest and kindness on the one side, and romantically loyal devotion on the other. Fanny Kingsley says discreetly, on the effect of this appointment, that press attacks in general became less frequent and less bitter. Tom Hughes, more forthright, commented that Kingsley then (and especially after the next two years, when the Prince Consort's influence helped him become a Cambridge Professor and one of the tutors to the Prince of Wales) became 'a Court favourite, a lion in the fashionable world, whenever he could be induced to appear in it, and a welcome and honoured guest in whatever society he chose to frequent. There have been many such changes in public opinion. I can myself remember several almost as complete, but none I think so rapid, or so unreasoning.'[2]

In spite of this proof of royal favour, Kingsley was exhausted most of that year. When he had a lecture to give he would work himself up to a pitch of intensity so that he could acquit himself wonderfully well, but would return to Eversley drained of energy. One outstanding lecture, given in July at Willis's Rooms, was for the first meeting of the Ladies' Sanitary Association, chaired by Lord Shaftesbury. Reprinted later in a collection,

Sanitary and Social Lectures and Essays, under the arresting title of *The Massacre of the Innocents*, it was powerful in cold print. Spoken by Kingsley, as Octavia Hill testified in a letter to her sister, Miranda, it was unforgettable.

What so terrible as war? I will tell you what is ten times, and ten thousand times, more terrible than war, and this is— outraged Nature. War, we are discovering now, is the clumsiest and most expensive of all games; we are finding that if you wish to commit an act of cruelty and folly, the most costly one that you can commit is to contrive to shoot your fellow-men in war. So it is; and thank God that it is so; but Nature, insidious, inexpensive, silent, sends no roar of cannon, no glitter of arms to do her work; she gives no warning note of preparation; she has no protocols, nor any diplomatic advances whereby she warns her enemy that war is coming. Silently, I say, and insidiously she goes forth; no! she does not even go forth; she does not step out of her path; but quietly, by the very same means by which she makes alive, she puts to death; and so avenges herself of those who have rebelled against her. By the very same laws by which every blade of grass grows, and every insect springs to life in the sun-beam, she kills, and kills, and kills, and is never tired of killing: till she has taught man the terrible lesson he is so slow to learn, that Nature is only conquered by obeying her.

This last point, that Nature can be conquered only by obeying her laws, was one which guided him in all his scientific interests and in his practical suggestions for the betterment of society. It guided him in such matters as how to conquer epidemics, typhus, cholera, diphtheria. It sustained him when he forced his parishioners to ventilate their cottages, sometimes to the point where he had to poke a hole in their thatched roofs with a carpenter's auger, or when he took round bottles of gargle to help ward off diphtheria. When his congregation, alarmed by the abnormally wet summer of 1860 and fearing a bad harvest, begged him to pray for fine weather, he preached instead the logic of sanitation. The rains, he explained, would clean drains, sewers and wells, purifying the drinking water so that if cholera and typhoid fever reappeared the infection stood less chance of spreading. He reminded his farming congregation that they had enjoyed better than average harvests in the preceding dry summers, so now they had to be prepared to take a poorer harvest, and be satisfied with the average. As for praying to God to change the weather over Eversley, Kingsley tried to make them understand that God was not a capricious wizard, turning physical phenomena off and on. 'Shall I presume, because I think it is raining too long here, to ask God to alter the tides of the ocean, the form of the continents, the pace at which the earth spins round, the force, the light, and speed, of sun and moon? For all this, and no less, I shall ask, if I ask Him to alter the skies, even for a single day.'[3]

It also guided him, as it guided F. D. Maurice, in giving a cautious welcome to the doctrine of evolution put forward in Charles Darwin's new book, *The Origin of Species*, which appeared in 1859. Kingsley's geological studies had prepared him for Darwin's theories, and the sober judgments which he and Maurice made on this subject helped to moderate Church resistance to Darwin's ideas, and to make it easier for men and women who accepted the new scientific ideas to retain also their old belief in God.

'Darwin is conquering everywhere, and rushing in like a flood, by the mere force of truth and fact. The one or two who hold out are forced to try all sorts of subterfuges as to fact, or else by evoking the *odium theologicum.* . . .

'But they find that now they have got rid of an interfering God—a master-magician, as I call it—they have to choose between the absolute empire of accident, and a living, immanent, ever-working God.

'Grove's truly great mind has seized the latter alternative already on the side of chemistry. Anstead, in his Rede lecture, is feeling for it in geology; and so is Lyell; and I, in my small way of zoology, am urging it on Huxley, Rolleston and Bates. . . .'
Thus Kingsley to Maurice.[4] He sighed as he learned that his friend, Philip Gosse, could not see it this way, and tried to

explain away the presence of fossils by declaring that these had been created by God as fossils from the start, and were not the remains of plants and animals.

While Kingsley's intellect was stimulated by these ideas, his conscience was troubling him over a different matter, adding to his generally depressed state of mind. Old Mr. Kingsley was very ill, dying likely, and his eldest son was remorseful, regretting those occasions when he had angrily resented his father's casual acceptance of Mrs. Kingsley's care and devotion. As the family watched the old man grow daily more frail Kingsley wondered whether he, too, would make old bones. On the whole, he hoped not. His state of mind is well described by John Martineau, who spent a week at Eversley in October 1859. He had graduated from Cambridge and was reading for the bar, and on the advice of Tom Hughes, was working in the chambers of Charles Pollock. In his spare time, Martineau was a volunteer teacher at the Working Men's College.

Mr. Kingsley is not *ill*; indeed, to all outward appearance he is as well as usual, and seeks rather than avoids society and exercise. But his brain is utterly worked out, his 'creative power,' he says, utterly gone for the time, and though he is beginning again to read moderately, and *take in*, he cannot produce, cannot even write a sermon. You may fancy how eagerly I am searching for a curate for him, for he has three services every Sunday and no help; two in church, and one in a schoolroom at the other end of the parish, where he preaches extempore. I think I never heard him more grand and more simple than in that schoolroom that Sunday evening. No one there but ourselves and the poorest labouring men and women, and there he speaks out his whole faith without fear or a thought of bigots and cavillers. Not a labourer there so dense and dull but was able to understand every word and carry it away too—a sermon for peasant and for prince. Truly, pedants and bigots little know how beautiful the Light is from which they would shut out themselves and their fellow-men. His great heart seems too large for his body, and for his brain too sometimes, powerful as that is, and if he is ever illogical or inconsistent it is because his intellect is too slight a rudder to his intense impulsiveness.

He has determined not to write for a long time—he says three years—and to see a good deal of society, going on with his parish work as usual, with a curate to save his Sunday work a little and to take his duty when he preaches at the Chapel Royal.

One day the hounds were to meet about six miles off, so he set to work to rig me out, putting me inside his leather inexpressibles, and outside his old horse, and a delightful morning I had in the forest of firs and heather, although we did not find till after I left and had no run.

Another day in walked Richard Trench and his geological companion Polwheel, who are located in the neighbourhood making a survey. Mr. Kingsley started off with them at once to show them what he knew of the geological features of Eversley, and another day they came again and we drove over to Mr. Walter[5] of Bearwood, who owns a great deal of Berkshire near there, lunched with him and his family, and examined the country.[6]

Indeed, there were constant visitors at Eversley, some dropping in for the day, others staying overnight. This picture of a socially busy but mentally lazy Charles Kingsley contrasts sharply with that of his brother, Henry, at the same time. Of course, Henry had no family responsibilities and no job to carry out, and devoted all his time to his novel. He worked at night, from about eleven in the evening until six in the morning, kept awake by a pipe and a jug of rum and water. Then he would sleep until lunchtime, spend a pleasant afternoon and evening walking, shooting, fishing or gardening, and be ready for the night's literary task.

Charles Kingsley's writing at this time extended to hardly more than keeping abreast of his extensive correspondence. He was always being approached by strangers who asked his advice on religious or moral problems, and he was quite prepared to do his best as an oracle. Certainly he had the common touch. People felt that he was *the* man who would understand their doubts and yearnings in a fast-changing age when all conventions were being questioned. He was consulted about book illustrations; about sewage plans; about women's emancipation; about marriage. To an unidentified correspondent, asking about marriage in a future world, he replied promptly, about himself and his wife: 'I know that if immortality is to include in my case identity of person, I shall feel for her what I feel now.' He and Fanny tended to disapprove of second marriages, chiefly because in their own case they could not imagine any second marriage for either of them being as happy as their existing union. Kingsley, indeed, entertained the fantasy that he and Fanny would be fortunate enough to die within a short time of each other, possibly days, so that the period of separation would be mercifully short. In practice, and with regard to other people, however, they did not condemn second marriages. F. D. Maurice had remarried when his first wife died, and in a period when so many men were left widowers with a family of young children, remarriage was often the only practicable solution.

Mr. Kingsley died in February 1860, aged seventy-eight. Kingsley broke the news to his elder son, Maurice, who was away at school. 'You must always think of him lovingly; and remember this about him, Maurice, and copy it—that he was a *gentleman*, and never did in his life, or even thought, a mean or false thing, and therefore has left behind him many friends and not an enemy on earth. Yes, dear boy, if it should please God that you should help build up the old family again, bear in mind that *honesty* and *modesty*, the two marks of a gentleman, are the only way to do it.' Kingsley composed the epitaph for his father's grave in Brompton Cemetery: '. . . With many friends and not an enemy on earth; Leaving to his children as a precious heritage The example of a Gentleman and a Christian.' F. D. Maurice wrote a kindly letter to comfort Charles, who in the bitterness of his sorrow could find no better phrase for death than 'an ugly damnable solecism'.

Fanny comforted the mother-in-law who had been so friendly

and understanding during the bleak days of her own courtship. The entire Kingsley family was very united, and Fanny was a warm and loving person, so her attentions to old Mrs. Kingsley were predictable. Martineau testified to Fanny's personality when he tried to explain to his slightly bewildered Unitarian relatives why he found the Kingsley home so appealing. 'The lady of the house was one in a hundred.' 'The Mother is the light and the moving spirit of the home.' 'It is a home blessed beyond expression.' Henry moved into his mother's cottage at Eversley to keep her company, leaving it only when he married a few years later. When Mrs. Kingsley was too old and infirm to live by herself she moved into the Rectory, where she lived until her death.

Meanwhile, Fanny went to Chelsea Rectory to supervise the final removal of the Kingsleys and their belongings, and Charles remained in Eversley, trying to discharge his emotional strain in physical activity. He and his churchwarden worked hard planting young shrubs in an addition to the churchyard.

Death was still close to the family circle. Anthony Froude sent an urgent summons to Fanny to go to her sister. The Froudes had leased Northdown House, Bideford, and Fanny dropped everything and hurried to Devonshire, but was too late. Charlotte Froude, who had been in bad health for some considerable time, died before Fanny's arrival. Froude was left with three young children. Kingsley had the melancholy task of officiating at the funeral of his sister-in-law, the first to lie in his newly planted churchyard. Then within weeks, it seemed, death claimed another of the Kingsley group—this time 'Little John' Parker. Kingsley wrote sorrowfully to John Skelton, a mutual friend and one of the chief contributors to *Fraser's*, 'Before our window lies the grave of one whom he adored, my wife's favourite sister. He was at her funeral. The next funeral which her widowed husband and I attended was his: Froude nursed him like a brother till the moment of death. His was a great soul in a pigmy body; and those who know how I loved him, know what a calumny it is to say that I preach "muscular Christianity"!'[6] Dr. Ackland wrote to say that Sir James Hamlyn-

Williams had died, and this, coupled with his father's death, made Kingsley feel that the whole Clovelly era had been broken up. Two more of the Grenfell family died that year: John Ashley Warre and Charles Grenfell.

But Charles Kingsley was left little time for repining, with honours now thrust fast upon him. The Regius Professorship of History at Cambridge fell vacant, following the resignation of Sir James Stephen, and in May 1860 Lord Palmerston offered Kingsley the chair. The Prince Consort, Chancellor of the University, had some influence in the affair. It was an appointment which Kingsley had neither sought nor anticipated, and in some embarrassment he hurried to Cambridge to take his M.A. degree, which he had never bothered to do, partly because of the expense and partly because he did not need it. He had not been to Cambridge since his undergraduate days, and found the university changed. He stayed as the guest of Dr. Whewell, Master of Trinity, of whom Sydney Smith used to say, 'Science was his forte and omniscience his foible.' Kingsley believed that the whole atmosphere in the colleges had changed for the better in two decades, and attributed it to the wholesome influence of Maurice and the 'band of brothers'. Kingsley looked optimistically into the future. He wrote to his wife: 'I feel much older, anxious, and full of responsibility; but more cheerful and settled than I have done for a long time. All that book writing and struggling is over, and a settled position and work is before me.' At forty-one he had lost his youthful *élan*, and although he would be hardworking, conscientious and public-spirited to the end of his days the ebullience of Parson Lot had largely vanished. All his friends were growing older, becoming more respectable, with distinguished grey hairs. Tom Hughes was even thinking of standing for Parliament as a Liberal when a suitable constituency presented itself. Anthony Froude had become an established and eminently readable historian. John Ludlow was sitting on important committees to examine the needs and legal position of trade unions. Maurice, of course, had always been a man of eminent respectability and social position, however unorthodox his doctrines. And even Carlyle was mellowing, although he often seemed to talk as much 'twaddle' as sense, thought Kingsley, who privately felt sorry for Mrs. Carlyle.

The rector gradually cheered up as the time for going to Cambridge approached. It would be undeniably pleasant to put 'Professor' before one's name; and nobody could overlook the fact that he would be paid almost as much for his lectures as he received for his work at Eversley. However, he felt some trepidation at lecturing in the university, where his new critics would be academics, and probably as hard on him as the journalists had been. To get himself mentally and physically toned up, he joined Froude on a fishing holiday in Ireland.

Fishing was a well-tried anodyne, and he had the thrill of catching salmon. 'I had magnificent sport this morning—five salmon killed (biggest seven pounds), and another huge fellow ran right away to sea, carrying me after him waist deep in water, and was lost, after running 200 yards, by fouling a ship's hawser! There is nothing like it. The excitement is maddening, and the exertion very severe. I am going to sleep for two hours, having been up at four.' And a few days later, he wrote: 'We have plenty of sea-boating and yachting, but I don't care for that since I have caught salmon; I can think of nothing else. . . .'

It was another of his family exaggerations. Even with the temptation of salmon before him, Kingsley could not entirely blind himself to the sight and the implications of the Irish peasantry. He had imagined sixteenth-century Irishmen, and described them in scathing terms, in *Westward Ho!*, but that referred to conditions over three hundred and fifty years ago, and one would have assumed that British rule and the English Protestant Church would have improved the Irish in body and spirit since then. Yet manifestly this was not the case, and Kingsley was upset by the discovery. His comments to Fanny are those of a man whistling in the dark to keep his faith alive. 'But I am haunted by the human chimpanzees I saw along that hundred miles of horrible country. I don't believe they are our fault. I believe there are not only many more of them than of old, but that they are happier, better, more comfortably fed and lodged under our rule than they were. But to see white chimpanzees is dreadful; if they were black, one would not feel it so much, but their skins, except where tanned by exposure, are as white as ours.' He was compelled to return to this theme later. 'But the country which I came through yesterday moves me even to tears. It is a land of ruins and of the dead. You cannot conceive to English eyes the first shock of ruined cottages; and when it goes on to whole hamlets, the effect is most depressing. I suppose it had to be done, with poor-rates twenty shillings in the pound, and the people dying of starvation, and the cottier system had to be stopped, but what an amount of human misery each of those unroofed hamlets stands for! Still it had to be done. There are magnificent farms growing up now, with roots and grasses, instead of the horrid potato in the black bog.'[7]

The summer of 1860 was interesting, among other things, for the meeting of the British Association in Oxford at which Bishop Samuel Wilberforce, with ill-inspired ridicule, tried to vanquish Thomas Henry Huxley and other supporters of the Darwinian theories. Kingsley followed all the arguments keenly, his sympathy on Huxley's side, and when, in September, Huxley's young son died suddenly, Kingsley was prompted to write to Huxley, hinting at Christian hope and consolation at such a moment of personal grief. Huxley was profoundly touched, although he replied stoically that he believed in the law of inverse squares, and could not rest his life and hopes upon weaker convictions. However, he added that he appreciated the truth and sincerity of Kingsley and Maurice, and felt that good must come from their efforts. The two men thus began a permanent epistolary friendship. They had a good deal in common: a love of science, a great talent for writing and lecturing, immense industry, a tendency to bouts of depression, and a blessedly happy marriage. Like Kingsley, Huxley had to write books and articles late at night after the day's work to pay household bills.

Charles Darwin had sent an advance copy of his book to Kingsley, whose reply began a friendship, similar to the one with Huxley. Darwin was particularly struck by a sentence in one of Kingsley's letters: 'I have gradually learnt to see that it is just as noble a conception of Deity to believe that He created animal forms capable of self-development into all forms needful . . . as to believe that He required a fresh act of intervention to supply the lacunae which He Himself had made. I question whether the former be not the loftier thought.' With Kingsley's permission, but not attributing it to him by name, this sentence was included in the preface to the second edition of *The Origin of Species*, as an answer to those readers who were likely to call the book irreligious.

In the autumn Kingsley took Fanny and Maurice with him to Cambridge, and prepared the inaugural lecture to be given in the Senate House. Word quickly spread that he was in Cambridge. 'I remember the thrill one felt as one November evening a man announced "in Hall"—"Kingsley is come; I saw him today in the streets; my father knows him, and I knew him in a moment." The man whose father knew Kingsley was a man to be envied, and to be asked to one's rooms at once. I remember there was a warm discussion as to some of the Professor's supposed views, and within a few days after he had stood up in the senate-house and delivered his inaugural lecture, men who were opposed to him began to say, "Whether we agree with this or that, we like Kingsley." ' John Martineau made a special journey to listen to his former tutor, and wrote a glowing account to his aunt. 'The great day is over, and the lecture more than worthy of its author. Mr. Kingsley has been in a state of unusual nervousness about it, and went up to the desk with a strange, half-frightened look that I never saw on him before; but as he went on and warmed to his work, his voice grew stronger and firmer, and he was listened to in perfect stillness for nearly two hours, and seldom, if ever, have I seen so great and intense interest. . . .

'The whole building was quite full and crowded. Mr. Maurice came this morning on purpose for the lecture. An undergraduate in the gallery recognised him and gave "Three cheers for Mr. Maurice" which was well received. Then there were "Three groans for Mr. Bright", also quite unanimous; "Three cheers for Garibaldi" was well received, in spite of a few groans and hisses of opposition. The Lecturer was received with deafening cheers upon the mention of his name before he came in, again when he came in, and a third time when he ended his lecture.'

This cheering became a feature of Kingsley's lectures, and created a lively atmosphere quite new to the university. A former undergraduate recalled Kingsley at the lecture stand. 'His eye used to glisten, his voice in its remarkable sea-like modulations to swell like an organ as he recounted something great, till his audience listened, quite spell-bound, fixed, till the climax came, and then rushed into a cheer before they were well aware of it. He was so modest and humble he could not *bear* our cheers. He would beckon for quiet; and then in a broken voice and with dreadful stammering say, "Gentlemen, you must not do it. I cannot lecture to you if you do." But it was no good—we did not mean to cheer—we could not help it.'[8]

In spite of his evident success with the students, Kingsley was in a state of collapse after the first lecture. Martineau called on the family in the evening, only to find Kingsley 'very tired and low in spirits. Mrs. Kingsley quite knocked up with neuralgia and gone to bed. The boy Maurice too is unwell with pleurisy, so they are all rather ailing just now.'

Kingsley had set forth in his first lecture, *The Limits of Exact Science as Applied to History*, how he would handle the subject. The academic gown barely concealed the preacher. 'I entreat gentlemen who may hereafter attend my lectures to bear in mind this last saying (*Homo sum, nil humanis a me alienum puto*). If they wish to understand History, they must first try to understand men and women. For History is the history of men and women, and of nothing else.... And you, if you would understand History, must understand men.' Like Carlyle, he advised studying history through biographies. The laws which in the long run governed history could be discovered through the lives of people and seeing whether they obeyed or disobeyed them. Human welfare, he insisted, was founded on morals, not on mind. 'The true subjective history of man is the history not of his thought, but of his conscience: the true objective history of man is not that of his inventions but of his vices and virtues.... As a people behaves, so it thrives; as it believes, so it behaves.' Kingsley was a product of the Victorian age in seeing an orderly progress in history—'inevitable sequence, orderly movement, irresistible growth.' 'God educating man . . . [to] discover for himself, as much as possible, fresh laws, or fresh applications of laws; and exercising his will and faculties, by trusting him to himself wherever he can be trusted without his final destruction. This is my conception of history, especially of Modern History—of history since the Revelation of our Lord Jesus Christ.'

The university academics who resented an outsider like Kingsley being appointed professor sneered at his lectures, but the students loved him. When Kingsley declared, 'I am not here to teach you history—I am here to teach you how to teach yourselves history,' they cheered him to the echo, and went off to the libraries to borrow books—almost a revolution in student habits. Kingsley held himself available to his students, believing that it was the duty of a university teacher to help his students in every possible way, which included counselling and friendship. This, too, was a new departure. He quickly became a cult figure among the students, and an object of suspicion, even derision, among the dons.

Now that he had achieved a measure of respectability, Kingsley's literary works were reassessed. The *National Review*, a periodical which in the past had glossed over his literary faults because he had an 'aim beyond amusing', surveyed the books more critically, and measured him against Scott, Trollope and George Eliot. *Adam Bede*, which appeared in 1859, had been an overnight popular and critical success, setting a standard for later novels, against which Kingsley emerged decidedly second-best. 'His ordinary style of workmanship is slovenly and slipshod . . . his ordinary standard is unfixed and low. . . . He "goes in" for quantity rather than quality, and trusts too much to "inspiration". . . . A genius like Mr. Kingsley's not only deserves the most sedulous culture but demands the most severe control . . . needs to be *employed*, not *indulged*.'[9] The word 'genius' was frequently used in connection with Kingsley, but always qualified.

He was sensitive to literary criticism, as he was to all other forms of criticism, but told himself his writing had never taken first place in his life. Indeed, when Sir William Cope inquired testily whether the rector's writing might not interfere with his parish duties Kingsley meekly replied that he did not start it until late at night when every other job had been completed. This was undoubtedly one reason for the uneven quality of his writing. So when Charles read carping reviews of his books, he told Fanny he could afford to stop writing novels; they had served their purpose in making known certain important problems, and indeed in making known a certain clergyman, who through royal patronage had now an even more prominent platform from which to preach. The literary work which he undertook in the future was, indeed, more appropriate to the interests and talents of a cultivated gentleman, with royalist and Anglican views, vehemently patriotic, who held socially progressive opinions, and was happiest in the role of amateur scientist. As for literature, the Professor believed that the honour of the Kingsleys was being well satisfied by Henry Kingsley, whose novel, *The Recollections of Geoffry Hamlyn*, had been excellently received in serial form, and was issued in a one-volume edition by Macmillans in 1860.

The Christmas vacation was spent back at Eversley, where some of the duties had been taken in Kingsley's absence by young Freddie Stapleton. Martineau joined the family, and described the fun and liveliness of Christmas holidays at the rectory for the benefit of his aunt.

'I am very happy. I have been here nearly a week. I have been out all day long, two days skating as well as snow would let me, and other days walking and playing at hockey. To-day I was to have gone hunting with Maurice. Mr. Kingsley has hired a hunter for himself, and would insist on *my* using him on the only day which appeared likely to be practicable! but the hard frost put hunting out of the question. We are all going up this evening to the great big house at Bramshill to Christmas-tree and dancing.

'The Rectory servants had their Christmas party on the last day of the old year, and they and their guests, consisting of the schoolmaster, etc. came into the drawing-room and were

entertained with dancing, games, etc. and we had the most
charming evening.' A week later, Martineau wrote: 'All the
children are late this morning in consequence of a charming
Christmas-tree which took place last night, followed by games
and dancing. I will tell you how I spent yesterday. I set off about
eleven with Maurice to Bramshill pond to skate. It is a glorious
lake, a mile round nearly, in a beautiful wild park, and near a
glorious old Elizabethan house. There I skated in extreme
enjoyment as hard as I could go till it was time to go on to meet
Mr. Kingsley on the road to Heckfield, where I found him, and
we walked on through Heckfield to Strathfieldsaye, where Mr.
Kingsley called, and I waited for him in the park till I saw some
one signalling to me from the hall-door, and I found it was to
bring me in to luncheon. I sat just opposite the Duchess, and had
nothing to do but look at and study that wonderful face.

'Thence we went to call on the Pigotts, who are going next
month to govern the Isle of Man and the tail-less cats, and then
to Lord Eversley (Speaker of the House of Commons), who
looks as young and as jolly as ever; then home across the moor
and through the fir-forest to the snug little Rectory, a five
o'clock dinner and a Christmas-tree and any number of children
to enjoy it.'

Kingsley's social status amongst the Hampshire notables had
certainly risen since the 'Chartist' days of 1848.

The professorship gave Kingsley the entrée into academic
circles at both the older universities, and he was welcomed in the
homes of the local gentry around Cambridge. He made friends
with Sir Charles Fox Bunbury, a noted botanist and geologist,
who had a famed collection of trees and botanical specimens at
Barton Hall, Suffolk. Sir Charles was fascinated by Kingsley's
wide-ranging conversation, and gave him an open invitation to
visit Barton Hall as often as he could. Kingsley did not have
much free time for visiting, but he kept up a warm association
by letter. Sir Charles told Mrs. Kingsley, after the rector's
death, that Kingsley had 'more than once said to me that, if
circumstances had allowed him leisure, botany, and natural
history, in general, would have been his favourite studies.'[10]

Circumstances never gave Kingsley leisure. His next assignment was to assist in the education of Bertie, the Prince of Wales. The Prince Consort had sent his eldest son for a year to Oxford, where a strict and boring course of study, deadened by a crushing protocol, took all the pleasure out of university life. Goldwin Smith, his history tutor, used to show the prince the textbook to be used, and stand silently by, turning the pages. He did not attempt to lecture or to explain the topics.[11]

The dismal failure of the Oxford experiment made the Prince Consort feel that his son was ineducable, but the young prince displayed poise and charm during a short courtesy visit to Canada and the United States, so his father decided to make a further attempt to instil into the young man a love of learning. The prince was nominally attached to Trinity College, but lived with his entourage a few miles outside Cambridge. Carefully chosen tutors, and even more carefully chosen undergraduates, were to associate with him. Kingsley was to tutor the prince in history, according to a syllabus arranged by the Prince Consort.

The prince visited Kingsley's house in Cambridge twice a week, to join a small history class. Once a week the prince rode over for a private tutorial during which Kingsley took the boy through the studies of the previous week. Kingsley was very solemn about this new responsibility. He had such a feudal regard for royalty that he could not consider the prince as just another man. He hoped to instil some 'sound literal principles', he said, into 'that jolly boy', but at the same time Kingsley was deeply conscious that he was tutoring a future king. The prince responded to Kingsley's style of teaching, the very opposite of Goldwin Smith's, and became very fond of the rector.

Kingsley did his best to follow the Prince Consort's wishes. He greatly admired that hard-working prince—wishing the English upper classes would follow his example. He felt a deep sense of loss at the prince's early death in December 1861. When the new Chancellor was installed at Cambridge, to succeed Albert, Kingsley composed an ode remembering the prince:

Can we forget one friend,
Can we forget one face,
Which cheered us toward our end
Which nerved us for our race?

Macmillans now wrote to say they were preparing a new
edition of *Alton Locke*, so Kingsley took the opportunity of
writing a new preface and revising the passages in the story
which dealt with Cambridge and the attitude of Cambridge
students to working-class men and women. His reasoning was
that working-class readers of the novel would have their notions
of the university and of Cambridge men moulded by the descriptions in the novel, and would be bound to assume that what
had been true in 1848 was still true in 1861. Now that Kingsley
had seen for himself that such was not the case he wanted to
present a truer picture. The changes he made were slight—of
emphasis rather than basic alterations—and he explained his
motives in a long, sermonising preface, specifically addressed to
the Cambridge undergraduates, young men on the brink of
professional life, who needed to be awakened to social problems
and to the just needs of the working class.

After ascribing the reasons for the generally improved moral
tone at the university to the influence of the High Church party,
of Dr. Arnold and of F. D. Maurice, Kingsley continued: 'Thirty
years ago, and even later, the young men of the labouring classes
were "the cads", "the snobs", "the blackguards"; looked on
with a dislike, contempt, and fear, which they were not backward
to return, and which were but too ready to vent themselves on
both sides in ugly words and deeds. . . . How changed, thank
God! is all this now. . . . The whole creed of our young gentlemen
is becoming more liberal, their demeanour more courteous,
their language more temperate.' Kingsley suggested that scholar-
ships should be provided at the university for sons of working
men, boys who had distinguished themselves in the National
Schools. 'As for the introduction of such a class of lads lowering
the tone of the University, I cannot believe it. There is room
enough in Cambridge for men of every rank.' He warned all

his readers against complacency. 'As for the social evils described in this book, they have been much lessened in the last few years, especially by the movement for Sanitary Reform; but I must warn young men that they are not eradicated; that, for instance, only last year attention was called by this book to the working tailors in Edinburgh, and their state was found, I am assured, to be even more miserable than that of the London men in 1848. And I must warn them also that social evils, like dust and dirt, have a tendency to re-accumulate perpetually; so that however well this generation may have swept their house (and they have worked hard and honestly at it) the rising generation will have assuredly in twenty years' time to sweep it over again.'

With regard to trade unions, a controversial subject at that time because of the Sheffield murders,[12] Kingsley argued calmly that this did not alter the fact that well-organised trade unions were desirable, and that the extension of the franchise to the working man was equally essential. Try to keep the unions down, he said, and 'You will not prevent the existence of combinations; you will only make them secret, dark, revolutionary.'

The new preface was a restatement of Kingsley's social and political stance, changed since 1848, as both the man and the times had changed. The preface was printed in edition after edition of *Alton Locke*, influencing many serious, impressionable young men and women of the upper and middle class. *Alton Locke* after 1862 was bought by a very different public from that of ten years earlier. Although Parson Lot had retired, his writings, sermons and lectures were still in print, and his transformation into Professor Charles Kingsley meant that his opinions reached a wider public than ever. When, in 1863, Macmillans acquired Kingsley's (and Maurice's) other works from the publishing firm of Parker, which went out of business, the book market was thereafter flooded with reprints, many in cheap editions, of the rector's books. A generation later, a new public appeared, the generation which had been made literate by the 1870 Education Act, which grew up hungry for enlightenment on social and humanitarian problems. Kingsley's style—dramatic, emotional, and often harshly bitter—won them immediately. The weaknesses deplored by critics and academics—his carelessness, his lack of subtlety, his lamentable habit of rushing into a fight without first checking his facts—were such universally human weaknesses that the broad reading public forgave him, caring only for what he meant to say, not for what he actually did say.

As a clergyman, and one who had welcomed new scientific theories, Kingsley was expected to take a position on a new collection of articles, *Essays and Reviews*, written by some progressive Anglicans, and intended to show that intelligent people, aware of scientific discoveries, could still remain in the Church of England. The Bible, like other research material, ought to be able to stand up to examination, and churchmen should not oppose such examination for fear that the result would be a loss of faith. A number of highly-placed Anglican bishops took fright at the book, calling it heretical. The controversy was part of the repressive campaign waged by orthodox Christians against the Darwinians. Kingsley and Maurice, both tolerant and far-sighted in these matters, insisted that the authors of *Essays and Reviews* were searchers after truth, and the bishops were behaving like men whose own faith was too weak to permit them to recognise the existence of other views.

As might have been expected, the protests of the bishops had the effect of drawing the attention of the lay public to the book. Maurice was alarmed in case it encouraged the spread of atheism and doubt, and he put together a collection of essays called *Tracts for Priests and People*. Kingsley was asked to contribute, but could not find enough time, although Tom Hughes wrote an attractive piece—*A Layman's Faith*—which Kingsley praised as being 'clear, hearty, and honest'.

A year or so later, another book appeared which had an even more unfortunate effect on a public whose faith was wavering— Bishop Colenso's examination of the first five books of the Bible. He added up figures and dates in the Old Testament, and made a ludicrous nonsense of any fundamentalist reading of the origins of the world according to the Pentateuch. Colenso had been a very close friend of Maurice since student days at Cambridge, but Maurice was so upset by Colenso's book, and what he regarded as its negative influence, that he broke entirely with his old friend. Indeed, Maurice (who had in 1860 been appointed priest of St. Peter's Church in Vere Street, London, by Lord Palmerston—to the great delight of his admirers and disciples) was so deeply unhappy at these doctrinal controversies within the Anglican establishment, that he declared he was ready to resign his living, in the hope that such a drastic renunciation would shame Colenso into a similar action.

The Prophet's friends, horrified at such an extreme stand, all begged him to reconsider, at the same time putting pressure on the government and on the Bishop of London to refuse such a resignation if it were offered. Kingsley wrote a letter to *The Times*, simplifying in Kingsleyan words the burden of the objections that Maurice had to Colenso's book, and he composed some new sermons, later printed in a volume and dedicated to Dr. A. P. Stanley. Kingsley's practical advice was to ignore inconvenient questions which had no obvious solutions, and instead concentrate upon the positive value and comfort to be found in the Bible. Maurice did not object to his ideas being interpreted by Kingsley. Indeed, in a letter of October 12, 1862, he asked Kingsley to do so, complaining that 'People will not hear me. My words they call strange and mystical.'

The outbreak of the American Civil War in 1861 had naturally claimed the attention of many people in Britain, and Kingsley felt that as a professor of modern history he had a moral duty to deliver a course of lectures on American history to his Cambridge students. His instincts of course aligned him with the South, although he expected and hoped the outcome of the war would be the end of slavery. He had for many years viewed the democracy of the Northern states as a money-grabbing 'arithmocracy', unleavened by the aristocratic element, permitting unbridled capitalism leading to exploitation. The American war was another issue on which he parted company with some of his oldest friends; Ludlow, Hughes and Alexander Macmillan being among the first in England to give public support for the North. In June 1861 Ludlow had written an article for *Macmillan's*

Magazine supporting the North, foreseeing that a victory for Northern democracy would encourage the progress of democracy in England. Indeed, the triumph of the Reform Act in 1867, extending the franchise to the town working man, was an indirect result of the success of the North. Kingsley, less politically astute, and certainly far less of a democrat, lined up with Gladstone, most members of the English upper class, and such formidable journals as *The Times* and the *Saturday Review*, in support of the South.

Still, America was three thousand miles away, and a foreign country after all, and Kingsley, as always, preferred to concentrate on matters closer at home. He read that a new governmental report on child employment had been issued, and asked Hughes to send him further details. Mainly through the efforts of Lord Shaftesbury, the scope of the investigation had been enlarged to include reports on climbing boys, the little chimney sweeps, whose fate William Blake had epitomised in a single verse:

> When my mother died I was very young
> And my father sold me, while yet my tongue
> Could scarcely cry, 'Weep! Weep! Weep! Weep!'
> So your chimney I sweep and in soot I sleep.

Charles Dickens in 1837 had shown how narrowly Oliver Twist had escaped the plight of apprenticeship to a master sweep.

The report of the government commission on this trade was truly horrifying. The use of climbing boys was actually on the increase throughout the country, as prosperous middle-class men had imposing mansions built for their families, and house-proud mistresses insisted on boys rather than machines to clean the chimneys because boys were more thorough and produced less dirt in the rooms. The master sweeps, more brutal now than in any earlier generation, liked to take children as young as possible, and found that six was 'a nice trainable age'. Younger than that, and there was a high risk that the child might die suddenly from weakness. The supply of orphaned or unwanted boys appeared limitless, especially in the great industrial towns, and the demand was continuous.

Deeply moved by these revelations, Kingsley preached on them before the Queen at Windsor, and again in his annual sermon at St. James, making the sardonic comment that we English, a kind-hearted race, were actually able to be sorry for one whole half-hour for those workers who were exposed to industrial diseases—'Sorry for the people whose lower jaws decay away in lucifer-match factories. Sorry for the miseries and wrongs which the Children's Employment Commission has revealed. Sorry for the diseases of artificial flower-makers,' etc., etc. He continued that 'we English' were relieved to hear that 'charitable people or the Government are going to do something to alleviate these miseries. And then we return, too many of us, each to his own ambition, or his own luxury, comforting ourselves with the thought that we did not make the world, and we are not responsible for it....'[13]

But sermons could not accomplish enough—even royal sermons which would later be published—and Kingsley was burning with indignation. A new literary form incubated in his restless mind—a fantasy for children—tomfoolery, with a serious purpose, 'to make children and grown folks understand that there is a quite miraculous and divine element underlying all physical nature; and that nobody knows anything about anything, in the sense in which they may know God in Christ, and right and wrong.' And the hero of the book was to be that pathetic product of Victorian industrialism, a climbing boy.

Mrs. Kingsley has a well-known passage in which she describes the birth of *The Water-Babies*. It was a spring morning in 1862, and the family was having breakfast in the rectory. Mrs. Kingsley reminded her husband of an old promise—'Rose, Maurice, and May have got their book, and Baby must have his.' Kingsley said nothing, but got up at once, and went into his study, locking the door. In half an hour he returned, with the first chapter of Tom's adventures in his hand, written without a correction. The book 'was more like inspiration than composition, and seemed to flow naturally out of his brain and heart, lightening both of a burden without exhausting either. Nothing helped the books and sermons more than the silence and solitude of a few days' fishing, which he could now indulge in.' The rest of the book was written with equal speed and fluency, with scarcely a correction, and as he wrote it, the instalments went to the printer to appear in *Macmillan's Magazine*. Alexander Macmillan, visiting Eversley around June, excited by the first chapter of the book, had written to his friend and business associate, James MacLehose: 'I am staying a day or two with the dear, noble Rector here. We are to have *such* a story from him for the Magazine—to begin in August when *Ravenshoe* is done. It is to be called *The Water-Babies*. I have read a great deal of it, and it is the most charming piece of grotesquery, with flashes of tenderness and poetry playing over all, that I have ever seen.' He read the instalments to his children, as they arrived for the printer, and his daughter in later years recalled it as 'the greatest excitement in the nursery world that I remember.'[14]

It was indeed a happy summer for Kingsley, with a story that cried out to be written, more physical strength than he had had for many months, and a wonderful holiday in Scotland as the fêted guest of lords and lairds. He stayed in Murthley Castle near Dunkeld, where the broad River Tay, filled with salmon, splashed over the rocks beneath the great house, and the historic woods of Birnham Hill could be glimpsed across the valley. 'We had reels last night, Lord John Manners and Sir Hugh Cairns both dancing,' he wrote to his mother. (Lord John Manners, at one time associated with Disraeli in the New England group, had spent much time on political work in connection with factory control and child employment.)

But the pleasures of Murthley, even though the laird was of the Royal Stewart family, soon paled before the grandeur of the Duke of Argyll's Castle at Inveraray, where the River Aray, Kingsley told his mother, contained more salmon than water. 'The loveliest spot I ever saw—large lawns and enormous timber on the shores of a salt-water loch, with moor and mountain before and behind.' As for the loch, it contained 'salmon, salmon trout, brown trout, solmoferox, sythe, herrings, sticklebacks, flounders, grayling (on my honour I ain't lying) and all other known and unknown fresh and salt-water fish, jumbled together

Eversley Church and Rectory

J. A. Froude

in thousands. Such a piece of fishing I never saw in my life. . . .'

It was something of a Kingsley family tour, as Fanny and young Maurice accompanied the rector, and for at least part of the time Henry Kingsley joined them, visiting Lanarkshire and Inverary at that time, acquiring local backgrounds for his new tale, *Austin Elliot*, which included some Scottish scenes. Henry was almost as keen a fisherman as Charles, and he had established himself in the London literary scene with a novel called *Ravenshoe*, to follow *The Recollections of Geoffry Hamlyn*.

Charles Kingsley returned to Eversley greatly refreshed, with memories of salmon, of grand castles redolent with history, of charming gentlefolk who enjoyed his jokes and listened respectfully to his views. He looked forward to a new year at Cambridge, and to some scientific honours which were going to be bestowed upon him. Nobody realised—he least of all—that little Grenville Kingsley's book was going to bring the rector a new kind of fame, dramatising the fate of the climbing boys in the same way that *Uncle Tom's Cabin* dramatised slavery.

This first chapter, full of incident, and certainly long enough to make it astonishing that Kingsley could have written all of it in half an hour, is set squarely in a thoroughly realistic countryside. Tom, the exploited child, is ignorant but tough, resigned to his fate since he cannot imagine any other, and when the story opens he is accompanying his master, Mr. Grimes, to sweep the chimneys of Harthover Place, where, 'in the frame-breaking riots, which Tom just remembered, the Duke of Wellington, and ten thousand soldiers to match, were easily housed therein; at least, so Tom believed. . . .' The pair of them are up at three in the morning on a midsummer's day.

So he and his master set out; Grimes rode the donkey in front, and Tom and the brushes walked behind; out of the court, and up the street, past the closed window-shutters, and the winking weary policemen, and the roofs all shining gray in the gray dawn.

They passed through the pitmen's village, all shut up and silent now, and through the turnpike; and then they were out

9

in the real country, and plodding along the black dusty road, between black slag walls, with no sound but the groaning and thumping of the pit-engine in the next field. But soon the road grew white, and the walls likewise; and at the wall's foot grew long grass and gay flowers, all drenched with dew; and instead of the groaning of the pit-engine, they heard the skylark saying his matins high up in the air, and the pit-bird warbling in the sedges, as he had warbled all night long.

All else was silent.

The naturalist's pen, already seen in *Glaucus*, was fulfilled in *The Water-Babies*, which is a joyous, merry book—a fairy tale, as the author kept insisting, and therefore not to be taken seriously —even if it were true. The book is full of brilliant cameos: the caddis fly building her water nest; the wonderful emergence of the dragon-fly; the stream in flood after a storm, crowded with water creatures being swept down to the sea. And when Tom, drowned in the beck, and turned into a water-baby, finally does his altruistic good deed by helping the lobster out of the pot (like the Ancient Mariner blessing the sea creatures unaware) he is rewarded by being able to see and hear the other water-babies, who had been near him all the time, only he was blind and deaf before. The task of the sea-shore water-babies is to keep the pools clean and tended like water gardens.

Only where men are wasteful and dirty, and let sewers run into the sea instead of putting the stuff upon the fields like thrifty reasonable souls; or throw herrings' heads and dead dog-fish, or any other refuse, into the water; or in any way make a mess upon the clean shore—there the water-babies will not come, sometimes not for hundreds of years (for they cannot abide anything smelly or foul), but leave the sea-anemones and the crabs to clear away everything, till the good tidy sea has covered up all the dirt in soft mud and clean sand, where the water-babies can plant live cockles and whelks and razor-shells and sea-cucumbers and golden-combs, and make a pretty live garden again, after man's dirt is cleared away.

Kingsley's fairy sisters, Mrs. Bedonebyasyoudid and Mrs. Doasyouwouldbedoneby, are two sides of the same lady, or Mother Carey herself, who lives in the icy wastes and creates life by making creatures make themselves. Tom's adventures, and the lessons he learns, still keep a magical flavour even when the moralising which Kingsley considered part of his social responsibility is no longer in fashion. His child readers did not always recognise his favourite targets, which bob up throughout the story—conventional education, for example, is satirised in the Isle of Tomtoddies, all heads and no bodies, where every night and morning the Tomtoddies sing their song to their great idol, Examination: 'I can't learn my lesson; the examiner's coming!' Then there is the great and jolly nation of the Doasyoulikes, which has dwindled in numbers and has taken to the trees like apes, so as to escape the prowling and predatory tree lions. Like Rabelais, Kingsley loved to string together long lists. Re-telling the story of Pandora's box, he wrote:

> And out flew all the ills which flesh is heir to: all the children of the four great bogies, Self-will, Ignorance, Fear and Dirt—for instance:
>
> | | |
> |---|---|
> | Measles, | Famines, |
> | Monks, | Quacks, |
> | Scarlatina, | Unpaid bills, |
> | Idols, | Tight stays, |
> | Whooping-coughs, | Potatoes, |
> | Popes, | Bad Wine, |
> | Wars, | Despots, |
> | Peacemongers, | Demagogues, |
>
> And, worst of all, Naughty Boys and Girls.

Nor could he resist a passing dig now and again at Papists. And, once more, there were his poems. The story became an immediate children's classic, to be followed by *Alice in Wonderland* and other satirical fantasies. Little Tom's story was an important milestone in Kingsley's journey away from the associations and activities of 1848, and towards what would be the achievements of his later years—teaching, preaching and popularising science.

12

The Clash with Newman

For the patriotic villagers of Eversley the great event of 1863 was the wedding of the Prince of Wales to Princess Alexandra of Denmark. The prince had recently appointed Kingsley as one of his private chaplains, and as he still held his appointment as one of the Queen's chaplains, Charles felt a dual devotion to the House of Windsor. Both he and Fanny were invited to the wedding in the chapel at Windsor, Fanny in a temporary gallery in the choir, and Charles in the household gallery, both close to the young couple. Kingsley's simple romantic heart throbbed sympathetically as he watched live Knights of the Garter and live princesses file into the historic chapel, and the solemnity of the occasion was ensured for him at least by 'the serious grace and reverent dignity of my dear young Master, whose manner was perfect. And one other real thing—the Queen's sad face. . . .'[1]

The Kingsleys had planned to hurry back to Eversley the moment the ceremony was over, for the village festivities had been carefully planned weeks previously, and the ever-willing John Martineau had been pressed into service to supervise things in the absence of the rector. It was a gala day. 'A sheep roasted whole, and abundance of food of all kinds for young and old, hurdle-races, foot-races, etc.; concluding with fireworks and the grandfather of all bonfires worth ten London's full of illuminations. At the height of the blaze come Mr. and Mrs. Kingsley (three hours later than they intended) in great delight at the Windsor doings, he from the breakfast at the Castle with a three-corner court-dress hat full of wedding cake and bonbons stolen for the children, feeling, he said, as if a scene in the Arabian Nights had turned into reality and brought crowned princesses and fairies and fairyland upon earth.'

All in all, a bright and genial experience for the rector—very different from the unexpected and extremely unpleasant encounter with Dr. Pusey, the High Church clergyman, and former associate of John Henry Newman, the same man whose influence had almost made Charlotte Grenfell a nun. Dr. Pusey was Professor of Hebrew at Oxford, and his voice was still a powerful one. Gladstone once used the adjective 'rabid' to describe him. Over the years, Dr. Pusey and F. D. Maurice had often crossed swords in the correspondence columns of newspapers and periodicals. Just lately they had been engaged in bitter exchanges in *The Times* over Maurice's championship of Benjamin Jowett's contribution to *Essays and Reviews*. Kingsley's letter to *The Times*, interpreting and approving of Maurice, would not have escaped Dr. Pusey's attention, and since in the public mind Kingsley was still indissolubly linked with Maurice, it may well have appeared to many people, not least to Dr. Pusey, that a blow at Kingsley would also be a glancing thrust at Maurice.

Such a blow became possible when the Prince of Wales, in connection with a visit to Oxford for the Commemoration by him and his bride, included Kingsley's name on the list of candidates for the honorary degree of D.C.L. Dr. Pusey at once loudly opposed Kingsley on the grounds that *Hypatia* was an immoral book. The charge of immorality was peculiarly wounding to Charles because it was completely untrue and unfair, tantamount to calling him a hypocrite. He felt that Pusey's attack was just one more instance of the underhand tactics used by the pro-Catholic group against its opponents. He was too self-conscious to risk becoming the centre of any personal scandal, and was determined to shield the Prince of Wales from the risk of any public scene. If Kingsley's name remained on the list, and if Dr. Pusey cried out '*Non placet*' from the body of the hall in the presence of the prince and princess, as he threatened, Charles would be deeply chagrined and would blame himself for the sorry business. His friends and supporters in Oxford urged him to fight—especially Dr. A. P. Stanley, and Max Müller, the philologist (who was now a family connection having married Fanny's niece)—rather as Kingsley had in the past urged Maurice to fight in situations of comparable delicacy. He refused, and withdrew his name. Of course, he and Fanny were deeply disappointed. The kudos of his Cambridge appointment would last only so long as he remained professor, but the glory of an Oxford doctorate would have accompanied him to the grave. Although he took a dignified stand he showed how deep the wound went by refusing to be associated with Oxford again, even to the extent of refusing to preach there when invited to do so a few years later.

We have no clue to Fanny Kingsley's frustrations at this juncture when her husband, for the first time in his career possibly on the threshold of worldly advancement, was thus publicly chastened. Her own relatives had done very well, by worldly standards, in the past twenty years, and here was Charles, more gifted, more deserving than they, still only a country rector, still forced by financial pressure to hold down two jobs. Could it be that he had something of his father in him—possessing every talent save that of knowing how to make use of them? She tried to put these selfish considerations behind her. 'Well, then, he is right and I am wrong in the great matters, which are, after all, the most important,' she had written to her 'Dearest Boy', John Martineau, on a lesser, but similar occasion.

Kingsley had no doubts as to his line of conduct. He deliberately turned away from any course which might lead to public life, considering that he had seen enough behind the scenes in ecclesiastical, political and now academic circles to take fright at the intrigues, hypocrisy and backbiting that went on in them. It was, alas, a world where old enemies might rise without warning, so he decided to please himself—one might almost say indulge himself—in the future, in scientific hobbies and pursuits, apart, of course, from his parish work. These pursuits were not a new departure, but he hoped to find more time for them, and he was fairly sure that scientists would not stab him in the back. He would turn his talents to the task of popularising science for schoolchildren and for working men and women, who had not had the chance to learn such things in schools.

He began to devote time to Wellington College, a newly

founded school near Eversley, in which the late Prince Consort had been interested. Maurice Kingsley was a pupil, and Charles helped to start the school museum, by writing begging letters to all his scientific friends and acquaintances, asking for money and trophies for the school collection. Dr. Benson, headmaster of Wellington College (and a future Archbishop of Canterbury), enjoyed his company. 'How bright some of my own photographs are,' he wrote to Fanny Kingsley, when she was compiling her memorial volume. 'Those evenings at Eversley—certain lyings on the grass—two or three sermons—a service at Bramshill—one or two rides—half a dozen walks—turns round the Wellington Cloisters—those lectures—some talks on Maurice—about classics—about History—about West Indies. Oh, dear Mrs. Kingsley, how I wish I could express half my gratitude to him. . . .'[2]

Kingsley preached at the school, lectured on natural history and geology, cheered on their football games, and was an eager spectator at the Kingsley steeplechase. He tried to communicate his own enthusiasm for science, and the need for accurate habits of observation. In one of his lectures to the boys he said:

Ah, that I could make you understand what an interest that is. The interest of the health, the wealth, the wisdom of generations yet unborn. Ah, that I could make you understand what a noble thing it is to be men of science; rich with a sound learning which man can neither give nor take away; useful to thousands whom you have never seen, but who may be blessing your name hundreds of years after you are mouldering in the grave, the equals and the companions of the noblest and the most powerful. Taking a rank higher than even Queen Victoria herself can give, by right of that knowledge which is power.

There is little doubt that had Kingsley been acceptable to the Grenfells by birth and bank account he would have devoted himself to science.

Dr. Benson was not the only person to remember Kingsley's

flow of talk. Sir Charles Fox Bunbury said: 'Much as I like and admire his writings—to many of which I return again and again with great pleasure—his conversation was much more delightful than his books.' Sir Charles's country house was close enough to Cambridge for Kingsley to visit occasionally, but the two men, although more friendly after Kingsley became a professor, had met briefly in 1857, and became more closely acquainted in 1859. This had been on the occasion of a visit by Sir Charles and his wife to Sandhurst College, where his cousin, General William Napier, was in charge. The Bunburys were driven over to Bramshill Park, where Sir William Cope was entertaining the local hunt, but Sir Charles's chief pleasure that day was in meeting Kingsley again, whose books he already admired. Kingsley walked Sir Charles to the rectory to meet the family and have lunch, and impressed Sir Charles with his intimate knowledge of the botany and geology of the district. Kingsley was an enthusiast for his home region within a radius of about forty or fifty miles from Eversley.

In 1855 he and Sir John Lubbock[3] had discovered the fossilised remains of a musk-ox in a gravel pit of the Thames valley not far from Maidenhead Station. This was an important find, because it proved that the old river deposits had been laid down during Arctic conditions. Kingsley had made a particular study of local geology ever since, and as Sir Charles was a leading member of the Geological Society, of the Geographical Society and of the Linnaean Society, the two men found immediately that they had common interests. Susbsequent meetings confirmed Sir Charles in his liking for the rector, and he noted them down in his diary. 'We drove over to Eversley and had a delightful visit to the Kingsleys. I am more and more charmed with him in each successive visit. He is a truly noble man. And the extent and variety of his knowledge are astonishing. He is not only an eloquent preacher and moralist, a poet and a novelist, but an accomplished naturalist and antiquarian, an eager sportsman. What is he not? All that he says bears the stamp at once of great intellectual power and of a lofty and noble nature. Unfortunately, his health has suffered from too great exertion of mind, and the physicians have ordered him to write nothing for the next three years.[4] He talked much of Darwin's new book on Species, expressing great admiration for it, but saying that it was so startling that he had not yet been able to make up his mind as to its soundness. But were it merely as the result of thirty years' labour of such a man, he observed it ought to be treated with reverence. He said that he had himself been disposed to question the permanence of species, and on the same ground to which Darwin has attached so much importance, namely, the great variations produced in the domestic races, but the very startling conclusions which Darwin has deduced from this doctrine have shown him the necessity of examining very carefully all the grounds of the reasoning. He is much interested also in the questions of the flint "hatchets" or "arrow heads" in the drift.'[5]

In April 1860 the Kingsleys had spent ten days at Barton Hall, and Sir Charles's diary again records the pleasure he took in Kingsley's company. Sir Charles Lyell, the eminent geologist, was both a friend and a family connection of the Bunburys. T. H. Huxley was their valued friend. When Fanny Kingsley writes primly but proudly in her memoir of Kingsley that he became friendly with eminent men of science, she is telling the literal truth. Kingsley was never a snobbish tuft-hunter who had to angle for social invitations. His warm personality, his amusing, often Rabelaisian conversation, racy but never crude, given an unexpected titillation by the stammer, combined with his propensity to hold forth on any number of subjects, made him a fascinating addition to any dinner party.

In 1863 Kingsley was made a fellow of the Geological Society, proposed by Sir Charles Bunbury, seconded by Sir Charles Lyell. It was an honour which the rector found most satisfying, and a great comfort when he licked his wounds over the Dr. Pusey episode. Kingsley spent much time in studying the glacial deposits in the Bagshot Sands district, and planned to read a paper on that subject. Darwin's book, *The Fertilization of Orchids*, interested Kingsley, and he wrote to the author: 'Ah, that I could begin to study nature anew, now that you have made it to me a live thing, not a dead collection of means. But my work lies elsewhere now. Your work, nevertheless, helps mine at every turn.' Many of his scientific friendships originated in his reviews for magazines, and as he had no shyness in writing to strangers in as friendly a manner as if they had just met as guests at a luncheon party, his circle of pen-friends increased yearly. It was his comparative isolation at Eversley that forced his gregarious soul to compensate in extensive letter-writing.

The months sped by, with a short break at Whitchurch in the spring to give him a rest. He enjoyed fishing the trout streams around Whitchurch, and often fished the Test on Lord Portsmouth's estate. He used the area as background for some of the scenes in *Two Years Ago*. He stayed at The White Hart, an old coaching inn, waiting for Anthony Froude to join him for a few days' fishing. Pelting rain kept him marooned in the inn in a 'low room with a beautiful Queen Anne ceiling', where he looked out at the crossroads and wrote letters.

It is unlikely that he realised that in December 1832 John Henry Newman had sat in that very room, also awaiting a Froude—Anthony's elder brother, Hurrell, preparatory to their Mediterranean cruise. Even if he had, there was of course no reason why he should find it a literary coincidence, for in May 1863 there was no indication that within a year he and Newman would be joined in duel.

Mrs. Kingsley tactfully suggests that Kingsley was again in the throes of illness and depression by the beginning of 1864, but there is little sign of it during 1863. In fact, the opposite is indicated by a letter from Henry Kingsley to Daniel Macmillan. Henry had taken his mother to stay in London with Lord and Lady Chelsea[6] and he told Macmillan that Charles was considering a new historical novel, to be set in the Babylon of Nebuchadnezzar. 'I am glad he has got out of the absurd idea that it was *infra dig.* to write novels. As I pointed out to him on Sunday night, Cabinet Ministers did. A man who has forced his way to the front rank of literature must not throw literature overboard. It won't do. Besides, with his literary reputation, it is actually wicked not to make use of that reputation to increase his fortune. I told him so some time ago, and now the leaven has worked. I need not tell you how sacred this little confidence of mine is. Don't let him know that I have discussed the matter with you: but I think that he ought to come before the public again with some carefully finished work. It won't do for him to be forgotten.'[7]

Henry was proud of his elder brother. Although, as was proper for an affectionate son, Henry dedicated his first book to his parents, he prefaced his second novel, *Ravenshoe*, 'To my brother Charles Kingsley I dedicate this tale In token of a love which only grows stronger as we both get older.' Helped initially by Charles's literary contacts, Henry had succeeded in earning a modest living as a freelance writer. He contributed to magazines, and frequently visited London, where, being a pleasant and likeable man, he was soon at home among the writers and journalists of the capital.

Charles Kingsley had not abandoned paid writing when he ceased to write novels, but he tried to ration his articles and restrict them to completely non-controversial topics. He was interested when Tom Hughes and others financed a new magazine *The Reader*, which they hoped would be an independent journal, dealing with serious problems, with Ludlow as its editor. Some familiar Christian Socialist names appeared as contributors, Kingsley's among them, but Ludlow discovered that the editorship was too time-consuming and resigned. Kingsley did not feel he could work with the new editor, Gerald Masson, in quite the same way. 'He is a good fellow,' he wrote to Ludlow, 'but you—You are one of the dearest friends I have and a man whom I know I can say anything to, even if we differ. . . .'[8] Ludlow was quite a successful freelance journalist, in addition to his legal work, although his first interest remained politics. 'I can only conceive of literature as a relaxation from politics,' he once told Maurice. In this he differed from Kingsley, who made use of literature not as relaxation but as a medium for propagating his religious, social and political views.

At the end of 1863 Kingsley was asked if he would review the latest instalment of Anthony Froude's *History of England* for *Macmillan's Magazine*. Kingsley had recently been very careful not only what he wrote, but for which periodical he wrote, since his name was so well known, and the press often so antagonistic, that he had suffered merely by having his name associated with journals. *Macmillan's*, although Protestant, was fairly moderate in its religious outlook, but Kingsley had refused to contribute articles even to that magazine, although he considered that serialised fiction was safe enough. Hence, when asked to write this review, he briefly hesitated and finally consented only because the author was his close friend. He prepared and delivered his Cambridge lectures, and then returned to Eversley where he read Froude's Volumes VII and VIII with great interest and enjoyment, blithely tossed off his article and posted it to London.

Over the years Kingsley had become set in his habits of thought towards the Roman Catholic Church. Apart from his psychological aversion to it on the grounds of its considering celibacy a higher spiritual state than a normal sexual life, he, like many of his friends, viewed the Vatican under Pope Pius IX as denying nationalist aspirations and ignoring social abuses. Mazzini and Garibaldi, heroes to the Italian patriots, were heroes to Kingsley and his friends. If the Pope saw Garibaldi as an enemy then the Pope was wrong. Kingsley's opinions were reinforced by F. D. Maurice. In a letter to the Rev. R. C. Trench (another friend of Kingsley), Maurice said: 'I hate Popery in two ways: as anti-Protestant, that is to say, anti-national, adverse to national distinctions and life: and, secondly, as anti-Catholic, adverse to ecclesiastical unity and universality.'

This, then, was the background of Kingsley's thoughts about the Church of Rome when he reviewed Froude's books on Protestant Tudor England, and in a mood of jaunty euphoria the Protestant professor quite gratuitously flung in a careless and ill-researched jeer at Dr. Newman. Perhaps Kingsley thought he was indirectly getting at Dr. Pusey. In the case of the rector of Eversley, it was an example of pride going before a fall; the only time in his life that such an incident occurred, and the only time that he was to be exposed to ridicule at the hands of a master.

The offending passage in the review of the January 1864 issue of *Macmillan's Magazine* (which appeared in December 1863) was as follows: 'Truth, for its own sake, had never been a virtue with the Roman clergy. Father Newman informs us that it need not, and on the whole, ought not to be: that cunning is the weapon which heaven has given to the saints wherewith to withstand the brute male force of the wicked world which marries and is given in marriage.'

An anonymous friend sent Newman a copy of the magazine with Kingsley's review marked. The article was not signed with Kingsley's full name, only with the initials C.K., but his name was in the list of contributors printed on the cover of the magazine. In view of the article, its subject, the style, and the initials, it might be assumed that interested readers would realise that C.K. was probably Charles Kingsley, since no other article by him appeared in that issue. However, Newman maintained that when he was shown the article he did not realise that the initials referred to Charles Kingsley, and presumably the anonymous sender did not know either, or if he did, he did not inform Newman.

Newman wrote privately to Macmillans, to object to the use of his name and the statement, and Kingsley, being shown the letter, replied in a private letter to Newman. From this point onwards, of course, the identity of the reviewer was plain to him. Kingsley explained that his generalisation had been made as a result of years of reading Newman's writings, but that he had had in mind specifically a sermon called *Wisdom and Innocence*. This was a sermon which Newman had preached at Oxford when he was still a Protestant clergyman. His text was: 'Behold, I send you forth as sheep in the midst of wolves; be ye therefore wise as serpents, and harmless as doves.' Newman described some weak animals who compensated by fleetness or by 'some natural cunning', but he expressly pointed out that such methods were forbidden to men. Nowhere in this sermon could there be found a passage which could be construed as having the meaning which Kingsley so casually suggested.

Newman insisted upon something stronger than Kingsley's first, private, letter of apology, so he wrote a second, to be published if necessary in the magazine as a public retraction. It was a curiously worded, indeed ambiguous, note, and Newman at once realised with a thrill of excitement that here was his chance to make his countrymen (although he was French Huguenot on his mother's side, he felt himself to be firmly English) understand completely why he had been led in his search for religious truth to become a Roman Catholic.

It had not been easy for a man with Newman's gifts to live in virtual obscurity, as he had done since his conversion, shunned by many of his former friends and associates, disregarded by the English public at large, and with no preferment offered in recompense by his adopted Church. Henry Tristram, in his introduction to *The Living Thoughts of Cardinal Newman*, says, 'In reality he was a man of action forced by circumstances to become a man of letters.' That statement might equally well have been made of Kingsley, and indeed the two men shared certain characteristics. Newman, writing on a variety of subjects, had laid himself open to a charge of being superficial; so had Kingsley. Both men had suffered in their careers for many years because of their publicly expressed beliefs. Both were highly sensitive, given to bursts of emotion. Both were powerful preachers; had won respect; had written novels but were better poets than novelists. Both felt they had missions to fulfil; both were periodically assailed by doubts and loneliness, and needed the security of Scripture to regain their confidence; both were conservative in politics. It is by no means inconceivable that if Charles Kingsley had not met Fanny Grenville, and had remained a bachelor, he would not have become an Anglo-Catholic—he was always attracted by the style and ceremony of the Catholic service.[9]

Thus far we may trace likenesses between Newman and Kingsley, but in almost every other way they were complete opposites. If we follow the Coleridge line, that every man is a born Platonist or a born Aristotelian, then undoubtedly Kingsley and Maurice were Platonists and Newman was an Aristotelian. All three men derived part of their thinking from Coleridge. Charles Kingsley had a winning way with women, and often declared that women were often superior to men, by reason of their greater sensitivity and capacity for tenderness and compassion. John Henry Newman always kept himself aloof from women. As a young man, Newman, graceful, delicate and ascetic, had been closely drawn to Hurrell Froude, a brilliant but unsatisfied young man with (according to his diary) repressed sadistic and homosexual yearnings. Hurrell was instinctively attracted to a dogmatic, authoritarian type of church, and had he not died young would most probably have preceded Newman into the Catholic Church. There is no evidence of any relationship between Newman and Hurrell Froude which could not survive public scrutiny. Anthony Froude, who became something of a protégé of Newman's after Hurrell's death, would surely have been aware of it had it existed, and his admiration and respect for Newman would hardly have persisted. Newman did not share Kingsley's high regard for women, and certainly Newman disapproved of married clergy. In his witty novel of Oxford life, *Loss and Gain*, 1848, he had given an amusing but very unattractive picture of a young parson and his bride buying hymn books and tracts in a stationer's shop. An uxorious, John Bullish, Protestant parson, snug in the rectory with his wife and brood, lazily tolerant of liberal attitudes in the Church and in politics, even sympathetic to the extension of the franchise (surely only a short step to tolerating agnostics) was anathema to Newman. Ever since the 1830s, when the great liberal reforms were passed by Parliament, Newman had opposed the spread of liberalism in general, believing that it must pave the way for false thought, what he sometimes called Rationalism. He believed that Christianity was doomed if the Church were liberalised; that a revealed religion like Christianity was of necessity a dogmatic religion, and that the vague, broad and flexible Anglican Church did not possess powerful enough principles to resist the onslaught of liberalism. Here, of course, he took the opposite view to Maurice and Kingsley.

Newman had watched, helpless, the spread of liberal opinions throughout the educated laity, products of Dr. Arnold (who was at Oriel College, Oxford, before Newman), and of whom it was said, 'He wakes every morning with the impression that everything is an open question.' The result, as Newman saw it, was that at the worst liberals were sceptical of religion; at the best they were indifferent to it. In 1863 he wrote privately, not for publication, that only saints could long endure a life of obedience when it had to be performed 'amid darkness, dryness and dejection, and I shall think myself most highly favoured of the God of grace and truth if He shall enable me to suggest anything useful to any one soul who is under this special visitation. If I attain this object by lawful means, I shall not stand in need of any other consolation.'

There is evidence that about the time that Kingsley wrote his review for *Macmillan's Magazine* Newman was holding himself in readiness for some important occasion when it would be appropriate to speak out and justify himself and his adopted Church to his countrymen. What, then, could have been more providential, more poetically ironic, than that the chief protagonist of the socially conscious wing of the Anglican Church should blunder towards him, ready for sacrifice? Here was Newman's opportunity, and in the duel of wit and words that followed Newman deliberately exaggerated, making it appear as if he took Kingsley's remarks more seriously than he did. As he later admitted, experience had taught him (as it taught all propagandists) that the public only took notice when points were over-emphasised. Newman, then, knew exactly what he was doing, whilst an examination of Kingsley's letters and actions during this exchange can only lead one to suppose that the rector of Eversley never really understood what was happening. The celebrated *bon mot* is that Kingsley was the fly embodied in the clear amber of Newman's *Apologia pro Vita Sua;* but this was the final product. Long before that stage was reached, Kingsley had to be the fly enmeshed in the shining web of Newman's subtle arguments.

Since Newman was using Kingsley as an instrument, rather than a person, he did not feel anger or indignation against him as an individual. Writing late at night, at white heat, barely pausing to rest, Newman wrote the instalments of his *Apologia*. In its original form it contained the Newman/Kingsley exchanges, but these sections were dropped in subsequent editions, so that there finally remained only the autobiography of an honest man in search of truth,[10] to capture the sympathies of a fair-minded reading public.

In February 1864, however, the *Apologia* was unwritten, and the situation was still that of a battle of words in the press. Newman printed a pamphlet called *Mr. Kingsley and Dr. Newman*, with a dialogue which he invented and which was extremely amusing, provided of course one were not Mr. Kingsley. To quote Augustine Birrell, 'In sarcasm Dr. Newman is pre-eminent. . . . His sentences stab, his invective destroys.' The agnostic intelligentsia was amused at the spectacle of two serious priests, no longer young, jousting at one another in print. Then Newman found an unexpected ally in R. H. Hutton, editor of the *Spectator*, a Protestant who had always been sympathetic to the views of Maurice and Kingsley, but who had read many of Newman's writings and greatly admired his integrity and literary talent. Hutton feared that because Kingsley represented so wide a spectrum of British opinion regarding the Roman Catholic Church, Newman might not receive a fair hearing. Accordingly, Hutton now entered the fray, with encouragement for Newman. What had begun as a piece of slipshod writing by Kingsley was turning into a time bomb, ready to explode in his face.

Newman's taunts brought Kingsley up sharply, and in a pamphlet of his own he discussed more carefully some general accusations against the Catholic Church and against the doctrines and histories which were taught as true by Catholic leaders and accepted as true by Catholics. In support of these later arguments Kingsley offered further quotations from Newman, from his sermons and from the *Lives of the Saints*. Kingsley argued that a man writing in the 1840s a book which he knew was bound to have some influence upon Oxford and Cambridge undergraduates should have written of saints and miracles in a moderately scientific manner, to say the least. Kingsley disapproved of the implications in Newman's statement in the 'Advertisement' or Preface, to the *Life of St. Walburga*, where he said, in reference to the question of whether these miracles should be accepted as facts, '. . . and in this day and in our present circumstances, we can only reply, that there is no reason why they should not be.' In 1843, in a letter to John Keble, Newman had said that the *Lives of the Saints* would help to stabilise the minds of people who were likely to be speculative. This was precisely the kind of thing that irritated Kingsley most. However, in the intervening years Newman had changed his views, since he hints in his *Apologia* that these *Lives* could be taken poetically or mythically.

On social grounds Kingsley believed he had an even stronger case against the Catholic Church. Newman had written that it was right from a religious point of view to be more occupied with personal than with social issues, and that this was particularly the case in backward Latin countries—Italy, for example, in the first half of the nineteenth century. Kingsley, on the other hand, admired countries which developed civic institutions, enforced law and order, and encouraged citizens to be socially responsible. He considered that the absence of such features in Catholic countries was the result of 'positive hindrance' by the Roman Catholic Church. Kingsley was infuriated by the vagueness and exaggeration which he thought he could detect in some of Newman's addresses, and singled out a passage in which Newman suggested that a highly imperfect beggar woman who went regularly to Mass stood a better chance of going to Heaven than 'mere natural virtue'.

But none of these wider implications (where Kingsley could make out quite a good debating case) were in fact ever answered by Newman. In the anti-Kingsley appendages to the first version of the *Apologia* Newman avoided Kingsley's broader issues, and wisely confined himself to the one rash accusation which Kingsley had made against his personal truthfulness, and to the hasty mis-quotation on which Kingsley had based his case. F. D. Maurice, who understood Newman better than Kingsley did, was most unhappy about the controversy, being sure that it was only Newman's subtle language that led to the suspicion that he twisted facts to suit his purposes, and that at heart he was supremely truthful.[11]

Nothing now could halt events. Kingsley, honestly amazed by the unexpected fury of Newman's attack, quite baffled by his opponent's refusal to agree to differ and leave it at that, was at a disadvantage. Mrs. Kingsley tells us that mutual friends told Kingsley that Newman was ill—it is possible that they were referring to the weakness Newman was experiencing as he wrote his autobiography—and that in chivalrous manner Kingsley wished to terminate the debate. (It is a statement which has the ring of a loyal wife defending her husband's memory.) Of course, Newman needed to prolong the debate, in order to finish his justification, but Kingsley was in no position to realise this.

Kingsley's family and friends thought it advisable for the rector to be conveniently removed as quickly as possible from the painful and nerve-wracking situation, and as Froude was about to cross to France, *en route* for Spain, where he was going to engage in historical research, it seemed sensible that Kingsley should go with him. Froude therefore invited him, and Kingsley replied eagerly: 'Dearest Anthony, This is too delightful. I had meant to offer myself to you, but my courage failed; but when you propose what can I do but accept? . . . I am ready, for my part, not only to go to Madrid, but on by mail to Alicant, and then by steamer to Gibraltar, *via* Cathegan and Malaga, coming home by sea. I have always felt that one good sea voyage would add ten years to my life. All my friends say, go, but I must not be the least burden to you. Remember that I can amuse myself in any hedge, with plants and insects and a cigar, and that you may leave me anywhere, any long, certain that I shall be busy and happy. I cannot say how the thought of going has put fresh life into me.'[12]

The two men departed towards the end of March, much to the relief of Kingsley's circle, especially Fanny and his mother. The rector's first letters home showed how he had not lost the knack of shrugging off annoyance by plunging into new enjoyment. There was great interest to be found in the sunny view of the crowded Tuileries from the top of the Hotel Meurice in Paris, he wrote—and how small the world was, for he had met, quite by accident, his fossil-hunting companion, John Lubbock, who was preparing to look for more fossils in the caves of the Dordogne. Froude and Kingsley pushed on south-west, where the towns

and landscapes were quite new to Kingsley, but his vision and
pleasure were enhanced by the recollections of talks with Fanny
about her European tour. 'The air strangely clear, the houses
low-roofed, and covered with purple-ribbed tiles like the old
Roman. I saw in an instant what you mean by the colouring
of the south.'

Kingsley's letters home from his holidays were very often
composed partly as notes which could later form the basis of
saleable articles or lectures. His descriptions were rapid word
sketches, notebook jottings for later reference. 'Little long-
wooled sheep, cows you could put under your arm, boys on
stilts tending them, with sheepskin coats (wool outside) and
sheepskin pads for their poor feet, else they would have to have
them asked after if there was anyone to ask, which there ain't—
the only birds magpies. But thrivingness and improvement
everywhere; immense new plantations of the pinus, neat clearings
for cultivation, new smart cottages, beautiful new churches,
railway stations laid out with shrubberies of foreign trees.
What a go-ahead place France is! It gladdens my heart to look
at it.'

At Biarritz, however, Kingsley collapsed, quite unable to
meet the exertion of accompanying Froude into Spain. The
rector made light of his disability, anxious that his wife should
not worry about him. 'I shall stop here for a week or so, to
botanise and breathe sea-champagne; Tulk, who is an M.D., will
take care of me.' As he had done at Torquay, Kingsley pottered
about on the sea-shore, collecting sea creatures and plants when
he did not fall asleep on the sands. His martial spirit flickered
bravely as he gazed upon old battlefields of the Peninsular
War, and his thoughts went to the descendants of the Iron
Duke at Strathfieldsaye. Full and vivid as his letters were, they
breathed loneliness as well. 'A day as pleasant as one can be
without you.' 'God bless you. I wish I was home again.' 'Love
to the darlings. . . .' 'Tell Grenville. . . .' '. . . picked up little shells
for Mary', and in answer to a letter from Grenville there was a
special reply, its style ideally suited to an intelligent little boy,
signed, 'Your own Daddy, C. Kingsley.'

Three days in the Pyrenees, part driving, part easy walking, brought a short return to bodily health, but had a strange effect on his spirits. 'We had had a good deal of snow going up, but a good road cut through it for timber carts. We climbed three hundred feet of easy down, and there it was right in front, nine thousand feet high, with the winter snow at the base—the eternal snow holding on by claws and teeth where it could above. I could have looked for hours. I could not speak. I cannot understand it yet. Right and left were other eternal snow-peaks; but very horrible. Great white sheets with black points mingling with the clouds, of a dreariness to haunt one's dreams.'[13] Of course, it was Kingsley's first experience of such great mountains, and he was unprepared for them. It was, after all, only his second journey abroad.

South he went to Toulouse, and then to Marseilles—'this wonderful place, the new Paris and new Liverpool, which is rising round the old Phocoean city.' To his pleasure, he bumped into Fanny's brother-in-law, Henry Glyn, just arrived from Nice, though the encounter heightened his homesickness. 'Lyons tomorrow. There I shall hear from my darlings, of whom I dream every night.' Carcassone, Narbonne and Nîmes captivated him with their traces of history, back to the Romans. He revelled in the sunshine—'I shall come back to you a different man. My brain is getting quite clear and well.' As soon as he was strong enough, he hurried home, although not quite fit, as he wrote to Maurice—'not well, and unable to take any mental exertion.'

On his return, as if timed to coincide with his reappearance in England, came the publication of the final section of Newman's book, entitled *General Answer to Mr. Kingsley*. Alexander Macmillan sent Kingsley a copy of all the sections published by Longmans, with the comment that he thought Kingsley ought to read it all through, and he, Macmillan, believed Kingsley would find it 'soothing'. Kingsley read it immediately, and at last wrote to Macmillan, inviting him to show that letter as his 'ultimatum on the Newman question' to anyone Macmillan chose, including Hutton. On his own ground Kingsley remained firm, finding it impossible, he told Macmillan, to understand a man who finally had to believe in 'the Infallibility of one Church, and in the Immaculate Conception.'

Editions of the *Apologia pro Vita Sua* after 1865 omit the sections about Charles Kingsley. Newman wrote in his preface that he would 'vanquish, not my Accuser, but my judges', and so it turned out. The reception of his book, especially by Protestants, was 'a wonderful deliverance'. The sympathy and admiration given to Newman now by liberals and intellectuals were for reasons largely outside Kingsley's comprehension. The far wider criticisms of the Catholic Church advanced by Kingsley, and never answered by Newman, remained in essence criticisms which most of the educated laity of Kingsley's day continued to find valid.

R. H. Hutton, writing just before Newman's death, and about fifteen years after the death of Kingsley, said, 'But there was something headlong about Kingsley, as there is something essentially reserved and reticent about Newman, and there, I fancy, was the secret of the repulsion between them. Kingsley's ideal always tended somewhat towards surrender to the glory of action and passion, towards embodiment in life, towards glow, and emphasis, and self-expansion. He had an odd theory, too, that a hearty English squire who does his duty, not only to the land, but to the tenants and the labourers on his estate, is the nearest thing to a saint which the world can produce, and it is not easy to imagine any ideal more different than Newman's. As far as I can judge, Kingsley and Newman have both been supremely truthful men, and Newman, I should say, though far the subtler and less easily understood of the two, not by any means less truthful than his rather random assailant.'[14]

Fenton Hort, who was deeply influenced by the life and teachings of Maurice and of Kingsley, could not help saying, 'Kingsley was much to blame for his recklessly exaggerated epigram, though it had but too sad a foundation of truth. Newman's reply, however, was sickening to read, from the cruelty and insolence with which he trampled on his assailant. Kingsley's rejoinder was bad enough, but not so horribly unchristian.'[15] Yet Newman in general shrank from inflicting pain, and his treatment of Kingsley was not meant to be personally vindictive.

Anthony Froude was probably in the best position to judge both men. He had told Kingsley that although Newman was supremely truthful on the personal level, 'No sane person could ever have divined the workings of his mind, or could have interpreted them otherwise than you, in common with so many others, did.' Writing twenty years later, after Kingsley's death, and trying like Hutton to assess the 'contest', if it could be called one, Froude wrote, 'Kingsley, in truth, entirely misunderstood Newman's character. Newman's whole life had been a struggle for truth. He had neglected his own interests; he had never thought of them at all. He had brought to bear a most powerful and subtle intellect to support the convictions of a conscience which was superstitiously sensitive. His single object had been to discover what were the real relations between man and his Maker, and to shape his own conduct by the conclusions at which he arrived. To represent such a person as careless of truth was neither generous nor even reasonable. . . .

'Kingsley, however, had passed through his own struggles. He, too, had been affected at a distance by the agitations of the Tractarian controversy. He, like many others, had read what Newman had written about ecclesiastical miracles. The foundations of his own faith had been disturbed. He was a man of science; he knew what evidence was. He believed that Newman's methods of reasoning confounded his perceptions of truth, disregarding principles which alone led to conclusions that could be trusted in other subjects, and which, therefore, he could alone trust in religion. His feelings had been, perhaps, embittered by the intrusion of religious discord into families in which he was interested, traceable all of it to the Oxford movement. He himself had determined to try every fact which was offered for his belief by the strict rules of inductive science and courts of justice; and every other method appeared to him to be treason to his intellect and to reduce truth, where truth of facts was before everything essential, to the truth of fable, of fiction, or emotional opinion.'[16]

We can be fairly sure that Kingsley did not bear any lasting grudge against Newman. Sir William Cope, who was a friend and admirer of Newman's, and often tried to act as a kind of intermediary between Newman and Kingsley (not, however, in the controversy), lent Kingsley a collection of Newman's poems in 1868, including *The Dream of Gerontius*. In his letter of thanks, Kingsley praised that poem in cordial and generous terms. He found the theme true and noble: the deepest longing of the soul to see God; and the poem filled him with 'awe' and 'admiration'. 'I am thankful to any man, who under any parabolic, or even questionably true forms, will teach that to a generation which is losing more and more the sense of reverence, and beginning confessedly to hate excellence for its own sake, as the Greeks ostracised Aristides, because they were tired of hearing him called the Just.'

The year 1864 was remembered in the Kingsley family less for the Newman controversy than for a happy personal event nearer home—Henry Kingsley's marriage. Although Henry had made himself a fairly respected novelist and writer, it did not bring him much money, and he was becoming reconciled to remaining a shy bachelor. He had little confidence in himself as a ladies' man, feeling that after all he was rather an ugly fellow at whom no woman would glance twice. His good friend, Henry Campbell, who had been in Australia with him, had for several years acted as a kind of literary secretary and adviser, rather as Fanny did to Charles, but Campbell felt it was time to return to Australia. The prospective loss of his friend forced Henry to realise how lonely he would be once Campbell had gone. Emotionally and mentally he was prepared for marriage, and, moreover, he had already met an attractive young woman likely to accept him. She was Sarah Maria Kingsley Haselwood, just twenty-two, the governess for the rector's children at Chelsea Rectory. Henry had first encountered the family on his sudden return to England, when he called at Chelsea Rectory, expecting to find his parents still there. The visit had begun a pleasant friendship with them.

The Kingsley in Sarah's name was no coincidence, for she was, on her mother's side, a distant cousin. She was intelligent and interested in books, admired Henry as a literary man, and was probably also impressed by the glamour of the relationship with Charles Kingsley. In his novel, *Silcotes of Silcote*, Henry Kingsley describes a young governess who resembles Sarah Haselwood: 'Here she was, and one must make the best of her; beautiful, attractive, boisterous, noisy; ready at any moment to enter into an animated and friendly discussion with a policeman, or for that matter a chimney-sweep; with a great tendency to laugh loudly at the smallest ghost of a joke . . . a mass of kindliness, vitality, and good-humour. . . .' Henry, a man who had roughed it in the colonies, found the girl's breezy sauciness distinctly appealing. Nor was she in any way stupid, and proved herself a very able assistant in her husband's literary projects.

The wedding took place at St. Mary's, Brompton, on July 19, 1864, and the party returned to Chelsea Rectory for the wedding breakfast. Charles and Fanny Kingsley, Dr. George Kingsley and his wife Mary, old Mrs. Kingsley, and the various children, were among the thirty odd guests. George Kingsley had a particularly warm regard for his brother Henry, and when he went on his frequent trips abroad, usually as physician companion to rich noblemen, he had the habit of placing his financial affairs temporarily in Henry's hands. Henry would thus look after his brother's household expenses until George returned to settle up. Nor was this assistance limited to money matters. George could take off for foreign parts in the knowledge that his wife and children could always turn to Henry in any emergency. It may well have been the grateful recollection of this brotherly assistance that led George Kingsley to exclaim on one occasion that it was Henry who was the great man, not Charles.

Henry's wedding day was a happy occasion. In the afternoon the guests went into the garden and played croquet. Everyone felt that there was something both romantic and sentimental in Henry setting out as a married man from the very house which had been his boyhood home. Henry did not intend to continue living in his mother's cottage, and he rented a house at Wargrave, on the River Thames, not far from Eversley. Fanny and Charles undertook the major responsibility for old Mrs. Kingsley, who soon afterwards moved permanently into Eversley Rectory.

It is most probable, although Fanny Kingsley is too discreet to say so in her book, that she at least was relieved that Henry and his bride were going to live outside Eversley. In her zealous safeguarding of Charles's energies she was a determined wife, and rightly so, for he was always prone to extreme over-exertion, and at forty-five was no longer the 'wild man of the woods'. Henry, on the other hand, was still vigorous, with much more leisure than the rector, and as for his wife, she was nearly thirty years younger than Fanny. With a generation separating them, and an abyss of social background (both Charles and Fanny deeply deplored Sarah's mother, Mrs. Haselwood, a widow, who soon looked upon Henry Kingsley as her meal ticket), it is not surprising that Fanny and Sarah Kingsley never became friends.

Charles devoted the rest of 1864, outside his normal parish duties, to preparing his Cambridge lectures and writing his university sermons, for he had been deeply gratified at being chosen as one of the preachers for the university for 1865. He took David, the Old Testament king, as his subject, since David had long been one of his heroes, and began accumulating notes for the sermon. He was only too well aware that his critics would follow his Cambridge sermons as assiduously as they read his lectures, and with the same idea in mind—to find some evidence of his unfitness to do whatever he happened to be doing at that time. Taking pot shots at the Rev. Charles Kingsley in 1864 was almost a fashionable pursuit.

A selection of his early Cambridge lectures was published in 1864 under the title *The Roman and the Teuton*, and brought Kingsley his worst press yet. Phrases and concepts which had sounded perfectly sensible, if not significant, when delivered in Kingsley's highly individual manner, were in cold print susceptible to all manner of academic criticism. The large-hearted professor was upset that so much of this criticism was what he considered to be niggling and petty. His opponents went to inordinate lengths to prove that his spelling of medieval German names was dubious. Kingsley's shortcomings, so recently made prominent in the Newman debate, were revealed again. E. A. Freeman, writing in the *Saturday Review*, a noted historian who would have appreciated Kingsley's Cambridge professorship for himself, attacked *The Roman and the Teuton* quite viciously, and for several years to come, no matter what subject he wrote upon, included sneers at Kingsley, at the Christian Socialists, and at the presumed ethos of the 'muscular Christians'. Kingsley's lectures, declared Freeman, were not history in the academic meaning of the word, because 'pages on pages of these lectures are simply rant and nonsense—history, in short, brought down to the lowest level of the sensation novelist.' A review in *The Times*, which Fanny Kingsley told F. D. Maurice was, she believed, written by a Mr. Woodham, a disappointed candidate for Kingsley's professorship, was just as acid.

Kingsley was definitely wounded by these reviews. He did his best as a history lecturer, spending as much as nine months of the year researching material for his lectures. His classes were crowded, students attending even when his lectures were not required for their courses. He was always ready to help students, to see them, and talk with them, and he would be glimpsed on the towpath, cheering on the boats. He realised his deficiencies as a historian, however, and clever, derisive reviews sapped his self-confidence. If he could have made up the Cambridge lecture fees in some other fashion, he would have resigned that year, but as long as the family needed the money, he felt bound to continue. In this he was encouraged by his friends at the universities, men like Anthony Froude and Max Müller, who had also borne their share of criticism, but did not take it so greatly to heart.

Kingsley's most truly satisfying relaxation was still science, in various aspects. He took the time to attend scientific meetings, and was gratified to be instantly recognised. He described himself modestly and truthfully as a 'camp-follower of science', pointing out that he, and others like him, contributed, however humbly, to the main body of scientific knowledge. He needed no urging by Fanny to refrain from all unnecessary emotional excitement and keep aloof from all controversial and political issues. His fingers had been well burnt by Dr. Newman. Science, though, was satisfying, and soothing.

He made few public comments on the American Civil War, now drawing to a close, although his sympathies remained with the South. He had convinced himself that victory for the South would in the long run benefit the negro, just as defeat of the kind of profit-seeking democracy which he considered the North to be must surely in the end benefit humanity. It was sad that the Civil War continued to deepen the gulf that had been opening up between him and his Christian Socialist friends. To his dismay, even F. D. Maurice finally came out for the North. Maurice's espousal of the Northern cause was a real blow to Kingsley, because both men had for years taken the same deprecating view of American industrial democracy. As for slavery, although in *Two Years Ago* Kingsley had made one of his minor heroes an abolitionist, he could never bring himself quite to feel that black men were the equals in intelligence or moral perception of white men. This is not the same as saying that he believed black races were predestined to be for ever inferior to white: but that he believed as far as he could see in his lifetime they were, for all practical purposes, inferior.

He toyed with the theory that the reason for white supremacy, by which he meant European and American supremacy, from the sixteenth century to the nineteenth, was because the geographical and climatic conditions of the homelands of these white races fostered the development of active, ambitious men and women. Black and brown peoples, living in enervating climates and luxuriant, fertile regions, were supplied too easily by Nature with the necessaries of life, so they had no need to struggle for existence, and were as a consequence usually weak, primitive and superstitious. This theory explained, to his satisfaction, the swift success of the Spaniards in Central America in the sixteenth century—the Indians were already in decline. From this, Kingsley further deduced that the conquest of the Indians by the Spaniards was an essential part of the divine plan for the development and civilising of mankind. He did not always take his ideas to their logical conclusions. He enjoying posing questions, but often did not stay for an answer.

He certainly never went as far as his brother Henry, who, in a light-hearted digression in *The Recollections of Geoffry Hamlyn*, imagined the pleasures of slave-ownership. The scene is the cool verandah of Captain Brentwood's sheep station on a burning hot Australian day:

Any man once getting footing there, and leaving it, except on compulsion, would show himself of weak mind. Any man once comfortably settled there in an easy chair, who fetched anything for himself when he could get any one else to fetch it for him, would show himself, in my opinion, a man of weak mind. One thing only was wanted to make it perfect, and that was niggers. To the winds with *Uncle Tom's Cabin*, and *Dred* after it, in a hot wind! What can an active-minded, self-helpful lady like Mrs. Stowe, freezing up there in Connecticut, obliged to do something to keep herself warm,— what can she, I ask, know about the requirements of a southern gentleman when the thermometer stands at 125° in the shade? Pish! Does she know the exertion required for cutting up a pipe of tobacco in a hot north wind? No! Does she know the amount of perspiration and anger superinduced by knocking the head off a bottle of Bass in January? Does she know the physical prostration which is caused by breaking up two lumps of hard white sugar in a pawnee before a thunderstorm? No, she doesn't, or she would cry out for niggers with the best of us! When the thermometer gets over 100° in the shade, all men would have slaves if they were allowed. An Anglo-Saxon conscience will not, save in rare instances, bear a higher average heat than 95°.[17]

It is probably safest to take this passage as ruefully humorous than as self-revealing, but it must be indicative of some Kingsley family feeling. Charles Kingsley did not forget, any more than his brother did, that on their mother's side they were descended from plantation slave-owners and that until 1833 slavery was an economic factor in running the family estate. Charles accepted the morality of emancipation but bemoaned the fact that his family had suffered financially therefrom, and apparently he saw no contradiction in these two attitudes. When an organisation to aid former slaves approached him for a donation, and he noticed that Tom Hughes was one of the sponsors, he informed Hughes sharply that the Kingsleys had paid their debt in that respect, and he did not feel called upon to pay any more.

In general terms, Kingsley agreed that American life in all its facets ought to be better understood in England so that when a Mr. Yates Thompson of Liverpool, thinking along similar lines, offered to finance a lecturership in American History at Cambridge, the lecturers to be supplied by Harvard University, Kingsley became one of the most enthusiastic and energetic supporters of the proposal. His fellow supporters were mainly liberals who wanted to see the North win the Civil War, but Kingsley did not regard this as any reason to withdraw. However, the ultra-conservative element in Cambridge rallied all its votes against the lectureship, and the proposal was rejected in case foreign radicalism and 'self-conceit' (this last was commonly held by the British upper class to be one of America's worst failings) should contaminate Cambridge. Once again Kingsley had found himself in a minority group, too advanced for his university.

The English Patriot

Fanny Kingsley realised that the Cambridge lectures were very exhausting for Charles, but she encouraged him to continue for a year or two longer, especially as Maurice Kingsley was in his last year at Wellington College and would be going on to Cambridge. She was sure that Charles would enjoy showing off the university to his elder son. Besides, the only alternative to the lectures, and the income they produced, was another long novel, which she feared would be even more tiring than the preparation of the lectures themselves. Meanwhile, they both hoped that Charles's university sermons would not be subjected to the academic strictures which had been applied to his lectures. The young men at the university did not criticise him harshly, and it was after all the young men who formed his congregation.

Fanny Kingsley was in seventh heaven as she wrote happily to John Martineau,[1] 'The University sermons were so successful, such noble sermons to such a glorious congregation—the object of my greatest ambition achieved—hearing him preach to the undergraduates in that pulpit of St. Mary's.'[2] When as older men these same undergraduates looked back to their university days, it was often Kingsley whom they recalled most vividly. Evelyn Shuckburgh remembered waiting in the throng of students for the church doors to open so that they could surge forward to claim the best seats. Dr. Stubbs, in his memoir of Kingsley published in 1899, recalled his first Sunday in Cambridge, and could still seem to hear that expectant hush as Kingsley entered, his face deeply lined for a man in his mid-forties, and with that strange intonation that made him a speaker not easily forgotten. His audience listened closely, and a thrill of half-expectation, half-amusement rippled round the church as he uttered the words, 'We have heard much of late about Muscular Christianity. . . .'

That phrase, apparently first used by T. C. Sandars, who contributed to the *Saturday Review*,[3] and taken up by many others, was an unwelcome label so far as Kingsley was concerned, rather as the 'Tom Brown' label was highly unwelcome for Tom Hughes. Although there was an element of appropriateness in each case, the underlying derision was unfair and hurtful. Certainly the picture of a 'muscular Christian' had no room for the sensitive, almost feminine, tenderness which was a very prominent feature of Kingsley's character. The rector detested the phrase, and in this sermon hoped to bury it. It could mean, he declared, this 'clever expression, spoken in jest by I know not whom', one of two things. The first was a healthy and manly Christianity, which did not exalt the feminine virtues to the exclusion of the masculine, one which led in the Middle Ages to the ideal of chivalry, and which contained the germ of Protestantism that conquered at the Reformation. The second meaning Kingsley considered to be untrue and immoral, and he did not elaborate upon it, except to warn his young congregation that the lesson they should draw from it was that self-control was the first and last of the virtues and graces.

David was his pattern of the heroic, God-fearing man. Kingsley described him as

> . . . warrior, statesman, king, poet, prophet. A man of many joys and many sorrows, many virtues and many crimes; but through them all, every inch a man. A man—heaped by God with every gift of body, and mind, and heart, and especially with strong and deep intense feeling. Right or wrong, he is never hard, never shallow, never light-minded. He is in earnest. Whatever happens to him, for good or evil, goes to his heart, and fills his whole song, till it comes out again in song.

Kingsley was tired by June, and the family took a holiday on the Norfolk coast, where he and the children could wander along the beaches. They made occasional excursions to towns like

John Stuart Mill, by G. F. Watts

J. H. Newman in 1868

Ely and King's Lynn, and of course as chaplain to the Prince of Wales Kingsley was invited to the prince's estate at Sandringham. There is a glimpse of the rector in these exalted social surroundings in Sir Charles Bunbury's diary: 'Kingsley said that the Prince and Princess of Wales in their house at Sandringham are most kind and pleasant hosts, very attentive to the comfort of their guests, and very simple and natural in their manners.'[4]

The Kingsleys returned to Eversley refreshed and ready to cope with the visit of Queen Emma of the Sandwich Islands.[5] The queen was recently widowed, and Kingsley had met her at Ely, where she was the guest of Lady Jane Franklin, widow of Sir John Franklin, the Arctic explorer. Kingsley knew Lady Franklin because she had donated many of her late husband's mementoes to the Wellington College museum. Queen Emma's son, had he lived, would have been sent to Wellington College. The queen was very interested to meet the author of *The Water-Babies*, which her husband used to read to their son, and when Kingsley learned that she was going to visit the Tennysons on the Isle of Wight he suggested hospitably that she should break her journey at Eversley and see how an ordinary Anglican clergyman and his family lived. It would also give her a chance to visit Wellington College.

The Kingsleys soon found that it was more taxing to entertain royalty, however unpretentious the royal personage might be, than foreign literary celebrities. Local gentry was shamelessly solicited for gifts of game, fruit and flowers ('Lord Eversley's grapes and Melon were magnificent'). Charles and Fanny met the queen's train at Wokingham Station, in company with Eversley villagers who tried not to show surprise at the queen's Lady-in-Waiting—'an enormous Dark (not to say Black) lady,' wrote Fanny to a friend. As the party climbed into the waiting carriages, the rain began to pour down, so that it was impossible even to glimpse the countryside from the carriage windows. Lunch was taken at Wellington College, where the cricket match was held, in spite of the pouring rain. Maurice Kingsley was in the team, to the pride of his father.

Then off to the rectory for a rest, and supper, Mary and

Grenville waiting at the rectory door to present the queen with a bouquet. The Kingsley china service was inadequate for such a grand party of guests, and Fanny had to make do with her drawing-room display china for the dessert, and rise early the next morning to help tidy and dust and put the china back in its show cupboard. By the time the guests left after lunch the following day the rector was longing for peace and quiet, although Fanny, in common with most of the villagers, had enjoyed the break in country routine.

Kingsley began to be conscious of the loss of friends. Old Judge Erskine, one of his father-figures in Eversley, whose companionship had been dear to him, died—though at his age death was to be expected. But almost within months his son, Henry, died, a man not much older than Charles. He wrote sadly to Tom Hughes that Henry Erskine's death made him value more greatly the friendship of his contemporaries, and Tom himself perhaps most of all. Kingsley's circle of close friends of his own age was not very large. It included Cowley Powles, his faithful friend to the last, his Cambridge friends, and the Christian Socialists from the 1848 days. His friends on Fanny's side were inevitably older than he, since Fanny was his senior, and the youngest of a large family; her relatives and acquaintances were nearly a generation his senior. The men Kingsley met as a professor at Cambridge were either older than he, men of substance and standing, or else students nearly young enough to be his sons. He had, like many busy breadwinners, made few close friends after passing the age of thirty, although he had as wide a circle of pen acquaintances and friends as anyone in England.

It was therefore all the more unfortunate for him personally that in the winter of 1865 he became involved in a new controversy which earned him the opprobrium of some of his oldest friends, dividing him very sharply, indeed permanently, from John Ludlow and Tom Hughes. It was connected with the action taken by Sir John Eyre, then Governor of Jamaica, in quelling a native insurrection.

Eyre, a one-time explorer in Australia, and a former Governor of New Zealand, had been sent out to Jamaica in 1862 as a temporary replacement for the then governor, Sir Charles Darling, who was going on leave. When Sir Charles did not return, Eyre was ordered to remain as governor. The situation in the island was by no means settled, for the economy had never been properly organised after the emancipation of the slaves, and by the 1860s there was extreme unemployment and poverty among the black Jamaicans. This situation was exacerbated by Government-sponsored immigration of Indian and Chinese labour to work on the plantations. There were no government plans for work and education of the Jamaicans, and the negroes had many well-justified grievances. When Eyre arrived he made a quick and unimaginative assessment of the unrest in the island, concluding that much of the rebellious talk was stirred up by Baptist missionaries. Governor Eyre was a stiff-necked Anglican, with strong prejudices against non-conformists, and he decided on very poor evidence that George William Gordon, a coloured Baptist preacher from Kingston, was the chief instigator of the unrest.

Eyre's officials advised him that a general uprising was imminent, an alarming prospect on an island where blacks outnumbered whites by thirty to one, particularly since a black rebellion had broken out on the neighbouring island of Haiti. The British government had sent a ship on loan to the Haitian authorities to help contain the rebellion, and this left Jamaica relatively unprotected, with one small ship and hardly more than a handful of regular soldiers. Some protest meetings were held on the island, and Eyre, hearing of these, immediately condemned them as seditious, heralding the start of an uprising. He acted with over-zealous promptitude, gave his officers considerable latitude in shooting and hanging blacks and setting fire to their houses. He was utterly convinced that he was acting for the best. In his report he wrote: 'So widespread a rebellion and one so effectually put down is not, I believe, to be met with in history, and speaks volumes for the zeal, courage, and energy of those engaged in suppressing it.'[6]

History has not vindicated the governor over the Jamaica Massacres and the summary trial and execution of George

William Gordon. Questions were asked publicly in Britain
about Eyre's conduct, just as they had been asked about Rajah
Brooke's conduct in Borneo, and people took sides, as convinced
of the justice of their cause as they had been over the head-hunters
and 'blood-money'. Queen Victoria followed the business closely.
Edward Cardwell, Colonial Secretary, sent copies of Eyre's private
letters to Sir Charles Phipps, the Queen's secretary, for her to read.
'They contain abundance of assertion of organised conspiracy to
massacre all the white and coloured inhabitants, but nothing in the
nature of proof: and I fear that it will not be easy to justify what has
been done.'[7] By December 7th the Colonial Secretary was writing
formally to the Queen about the need to appoint a Commission
of Enquiry to proceed to Jamaica. Eyre had to be present on the
island to reply to questions, but he could not continue as governor,
and Sir Henry Storks, governor of Malta, was made temporary
governor of Jamaica and instructed to head the Commission.

The Queen read through the documents with deep interest,
and let it be known that she found Cardwell's dignified summary
of the case 'excellent'. Sir Charles Phipps wrote: 'Whatever
may be the result of the inquiry, there can be no question that
the tone of some of the letters is, to say the least of it, exceedingly
to be regretted. It is curious that on not one of these papers is
there the slightest appearance of an expectation that anything
that had been done could be questioned in England. On the
contrary, the only anxiety appeared to be to claim the largest
share in acts which are here supposed to entail so heavy a
responsibility.'[8]

John Stuart Mill led the protests in England over Eyre's
behaviour, making the point that men who apparently could not
conceive of negroes as being human beings like themselves
ought not to be allowed power over them in colonial administration. Thomas Carlyle, predictably, was the first to thunder in
defence of Eyre. As far back as December 1849 Carlyle had held
forth on Jamaica, insisting that the island's problems were due to
the natural laziness of the blacks. His views, published in *Fraser's*,
as one of the 'Latter Day Pamphlets', were set forth in his
Occasional Discourse on the Nigger Question, and he spoke for many

people in England at that time. His views were widely circulated among Colonial Office civil servants, and not surprisingly influenced Colonial Office policy. Both Mill and Carlyle, of course, took their stand before the findings of Cardwell's commission were published in April 1866. From this report it appeared that Eyre had maintained martial law for the maximum period of two months. Five hundred and eighty-six 'rebels' had been executed. Floggings were too numerous to be counted. Over a thousand houses belonging to 'suspects' had been burned. The Commission concluded that Eyre had been too severe; that Gordon's trial had been illegal and his execution unjust.

Mill, who was then an M.P., denounced Eyre in the House of Commons. The government dismissed Eyre and withheld his pension, but Mill, in no way appeased, began to rally support to bring a law suit against Eyre for murder. The Jamaica Committee formed in London for this purpose included, besides Mill, Ludlow and Hughes, T. H. Huxley and Herbert Spencer, among others. It led to a counter-committee, the Eyre Defence Fund, which numbered Carlyle, Tennyson, Sir Charles Lyell, Ruskin, and later Henry and Charles Kingsley, although Charles tried to keep his name from appearing publicly.

Henry Kingsley was one of the most enthusiastic supporters, because it so happened that he had for long admired John Eyre, and had written a gripping account of the explorations round the Great Australian Bight which Eyre had undertaken in 1840-1841, during his career there as a sheep farmer. In those days Eyre had earned considerable respect as a defender of the rights of the Australian aborigine. Henry was working on a literary project about Australian explorers, and had in 1862 completed an article entitled *Eyre's March*. It was not published until October 1865, in *Macmillan's Magazine*, and he had assumed without checking that Eyre was dead. It was a considerable surprise to him to find that in that same month not only was his hero alive but he was being accused of actions which seemed quite impossible to reconcile with the character of the explorer. As might be expected, Henry threw himself into the Eyre controversy, embarking upon correspondence in *The Times*. He wrote to Alexander

Macmillan: 'Meanwhile our poor Eyre is in a great mess. There is no disguising it. The next time I am made Governor of Jamaica they shall burn the island about my ears before *I* begin to stop them. There shall be nothing like promptitude or vigour about *my* proceedings. Not a shot shall be fired until I have written home and got instructions. But then I shall be gibbeted just the same by the other party. I suppose, by the way, that I shall have a twister from *The Saturday* about this business. I must endeavour to survive it.'[9] Charles Kingsley was easily brought round to agree with his brother. In Charles's eyes Eyre was merely copying Rajah Brooke: even, one might say, behaving like Raleigh in Ireland. Possibly, had Kingsley lived in London, closer to the heart of information, and not relatively isolated in Eversley, he might have at least refrained from taking sides at all. His deepest instincts, however, unhindered by facts, made him support the governor.

In August 1866 Eyre returned to Britain. He was dignified, accepted responsibility for giving the orders, and retired to the Conservative rural fortress of Shropshire, where he lived quietly without taking any part in the debates which centred around him. Mill tried for another two years to get at Eyre, only to discover that the government, whatever its complexion,[10] protected Eyre by means of judicial decisions and rulings. Finally, the Jamaica Committee was disbanded and the matter dropped. In 1872 the Commons voted to pay compensation to Eyre to cover his legal costs in cases brought against him by the Jamaica Committee, and in 1875 he was given back his pension rights.[11]

Charles Kingsley in 1866 would have been bound to identify with Governor Eyre in his difficult situation. As descendants of West Indian plantation-owners, both Charles and Henry felt sympathy with the complaints and apprehensions of the white community in Jamaica. The Eyre debates formally snapped Kingsley's last slender link of friendship with Ludlow, who wrote coldly in 1865, after the Eyre Defence Fund was started, and Ludlow had noticed Kingsley's name in support, that their paths had diverged so much that it was useless to continue corresponding. Although Ludlow did not say so, he could not help being influenced by the knowledge that as Kingsley became more of a literary lion, so he appreciated less and less any criticisms of his writings and ideas, however well meant. Kingsley replied, with dignity and sadness, that he regretted Ludlow's decision, but would continue to value the memories of their past association.[12]

Unlike Ludlow, who took a rigid position, Kingsley was tolerant towards people whom he respected but whose views differed from his own. Henry Dunn, an author of religious studies, recalled how, on a long walk around Eversley, Kingsley talking to him the entire time, they passed a farm-worker labouring in the field. Charles pointed this man out to Dunn, with the comment, 'He is one of my dissenting parishioners, a Baptist and a high Calvinist. He is ignorant and often mistaken in his interpretations of Scripture, but I honour him. He is a good man, well acquainted with his Bible, and conscientiously living according to the light he has. Why should we quarrel?'

Tom Hughes sympathised with Ludlow over his disappointment at finding Kingsley on the opposite side in the Eyre affair, but he did not go to the extent of breaking off relations, although he saw less and less of Kingsley from this time. He agreed with Ludlow that Charles was very sensitive to what people thought of him—he freely confessed this weakness himself—but Hughes admired him for not being warped by it, a man 'who wavered less in saying or doing the word or thing which he felt it was true and right to say or do, looking the storm, which he knew it would bring about his ears, straight in the face all the time.' Hughes knew that Charles had been bred in the gentry tradition, where a man paid great attention to what Lord A. and Lady B. said about him and his actions, and he gave full credit to his strength of character in going against the training and teaching of his boyhood.

Even if all three men had reacted the same way on the Eyre controversy, their preoccupations gave them less and less spare time to meet as they had done when they were younger. Hughes was a Member of Parliament as well as a barrister ('Vote for

Tom Brown,' his election posters had said, much to his annoyance) and he and Ludlow worked hard for the co-operative movement, taking on many speaking engagements throughout the country. Kingsley's time was also heavily subscribed, and each year he needed several weeks of enforced leisure when he could recuperate. Their activities would have parted them anyway. Sir Charles Bunbury was another of Kingsley's friends who disagreed with him over Eyre. Sir Charles wrote in his diary, after Kingsley's death, 'I think him mistaken and even inconsistent with himself in the view he took of the Civil War in America, and seriously mistaken about Governor Eyre. But in both cases, supposing he *was* mistaken, I believe he was misled by a chivalrous feeling.'

That Kingsley felt warmly over Eyre there is no doubt whatsoever. He wrote in October 1866, to a Mr. T. Dixon, a corkcutter of Sunderland, with whom he carried on a lengthy correspondence, mainly on very practical agricultural topics, 'I do not quite understand the end of your letter, in which you are kind enough to compliment me for following Carlyle's advice about one "sadly tried". I *have* followed the sage of Chelsea's teaching, about my noble friend, ex-Governor Eyre of Jamaica. I have been cursed for it, as if I had been a dog, who had never stood up for the working man when all the world was hounding him down in 1848–9, and imperilled my own prospects in life in behalf of freedom and justice. Now, men insult me because I stand up for a man whom I believe ill-used, calumniated, and hunted to death by fanatics. If you mean Mr. Eyre in what you say, you indeed will give me pleasure, because I shall see that one more "man of the people" has common sense to appreciate a brave and good man, doing his best under terrible difficulties; but if not, I know that I am right.'

Still, the Eyre matter was only one of Kingsley's extensive interests, and Ludlow appears to have been the only person to make a ceremonious break over it. Ludlow indeed regretted this impulse in later years, and was glad that when they next met (it was at Maurice's funeral) they could be on perfectly friendly terms.

This was the time when Kingsley wrote the last of his novels—
Hereward the Wake, 'Last of the English', dedicated to Thomas
Wright, the historian who had disinterred Hereward 'long ago,
when scarcely a hand or foot of him was left standing out, from
beneath the dust of ages.' *Hereward the Wake* appeared first in
serial form in *Good Words*, and then in book form in 1866.
Kingsley hoped that it would be financially successful and allow
him to resign the professorship. It was the last of his historical
novels, and in the frequent footnotes it shows traces of Kingsley
the Professor, so often challenged to give chapter and verse for
his assertions or conjectures. Much of the story is set in the Fen-
lands, so familiar to him from boyhood. He describes the land
with loving detail, in the fashion of a man deeply versed in the
life and past of the region, tracing the growth and decay of
settlements as if they were actual families. So clear and accurate
are the topographical details that a devout reader can easily
retrace the actions and events in the plot.

Kingsley admired the Danes much as he admired the Teutons
in *Hypatia*, and the Danes are almost as much the heroes of his
book as the Saxons—'the free norsemen, among whom there was
not a single serf.' Hereward himself, second son of Lady Godiva
and Earl Leofric, is an anti-hero, handsome, self-willed, rebellious,
who becomes an outlaw rather than obey his devout mother
and become a monk. Forced to flee from his Fenland home,
Hereward earns a fearsome reputation as a fighting man, gaining
his famous soubriquet—'the Wake'—a man ever watchful of
envious enemies. In Flanders he marries a Flemish princess,
Torfrida, who is strangely like Kingsley's other heroines (almost
an eleventh-century Fanny Grenfell): 'Pure she was all the while,
generous, and noble-hearted; with a deep and sincere longing—
as one soul in ten thousand has—after knowledge for its own sake;
but ambitious exceedingly, and that not of monastic sanctity.'
The pair marry, and have a daughter.

When William of Normandy invades and conquers England,
Hereward remains on the Continent, but three years later he is
persuaded to return, in a last-ditch attempt to free the Saxons
from the Norman rule. He lands secretly in England on a

reconnaissance mission, accompanied by his mysterious man-servant, Martin Lightfoot, and takes his widowed mother to the monks at Crowland.

Ere the morning light, the war-arrow was split into four splinters, and carried out to the four airts, through all Kesteven. If the splinter were put into the house-father's hand, he must send it on at once to the next freeman's house. If he were away, it was stuck into his house-door, or into his great chair by the fireside, and woe to him if, on his return, he sent it not on likewise. All through Kesteven went that night the arrow-splinters, and with them the whisper, 'The Wake is come again'; till, before mid-day, there were fifty well-armed men in the old camping-field outside the town, and Hereward harangued them in words of fire.

A chill came over them, nevertheless, when he told them that he must at once return to Flanders.

'But it must be,' he said. He had promised his good lord and sovereign, Baldwin of Flanders, and his word of honour he must keep. Two visits he must pay ere he went; and then to sea. But within the year, if he were alive on ground, he would return, and with him ships and men, it might be with Sweyn and all the power of Denmark. Only let them hold their own till Danes should come, and all would be well. So would they show that they were free Englishmen, able to hold England against Frenchmen and all strangers. And whenever he came back he would set a light to Toft, Manthorpe and Witham-on-the-hill. They were his own farms, or should have been; and better they should burn than Frenchmen should hold them. They could be seen far and wide over the Bruneswold and over all the fen; and then all men might know for sure that the Wake was come again.

'And nine-and-forty of them,' says the chronicler, 'he chose to guard Bourne' (seemingly the lands which had been his nephew Morcar's) till he should come back and take them for himself. His own lands of Witham, Toft, and Man-thorpe, Gery his cousin should hold till his return; and they should send what they could of them to Lady Godiva at Crowland.

Then they went down to the water and took barge, and laid the corpse therein; and Godiva and Hereward sat at the dead lad's head;[13] and Winter steered the boat and Gwenoch took the stroke-oar.

And they rowed away for Crowland, by many a mere and many an ea; through narrow reaches of clean brown glassy water; between the dark-green alders; between the pale-green reeds; where the coot clanked, and the bittern boomed, and the sedge-bird, not content with its own sweet song, mocked the notes of all the birds around; and then out into the broad lagoons, where hung motionless, high over head, hawk beyond hawk, buzzard beyond buzzard, kite beyond kite, as far as eye could see. Into the air, as they rowed on, whirred up great skeins of wild fowl innumerable, with a cry as of all the bells of Crowland, or all the hounds of the Brunewold; while clear above all their noise sounded the wild whistle of the curlews, and the trumpet note of the great white swan. Out of the reeds, like an arrow, shot the peregrine, singled one luckless mallard from the flock, caught him up, struck him stone dead with one blow of his terrible heel, and swept his prey with him into the reeds again.

'Death! death! death!' said Lady Godiva, as the feathers fluttered down into the boat and rested on the dead boy's pall. 'War among men and beast; war on earth; war in air; war in the water beneath' as a great pike rolled at his bait, sending a shoal of white fish flying along the surface. 'And war, says holy writ, in heaven above. O Thou who didst die to destroy death, when will it all be over?'

And thus they glided on from stream to stream, until they came to the sacred isle of 'the inheritance of the Lord, the soul of St. Mary and St. Bartholomew; the most holy sanctuary of St. Guthlac and his monks; the minster most free from worldly servitude; the special almshouse of the most illustrious kings; the sole place of refuge for any one in all tribulations; the perpetual above of the saints; the possession of religious men,

especially set apart by the Common Council of the kingdom;
by reason of the frequent miracles of the most holy Confessor,
an ever-fruitful mother of camphire in the vineyards of Engedi;
and by reason of the privileges granted by the kings, a city of
grace and safety to all who repent.'

As they drew near, they passed every minute some fisher's
log canoe, in which worked with net or line the criminal who
had saved his life by fleeing to St. Guthlac, and become his
man forthwith; the slave who had fled from his master's
cruelty; and here and there in those evil days, the master
who had fled from the cruelty of Frenchman, who would
have done to him as he had done to others.[14]

In passages such as this we detect Kingsley's saga style, but there
is a difference between his earlier heroes, such as Amyas Leigh
and Philammon, and the mature mercenary, Hereward. For one
thing, history compelled Kingsley to use the theme of marital
infidelity, something he had shunned in earlier stories. And for
another, life had taught him that human relationships were sadly
complex, and in *Hereward the Wake* for the first time he approaches
maturity in his delineation of the relationship between Hereward
and Torfrida, in the difficult months preceding Hereward's
final capitulation.

The weary months ran on, from summer into winter, and
winter into summer again, for two years and more, and neither
Torfrida nor Hereward was the better for them. Hope deferred
maketh the heart sick; and a sick heart is but too apt to be a
peevish one. So there were fits of despondency, jars, mutual
recriminations. 'If I had not taken your advice, I should not
have been here.' 'If I had not loved you so well, I might have
been very differently off.' And so forth. The words were wiped
away the next hour, perhaps the next minute, by sacred kisses;
but they had been said, and would be recollected, and perhaps
said again.

Then again, the 'merry greenwood' was merry enough in
the summer tide, when shaughs were green, and

'The woodwele sang, and would not cease,
Sitting upon the spray,
So loud, it waken Robin Hood
In the greenwood where he lay.'

But it was a sad place enough, when the autumn fog crawled round the gorse, and dripped off the hollies, and choked alike the breath and the eyesight; when the air sickened with the graveyard smell of rotting leaves, and the rain-water stood in the clay holes over the poached and sloppy lawns.

It was merry enough, too, when they were in winter quarters in friendly farmhouses, as long as the bright sharp frosts lasted, and they tracked the hares and deer merrily over the frozen snows; but it was doleful enough in those same farm-houses in the howling wet weather, when wind and rain lashed in through the unglazed window and ill-made roof, and there were coughs and colds and rheumatism, and Torfrida ached from head to foot, and once could not stand upright for a whole month together, and every cranny was stuffed up with bits of board and rags, keeping out light and air as well as wind and water; and there was little difference between the short day and the long night; and the men gambled and wrangled amid clouds of peat reek, over draught-boards and chessmen which they had carved for themselves, and Torfrida sat stitching and sewing, making and mending, her eyes bleared with peat smoke, her hands sore and coarse from continued labour, her cheek bronzed, her face thin and hollow, and all her beauty worn away for very trouble. Then sometimes there was not enough to eat, and every one grumbled at her; or some one's clothes were not mended, and she was grumbled at again. And sometimes a foraging party brought home liquor, and all who could got drunk to drive dull care away; and Hereward, forgetful of her warnings, got more than was good for him likewise; and at night she coiled herself up in her furs, cold and contemptuous; and Hereward coiled himself up, guilty and defiant, and woke her again and again with startings and wild words in his sleep. And she felt that her beauty was gone, and that he saw it; and she fancied him (perhaps it was only fancy) less tender than of yore; and then in very pride disdained to take any care of her person, and said to herself, though she dare not say it to him, that if he only loved her for her face, he did not love her at all. And because she fancied him cold at times, she was cold likewise, and grew less and less caressing, when for his sake, as well as her own, she should have grown more so day by day.

Alas! for them. There are many excuses.[15]

The book did not make as much money as his earlier novels. Kingsley always considered *Hypatia* his best historical novel, but many readers preferred *Hereward the Wake*, which has a single thread and practically no philosophising. Without aspiring to the grandeur and sweep of *Hypatia* it constructs a convincing picture of eleventh-century Europe, and in his depiction of a greatly loved landscape and the careful analysis of human relationships we see Kingsley in a thoughtful mood. *Hereward the Wake* was not written with his heart's blood, or dictated from on high, but its honest vigour has earned it a permanent place in juvenile fiction. 'The Wake', by which Hereward has been universally known since Kingsley's novel, is, incidentally, a fifteenth-century term. In his own day he was called Hereward Leofricsson.

Perhaps Hereward should be regarded not so much as the 'Last of the English' but as the first of the literary Vikings, as Andrew Lang suggests. In all his stories, even though he so often overstates his case, it is this spirit of Kingsley which counts and which persists in the memory, the Berseker robustness of his heart and the bright spark of his poetry.

Hereward the Wake was an opportunity to pay tribute to 'that able antiquary, E. A. Freeman, Esq. By him the facts of Godwin's life have been more carefully investigated, and his character more fully judged than by any author of whom I am aware: and I am the more bound to draw attention to these articles, because some some years since, I had a little paper controversy with Mr. Freeman on this very subject. I have now the pleasure of saying that he has proved himself to have been in the right, while I was in the wrong.' Circumstances led to Kingsley and Freeman meeting socially, and they found to their mutual surprise and relief that they could be congenial fellow dinner guests.[16]

In 1866 Kingsley was happy to help honour F. D. Maurice by voting to have him elected as Knightsbridge Professor of Casuistry, Moral Theology and Moral Philosophy at Cambridge. Maurice did not relinquish the principalship of the Working Men's College when he moved to Cambridge, but clearly could not devote much time to it, and the office of vice-principal was established. Kingsley took great trouble to make sure that Cambridge students could meet Maurice, a shy man under the best circumstances, and grow to love and revere him as Kingsley and so many others did. Both men used the same lecture hall, but on different days, and it was an abiding pleasure to Kingsley to attend Maurice's lectures or to run into him accidentally in the street. The Master, never strong, looked increasingly delicate, and whenever Kingsley met him the younger man insisted on carrying his 'beloved Master's' books, and holding his arm. When he attended Maurice's lectures Kingsley would sit meekly among the undergraduates, sometimes moved to tears by the depth and sincerity of Maurice's words. He would make references to Maurice's lectures in his own—'You who come to this room on the other days of the week, know from one who can teach you, and me also—(God grant that we may learn)—what *duty* is.'

Maurice Kingsley was a student at Trinity Hall, but no more a scholar than his Uncle Henry had been. His father, who always saw his ducklings as swans, continued to write enthusiastically about Maurice's academic potential. 'Ah, what a blessing to see him developing under one's eyes and to be able to help him at last by teaching him something one's self! It is quite right that the schoolmasters should have the grounding and disciplining, but the father who can *finish* his boy's education, and teach him something of life besides, ought to be very thankful.' Fairly soon, however, it was to become obvious that Maurice was more suited to travel and an outdoor life than study and an office, and the family seriously considered emigration for him.

Maurice envied his uncles, who managed to take such interesting trips abroad. In the summer of 1866 his Uncle Henry had spent several weeks in France watching army manœuvres, gathering material for a novel about the battles of Magenta and Solferino. And early in 1868 his Uncle George embarked upon an exploring trip with the Earl of Pembroke, breaking new ground in Polynesia. Dr. Kingsley had given all his relatives a fright the previous year by falling desperately ill—'my poor brother, my earliest, best, and dearest friend,' wrote Henry Kingsley, but now he was fit again. Understandably, as he found his university studies tedious, young Maurice felt that he could best finish his education by foreign travel. He was a sturdy young man, not afraid of hard work, and after long family discussions it was decided he should leave Cambridge. He went to a farm, to see what was involved in the farming life, and in the late summer of 1868 set sail for South America, to work on a cousin's estate.

Charles Kingsley was, as usual, filling every second of his time. He did not yet feel able to afford the extravagance of a curate (even though one might be had for as little as £80 a year, or part of a year), and apparently nobody made the point that in view of Kingsley's periodic collapses the assistance of a curate was a necessary precaution and not a selfish indulgence.

One day, depressed beyond measure at the drab monotony of the country labourer's life compared with the variety of pursuits open to a middle-class family, Kingsley began a series of Penny Readings in the Eversley schoolroom. He could hardly blame the men for spending their time in the public house when there was practically no other recreation open to them. It was even worse for the women, who could not even frequent the public house if they valued their respectability. The Readings were another example of Kingsley's pioneering efforts on the social welfare side of his parish work. The first meeting, called to discuss the matter, was crowded with men and boys, but the women had been left behind. Kingsley appealed to his audience on behalf of their wives and mothers, telling the men that women needed a respite from a life of drudgery too. Since the women had no money to pay the penny entrance fee, it was arranged that their menfolk would pay to attend, but wives and mothers would be allowed in free of charge.

The meetings were held fortnightly, and although originally intended as recreations for the poorest members of the parish, were so enjoyable that they provided a focal point for the whole parish during that autumn and winter. There were concerts, poetry readings, story-telling, all at the highest level Kingsley could organise. He wrote to Maurice in South America asking the young man to write letters which could be read aloud to the villagers. Friends from London would join with the Kingsley family to give musical evenings. The schoolroom, brightly lit and decorated, was a warm haven to parishioners whose only light was a farthing dip candle in a dark cottage. Kingsley was always touched and astonished by the effect that music had on some of his apparently impassive parishioners, who would walk several miles on a dark wet night and then sit spellbound for two hours, revealing their enjoyment silently by a kindling expression, and perhaps a low hum of approbation which hinted at some 'deep musical undercurrent beneath that rugged exterior'. A response like that amply repaid all his time and trouble for those evenings. Encouraged by the early success, Kingsley opened an evening reading-room for the men, with books, bagatelle-boards and various games. This would in effect be a village club, to be self-governing with the men making their own rules, and he allowed the managers to buy a cask of good beer, each glass to be paid for as it was drunk, hoping in this way to avoid the temptation of the men dropping into the public house on their way home.

The experiment worked fairly well for a year or two, but Eversley was such a scattered parish, being virtually three villages in one, and so well endowed with public houses, seven of them to serve a population of eight hundred, that the reading-room and the club gradually languished and finally closed.

Kingsley's pen was kept busy: he gave two lectures on Science and Superstition at the Royal Institution, and preached special sermons in London, including one in Westminster Abbey. His wife wrote: 'His London congregations were enormous, and it was striking when he preached for a hospital to see medical students standing the whole length of the service, watching him with rapt attention.' His sermons were printed in collections which sold well overseas as well as in Britain. Sometimes his lectures were used as propaganda material for specific campaigns, and circulated in this form. The success of *Glaucus* and *The Water-Babies* encouraged him to write another set of simple science articles, *First Lessons in Earth Lore*, which were printed serially in *Good Words for the Young* and appeared later as a volume entitled *Madam How and Lady Why*. These lectures began as talks to his son, Grenville, then a pupil at Winton House, the preparatory school kept by C. A. Johns, Kingsley's former botany teacher at Helston. The finished book was dedicated to Grenville and his schoolmates. The title referred to Lady Why, Nature herself, whose reasons lie too deep for mere mortals to understand, and Madam How, the servant of Lady Why, who works ceaselessly at landscaping the earth. We can see what a gift Kingsley had for writing popular science for young people, one of the first scientific writers to address that audience. Here he is, describing the effect of ice on rock, and holding the boys' attention by taking a piece of limestone or marble, which was roughly broken off at one end but rubbed smooth with fine grooves at the other. How, he wonders aloud, could it have been done?

Of course a man could have done it, if he had taken a large round stone in his hand, and worked the large channellings with that, and then had taken fine sand and gravel upon the points of his fingers, and worked the small scratches with that. But this stone came from a place where man had, perhaps, never stood before,—ay, which, perhaps, had never seen the light of day before since the world was made; and as I happen to know that no man made the marks upon that stone, we must set to work and think again for some tool of Madam How's which may have made them.

And now I think you must give up guessing, and I must tell you the answer to the riddle. Those marks were made by a hand which is strong and yet gentle, tough and yet yielding, like the hand of a man; a hand which handles and uses in a grip stronger than a giant's its own carving tools, from the great boulder stone as large as this whole room to the finest grain of sand. And that is ICE.

That piece of stone came from the side of the Rosenlaui glacier in Switzerland, and it was polished by the glacier ice. The glacier melted and shrank this last hot summer farther back than it had done for many years, and left bare sheets of rock, which it had been scraping at for ages, with all the marks fresh upon them. And that bit was broken off and brought to me, who never saw a glacier myself, to show me how the marks which the ice makes in Switzerland are exactly the same as those which the ice has made in Snowdon and in the Highlands, and many another place where I have traced them, and written a little, too, about them in years gone by. And so I treasure this, as a sign that Madam How's ways do not change nor her laws become broken; that, as that great philosopher Sir Charles Lyell will tell you, when you read his books, Madam How is making and unmaking the surface of the earth now, by exactly the same means as she was making and unmaking ages and ages since; and that what is going on slowly and surely in the Alps in Switzerland was going on once here where we stand.

It is very difficult, I know, for a little boy like you to understand how ice, and much more how soft snow, should have such strength as to grind whole mountains into plains. You have never seen ice and snow do harm. You cannot even recollect the Crimean Winter, as it was called then; and well for you you cannot, considering all the misery it brought at home and abroad. You cannot, I say, recollect the Crimean Winter, when the Thames was frozen over above the bridges, and the ice piled in little bergs ten to fifteen feet high, which lay, some of them, stranded on the shores, about London itself, and did not melt, if I recollect, until the end of May. You never stood, as I stood, in the great winter of 1837–8 on Battersea Bridge, to see the ice break up with the tide, and saw the great slabs and blocks leaping and piling upon each other's backs, and felt the bridge tremble with their shocks, and listened to their horrible grind

and roar, till one got some little picture in one's mind of what
must be the breaking up of an ice-floe in the Arctic regions, and
what must be the danger of a ship nipped in the ice and lifted
up on high, like those in the pictures of Arctic voyages which
you are so fond of looking through. You cannot recollect how
that winter even in our little Blackwater Brook the alder
stems were all peeled white, and scarred, as if they had been
gnawed by hares and simply by the rushing and scraping of
the ice. . . . [17]

Kingsley was the kind of teacher who always tried to broaden
his students' horizons. He did not pretend he had the answers,
but he did hope he had some of the questions.

Christmas 1868 was the first time that there had been a break
in the rectory circle. With Maurice now financially independent,
Kingsley yielded to family persuasion and employed a permanent
curate, the Rev. William Harrison. It was a fortunate choice,
the two men quickly became great friends and Kingsley was able
to leave his parish in good care. To some extent Harrison compensated for the loss of the companionship of Ludlow and Hughes,
and in the first relationship of Kingsley and Harrison there is a
faint reflection of the relationship years before of Maurice and
Kingsley. Best of all, Kingsley could risk resigning his Cambridge
professorship, although it would be a year before the resignation
became effective. There were certain formalities, letters to Dr.
Thompson, Master of Trinity and Vice-Chancellor of the
university; a letter to the Queen; one to Mr. Gladstone; but the
decision was final.

When it became known that this was to be Professor Kingsley's
last year at Cambridge, his lectures were more crowded than
ever. He lectured upon Comte and the positivist school because
he believed the school posed an important atheistic challenge.
He hoped to do something, however slight, to counteract their
influence, and was happy to notice that Huxley regarded Comp-
tism much as he did—'Catholic organization without Catholic
doctrine, or in other words, Catholicism minus Christianity.'

Almost as soon as he offered his resignation, out of the blue came the long-awaited preferment, a canonry at Chester, which Kingsley accepted gratefully. Although for several years Queen Victoria had sought to help him in his career, the Conservative governments had considered him too dangerous. Disraeli was particularly stubborn in refusing to jeopardise his government, though a number of Kingsley's ideas had been similar to those of Disraeli's own Young England group, and Lord John Manners, a prominent member of that group, had long been a friend of Kingsley's. When Gladstone became Prime Minister after the 1867 reform act which gave the vote to the urban working man, he had a legislative programme dealing with many social problems dear to Kingsley's heart, and the one-time 'Chartist' cleric did not alarm him. Gladstone was an admirer of F. D. Maurice, although he did not always understand him, and since in the public mind Kingsley and Maurice were inextricably mixed this was an additional reason for showing favour to Kingsley.

J. R. Seeley, a far better historian than Kingsley, succeeded him at Cambridge, but his lectures were much less popular. Dr. Thompson, one of Kingsley's most loyal supporters, was maliciously pleased to note that in their initial disappointment at Seeley's performance the university critics were at last prepared to give due credit to Kingsley.

Charles was now fifty years old, the age his father had been when he went to Chelsea, and he was quite happy to look on the Chester canonry, coupled with the Eversley duties, as the apex of his clerical career, although his friends were ambitious for him and thought he should have been offered something better. The joy of Chester, so far as Kingsley was concerned, was that four canons shared the duties and the house near the Cathedral in turn, so that he would be away from Eversley only one-quarter of the year. Although not as well paid as his Cambridge professorship, there was no comparison in terms of strain and work-load.

1869 ended in a positive cascade of honours, excitement and glory. Kingsley had taken Fanny to London in the summer to attend the first Women's Suffrage meeting, staying the night in the home of John Stuart Mill. Although Kingsley and Mill had been opponents over Governor Eyre, Mill did not react like

Ludlow where Kingsley was concerned and welcomed him to his cause. Both men admired and respected women. Kingsley had for many years advocated medical education for women, and he greatly admired Mill's book, *The Subjection of Women,* for its blend of boldness and moderation. Mill was a courteous host, who won over his two guests by his manners and his vast erudition. Kingsley was fascinated by his face, holding the artistic belief that a trained painter could discern a man's entire character from his face. 'When I look at his cold, clear-cut face, I think there is a whole hell beneath him, of which he knows nothing, and so there may be a whole heaven above him,' said Kingsley of Mill.

There were other reasons beside the women's cause why Kingsley should admire Mill. Influenced by Robert Owen and Louis Blanc, Mill had advised co-operation in production as well as in distribution. Mill too had been aware of the power of Carlyle as a poet and as an intuitive thinker. On colonial matters he tended to agree with Carlyle, again a tendency which Kingsley would find sympathetic. Mill's outstanding characteristic was his logical mind, which synthesised the ideas of his time. His *System of Logic*, published in 1843, was a powerful influence upon a generation of young men with liberal inclinations.

John Stuart Mill fully understood the importance of women. He waited twenty years for Mrs. Taylor to be free to marry him, and when a few years after their marriage she died at Avignon, where Mill had a cottage, he was dominated by her memory in death as much or more than when she was alive. The inscription on her tomb at Avignon read, 'Were there even a few hearts and intellects like hers this earth would already become the hoped-for heaven.' It was a sentiment which Charles and Fanny Kingsley could echo with all their hearts. With his *Subjection of Women* Mill galloped into the arena, a literary knight errant, his heroine being subject woman held captive by the monster man for so many years that the bondage had entered into her soul and neither she nor the rest of the world was aware of her full potential. Mill did not succeed in bringing about women's suffrage, but the liberating legislation of the Married Woman's Property Act of

1882 was in large measure due to him. Kingsley's initial ardour was well received by the movement, which reprinted one of his lectures as a pamphlet. But his enthusiasm was soon dampened by some of the activities of leading militants as the women's suffrage campaign got under way.

Kingsley kept to an old-fashioned idea of what constituted seemly feminine conduct, and he and Fanny were shocked by some of the militants. He wrote in 1870: 'I do not hesitate to say that a great deal which had been said and done by women, and those who wish to support women's rights, during the last six months, has thrown back our cause.... We shall not win by petitions. The House of Commons cares nothing for them. It knows too well how they can be got up, and takes for granted that we shall get up ours in the same way.' He regretted that men and women who were prejudiced against women's rights but who might be persuaded to see the justice of the cause were allowed to sink back into their former way of thinking because of some of the violent language and methods used by the women themselves.

Mill did not share this instinctive distaste, and wrote to ask why, after his first eagerness, Kingsley had more or less withdrawn from the movement. Kingsley replied in a long letter, explaining that he thought the violent methods were counterproductive, and that many women would be frightened by having to air their chief problems in public. He preferred a gradualist approach where women would take their place in the professions, starting with the medical profession, and in the course of time all women would be educated to take their place in society free from inhibitions. In the meantime he believed he could do more for the cause of women by writing about them in their highest role as the teachers and inspirers of their menfolk. (It is undoubtedly true that a survey of Victorian fiction from about 1850 to 1870 is unlikely to show another novelist with as fine a record as Kingsley in portraying intelligent and independent heroines. It was not for nothing that he thought *Hypatia* his best novel.)

Kingsley's reactions in connection with women's suffrage resemble his reaction to the Chartist movement: sympathetic in principle but unable in practice to conquer an inbred repugnance to the methods employed. He did not entirely desert the women's cause, but concentrated his fire on the right of women to become doctors. He had been a campaigner in this cause for some time, and was a great admirer of women pioneers in medicine, such as Dr. Elizabeth Blackwell.

What women's suffrage lost, the Education League gained. Belief in education had been a keynote of his life since Chartist days. His entire career, except for his poetry, was that of the teacher/preacher. He had helped a promising Eversley boy go on to further training so that the young man could return as schoolmaster to the village, and many of Eversley's lessons for children and adults had been given personally by the rector or members of his family. He used striking phrases which stayed in the memory. A sermon preached on behalf of the Kirkdale Ragged School was remembered because he spoke of 'human soot':

Capital is accumulated more rapidly by wasting a certain amount of human life, human health, human intellect, human morals, by producing and throwing away a regular per-centage of human soot—of that thinking and acting dirt which lies about, and, alas! breeds and perpetuates itself in foul alleys and low public-houses, and all and any of the dark places of the earth. But as in the case of the manufacturers, the Nemesis comes swift and sure. As the foul vapours of the mine and manufactory destroy vegetation and injure health, so does the Nemesis fall on the world of man—so does that human soot, those human poison gases, infect the whole society which has allowed them to fester under its feet. Sad; but not hopeless. Dark; but not without a gleam of light on the horizon.

I can yet conceive a time when, by improved chemical science, every foul vapour which now escapes from the chimney of a manufactory, polluting the air, destroying the vegetation, shall be seized, utilized, converted into some profitable substance, till the Black Country shall be black no longer, and the streams once more run crystal clear, the trees be once more luxuriant, and the desert which man has created in his haste and greed, shall, in literal fact, once more blossom as the rose. And just so can I conceive a time when, by a higher civilization, founded on political economy, more truly scientific, because more truly according to the will of God, our human refuse shall be utilized like our material refuse, when man as man, even down to the weakest and most ignorant, shall be found to be (as he really is) so valuable that it will be worth while to preserve his health, to the level of his capabilities, *to save him alive,* body, intellect, and character, at any cost; because men will see that a man is, after all, the most precious and useful thing in the earth, and that no cost spent on the development of human beings can possibly be thrown away.[18]

He was elected President of the Education Section of the Social Science Congress held at Bristol, and he and his wife were guests of the headmaster at Clifton School, then only about four years old. Kingsley made a great impression as a speaker and also as a gifted raconteur of Devonshire stories told in dialect. He supported state compulsory education, and thundered about the '1,280,000 children growing up in ignorance, in a country which calls itself civilized.' Perhaps the two most unexpected points he made, considering he was a clergyman, were first that in an increasingly secular age teaching should be secular, and the clergy should confine themselves to teaching about God, and that secondly unless that religious teaching was accompanied by sensible physical teaching, based on a substratum of truth, reason, and common sense, then religion itself would become stunted and shrivelled.

The Education League was rightly pleased by its new recruit, and printed 100,000 copies of his address as a propaganda leaflet. When, in 1870, his friend W. E. Forster introduced an elementary education bill in Gladstone's ministry Kingsley supported it even though it did not go as far as he wished and make schooling compulsory. Some members of the Education League indeed opposed this bill because of the principle of non-compulsion, but Kingsley, always pragmatic, supported Forster on the ground that the government had at least taken notice that education was a social need, and this bill was the first step.

Both Charles and Fanny Kingsley looked forward to 1870 as the dawn of a new and easier chapter in their lives. Meanwhile, as an unexpected treat, Charles was invited by Arthur Hamilton Gordon, governor of Trinidad, to spend a few weeks there as his guest. Gordon had married Lord Eversley's daughter, and had made Kingsley's acquaintance some two years earlier. Such a visit had been one of Kingsley's dreams. The jungle scenes he had re-created from musty old chronicles for *Westward Ho!* would appear before his eyes. He would write copious letters home, to be serialised in *Good Words*, and edit them at his leisure for another book for Macmillans. (When this appeared, it bore the significant title *At Last.*) Preparations were made for him and Rose, his elder daughter, and in December 1869 they boarded the steamer for Trinidad.

14

Canon of Chester

It would be virtually impossible to find a greater contrast in colonial administrators than Kingsley's host in Trinidad, Arthur Hamilton Gordon, and Sir John Eyre, and it is fascinating to speculate whether Kingsley would have backed the Eyre Defence Fund had he been friendly with Gordon at that time. Gordon was the youngest son of the fourth Earl of Aberdeen, a graduate of Trinity College, Cambridge, and an admirer of Mr. Gladstone. His father had been a Tory Member of Parliament, but Gordon sat as a Liberal member for Beverley from 1855 to 1857. The following year he had accompanied Gladstone as his private secretary on a visit to the Ionian Islands, and in 1861 was appointed lieutenant-governor of New Brunswick. He contributed a section about New Brunswick for a travel book edited by Francis Dalton, thereby setting a pattern for his future life: colonial government and writing.

Gordon held liberal and progressive views on colonial administration, disapproving of the notion that native races existed in order to be exploited by the whites. His policies were often criticised by white settlers during his tours of office, but he remained unmoved and his example was followed by other colonial administrators. He became governor of Fiji in 1875, remaining there until 1880, and upheld native customs and the authority of the chiefs. In retirement, he devoted himself to writing. Charles Kingsley's ideas on colonial administration were unquestionably modified as a result of contact with Gordon, and his visit to the West Indies in 1870 was an education in the widest sense of the word.

Many deep-seated emotions rose to the surface as Charles approached his mother's homeland, and he responded impetuously to the lush beauty of the tropics where the 'bride-look' had not yet died—'and a fresh Dryad gazed out of every bush, and with wooing eyes asked to be wooed.' Just as in Europe he had gazed on many scenes primed by his wife's recollections, so now he gazed at Trinidad and the other islands with remembrance of family relics and stories told years before by his mother. His boyhood memories were coloured by romance, but looking at the reality as a man he derived social and moral lessons from the islands as well as appreciation of their beauty.

Meanwhile it was a comfort to one fresh from the cities of the Old World, and the short and stunted figures, the mesquin and scrofulous visages, which crowd our alleys and back winds, to see everywhere health, strength and goodly stature, especially among women. Nowhere in the West Indies are to be seen those haggard down-trodden mothers, grown old before their time, too common in England and commoner still in France. Health 'rude' in every sense of the word is the mark of the negro woman and of the negro man likewise. Their faces shine with fatness; they seem to enjoy, they do enjoy, the mere act of living. . . . Let us, before we complain of them for being too healthy and comfortable, remember that we have at home here tens of thousands of paupers, rogues, whatnots, who are not a whit more civilised, intellectual, virtuous, or spiritual than the Negro, and are meanwhile neither healthy nor comfortable. The Negro may have the *corpus sanum* without the *mens sana*. But what of those whose souls and bodies are alike unsound?[1]

This was a moralising reflection intended for public consumption, but in a private letter to his mother he had to admit that he could not bring himself to like the negro women, they were simply too independent and overwhelming. 'Their masculine figures, their ungainly gestures, their loud and sudden laughter, even when walking alone, and their general coarseness, shocks and must shock.'

His joy in being in the islands of his maternal ancestors, where the Elizabethan sea-dogs had sailed, was continually haunted by the reproach—'What might the West Indies not have been by now, had it not been for slavery, rum and sugar?' He comforted himself with the thought that perhaps after all it was for the best, since British ownership of Trinidad must have saved it from becoming a 'slave-holding and slave-trading island, wealthy, luxurious, profligate' like Cuba, or incorporated into Venezuela to become part of a typical South American republic 'combining every vice of civilisation with every vice of savagery'. He was in the main indulgent towards the many individuals whom he observed with apparently nothing to do, commenting drily, 'If a poor man neither steals, begs nor rebels (and these people do not do the two latter) has he not as much right to be idle as a rich man? To say that neither has a right to be idle is, of course, sheer socialism, and a heresy not to be tolerated!'

His remarks about the employer-employee relationship in society, arising out of his observations on the labour situation in Trinidad, show that he still deeply disapproved of the existing economic system in Britain, hoping one day for a 'nobler bond' between men than the cash nexus which was weak and mean and produced a society which left 'the poor man who cannot wait to be blockaded and starved out by the rich who can.'[2]

In general, Kingsley was overwhelmed by the tropics. Although very well-read, and steeped in incidental information about the West Indies, its history, its flora and fauna, he was totally unprepared for the grandeur of Trinidad. He had travelled so little outside the British Isles that he was 'awestruck' by the islands, as he had been awestruck by the Pyrenees, and as he would be awestruck later by the Yosemite Valley. The famous Pitch Lake evoked a thoroughly conventional response: 'All that the scientific man can do is, to confess the presence of mystery all day long; and to live in that wholesome and calm attitude of wonder which we call awe and reverence.'

Influenced by the governor's gentle, moderate views, Kingsley lost his feudal attitudes and faced the fact that if the Negro seemed in many ways an inferior being it was unfortunately because the white man had made him so. Kingsley met a number of negroes who by ability and appearance so impressed him that he saw the future solution for the island, even for the entire Negro people, as lying in complete equality of opportunity in jobs and professions so that able Negroes could rise to the top. He believed that the effect in that case would be that the general level of education and attainments throughout the island would also rise. He examined the island school system, to admit with a rueful dig at himself that in Trinidad the Roman Catholic influence was the chief, if not the only, civilising and Christianising influence on the poorest islanders, and in the case of a new Education Act then being considered for the island it was the Protestants with sectarian bigotry who were trying to sabotage some good and essential legislation.

These were the serious sides to his visit, but of course the Kingsleys were on holiday, even though Charles would have to write it up for his 'daily bread' later on. He abandoned himself where possible to sheer sensual enjoyment, and fell back on homely comparisons when trying to explain to the family what the landscape really looked like—'To conceive it the reader must fancy himself at Clovelly. . . . Magnify it four or five times, pour down a tropic sunshine and a tropic haze, and you had it.' He told his mother, who although over eighty and infirm was in full possession of her mental faculties and still fussed over her first-born son, that he was taking no chances with his health. 'Tonight we start for the north coast and glorious mountain shores. We sleep at a planter's, and ride off tomorrow morning for three days, with cutlass, mackintosh, botany-box and quinine-bottle, into the forests. The riding here is very wild—rock, roots, fallen timber, and abysses of mud. But the horses are very sure-footed, and I *can* ride, so I have not had a fall yet.'[3]

His letters to Fanny Kingsley fairly sparkled with health and vitality. 'I have not been so well this seven years. I have been riding this week six to eight hours a day, through primeval forests, mud, roots, gullies, and thickets, such that had I anticipated them, I would have brought out breeches and boots.—English mud is but a trifle to tropical. But I have had no fall, and never got wet, and as for what I have seen, no tongue can tell. We have got many curiosities, and lots of snakes. I have only seen one alligator, and about five to six feet long, and marks only of deer and capo. But I have seen one of the mud volcanoes! As for scenery, for vastness and richness mingled, I never saw its like. Oh that I could transport you to the Monserrat hills for one hour. We can get no photographs, so that I know not how to make you conceive it all'. (In 1870 photography was still in its infancy.) By the end of February the short holiday was over and Kingsley and his daughter were homeward bound, together with a parrot, a kinkajou, many plants and other sundry mementoes, many of them for friends. At Southampton the Kingsleys were treated like very special arrivals and were among the first to leave the dock, to the Canon's mingled pride and amusement. Maurice Kingsley arrived at Eversley on a visit, and the three travellers shivered in the Hampshire winter, exchanged experiences, and prepared their talks for the Penny Reading evenings.

Kingsley was cheered by military manœuvres which took place around Eversley just then, with sights and sounds which thrilled him to trumpet pitch, and the entire rectory, including the servants, fell victim to the contagion. 'We've all had scarlet fever,' as Fanny Kingsley gaily described it. The Prince of Wales was on duty with his unit during these troop movements, and enjoyed himself by slipping away for a fleeting visit to his old tutor.

It was nothing new for soldiers to march through Eversley. Officers from Sandhurst College, and from Wellington College, regularly joined Kingsley's congregation. The rector was torn between satisfaction at seeing his church full and dismay at being a public personality. Even in Eversley church he suffered from shyness and nerves, and a side gate was cut in the rectory garden wall which bordered the churchyard to allow him to avoid the crowds after the service and bolt to safety.

On May 1, 1870 the Kingsleys took up residence in Chester. It was Race Week, when the historic town was filled with racegoers and the public houses did their best trade. This slightly unfortunate first impression did not last, since Charles found so many other things about Chester which he enjoyed. His father's family had always traced its ancestry back to the Kingsleys of Delamere Forest, so he had the satisfaction of feeling that just as he had spent a short time in his mother's native background, now he was returning to the land of his fathers. It was a sentiment which was well received by the good people of Chester. Kingsley was also pleased to discover that the Huxley family derived from the same district. The city did not then present the picturesque aspect familiar today, for the extensive rebuilding of the famous black and white houses had not taken place nor had the cathedral received its Gilbert Scott ornamentations. But the palatial town hall had just been built, an ornate witness to the civic dignity of the Chester corporation.

Kingsley arrived at a critical moment in Chester's intellectual life. His interest in botany and in the natural sciences was eagerly welcomed by an influential knot of educated middle-class men who wanted to ensure that their city had her share of scientific societies. There had been several attempts to organise such societies in the previous half century, but none had survived. 'The Mechanics' Institute, Library, and Reading Room', founded in 1835, had flourished for twenty years and then flagged, although the library continued to function. A School of Art and an archaeological association had both been established only to fall gently into the doldrums. But around the time when Kingsley's appointment as the next canon was announced, the Library Committee approached the Very Rev. Dean Howson with the proposal that a series of popular lectures be given to raise funds for the public library. The idea was opportune, the Dean made the obvious connection, and Kingsley was asked to assist with the lectures, an invitation which he naturally accepted. Dean Howson was pleased because he was hoping to make the cathedral more important in the secular life of the city.

All four canons came under the orders of Dean Howson, who was, like Kingsley, a Cambridge man. He awaited Kingsley's arrival with trepidation, recalling how appalled he had been by Kingsley's 'I am a Chartist' avowal in 1849, by the deliberately provocative style of *Yeast* and *Alton Locke*, and most especially by the Cambridge scenes in the first edition of *Alton Locke*. It was true that in the following twenty years Kingsley had ceased to thunder in justification of Chartism, but then Chartism itself had become a dead cause, and attenuation of the Chartist campaign had not weakened his propensity to lash out whenever he scented an honourable cause. Dean Howson, against all evidence, still expected to meet an iconoclastic firebrand who would enjoy disturbing the harmony and tradition of a cathedral close. He could not forget occasions when Kingsley had declared that empty cathedrals should be used as museums for the people. Howson had by coincidence been Hulsean Lecturer at Cambridge during part of the time when Kingsley was Professor of Modern History, and there had actually been one brief meeting between the two men when Howson had been surprised to find that Kingsley was a warm, agreeable man—but such was the strength of prejudice built up by years of orthodox disapproval and press antagonism that Howson remained deeply uneasy about Kingsley.

Of course none of his forebodings proved justified. Kingsley was infinitely deferential and so sensitive to ecclesiastical hierarchy that he was profoundly embarrassed when enthusiastic vergers showed him off to visiting tourists as the city's most famous literary lion and extolled him out of all proportion to his relatively humble position as one of four canons. His self-consciousness was all the more troublesome because he could not resist a hidden pride at his fame, ashamed of such weakness as he was. It peeped out in rather unexpected ways, like his insistence that he should be addressed in print by his new full title—The Revd. Canon Charles Kingsley.

Relations between the new canon and the citizens of Chester opened on the most favourable note possible and continued at the same high level. Rarely if ever can an outsider have made such a deep and lasting impression upon the social and cultural life of any city as did Charles Kingsley upon Chester, and it is even more remarkable when we notice that his total life in Chester amounted to three months in each of three years. By the time Kingsley arrived the Library Committee had already compiled a list of some forty young men who wished to join his proposed class. Kingsley chose botany as his subject, stipulating that the course of

twelve weekly lessons should be limited to men, for he thought
that 'the presence of young ladies would prove too strong a
counter-attraction. "Let Mr. John Price form a Class and take
the ladies: he is the nicest man, and should have the nicest
pupils." '4

The lectures were held alternatively indoors and in the
fields. Asked what price to charge, Kingsley observed that
'they ought to be worth threepence a time', and Fanny Kingsley,
present at that discussion, offered to pay the fees of anyone who
could not afford the three shillings for the whole course. Early in
May Kingsley took the chair at a meeting of the Archaeological
Society, and insisted that he was 'at the service of the good
citizens of Chester, without any regard to creed, politics, or rank,
in any way whatsoever'. He was applauded wherever he went, the
right man in the right place at the right time, and the Chester
duty became immensely satisfying. He wrote to Froude: 'I am
very happy here. I have daily service. Plenty of work in the place.
I have started a Botanical Class for middle-class young men,
which seems to go well; an opportunity of preaching to shrewd,
able northern men, who can understand and respond; and time
to work at physical science; the only thing I care for much
now. . . .'

The botanical classes were so successful that they had to be
moved from a small room in the library basement to a larger
room upstairs. Kingsley used *Flowers of the Field* as a textbook.
Written by his old friend C. A. Johns, it was one of the most
successful books on its subject. Kingsley illustrated everything
with chalk and blackboard, and insisted that his students should
not use living specimens except on their walks and nature
rambles. He never narrowed himself to one subject, but extended
botany so that it embraced geology, foreign travel, evolution,
natural history and morality generally. So successful were the
classes and so charmed with their new canon were the cathedral
dignitaries and the Chester citizens that during the following
winter ambitious plans were laid to form a new natural history
society. Aware that similar societies had failed, although begun
with equally high hopes, the Chester intelligentsia suggested

that the proposed new society might have healthier prospects if Kingsley himself took the initiative. So it proved. In May 1871, taking up residence, he called a nucleus of a committee to his house in Abbey Square, a General Meeting was called there three weeks later (by a happy chance it was Kingsley's birthday) and the Chester Society of Natural Science was born.

The canon's name was rarely out of the local newspapers from that time on. In February, at Dean Howson's request, he had composed an open letter to the young men of Chester, pointing out the evils of gambling and hoping to make an impression which would last until the May races. Kingsley felt strongly about gambling. Ever since a night of drinking and gambling at cards during his student days, when he awoke the following morning to find he had won a considerable amount of money but had no recollection of how or when, he had been convinced that gambling was morally wrong. He loved horse racing, because he loved horses, but hated the betting which accompanied it. His letter was simple and to the point. 'Betting is wrong: because it is wrong to take your neighbour's money without giving him anything in return. Earn from him what you will, and as much as you can. All labour, even the lowest drudgery, is honourable; but betting is not labouring or earning; it is getting money without earning it, and more, it is getting money, or trying to get it out of your neighbour's ignorance.' He saw a vast difference between commercial race-track betting and friendly wagers, or a rubber of sixpenny whist. But he insisted that when the gambling fever, like drink, took hold of a man it was the honourable man who always suffered most, being no match for the scoundrel who did not scruple to cheat. 'If any young man will not believe me, because I am a parson, let him read, in the last chapter or two of *Sponge's Sporting Tour*, what was the thought of the Enoch Wriggles and Infallible Joes, by a better sportsman and a wiser man, than any Chester betting young gentleman is likely to be.'

Kingsley loved the new science society and called it 'the dream of years'. He begged his famous friends and acquaintances in the scientific world to become honorary members and thereby give the Chester members 'the feeling that they are initiated into the great freemasonry of science, and that such men as you'—he was writing to Sir Henry Lyell, the geologist—'acknowledge them as pupils.' He signed himself, 'Your most faithful and loyal pupil, C. Kingsley.'

His postbag continued to claim much of his time, and with a friend like Sir Charles Fox Bunbury the correspondence was wide-ranging. His recent travels in the tropics were leading Kingsley to the belief, he told Sir Charles, that in distant geological times there had been a continuous belt of land round the tropics and that life, human and animal, would have originated in some such warm clime. This theory appeared to explain the existence of similar species in vastly separated continents. The two men also discussed at length the feasibility of '*la petite culture*' as a solution for agricultural poverty. Kingsley had retained his interest in this subject since *Yeast* and never resented taking time to reply to strangers who wrote to him about agricultural topics. So many-sided was he that many people who knew only one side of him were unaware that he was accounted an authority on some other facet. Fanny Kingsley tells the anecdote, quoted later by Julia Wedgwood in an article in the *Spectator*, ' "What an unintelligible mystic Kingsley is!" said a guest at some dinner party. "I wonder if he himself understands his own writings." His hearer did not see the appropriateness of the description, and the conversation took a line on which the speaker had more to say—a subject connected with agriculture. "There is an admirable article on that subject," he continued, "in such and such a Review; it throws more light upon it, and gives more practical suggestions concerning it, than anything I have read for years." "It was written by Kingsley," said the other—and the first speaker took refuge in his dinner.'

The outbreak of the Franco-Prussian War revived all Kingsley's well-established Teutonic sympathies. He considered that Napoleon III had betrayed the 1848 French revolution and the events of 1870 were Nemesis at work. Had the Prussians taken the initiative in declaring war he might have doubted its morality, he confessed, but since it was the French who had done so he believed that it was a case of the French nation surrendering to war fever in the hope that they would avenge their defeats of 1813 and 1815, and through war keep Germany weak and divided. Holding such views, it was not difficult for Kingsley to forgive Bismarck for divulging the terms of the secret Biarritz meeting with Napoleon, and, like many of his circle, Kingsley was convinced that a Europe which included a unified Germany whose moral tone was set by industrious, Protestant Prussia, was a Europe to be respected.

Henry Kingsley shared his elder brother's interest in the war. In 1870 Henry was in Edinburgh editing *The Daily Review*, the organ of the Free Church Party. Henry did not possess the patience or the skill to make a good editor, and as an Englishman and a convinced Anglican he was hardly the man for *The Daily Review*. When he proposed to go to France as a roving war correspondent his employers gladly agreed, and in August Henry was roaming over the battlefield of Sedan. His war despatches, sensitive and impressionistic, were excellent, and read by a large public including, of course, his elder brother. Kingsley wrote strongly to Sir Charles: 'Since Waterloo, there has been no such event in Europe. I await with awe and pity the Parisian news of the next few days. As for the Emperor, while others were bowing down to him, I never shrank from expressing my utter contempt of him.' 'Another interesting letter from Kingsley,' jotted down Sir Charles admiringly in his diary. Most of his associates were scientists, and Kingsley's wider knowledge and interests were a source of never-ending astonishment to him.

Kingsley began a series of geology classes in Chester, given fortnightly at the King's School. The following year they were printed in a volume entitled *Town Geology*. A charge of three shillings was made for the six lectures, and doors opened at 7.30 p.m. In addition to the lecturer the platform usually held Mrs. Kingsley, or one of the daughters, Dean Howson, and one or two other friends, and the hall was always full. The entire course made a profit of fifty pounds, which was divided among the City Library and other institutions. Geology was a subject which Kingsley personally found exciting and he communicated this to his audience. One listener said of those lectures: 'Many of those who were then present must recall the look of inspiration with which the Lecturer's burning words were accompanied.' Women were not excluded from these geology lectures: 'each member was allowed to bring a lady friend.' Natural history expeditions were organised to supplement the botanical and geological studies, and Kingsley surveyed the ground carefully beforehand, not forgetting to arrange for resting-places and refreshments and to make sure of train connections.

If his popular lectures made the people of Chester proud of their canon, the field excursions made them love him. Siddall remembered 'the bright sunshine and sweet fresh air of the hill top; and the Canon stretching out his chest and breathing it in, and bidding us to do likewise, and thank God for it all, and get rid of some of the stuffiness of "Rare old Chester".... Then, the tea in the Village School, and the Canon's delightful review of all we had seen; the comparing of the finds, fossil and fresh, and all this to an audience of beginners, to whom all was new and wonderful. Then the journey home, and a loving goodnight. The gates of a new and wonderfully beautiful world were opened to us on this and other such days, and we were invited to enter freely into it, and rejoice and be thankful.'[5] (Kingsley's outings were strongly reminiscent of the weekend outings and rambles organised by the Working Men's College in London, one or two of which he had attended.) Parties of upwards of a hundred set out, led by Kingsley and his daughters, he with a botany box over his shoulder (shades of the Helston schoolboy) and a geological hammer conveniently to hand.

On July 28, 1871 the first of another successful series of events was held—a Conversazione—attracting almost three hundred members and friends to the Town Hall. There was a fine selection of drawings, etchings and photographs lent by Kingsley and others; collections of shells and fossils; and, most intriguing of all, the Microscopical Exhibition. 'Be sure and see the men with the microscopes,' Kingsley used to say. Mary Kingsley labelled a brush which had been left behind by the cleaners as '*Dustbroomia vulgaris*, kindly lent by the Corporation'. The social intercourse created by these exhibitions rejuvenated the intellectual climate of the entire city, for which Kingsley received most of the credit. Preparations were made to establish a museum and further lectures were given at the King's School in the autumn, continuing the Kingsley tradition.

The Coal in the Fire was one of his most popular lectures, and shows how he interwove personal reminiscence with popular science.

I myself once saw a scene of that kind, which I should be sorry to forget; for there was, as I conceived, coal, making or getting ready to be made, before my eyes: a sheet of swamp, sinking slowly into the sea; for there stood trees still rooted below high-water mark, and killed by the waves; while inland huge trees stood dying, or dead, from the water at their roots. But what a scene—a labyrinth of narrow creeks, so narrow that a canoe could not pass up, haunted with alligators and boa-constrictors, parrots and white herons, amid an inextricable confusion of vegetable mud, roots of the alder-like mangroves, and tangled creepers hanging from tree to tree; and over-head huge fan-palms delighting in the moisture, mingled with still huger broad-leaved trees in every stage of decay. The drowned vegetable soil of ages beneath me; above my head, for a hundred feet, a mass of stems and boughs, and leaves and flowers, compared with which the richest hothouse in England was poor and small.

To show his listeners what he meant by 'Nature's poetry', Kingsley spoke of the coal, first as an ordinary black object.

Man digs it, throws it on the fire, a black, dead-seeming lump. A corner, an atom of it, warms till it reaches the igniting point; the temperature at which it is able to combine with oxygen.

And then, like a dormant live thing, awaking after ages to the sense of its own powers, its own needs, the whole lump is seized, atom after atom, with an infectious hunger for that oxygen which it lost centuries since in the bottom of the earth. It drinks the oxygen in at every pore; and burns.

And so the spell of ages is broken. The sun-force bursts its prison-cells, and blazes into the free atmosphere, as light and heat once more; returning in a moment into the same forms in which it entered the growing leaf a thousand centuries since.

Strange it all is, yet true. But of nature, as of the heart of man, the old saying stands—that truth is stranger than fiction.[6]

Kingsley used the preface to *Town Geology* as a forum to advocate science education for all classes of men and women and to explain why he had changed his political views since 1848. It is an interesting document, repaying close study as an indication of Kingsley's social and political beliefs at this time, beliefs which remained unchanged until his death. The laws of physical science, he wrote, were none other than the Word of God revealed in facts, quoting Lord Bacon centuries earlier. Kingsley spoke of the healthy benefits of sanitary reforms and of new types of jobs resulting from the scientific discoveries. Acquire the scientific habit of mind, he declared and 'you will find yourselves enjoying a freedom, an equality, a brotherhood, such as you will not find elsewhere just now. Freedom: what do we want freedom for? For this, at least; that we may be each and all able to think what we choose; and to say what we choose also, provided we do not say it rudely or violently, so as to provoke a breach of the peace. That last was my poor friend Mr. Buckle's definition of freedom of speech. That was the only limit to it which we would allow: and I think that this is Mr. John Stuart Mill's limit also. At all events, it is mine.'[7] Kingsley advised the study of Natural Science ('common sense well regulated', in Huxley's phrase) because it would give people the free habit of mind. As for equality, Kingsley declared that at the very least every boy and girl should have an equal and sound education. 'If I had my way, I would give the same education to the child of the collier and to the child of the peer.

I would see that they were taught the same things, and by the same method. Let them all begin alike, say I. They will be handicapped enough as they go on in life, without our handicapping them in their first race. Whatever stable they come out of, whatever promise they show, let them all train alike, and start fair, and let the best colt win.'

Fully aware that these pleas for education and moderation were likely to irritate his younger readers, Kingsley addressed himself particularly to that group. 'I, at least, shall certainly not be angry with them. For when I was young, I was very much of what I suspect is their opinion. I used to think one could get perfect freedom, and social reform, and all that I wanted, by altering the arrangements of society, and legislation, by constitutions, and Acts of Parliament; by putting society into some sort of freedom-mill, and grinding it all down, and regenerating it so. And that something can be done by improved arrangements, something can be done by Acts of Parliament, I hold still, as every rational man must hold.

'But as I grew older, I began to see that if things were to be got right, the freedom-mill would do very little towards grinding them right, however well and amazingly it was made. I began to see that what sort of flour came out at one end of the mill, depended mainly on what sort of grain you had put in at the other; and I began to see that the problem was, to get good grain; and then good flour would be turned out, even by a very clumsy, old-fashioned sort of mill. And what do I mean by good grain? Good men, honest men, self-restraining men, fair men, modest men. Men who are aware of their own vast ignorance compared with the vast amount that there is to be learned in such a universe as this. Men who are accustomed to look at both sides of a question.' Otherwise, he believed, society would degenerate until it was governed by 'organised brute force and military despotism. And, after that, what can come, save anarchy, and decay, and social death?' His solution was a society composed of men and women, students of Natural Science, believers in God, employing the brute force of Nature because they had understood her laws and obeyed them, and living together in a society which was just because it followed the teachings of Jesus Christ.

Kingsley's belief that obedience to the laws of hygiene would benefit the population as much as or more than obedience to the laws of Parliament was sadly reinforced when not long afterwards the Prince of Wales suddenly collapsed with fever. Prayers for the prince's recovery were offered throughout the country, and Kingsley felt so emotionally involved that he could not stay still at Eversley but went to King's Lynn so as to be close to Sandringham, where the prince lay sick. Kingsley telegraphed daily bulletins home, where they were posted at the church door and in the window of the village shop. After the prince's recovery, Kingsley made the need for sanitary reform the theme of his royal sermon, 'Loyalty', preached at St. James's. By now his reputation made him a personality to be treated seriously if not sympathetically by the press, and his body of writing, mostly polemic, had over the years helped to produce changes in the thinking of a generation. His public sermons reached a large congregation. 'Two hundred thousand persons, I am told, have died of preventible fever since the Prince Consort's death a few years ago. Is not that a national sin to bow our hearts as the heart of one man?' At least, he commented, the illness of the Prince of Wales would have had one good aspect if it awakened public opinion to the need for clean water, drainage, air and housing, so that unborn generations would live instead of die.

He was much in demand as a speaker for sanitary reform, and as President of the Midland Institute for 1872 gave the inaugural address in Birmingham. Under the radical mayoralty of Joseph Chamberlain that city had become an example to all civic-minded people, and Kingsley had considerable respect for what had been accomplished there. Lord Lyttleton chaired the meeting, which was attended by London reporters for the national press. *The Times* actually used Kingsley's lecture as the basis for a leader on science institutes and lecturers, although it could not resist the unnecessary comment that readers might have expected Canon Kingsley to use very picturesque imagery whilst what he had done was far more useful—he had taken the bull by the horns and told the townsfolk some very simple truths. It was in Birmingham that Kingsley used the phrase 'divine discontent', meaning that every member of the population should feel this and aspire towards higher things. The expression was frequently repeated, often by Kingsley's opponents, who assumed that it was to apply to the poor, calling them to awaken to their condition.

The most gratifying result was the immediate response by a Birmingham manufacturer who listened to Kingsley's lecture and donated £2,500 to establish classes and lectures on 'Human Physiology and the Science of Health'. Fanny Kingsley tells us that this 'was perhaps *the* highest earthly reward ever granted to him', and we must assume that she is repeating what her husband said. Arthur Ryland was put in charge of the project, with Professor Huxley and Dr. Lyon Playfair as scientific advisers. These Birmingham classes were examples followed at Wolverhampton and elsewhere. As at Chester, Kingsley had risen at a most propitious moment like a prophet of old to point the way. Science was on the march and to Kingsley, as to so many other Victorians, it appeared that science was God's plan for man's progress.

In the following January Kingsley went to Chester to attend the opening of the cathedral, which had been closed for a long period while the nave was being repaired. The cathedral was full; the Canon was warmly greeted; and everyone asked after kind Mrs. Kingsley. 'I do love this place and people, and long to be back here for our spring residence,' he wrote home.

Before that date Kingsley had to face the loss of F. D. Maurice, who died on April 1, 1872. Kingsley had noticed with concern Maurice's frailty fully two years earlier, and for his dear Master's sake he now tried to be glad that he was granted peace. Maurice's sensitive, handsome features had been honed by experience to a rare delicacy, remarked upon by everyone, and 'beautiful' was not an inappropriate adjective to describe him in his last years.

The funeral took place on the afternoon of Easter Monday at

Highgate Cemetery where men who had not met for years for-
gathered to pay tribute. As Kingsley stood by the grave, tears
blinding his eyes, John Ludlow approached him, and the pair,
united by common grief, thrust aside the disputes which had
separated them. Tom Hughes was there too, and among the
other mourners in the western sunlight were Chartists, bringing
back memories nearly a quarter of a century old. But for all his
grief Kingsley could not truly wish his Master alive again.
Maurice had done his life's work: he deserved his rest.

Most of Kingsley's life's work was done by this time also, and
he was tired, a man of fifty-three, prematurely aged. In his
frequent moods of depression and melancholy he always regarded
death as a welcome friend, opening the door to an after-life that
must be better than the one on earth. Clifford Harrison wrote in
Stray Records about Kingsley that 'for one day when he was in
the mood that cried "Welcome wild North-easter", there were
twenty when his heart sang: "Oh that we two were maying
Over the fragrant leas." '8 Dr. Norman McLeod, editor of
Good Words, and an old personal friend, died the same year,
leading Kingsley to remark that McLeod's death was 'an instance
of a man who has worn his brain away, and he is gone as I am
surely going'. For as the Canon became increasingly respectable,
uncontrovertibly a man of decent, sensible views, expressing
those of so many of his fellow countrymen, he became even
more in demand for lectures and sermons. He had more invitations to visit and stay with friends than he could possibly
accept. His wife tried to shield him from unnecessary exertions,
but she was a delicate woman, who had suffered from a number
of miscarriages, and the entire Kingsley family was prone to
chronic coughs and colds because of the cold, damp site of
Eversley Rectory. Kingsley's intense restlessness—he could barely
sit through a meal without getting up at least once to pace
round the room—made him a prey to digestive disorders.
With Maurice's and McLeod's deaths fresh in her mind, Fanny
became fearful for Charles's health, and wished he could be
given a more lucrative canonry than Chester so that he could
stop writing altogether. Her fears were not groundless, as she

hints in the second, revised biography: 'over-work of the brain brought on symptoms, which led him to apprehend paralysis,'[9] a condition which Kingsley may have been referring to obliquely in a letter saying he had only just regained the use of a hand. Fanny Kingsley foresaw her husband one day dropping in his tracks, a fate she hoped to avert for as long as possible, taking no comfort in Kingsley's humorous remark, always made when she introduced the subject, that it was 'better to wear out than rust out'.

The Kingsley's youngest child, Grenville Arthur, was being coached for public school by a young German, Karl Schulze, who fell under Kingsley's spell just as young John Martineau had done twenty years earlier. The tutor was in the country to perfect his English before taking up an appointment as a professor in Berlin. Thanks to Schulze, Grenville, a rather lazy, unscholastic boy, passed the entrance examination for Harrow School. Kingsley, who was always optimistic about his children, was convinced that Grenville would outgrow any early physical or intellectual difficulties, ending up a strong, successful man, whatever profession or country he adopted. Maurice Kingsley was now supporting himself as a surveyor for a railway company in Mexico. The earlier hope of buying a farm for Maurice had been dropped when Fanny Kingsley's trustees refused to release any of her capital.

Meanwhile, Kingsley found time to scribble some comments on a new hymn book compiled by Dr. Monsell and submitted to him. As he grew older his tastes grew simpler, and he disliked the exaggerated revivalist language of many of the modern hymns. 'People do *not* hear the angels sing over fields and seas,' he objected reasonably. Faith and simple worship were becoming his bulwark, and the absence of F. D. Maurice, the rock to which he had clung most of his thinking life, left only one source of strength and comfort. Kingsley the middle-aged man looked to the Bible in a way that he had never been able to do as a young man plagued by doubt.

He was enjoying also the worldly pleasures of high society. At Chester, for example, the Duke of Westminster, influential

patron of the scientific societies, was a personal friend. The Duke
of Argyll was an old companion from sanitary reforming days.
Lord Carnarvon took Kingsley on his yacht. The Duke of
Wellington at Strathfieldsaye was always pleased to see him,
and there were many other great houses where Kingsley was an
honoured visitor for his quick wit and informative conversation.
The network of family relationships within the aristocracy and
the scientific and academic professions meant that friendship
with one member usually led to introductions to others within
the group. The two sides of Kingsley's life emerge from a letter
written by Octavia Hill on March 23, 1873. 'We have heard
to-day a sermon of Kingsley's for the Girls' Home. It was almost
wholly about Mr. Maurice and gave him fully the place one
believes he has. It was a sermon full of Kingsley's own peculiar
power; and there was not a word in it that was not true and
beautiful. It was to us a sight of deepest solemnity. The church . . .
was crammed with people, and one knew every second face.
It was filled with the old Lincoln's Inn and Vere St. people,
and with their spiritual inheritors of all that teaching. . . . Did I
tell thee about dining at the Cowper Temples and meeting
Kingsley and Lord and Lady Ducie?'[10]

One of the lesser Kingsley family irritations which now began
to be very irksome for Charles and Fanny was Henry Kingsley's
shortage of money. It was not Henry's fault that he could not
make ends meet by writing, and certainly not for lack of trying,
but the hack journalism which he was forced to accept to pay the
household bills stifled his true creative gift, and the quality of his
novels showed a depressing decline. Several times he was forced
to write what Charles and Fanny Kingsley censoriously considered
to be begging letters to titled patrons of the arts. Charles himself
helped his brother financially, but there came a time when
Fanny Kingsley objected, and objected strongly. In her biography
she indicates discreetly that Henry was the victim of an unsuitable marriage, and that not only his wife but more particularly
his mother-in-law made extravagant demands upon him. Sarah
Kingsley was often ill, also had several miscarriages, and needed
constant medical care. Like Charles, Henry was forced to write

incessantly merely to keep abreast of his debts. That freshness and skill which gave life to his Australian stories, and made some critics say he was a better novelist than Charles, became sadly eroded and lack-lustre. Charles referred to Henry and his two women in the last line of one of his few entirely private and domestic poems written at this time. The boy of the poem is Grenville; the grandmother, old Mrs. Kingsley; the 'foot of all feet' belonged to Fanny (her husband had something of a fetish about a woman's foot, and it appears as a symbol of desirable femininity frequently in his novels):

THE DELECTABLE DAY

The boy on the famous grey pony,
Just bidding goodbye at the door,
Plucking up maiden heart for the fences
Where his brother won honour of yore.

The walk to 'the Meet' with fair children—
And women as gentle as gay—
Ah! how do we male hogs in armour
Deserve such companions as they?

The afternoon's wander to windward,
To meet the dear boy coming back;
And to catch, down the turns of the valley,
The last weary chime of the pack.

The climb homeward by park and by moorland,
And through the fir forests again,
While the south-west wind roars in the gloaming,
Like an ocean of seething champagne.

And at night the septette of Beethoven,
And the grandmother by in her chair,
And the foot of all feet on the sofa
Beating delicate time to the air.

> Ah, God! a poor soul can but thank Thee
> For such a delectable day!
> Though the fury, the fool, and the swindler
> To-morrow again have their way!

Normally, however, Charles showed a mellowness in his approach, including new thoughts on theology. The Athanasian Creed ('that Knowledge of God, and it alone, is everlasting life') had once disturbed him, but now became the absolute basis for his teaching in and out of the pulpit, although he did not condemn others for not doing the same. Like Newman and Hurrell Froude thirty years earlier, he surveyed the historic roots of the Anglican Church and derived comfort from an old Catholic doctrine of an intermediate state after death. One of his main difficulties with the Athanasian Creed was that most people had defined it in an illiberal, Puritanical manner, dividing human beings into the damned and the elect. This made it a doctrine no better than that held by Dissenters. The intermediate state after death (not to be confused with the Roman Catholic state of purgatory) might overcome this problem by giving the soul another opportunity to know God after death. It is possible that this was the point in John Henry Newman's mind when he told a friend, after Kingsley's death, that he believed that of late years Kingsley had been moving nearer to the Roman Catholic Church.

When Grenville entered Harrow his parents rented a house at Harrow-on-the-Hill. Charles liked living there, partly because the house was much healthier than Eversley Rectory, but also because it was closer to London and he could visit friends knowing there was a midnight train to get him safely home. He obtained a special dispensation from the Bishop of Winchester to live outside Eversley parish on the condition that he took the Sunday services. He went down every weekend, often accepting Sir William Cope's hospitality at Bramshill. These two men, who had disputed and bickered so often, settled into an unexpectedly friendly relationship, drawn closer by the deaths of so many mutual friends.

A poem, 'Drifting Away', written in the autumn of 1867, reflects an elegant mood:

> They drift away. Ah, God! they drift for ever.
> I watch the stream sweep onward to the sea,
> Like some old battered buoy upon a roaring river,
> Round whom the tide-waifs hang—then drift to sea.
>
> I watch them drift—the old familiar faces,
> Who fished and rode with me, by stream and wold,
> Till ghosts, not men, fill old beloved places,
> And, ah! the land is rank with churchyard mold.
>
> I watch them drift—the youthful aspirations,
> Shores, landmarks, beacons, drift alike.
>
> I watch them drift—the poets and the statesmen;
> The very streams run upward from the sea.
>
> Yet overhead the boundless arch of heaven
> Still fades to night, still blazes into day.
>
> Ah, God! My God! Thou will not drift away.

In these autumnal years Kingsley re-read the authors and poets whom he had loved, concluding that Wordsworth's influence had been crucial, for it had preserved him from 'those shallow cynical and materialist views of the universe, which tempt the eager student of science in his exclusive search after the material and the temporary to neglect the spiritual and the eternal....' When his Chester students went out on their scientific expeditions, he advised them to take 'a volume of good poetry, say Wordsworth's "Excursion"—above all modern poetry.'[11]

15

The Treasures of Westminster

With the lengthening days Kingsley's thoughts turned to his spring duty in Chester. On March 24, 1873 he wrote to Mr. Shepheard, 'Give my love—that is the broadest and honestest word—to all the dear Chester folk, men, women, and children, and say that I long for May 1st, to be back again among them.' Two days later a letter from Mr. Gladstone was delivered to Kingsley at the Harrow house offering him a vacant canonry at Westminster Abbey. Charles was taken entirely by surprise. There was no comparison between the two stalls, Westminster paying twice as much as Chester and giving him the pulpit of England's most prestigious church. Every sound reason could be advanced for him to accept, and of course he was bound to do so, although he regretted giving up the quiet happiness of Chester. On March 27 he wrote again to Shepheard, 'I have just accepted the vacant stall at Westminster. I had to take it for my children's sake. Had I been a bachelor I would never have left Chester, meanwhile I had sooner be Canon of Westminster than either Dean or Bishop; but I look back longingly to Chester.'[1]

His friends regarded his new appointment in a different light. The Dean of Westminster, A. P. Stanley, was eager to have Kingsley associated with the Abbey, knowing that the association would strengthen his own efforts for a broad, informal alliance of churches, and, further, that Kingsley's reputation would attract a new congregation to the Abbey. 'How many waters, as the French say, have run under the bridge since we first met at Exeter College, many years ago. What a meeting of those waters here, and what a world of interest have they now to run through from this happy confluence!'[2] A. C. Tait, Archbishop of Canterbury, wrote warmly: 'It is a great sphere for one who, like you, knows how to use it.' Bishop Wilberforce joined with his good wishes. The people of Chester were so distressed at their own loss that they almost forgot to congratulate Kingsley, 'All Chester mourns,' wrote one of the Society members sorrowfully. To make up for his absence, Kingsley arranged to attend Chester for the Society's annual excursion in July, and it was indeed a day to remember.

Guests from the Cradoc Field Club met the two hundred or so members and friends as they reached Church Stretton railway station. 'Then to have a natural history ramble of eight or nine miles up the glorious Longmynd and Lightspout Valley, with the Canon, Dr. Wilding, Mr. Walker, Mr. Strahan, Mr. Shrubsole, Mr. Shone, and many others, to point out everything of interest *en route*; then tea before returning home.' It was clearly a splendid outing, with only one lament to mar the day: 'anticipation, alas, far exceeded realisation as to the much-desired tea. An afternoon cup alone is a poor offering to nature for creating an appetite worth at least a shilling. Why had our Secretary and Treasurer refused to pay more than tenpence?'

The Kingsleys stayed a few days in Chester so that Kingsley could speak at their third Conversazione, where he repeated that he was leaving a little of his heart behind in Chester. The Society would flourish, he felt sure, and prove to be one more centre of civilisation in Chester. 'The thing was to get their young people to worship Nature that they might worship God.' It was the last time Kingsley ever spoke in Chester. The Society did indeed continue and prosper along the lines Kingsley had indicated, forming a connection with the neighbouring Wrexham Society, publishing its proceedings, and getting the City Library on a sound basis.

Charles never lost the enviable knack of being able to live in the present. Once a new course of conduct was opened to him he moved forward like a soldier under orders. His happiness in Chester had been warm and genuine, but his happiness in being part of Westminster Abbey, with its hallowed place in English history, was solemn and profound. 'It was like coming suddenly into a large inheritance of unknown treasures,' he told Dean Stanley.

He had already preached various sermons in the Abbey before his appointment. That April he had preached a sermon for the Temperance Society, although he was far from being teetotal himself or advocating it for others. It was drunkenness which he abhorred, both for the sake of the drunkard and for his or her family. He pleaded now for the opening of the public art galleries, pointing out that if people were caught in a shower in London on a Sunday there were only the public houses open to provide them with shelter. Twenty-five years earlier he had said much the same thing in his Christian Socialist letters, but although his phrases were as youthfully fierce as ever it was now an elderly man who delivered them. Fanny Kingsley described him in these last two years as a candle spluttering in its socket.

His son, Maurice, home on a visit, was appalled at the rapid deterioration which he noticed in his father, and insisted that a sea voyage was vital to restore his health. This was easier said than done. Kingsley's way of life and financial status had never made annual recuperative holidays easy. He agreed that a sea voyage was desirable but refused to leave England while his mother was alive. Mrs. Mary Kingsley was almost eighty-six, very weak physically, but mentally alert enough to be proud that her eldest son had reached the Abbey.

As news of his appointment became more widely known he received a fresh batch of congratulatory letters, one of them from the Rev. Peter Wood, his old Cambridge friend. Kingsley was touched: '... it is a comfort to me to know that an old friend like you still thinks of me, and rejoices in my real good fortune.... God bless you; shall we not kill a trout together again? My mother, who is 86, is living, or rather, alas, dying with us. She often speaks of you.'[3]

Mrs. Mary Kingsley died soon afterwards. Henry Kingsley attended the funeral, coming from London where he and his wife now lived, thanks apparently to a small legacy.[4] Henry had heard literary gossip for months that Charles was ill, but his mother never mentioned this in her letters, and the funeral seems to have been the first time the brothers had met for a considerable period. Henry Kingsley, like Maurice, was shocked at the change in Charles's appearance. Nor was Fanny Kingsley well, for she had suffered an attack of angina pectoris, and her husband made light of his own weakness in an attempt to save her anxiety. Kingsley now had no reason to object further to a lecture tour of North America, which would give him a change of scene and a sea voyage, and enable him to pay his way.

His duties as Canon at Westminster Abbey covered the months of September and November and he often preached two sermons on Sundays. These were unfashionable months in the capital, but even so his name attracted such large congregations that he sometimes wondered how much larger they could possibly be if he were Canon during the high season of May and June. He preferred the unfashionable months, as he disliked society congregations, and in this instance had not changed since he was a young man in his father's Chelsea parish. Apart from this he believed he could accomplish more by preaching to the 'middle and lower class', as he thought they were most in need of the ideas and religious comfort which he hoped he could bring and were also in a better position to take advantage of them.

As Fanny Kingsley was too ill to move into the Canon's house in Westminster Cloisters, Rose acted as her father's housekeeper and hostess, leaving Fanny to regain her strength slowly in the country. Kingsley wrote comforting letters to her, assuring her that she would find the house charming and spacious, with an attractive view from the windows in the 'delicious gleamy weather' of November. In spite of his careful phrasing a familiar warning note escaped him at the end: 'I regret much that I am leaving just as I seemed to be getting hold of the people. But I do not think I could have stood the intense excitement of the Sundays much longer.' His last sermon at the Abbey that year had a Maurician theme—'Fix in your minds—or rather ask God to fix in your minds—this one idea of an absolutely good God; good with all forms of goodness which you respect and love in man; good as you, and I, and every honest man, understand the plain word good. Slowly you will acquire that grand and all-illuminating idea; slowly and most imperfectly at best; for who is mortal man that he should conceive and comprehend the goodness of the infinitely good God?'

He managed to complete three important articles on health and sanitary reform (later to be collected in a volume by Macmillan) and wearily returned to Eversley, willing to leave the travel details of the American trip to his capable daughter. Rose Kingsley was now thirty, a tall, adventurous young woman, with a strong resemblance to her father, and a definite taste for travel. The previous year she had gone to the United States and Mexico, visiting her brother, and was delighted at the prospect of another trip. She inherited the family gift for writing and sketching and had written, anonymously, a book about her travels with an introduction by her father.

The Kingsleys travelled on the S.S. *Oceanic,* one of the newest of the White Star Line's high-speed luxury ships, and if the fare was high the saloon accommodation was certainly luxurious. Dean Howson took advantage of the nearness of Chester to Liverpool to see his friends off, and Thomas Henry Ismay, owner of the White Star Line, met Kingsley in Liverpool in order to introduce him to the ship's captain: a happy start to the voyage. Kingsley logged the journey meticulously on the back of a passenger track chart and sent it home for Grenville in the hope that it would 'interest and teach' him. Gales and high seas slowed the ship down, although it did not deviate from its course.

Kingsley made friends with Americans on board and was pleased to hear that he could expect to command high lecture fees. 'Thus there seems little difficulty in making $500 to $1,000 a week, if God give me health and luck,' he wrote optimistically to his wife. As soon as they landed he felt better immediately, with the air 'like Champagne, as poor Thackeray used to say' and a blazing hot sun—'It is a glorious country, and I don't wonder at the people being proud of it.'

He was guest speaker at a gala dinner given by the Lotos Club of New York[5] and delivered his Westminster Abbey lecture amid great applause. Afterwards he was escorted to the Century

Association by the American poet, William Cullen Bryant, whose work he admired. Most of his lectures were arranged by the Redpath Lyceum Bureau and on the whole they were well attended, sometimes exceptionally well attended. In Philadelphia he lectured in the Opera House to an audience of nearly 4,000, every seat being taken and the aisles and steps crowded with people standing. As the *Philadelphia Inquirer* said, 'It is Kingsley the author who is admired, and not the Canon of Westminster,' and since he never wore clerical dress unless he was in the pulpit, it was Kingsley the author whom most Americans believed they were meeting.

Several reporters criticised his style of delivery, assuming that its slow monotone must be a particular kind of English cathedral delivery and not realising it was mainly due to Kingsley's patient attempts to conquer his bad stammer. His accent, not being American, also came in for criticism: it was 'too broad', or 'too Scottish', or 'too Yorkshire' or 'offensively English'—and some reporters objected because he read his lectures. The agonies of shyness and emotional strain which Kingsley endured when lecturing are seen in an account from the *New York Daily Tribune* on February 28, 1874: 'While the Rev. Mr. Potter is introducing him, he shrinks, covered with confusion, blushes in his arm-chair, and when the time comes, rolls himself off his cushion, seizes his manuscripts as a sheet anchor, fumbles off his last kid glove, straightens himself up, and launches out with a voice that sounds like the wail of miserable sinners in his own Abbey service. For an hour and a half this mournful cry keeps on, with scarcely a change of note, with hardly a dying fall, and with such wide-mouthed rolling vowels and outlandish accent that many a time what he is saying might as well be Greek for all that can be made of it. There is but one gesture; the right elbow supported by the left hand, and the right hand or its forefinger waving like a pennon, appealing, threatening, emphasizing, doing all the work of two hands and answering the awkward angularity of the body's swaying back and forth.'[6] Although this is close to caricature there is an element of truth in it, but if Kingsley were really such a figure of fun it is surprising that people even stayed to listen, and this same reporter ended his account by admitting that the audience was none the less 'bound by the spell of the eloquent thought and tender feeling, listened all the time and could have listened twice as long.'

As soon as Kingsley received his first fees he changed the money into pounds sterling and sent it home to repay a loan of £200 from Cowley Powles,[7] and £100 to Fanny. As soon as he could he sent $500 to Maurice, who was just about to marry an American girl, Marie Yorke, in Mexico City. The letters which crossed the Atlantic during this longest of all Kingsley's absences speak of preoccupation with household and family matters and nagging anxieties over small domestic sums of money. Obviously Fanny Kingsley worried about Maurice, so far away, without professional qualifications, with no money to establish himself. Charles wrote back in optimistic mood, but none of his hopes for his son matured, and finally Maurice took a position as a civil engineer in Tennessee. Kingsley had to reassure Fanny about Grenville also. His first year at Harrow was so far from being promising that it was decided to remove him. His fond father stoutly maintained that the only problem was some childish weakness which Grenville would surely outgrow. In the meantime he should have nothing except 'idleness and food and fresh air'. In due course he would make 'a huge man and a clever one.'[8]

News about Mary, his younger daughter—Polly, as she was called in the family—was certainly happier, for she had just become engaged to William Harrison. The young man had been almost an adopted son when he was Kingsley's curate, now he was a rising young clergyman and Kingsley looked forward to the day when he would be a son-in-law. In the meantime, hearing that Harrison had attended David Livingstone's funeral on Kingsley's behalf as well as his own, Charles asked that Harrison be thanked for his thoughtfulness. He was especially pleased about Polly's engagement because he had feared that Rose might become engaged to a Captain Howard Schuyler and marry and settle in America. This came to nothing, as the dashing captain was already engaged to another, much to Kingsley's relief. We do not know how Rose regarded it; she never married. The irony of Polly's marriage (which Kingsley never lived to see) was that it did not last, and after a few years together the Harrisons separated, apparently amicably.[9]

In America Kingsley was delighted to meet and talk with every kind of person in every walk of life. He met John Greenleaf Whittier in Boston, a poet he deeply admired. Whittier had been looking forward to a long talk about problems of writing poetry and was astonished when Kingsley abruptly broke the chain of their conversation to speak in grave tones about life and death. As Whittier wrote later to Fanny Kingsley, 'The solemn questions of a future life, and the final destiny of the race, seemed pressing upon him, not so much for an answer (for he had solved them all by simple faith in the Divine Goodness), as for the sympathetic response of one whose views he believed to be, in a great degree, coincident with his own. "I sometimes doubt and distrust myself," he said, "but I see some hope for everybody else. To me the Gospel of Christ seems indeed Good Tidings of great joy to all people; and I think we may safely trust the mercy which endureth *for ever*." '[10] It is impossible not to conclude from this unusual behaviour that Kingsley was becoming increasingly preoccupied with death and what might lie ahead.

One of Fanny's early letters to Kingsley in America gave the news of the death of Anthony Froude's second wife, completely unforeseen, as she had not been ill, and sympathy for his friend revived memories of the first Mrs. Froude, Fanny's sister. Replying to Fanny, Kingsley wrote: 'Surely God must have great things in store for one on whom He inflicts *two* such tremendous blows. But do not *you* die, oh my Fanny, do not you die.' Kingsley cherished the romantic notion that marriages as blessed as his and Fanny's could not end in this world but must surely continue in another. The perfect ending for married lovers was to die within a brief space of each other, but failing that he hoped that the period of waiting for the partner dying first might perhaps, through the dispensation of a merciful and loving God, have no temporal significance. Thus years could pass in a flash. Kingsley never wished to survive his wife, although the likelihood was that he would do so, since she was five years his senior and a semi-invalid, and when they had discussions about the future he always promised her he would try to live, if she died, for their children's sake. This of course could not now be as pressing a consideration as it once was. Maurice was married, Polly engaged, Rose well able to control her life, and clearly Grenville would never need money for a university training. If both his parents died, Grenville would have the faithful John Martineau as guardian, with Cowley Powles and Anthony Froude on hand in the event of any crisis.

John Greenleaf Whittier could not have dreamed of this intimate family background when he spoke with Kingsley in Boston, and so was naturally taken aback by Kingsley's obsession with final causes. For his part, Charles had no idea he had made such a strange impression upon the American poet, for he wrote about Whittier '. . . we had a most loving and like-minded talk about the other world. He is an old saint.'

A similar incident took place in Canada, where Kingsley was taken by Colonel Strange to view the impressive falls of Montmorency near Quebec. The colonel noticed how very moved the rector was and had the tact to remain silent. This sympathy encouraged Kingsley later that day to speak his mind to the colonel much as he had done to Whittier; as the colonel said, 'pacing the little room with brave, kind words to me, upon my dear mother's death. He spoke then of his readiness to go to his own place.'

The stimulation of new faces and old friends was like a tonic to Kingsley, although he tried conscientiously to follow the advice of American friends like Henry Wadsworth Longfellow not to overwork. 'One feels ready to do anything, and then suddenly very tired,' he wrote in February at the start of the tour which was to last until July. He was still confident a few weeks later: 'But it is infinitely healthy, at least to me. Rose looks quite blooming, and seems years younger, than when she started—and I am suddenly quite well. All those sucking craving feelings gone, and my old complaint so utterly vanished, that I am rather in the opposite trouble at times. I never want medicine or tonic, and very little stimulant. But one cannot do as much here as at home. All say so and I find it. One can go faster for a while but gets exhausted sooner.' These comments were surely reflections of a man approaching the end of his strength, impelled more by spirit than by body. Without Rose's stalwart companionship and organising skill, Kingsley could never have kept up the pace, even with the generosity of men like Cyrus Field giving them free railway passes and every kind of help and hospitality.

Kingsley was constantly writing to assure Fanny that American trains were perfectly safe, although he and Rose did have a narrow escape in April. According to Rose, 'Our first halting place was Ithaca (Cornell University), which we should have reached on the evening of the 20th, but on the Erie railroad we were stopped for six hours by a huge rock falling on the track as a coal train was coming towards us, round sharp curves, and we should have had a frightful accident but for the presence of mind of the engineer, as his engine ran over the rock, jamming itself and the tender across both lines of rail; he being unhurt, and remembering our train was due at that moment, ran down the line seeing us coming, and we pulled up within 100 yards of the disaster. It happened in the midst of the finest scenery on the Delaware, above Port Jervis, where the railway follows the windings of the river, and is in many places blasted out of the cliffs. And as there was no possibility of getting on till the disabled train and broken trucks were removed, my father and I spent the hours of waiting in wandering about the rocky woods above the railway, botanizing and geologizing.'

In March Kingsley was in Washington, where he met Charles Sumner, the famous anti-slavery Senator from Massachusetts. They had at one time been close pen-friends, but had drifted apart over the Civil War. Sumner had recently suffered a heart attack, but attended the Senate that day, against his doctor's advice, and he and Kingsley enjoyed a reconciliation. An hour later Sumner had another attack and died the following day. The news of his death was particularly shocking to Kingsley, removing the pleasure he would otherwise have felt when as a visiting celebrity he had been given the honour (not entirely uncommon for foreign clergymen) of opening the Session of the House of Representatives with prayer.

The Kingsleys crossed the border to Canada, where Montreal, 'this magnificent city', sparkled in frost, snow and sunshine. He gave a few lectures and took a week off to rest. He and Rose stayed for the Easter holiday with the Governor-General in Ottawa ('the delightful Dufferins'—who invited them back) and then returned to Washington where the President arranged 'a regular dinner party for us—so we shall have seen quasi-royalty British and Yankee both in one week.' He spent time at Niagara and was overcome by the splendour and beauty of the falls, but he was already homesick. He was not normally absent from Fanny for long periods and anxiety about her health made him even more tender towards her. 'My own, I love you, and dream of you every night; but my feeling comes out in my dreams, that I have not been what I ought to have been to you in this world— Oh God grant that I may make up for it all in some other.'[11]

By May the Kingsleys were heading West across the 'huge rushing muddy ditch' of the Mississippi, and most comfortably installed in St. Louis, then a growing city of 470,000 souls. They inspected one of the famous Mississippi steamers which plied between St. Louis and New Orleans ('She will *not* blow up at the quayside'), visited a Botanic Garden, and then set off for Omaha, on the way to Denver, Salt Lake City and the west coast. His lectures went down so well in St. Louis that he was asked to give an additional one.

His most popular lecture was entitled *Westminster Abbey*, and he had written it with Americans especially in mind. 'I know few more agreeable occupations than showing a party of Americans round our own great Abbey; and sentimentalising, if you will, in sympathy with them, over England's Pantheon.' After a graceful tribute to Washington Irving's *Sketchbook*, with its essay on the Abbey, Kingsley took his audience on a guided tour. and we can glimpse something of his love for that storehouse of riches. He praised the Abbey as a place of peace, where Queen Elizabeth I lay in the same vault as her half-sister, Queen Mary, just across the aisle from Mary, Queen of Scots. And after assuring his audience that the American Congress was as much a child of the English Magna Carta as was the Parliament at Westminster, he continued,

> Yes—and I do not hesitate to say that if you will look through the monuments erected in that Abbey, since those of Pitt and Fox—you will find that the great majority commemorate the children, not of obstruction, but of progress; not of darkness, but of light.
>
> Holland, Tierney, Mackintosh, Gratton, Peel, Canning, Palmerston, Isaac Watts, Bell, Wilberforce, Sharp, the Macaulays, Fowell Buxton, Francis Horner, Charles Buller, Cobden, Watt, Telford, Locke, Brunel, Grote, Thackeray, Dickens, Maurice[12]—men who, each in his own way, toiled for freedom of some kind; freedom of race, of laws, of commerce, of locomotion, of production, of speech, of thought, of education, of human charity and of sympathy—these are the men whom England still delights to honour.[13]

So far as poets were concerned, Kingsley observed, 'They are the heritage, neither of us, nor you, but of the human race'— and in a highly personal aside he made it clear that he would not want to be buried in the Abbey, however greatly it stirred him, for the poet went not to the town but to nature for inspiration and therefore Kingsley quoted Burke with approval: 'After all I had sooner sleep in the southern corner of a country churchyard than in the tomb of all the Capulets.'

The *Westminster Abbey* lecture displayed Kingsley as the Canon of Westminster, royal chaplain, poet, scientist, spokesman for freedom, but in his other favourite lecture, *The First Discovery of America*, we see the other side of the man—Kingsley the lion, the Viking, the warrior fighting to the death. He began with a quotation from the Norse sagas and told the story of Leif the Fortunate finding the wild fox-grapes on the shores of New England and calling that land Vinland the Good. Next he reflected on the ethics of the Vikings, rather as he had done in *Hypatia*, concluding, 'And yet one loves them, blood-stained as they are.' Kingsley believed there were similarities between the Western tales of Bret Harte and Colonel John Hay and the tales of the old Norse heroes, and to prove his point he ended with an exceedingly bloodthirsty yarn of Norway around the year 1030. 'Yes, as long as you have your *Jem Bludos* and *Tom Flynns of Virginia City*, the old Norse blood is surely not extinct, the old Norse spirit is not dead.'

His other lectures included *The Stage as It was Once, The Servant of the Lord* and *Ancient Civilization*, but there is no doubt that the first two were more characteristic of Kingsley.

The contrast between the cold of Detroit and the intense heat of St. Louis upset him, although he had to be careful not to alarm Fanny by grumbling about his health. 'The heat is tremendous—all of a sudden. But it will be cooler as we rise to the Prairies out of the Mississippi Valley. Rose seems well, though we both have had little colds—nothing but the heat—' In spite of his brave words, his cold remained troublesome.

On May 11th Kingsley headed his letter Omaha, a fast-growing town since the railway first called there five years earlier. Kingsley felt a sentimental pang as he gazed upon Council Bluffs, and recalled how as a poor student he had considered emigrating there. Fortunately Fanny had come along to save him and dutifully he wrote to remind and thank her. The Kingsleys continued their progress to Salt Lake City, where Brigham Young, President of the Mormon Church, offered Kingsley the tabernacle to preach in—'but of this offer he of course took no notice whatever,' wrote his daughter. Plural marriage was almost as revolting as celibacy to Kingsley. 'What horrors this place has seen. Thank God, it is all breaking up fast. The tyrant is 70, and must soon go to his account—and what an awful one.' On went the Kingsleys and their entourage, for now Cyrus Field and other friends accompanied them, to the Yosemite Valley, stopping briefly in Virginia City for Rose to go down a silver mine although Charles had strength only to go for a drive round the town.

The party was mounted for the Yosemite trip and members had to be ready on their horses by six in the morning. The mountain air and outdoor régime suited Kingsley, who was always one of the earliest and fittest of the group. On Whit Sunday he conducted a short service in the glorious mountain forest, a setting which he had often declared was more suitable to religious worship than were great cathedrals. On the same day, in England, Dean Stanley seized the chance of preaching co-operation when he said in his sermon in the Abbey that day that 'a gifted member of this Collegiate' was preaching in one of the most beautiful spots in the world. 'Let me, from this pulpit, faintly echo the enthusiasm which I doubt not inspires his burning words. Let us feel that in this splendid Psalm (Psalm 104) and this splendid festival, the old and the new, the east and the west, are indeed united in one.'

By the time the Kingsleys reached San Francisco the rector's exertions and his neglected cold made him highly susceptible to the chilly evening fogs. He delivered his lectures, but these did not seem to go down as well as in the East, partly because there were other leisure distractions in the city and partly also perhaps because he was getting bored with repeating them. He gave a very successful talk to students of Berkeley University, but he was extremely tired and his medical advisers insisted that he return to the mountains. In mid-June the Kingsleys reached Denver, Colorado, and Kingsley was pining for his wife as well as weak in health. He tried to interest himself in a collection of plants and seeds he was making for friends like Lord Eversley and Sir Charles Bunbury, and he kept comforting himself with the knowledge that they had at least turned eastwards and were on the homeward lap.

By a happy accident Charles and Rose met Dr. George Kingsley, who was shooting bear in the Rockies with a companion. George quickly diagnosed his brother's complaint as pleurisy and sent him to convalesce at the ranch of Dr. Bell at Manitou, near Colorado Springs. At the Bell ranch Charles received the attention due to an honoured guest and an ailing man, enjoyed English food and the companionship of English travellers. He realised that he was becoming irritated with the American accent and homesick for the slower English inflection. George gave him news of home, including a welcome item about their brother,

Henry, who George thought had taken on a pupil to help with household expenses. There were letters from the rectory and one from John Martineau. Charles and Rose remained in the area for several weeks, part of the time at another ranch, and part at the castle-like home of an eccentric railway promoter called General William J. Palmer.

The time for departure was now close—'I cannot believe that I may see you within 21 days. I never longed so for you and home'—and the Kingsleys began to plan their future in the Westminster house for the autumn. Fanny had found the strength to inspect it and found it every bit as charming as Kingsley had said. He could not wait to move in there. 'Yes, we shall rest our weary old bones there for awhile, before kind death comes,' he wrote, 'and perhaps see a bevy of grandchildren round us there— Ah please God *that*.'[14] During his enforced rest in Colorado Charles had a last burst of poetic activity and composed a strange, haunting ballad about an unfortunate girl, Lorraine, who is killed riding a dangerous horse. The poem has a relentless, thudding rhythm which led Anthony Froude to place it high among his favourite poems by his friend, but although it has a stirring theme —an important race—it is tragic because Lorraine is a doomed figure.

In August, with Kingsley home at last in his beloved Eversley, he, too, seemed a doomed figure. Bowed, shrunken, visibly older, he had not benefited by the journey and the sea voyages. Worse, the summer in England that year was hot and dry with a persistent wind which gave Kingsley a troublesome cough, and the villagers fell sick with the fever which so frequently accompanied dry summers in those years before national sanitary legislation.[15] The rector began his usual cottage visiting, encouraging the sick, opening windows, ordering water to be boiled, explaining the elementary laws of hygiene. The little strength he had garnered painfully in Colorado was soon dissipated and he had still to face his tour of duty at Westminster.

Somehow he dragged himself through September at the Abbey, although he was weakened by a severe attack of 'congestion of the liver'. He made light of it, wishing to spare Fanny distress and hoping not to disappoint his Abbey followers, but he was not strong enough to give two sermons in one day. Just as he was beginning to recover Fanny had another heart attack, and Charles spent all his free time by her bedside, filled with apprehension. As soon as she was over the worst she insisted that Charles go to friends in Norfolk for a few days' rest and change of air.[16] He returned to London in November, ready to start his second month's work. It was unfortunate that Dean Stanley was detained in Paris at this time and extra responsibility fell upon Kingsley in the Dean's absence. His congregations were bigger than ever, a fact which normally would have pleased him, but which now seemed overwhelming, forcing him to take even greater pains with his sermons. He chose texts, and it can hardly be a coincidence, from passages of the Bible dealing more with the next world than with the present one. He was preoccupied with thoughts of God, and the goodness and mercy of God to human sinners, and would interpose sudden exclamations to this effect no matter how irrelevant it might seem. It was as if he were easing himself out of this existence and preparing himself for the next.

His last sermon of the month was preached on November 29th, while a howling gale outside tugged at the foundations of the great church. Kingsley had always responded with excitement to storms and this occasion was no exception. He preached in a highly emotional strain on the text of Luke XXII, 41—Christ weeping over the doomed city of Jerusalem. He told his packed congregation that individuals resembled nations and institutions; each separate human being like a thought of God, and when that life was in harmony with itself and with God, it would be a 'microcosmic City of God'. Men and women, however, were not doomed like the doomed city of Jersualem, because they could be redeemed at any time by a visitation of Christ, whispering as he came 'Come unto Me, thou weary and heavy-laden heart, and I will give thee *Rest*.' We can imagine how solemnly Kingsley would have uttered these last words, feeling at that juncture how appropriate they were to himself.

Fanny Kingsley had not felt strong enough to attend the Abbey that afternoon for his last sermon, although he had deliberately

12

chosen her favourite text. She was obeying doctor's orders and resting in her room every afternoon. Charles had one or two duties still to perform in connection with the Abbey. On the following day he attended a Deanery dinner and an evening lecture, and caught a fresh chill on the way home. Out of the habit of a lifetime and for Fanny's sake he made light of his ailment. The servants were busy packing for the return to Eversley, and on December 3rd Charles took Fanny home. In spite of the very greatest care on the journey Fanny suffered another heart attack, this time so serious that the doctor informed Charles that there was very little hope of her recovery. The end was merely a question of time. He telegraphed his children to hurry home, informed Queen Victoria that he could not preach at Windsor that weekend as she had requested, and remained at Fanny's bedside, comforting her as he had comforted so many of his parishioners.

As news went round the village that Mrs. Kingsley was ill, messages of condolence and hopes for her recovery arrived. Mr. Stapleton, for many years a friend of the Kingsleys, who had, however, ceased visiting them some years back when he and Charles fell out over some controversial matter, was so concerned about Fanny that he called at the rectory, wishing to heal the breach before it was too late. Kingsley had seen him coming through the window and was waiting at the front door to greet him and thank him for his consideration. Stapleton was greatly touched. Kingsley gave him the impression of a man quietly making his peace with everyone, and Stapleton was happy that he had yielded to his impulse. John Martineau rode over from Heckfield every day for news of the woman who had been a true second mother to him. On the days when the snow was too thick for his horse Martineau would ride as far as a small inn on the Eversley road, stable his horse there and walk the rest of the way.

On her death-bed, as she and Charles had been led to suppose, Fanny was ashamed to discover that at the final moment she was a coward who shrank from the unknown. Charles comforted her, assured her there was no need for shame, read aloud all their favourite poems, relived with her all the significant episodes

of their happy marriage. They discussed arrangements for the
funeral quite calmly, the coffin to be carried by village men, and
the Latin motto which they had agreed long ago summed up their
life to commemorate their common grave. At this point, of
course, Charles still had faith in his own powers of recuperation
and believed he had many lonely years ahead of him.

Christmas came and went, a family festival still, but this year
a sorrowful one. Thinking only of Fanny, Charles neglected his
own health. The rectory bedrooms were ice-boxes with spots of
warmth, and Fanny's bedroom was especially cold since when one
of her attacks seized her the servants would fling open the windows to give her more air. At the end of December Kingsley
himself was on the point of collapse and Mr. Heynes, for years his
local medical adviser, diagnosing pneumonia, ordered him to
remain in one temperature and preferably to stay in bed. '. . . yet
one day he leaped out of bed, came into his wife's room for a few
moments, and taking her hand in his, he said, "This is heaven,
don't speak."; but after a short silence, a severe fit of coughing
came on, he could say no more, and they never met again.'[17]
For a few days they maintained daily contact by written notes,
but this proved physically and emotionally tiring, 'too tantalising'
was Kingsley's phrase.

The weather improved on New Year's Day and the grass on
the mount opposite the rectory showed green beneath its sprinkling of snow. Charles could lie in bed and watch the sun on the
slope and reflect once more how quietly beautiful the Eversley
countryside was. A trained nurse from Westminster Hospital,
London, sat with him at night, and his children and the servants
shared the day duty. Their old family nurse stayed by Fanny's
side. Mr. Heynes kept Charles under constant sedation and he
dreamed away the days and nights, travelling once more in the
West Indies and the United States. It was a strange imitation of
his fictional character, Alton Locke, and the three weeks passed
like three days.

The rector's illness became public knowledge and, again,
messages of goodwill arrived by every post. At Chester prayers
were said daily for both the Kingsleys and a daily bulletin was

posted outside the cathedral. The doctor kept all letters away from Charles, so as not to disturb him, but made an exception in the case of two letters with drawings sent by the young sons of the Prince of Wales. Charles summoned up strength to reply personally: almost the last message he sent. His family watched him slipping into a mood of peace and acceptance—'All *under rule*,' he murmured repeatedly to himself. The Prince of Wales sent his physician down to Eversley, an event sufficiently newsworthy for *The Times* to report it. Up to that time, January 20th, it was generally believed that Kingsley would pull through in the end, although it was felt that Mrs. Kingsley would die.

However, on the night of Dr. Gull's visit Charles had a serious haemorrhage, and both he and Heynes knew the end was near. Characteristically Charles spoke in fighting language. 'Heynes, I am hit: this last shot has told.' He gave the doctor details of the funeral arrangements. They had been intended for Fanny: they would serve for him. The family nurse snatched a moment to leave her mistress in order to pay a last visit to her dying master, and in his confused state of mind Charles appears to have misunderstood her and gained the impression that she had come to his bedside because Fanny was already dead. This belief helped him reconcile himself to his own impending death, seeing that it corresponded to one of his deepest fantasies. 'Ah, dear nurse, *and I, too,* am come to an end; it is all right—all as it *should be*,' he told her. There was a slight rally on January 22nd, and Rose, Heynes and William Harrison sat with him throughout the night. He prayed, apparently oblivious of them, and once exclaimed quite loudly, 'No more fighting; no more fighting.' At 5 a.m. the others rested while the hospital nurse took over, and Charles could be heard reciting the burial service. This seemed to ease him, and he turned on his side. He lingered for a few hours and died before midday on January 23rd, so peacefully that neither Rose Kingsley nor the nurse could determine the exact moment.

A messenger rode over to Heckfield to tell Martineau that Kingsley was dead, and Martineau and his wife hurried to the rectory. The village had already heard. Telegrams were sent to Windsor, Sandringham, Westminster, Chester. The cathedral bell at Chester tolled for him and the Abbey bell at Westminster. Queen Victoria noted in her journal:

Osborne, 23rd Jan. 1875. Poor Canon Kingsley, who has been alarmingly ill for the last three or four weeks, died to-day, and is a sad loss! His wife was very ill at the same time, and neither could go to the other, which was dreadfully sad, and terrible for the two daughters. He was full of genius and energy, noble and warm-hearted, devoted, loyal and chivalrous, much attached to me and mine, full of enthusiasm, and most kind and good to the poor.

With Fanny still ill, the burden of business arrangements fell upon Martineau, executor of Kingsley's will. Dean Stanley telegraphed at once his willingness to have Kingsley buried in Westminster Abbey, but Fanny and Martineau knew that the rector wished to be buried in Eversley. He had died on a Saturday, and on the following Sunday references to his life and work were numerous in church and chapel up and down the country. John Henry Newman said a mass for him. Sir William Cope, himself an ordained clergyman and churchwarden at Eversley, preached in the church on the Sunday, a grieving friend who had forgotten the sharp exchanges of their early association. In Westminster Abbey Dean Stanley described him as one of the most conspicuous teachers of his age with 'the power of reaching souls to which other preachers and teachers addressed themselves in vain.'[18] At the Cooperative Congress held in London shortly after Kingsley's death, Tom Hughes paid tribute to 'the brave minister of God, the accomplished scholar, and gentleman, and the brilliant author, whose place is empty.' The delegates stood in silence for a few moments. In the Official Report, it was recorded —'He has become one of that illustrious band who "being dead still speaketh".'

The funeral took place on January 28. *The Times* reported it in detail. 'Though the funeral was, by the special desire of the deceased, conducted privately, the occasion was made one of such an exhibition of sympathy and respect as is rarely witnessed.

As the distance from the rectory to the churchyard is only some 50 yards, the large concourse of spectators and mourners occupied but a small space, and the road was nearly blocked by carriages. Shortly before half-past 2, the time fixed for the ceremony, a large assemblage of clergymen and mourners appeared on the broad gravel road facing the rectory. Eight villagers carried out the coffin, which was of oak, and on this was placed a profusion of wreaths and crosses of camellias. Sir William Cope, church-warden of the parish, headed the cortège, Dean Stanley reading the opening service in a most impressive manner and the Bishop of Winchester following. Besides the relatives and friends of the deceased and a large number of clergy, there were present Mr. Macmillan, Sir Charles Russell, Professor Max Müller, the Deans of St. Pauls and Chester, and Colonel the Hon. A. Fitzmaurice representing the Prince of Wales.' Max Müller, in his introduction to *The Roman and the Teuton*, added further touches: '... close by, the gipsies of Eversley Common, who used to call him their "Patrico-rai" (their Priest King). There was the squire of his village, and the labourers young and old, to whom he had been a friend and a father. There were governors of distant colonies, officers, and sailors, the bishop of his diocese and the dean of his abbey; there were the leading Nonconformists of the neighbour-hood, and his own devoted curates, peers and members of the House of Commons, authors and publishers, and the huntsmen in pink; and, outside the churchyard, the horses and the hounds. . . .'

The Times account ends: 'By special desire of the deceased the grave was not bricked, his wish being that his body might be committed to mother earth without that formality.'

16

Summation

John Martineau took charge of all the business matters attendant upon Charles's death, organised the removal of the Kingsley family from Eversley Rectory and accepted the guardianship of young Grenville. Fanny Kingsley, still very ill, went to Byfleet for a period until a permanent home was found for her in a charming manor house at Tachbrook Mallory, near Leamington, where she lived for a further sixteen years, a semi-invalid, until her death in 1892.[1] Although she was always physically weak, her mind and resolution were strong and she overcame her grief at bereavement by compiling a memorial volume of the life and letters of her husband. This tribute seemed to some readers to be more in the nature of an essay in canonisation than a simple biography, yet enough of Kingsley's energy and complex character shone through it to make the book an instant best-seller, reprinted many times and finally available in an abridged edition.

With typical Victorian wifely diffidence, Fanny Kingsley had doubted her judgment in selecting material, and relied upon the advice of four trusted friends: Cowley Powles, Max Müller, John Martineau and the Hon. Gerald Wellesley, Dean of Windsor. In obedience to Victorian standards of decency and good taste in biographies, only a hint of personal and intimate details were included: a reticence which we may regret, but which contemporary men of letters like Leslie Stephen strongly admired. The first edition, published in 1876, rapidly sold out, and since a second edition in January 1877 bid fare to follow suit Macmillans quickly prepared a third edition. A jubilant Fanny wrote to Martineau: 'The voice from the grave seems daily more powerful'. She found it comforting although ironic that it was she who now received letters from strangers, as her husband had done all his life, and many of these correspondents confessed that whilst they had refrained from reading Kingsley's books during his lifetime because of religious prejudice, now that he was safely dead they were reading him for the first time. Naturally they did not find the social revelations in _Yeast_ and _Alton Locke_ as shocking as their fathers had done thirty years before, since so many of Kingsley's opinions now reflected majority views and reinforced them in a comforting manner instead of preceding them at an alarmingly advanced pace.

Thomas Woolner, one of the leading sculptors of the day (and an associate of the Working Men's College), was commissioned to design a marble bust which would stand in Westminster Abbey, fittingly near the memorial there to F. D. Maurice. The artist deliberately omitted Kingsley's side-whiskers on the grounds that these were only a fashionable fad, doubtless transitory, and the real man would be best represented without them. Close friends and family agreed with Woolner and found the likeness spirited and faithful, although strangers were disconcerted by the clean-shaven rector. A bust of Kingsley in a new science museum which was built at Chester, the Grosvenor Museum, showed him with the bushy side-whiskers which had been a feature of cartoons of the later Kingsley. Since Fanny's health made it extremely unlikely that she would ever have the strength to travel to London where she could see the bust in the Abbey, Woolner sent it down to Byfleet for a few hours before its official installation, an act of kindness which she deeply appreciated.

Additional tributes to Kingsley's memory found concrete expression in places which had been particularly associated with him. A bas-relief was affixed to the wall inside Eversley Church. The ladies of Chester collected money to pay for the renovation of a seat in the choir stalls at the cathedral, and a fund was started for a Kingsley Memorial Medal and another to encourage science in the Chester district. A special stained-glass window was designed and installed in Holne Church. An impressive marble statue of the rector in academic robes was erected at the end of Bideford Quay. Countless roads and buildings were named after him. Two Metropolitan horse drinking-troughs were set up in

London in his memory—one still exists by the Round House in Chalk Farm.

Fanny Kingsley discovered as she read over her late husband's correspondence and tried to edit her chapters that it was almost impossible to pin down such a many-sided man. 'A mystic in theory, and an ultra-materialist in practice,' he once said of himself. Monkton Milnes (later Lord Houghton) had remarked that Kingsley had literally '*rowed* himself to death', and there is a strong element of truth in that statement, just as there would be in a comment that he worried himself to death. So far as Fanny Kingsley and John Martineau were concerned there was no real problem. He was simply one of the world's saints. After she read Martineau's personal recollections of those early days at Eversley she wrote to him: 'When I read yours now again and again, it makes me shiver, it is so like him.' Tom Hughes, remorseful that he had turned aside from his old friend after the American Civil War, tried to make amends by writing a warm and personal memoir as introduction to a new edition of *Alton Locke*. Some years afterwards, however, in 1888, when he had become a judge at Chester, Hughes was invited to write an article on Kingsley and he consulted with Martineau as the man closest to the rector. In a surprising admission Hughes explained to Martineau, 'I saw so little of him after (about) 1860, and was never, I take it, intimate enough to know the real man.' It is no wonder that Hughes abandoned the attempt to reveal a personal truth about Kingsley, finding it easier and less painful to portray the man through his writings, where he saw sadness as the key to the rector's character. He quoted Kingsley's line, 'It is a sad world, a sad world, and full of tears', and added, 'All his noble songs had a deep melancholy in them. But he was bent on arousing an eating and drinking generation to the perils ahead.' This Kingsley undoubtedly succeeded in doing. William Morris, writing in 1883 and looking back on his student days at Oxford in the 1850s, said, 'I was a good deal influenced by the works of Charles Kingsley, and got into my head therefrom some socio-political ideas which would have developed probably but for the attractions of art and poetry.' Frederic Harrison spoke of Kingsley and his effect on young people: 'He woke them up in all sorts of ways, about all sorts of things.'

It was the combination of seer and poet in Kingsley which caused his readers to feel, protest and turn to action. His social-problem novels gave genuine expression to the grievances of the poor, and he was almost alone in speaking out on the unavoidable sexual squalor of the very poor. He was convinced that a great part of man's inhumanity to man lay in denying to a poor man his intrinsic human dignity by forcing him to live in degrading circumstances, and although Kingsley never saw the solution to this problem as lying in a social revolution (a moral revolution was a different matter) his forthright prose had an influence on readers late into the century, often turning their thoughts and actions into paths which did not exist during his own lifetime. To readers of this type it was not particularly important that Kingsley contrived, for example, a sermonising ending to *Alton Locke* and *Yeast*, because the real meat lay open for all to see in the body of the books and was ammunition for co-operators, trade unionists, Fabian Socialists and most especially for the various groups of concerned Churchmen who formed a late Christian Socialist revival at the end of the nineteenth century.

Stewart Headlam, whose Cambridge tutor, William Johnson, had been a friend of Maurice and Kingsley, became a Fabian Socialist as well as a clergyman, and founded the Guild of St. Matthew in 1877, a ginger group of Christian radicals. Its first object, as Headlam described it, 'borrows a phrase of Kingsley's ("to justify God to the people") and sums up what was to be our work.'

Men like Charles Gore and Henry Scott Holland followed in the Kingsley-Maurice tradition. Scott Holland had been a student at Balliol under the philosopher T. H. Green, whose favourite authors before he entered Balliol himself as a student under Benjamin Jowett were Maurice, Kingsley and Carlyle.[2] The Christian Social Union, in the first issue of its journal, *The Commonwealth*, dated January 1896, set a quotation from a letter Kingsley wrote to John Bullar in 1857 at the head of its section entitled 'Texts for the Times':

It is my belief that not self-interest, but self-sacrifice, is the only law upon which human society can be grounded with any hope of prosperity and permanence. That self-interest is a law of nature I know well. That it ought to be root law of human society I deny, unless society is to sink down again into a Roman Empire, and a cage of wild beasts. . . . I shall resist it, as I do any other snare of the devil, for if I once believed it I must carry it out. I must give up all which I have learnt most precious concerning political freedom, all of which keeps me content with the world because I look forward to a noble state of humanity.

Cosmo Gordon Lang, a future Archbishop of Canterbury but in the 1880s merely a poor young man in London wondering what place he would ultimately occupy in the Church of England, was attracted by High Church teaching but equally determined to combine this teaching with that of Maurice and Kingsley. In some autobiographical notes dealing with this period of his life, Lang wrote: 'The mention of Kingsley is the mention of the only personality which had so far got a hold of such religious life as I had. I remember reading his life in the dingy little lodgings. . . . Well, that book spoke to me as no living voice ever had, and I remember distinctly closing it with the feeling that had I been good enough, I should have liked to take Orders and witness to the Kingsley ideal of Christianity.'[3]

It was an unavoidable weakness of the Christian Socialists of the 1850s that coming from a middle-class background they tended to patronise the working class without in the least meaning to do so. It was this aspect which has led some later critics to complain that Kingsley's greatest aim was to wash the British working class clean with middle-class soap and water, like Tom the chimney sweep.[4] Children who received the baptismal name of Kingsley because of their parents' admiration for the rector did not always grow up to appreciate the sentiment. Kingsley Martin was named by his father, Basil Martin, a Congregational minister, and a pacifist and socialist who admired Kingsley as 'a great Liberal, a Christian Socialist, a Chartist supporter and a champion of the poor.' Martin's biographer remarks that when he had become editor of the *New Statesman and Nation* he did not share his father's reverence for the man, because, as he understood it, Charles Kingsley had been 'contemptuous about George Eliot and Goethe and got his Cambridge Professorship of Modern History on the strength of his having written three historical novels, none of them "modern", and on the patronage of Queen Victoria, in which he had basked like any sycophantic Balmoral ghillie.'⁵ This quick assessment, which probably reflects the majority opinion of the Left in this country, is as misleading and ill-informed as was Kingsley's judgment of Newman in 1864, although there is a little substance in it.

Kingsley was undoubtedly prejudiced against George Eliot on moral grounds because of her relationship with George Henry Lewes, and he would also class her, as the translator of Strauss and the friend of Herbert Spencer, as a dangerous and influential supporter of the Positivists and atheists. Among the woman novelists of his day Kingsley set Mrs. Gaskell at the head. Her social and religious views were close to those of the Christian Socialists, and she admired his books. Writing to her friend Miss Fox around 1849, Mrs. Gaskell declared, 'I mean to copy you out some lines of my *hero*, Mr. Kingsley.'⁶ When Mrs. Gaskell sent him her life of Charlotte Brontë in 1857 he thanked her for having shown him how he had misjudged Miss Brontë. 'I shall now read carefully and lovingly every word she has written,' he promised. It was particularly pleasing for Mrs. Gaskell when Kingsley praised her novel, *Ruth*, the social realist novel in which Mrs. Gaskell was courageous enough to make her heroine an unmarried mother. Most of her readers wrote in protest, outraged that she should deal with such a theme.

When Mary Russell Mitford, authoress of *Our Village*, moved to Swallowfield, next to Eversley, in 1851, she met Kingsley, who became a good neighbour to her. She wrote: 'Mr. Kingsley took me quite by surprise in his extraordinary fascination. I have never seen a man of letters the least like him. . . . Mr. Kingsley is not only a high-bred gentleman, but has the most charming admixture of softness and gentleness with spirit, manliness and frankness—a frankness quite transparent—and a cordiality that would win any heart.'[7]

As for the belief that it was Queen Victoria who had Kingsley appointed professor, it was in fact the Prince Consort who had done so, and at that time Kingsley had written three extremely contemporary and controversial modern novels dealing with social issues, whilst his first historical novel, *Hypatia*, discussed a Victorian religious debate, but in period dress, rather as Arthur Miller's play, *The Crucible*, took a modern political problem. *Westward Ho!* (which the Macmillan brothers thought was in the 'modern idiom') was Kingsley's other historical novel at the time of his appointment. However, Kingsley Martin was unquestionably right when he spoke of Charles Kingsley as 'basking' in royal favour. The rector's loyal, not to say feudal, views deepened over the years.

In all fairness it should be recognised that Kingsley extended the subject matter of the Victorian novel, and for this he should be given credit as a liberating force. One of the features of the mid-nineteenth-century novelists was their liking for experimentation. Just as the age itself was one of rapidly changing fashions and ideas, with traditional modes of life and thought under challenge from scientific discoveries and inventions, so the writers, particularly those concerned with the 'condition of England', used a variety of forms in which to express themselves. Bulwer Lytton and Kingsley (leaving apart the giants, Thackeray and Dickens) were outstanding as writers who tried their hand at different types of books. In this, as in so much else, Kingsley showed himself a man of his time.

T. H. Huxley saw him as a fellow campaigner in the fight against superstition, and urged him to show up the superstitions of men of science. 'Their name is legion and the exploit would be a telling one. I would do it myself only I think I am already sufficiently isolated and unpopular.'[8] How well Kingsley sympathised with that last heartfelt remark. He was always in the public eye, which was sometimes approving and sometimes disapproving, and his name stands out so that wherever the Christian Socialists of 1848 are briefly referred to it is Kingsley's name that is mentioned.[9]

In writing an account of Kingsley's life from a social point of view, one is bound for reasons of space to omit many of the famous anecdotes. Kingsley in the pulpit, breaking off in mid-sermon to step down and rescue a bruised butterfly. Kingsley the forgetful preacher, leaving his sermon behind in the locked rectory and rushing from the church, to sit despairingly in the churchyard until his practical wife could deal with the crisis. Kingsley the belligerent patriot taking pot-shots at rabbits and wishing they were enemy Russian soldiers on the heights of Alma. Kingsley the humorist, declaring that the Almighty must have had a sense of humour or He would never have created the crab.

A story was handed down from his Cambridge days that faced with the question in a mechanics examination, 'Describe the Common Pump', Kingsley decided to answer with a blithe sketch. He drew an elaborate village scene, with a fine pump on the green opposite the church, and a pompous beadle standing at the side of the pump, keeping back a queue of women and children with buckets and other vessels. The pump was securely padlocked and bore the notice, 'This pump locked during Divine service.' We do not know how the student fared, but apparently the examiner appreciated the wit of the answer so much that he had it framed and hung in his rooms.

There are many stories that illustrate Kingsley's love of nature in all her aspects and especially in her most boisterous moments. Harrison remembered him flinging open the rectory study door on a night of autumn storms and exclaiming, 'What a night! Drenching! This is a night on which you young men can't think or talk too much poetry.' Kingsley was a happy father, patient and tender with his children. 'I wonder if there is so much laughing in any other home in England as in ours,' he said. When Maurice Kingsley heard in the United States of his father's death and his mother's grave illness, he felt as if 'a huge ship had broken up, piece by piece, plank by plank. . . .' In spite of Kingsley's inner doubts and sadness, he gave an impression of strength and optimism to others. Fenton Hort, who became acquainted with the Maurice group at the end of 1849, and was afterwards a friend of Kingsley's, said about him, 'It seems impossible to despair of anything while he is among the living.' To those who knew him at home, Kingsley was also the lover of animals, surrounded by the rectory cats and dogs, protecting the toads that lived year after year in the same safe hole in the rectory lawn, and protecting also a harmless slow-worm that lived in the churchyard, and which the parishioners were forbidden to hurt. Magdalene tradition has it that Kingsley kept a dog in college, which would get up early to accompany him on fishing expeditions. Following John Wesley, Kingsley liked to think there was some provision made for animals in a hereafter.

In his funeral sermon on Kingsley, Dean Stanley said, 'He was what he was, not by virtue of his office, but by virtue of what God made him in himself. He was, we might almost say, a layman in the guise or disguise of a clergyman.'

Kingsley's belief that a working man who improves himself should remain within his class and try to help his fellow workers to elevate themselves sprang from his belief that God had produced a unified pattern for mankind, and so all men were brothers whether they liked it or not. The upper classes had a social responsibility to use their better fortune and privileges for the benefit of others. Co-operation was the obvious path for the future, and decent sanitary conditions would do more than almost anything else to help working people to a healthy, dignified life. Kingsley was one of the great humanitarians of his day, always compassionate, and optimistic to the last even when, as he grew older, he felt the world was becoming worse instead of better. The growing conservatism which he exhibited in his final years does not cancel out the importance of his message that true happiness lay in love and justice for one's fellow-men—'the sure riches, either for a man or for a nation, are not money, but righteousness, love, justice, wisdom.'[10]

If we agree that people need a theme to live for, a goal to strive towards, then Kingsley provided such a spur for many. G. M. Young quotes him as saying, 'I have a certain artistic knack of utterance (nothing but a knack)', but as Young continues, it was 'the knack of uttering what the new age wanted to hear. A

Royal Commission in 1860 asked an undergraduate what books he read at school. "Scott, Dickens, Macaulay, Tennyson; Kingsley of course." '11

In Kingsley's life and work there is much that came to a full flowering in late Victorian England after his death. Some of these ideas seem contradictory—socialism and imperialism, for example. Others do not seem to have any close connection—feminism and sanitary reform. Some have a more obvious link—say science and education. Even his life and reputation show these contradictory flashes, from the days when he was considered a dangerous revolutionary to the years when he had become a national institution. Most of the causes and campaigns he pioneered have become completely accepted as part of the fabric of our society, although if Kingsley were alive it is unlikely he would find much to be complacent about, and among the various causes we might expect him to support, there are—alas—still a number which he would find only too familiar.

A man who has had as much influence on the thought and actions of his fellow men as Kingsley had cannot be lightly disregarded.[12] Much of his humanitarian teaching is in his sermons and lectures, which, although obscure to us, were far-reaching and influential both during and shortly after his death. This is one reason why his reputation has suffered. For one reader today who has dipped into Kingsley's printed lectures and remembers a phrase like 'Human Soot', there are twenty who recall only *Westward Ho!* and the fights with the Spaniards. Kingsley the poet is almost as many-sided as Kingsley the man, and as a consequence although he features in many kinds of poetry anthologies, including the most modern collections, the reader can never anticipate which poem, or even which type of poem, will be the editor's choice.

Had he, perhaps, been more single-minded, more personally ambitious, less sensitive, then with his abundant gifts he might have achieved a higher rank in English literary history or a more important position in the Church of England or a more clearly defined place among popular scientists. But in that case, of course, he would not have been Charles Kingsley, rector of Eversley.

References

Chapter 1

1. Matthew Arnold, for instance, who thought Kingsley too coarse a workman for a poet, was touched by his quite exceptional generosity, unusual from one poet to another, in Arnold's experience. '... I send you an unexpected note from Kingsley, which well shows the generous and affectionate side of his dispositions.' *Letters of Matthew Arnold 1848–1888*, George W. E. Russell. Vol. II (Macmillan, London, 1895) p. 43.
2. She once met Lord Byron at a dance in Norwich.
3. The rectory stood a little distance from the village, its garden sheltered by a high bank, and affording a panoramic view across the valley whose aspect would change dramatically in the sudden shifts of Dartmoor weather. Mrs. Mary Kingsley would steep herself in the beauty of the landscape during her pregnancy, hoping to imprint a love of nature on her unborn child. Today the rectory is a private residence.
4. Kingsley would probably have agreed with Sir Norman Moore in the *Dictionary of National Biography* that if Maurice should be regarded as the holy abbot, then Kingsley was his travelling friar.
5. *F. D. Maurice*, Florence Higham, (C.S.M. Press, London, 1947) p. 142.
6. Kingsley had been impressed by Carlyle's views in his book on Chartism.

Chapter 2

1. After Gerald Kingsley died on active service in the Royal Navy in 1844 Charles had vivid dreams. He wrote to his wife: 'I saw him twice last night in two different dreams—strong and well—and so much grown—and I kissed him and wept over him—and

woke to the ever-lasting No!' *Charles Kingsley. His Letters and Memories of his Life*, Fanny Kingsley Vol. I (C. Kegan Paul, London, 1878) p. 134.

2. *Alton Locke*, Chapter XXXVI.

3. *Charles Kingsley. His Letters and Memories of his Life*, Vol. I, p. 8.

4. Anecdote told by a clergyman friend of Charles Kingsley's father. *Charles Kingsley. His Letters and Memories of his Life*, Vol. I. p. 8.

5. Illustrated by a letter to his nurse, Mrs. Knowles, in collection of National Library of Scotland.

6. *The Dust of Combat*, R. B. Martin (Faber, London, 1959), p. 24.

7. *Hereward the Wake. Prelude. Of the Fens.*

8. *Prose Idylls* (Macmillan, London, 1874) pp. 95–96.

9. *Prose Idylls*, pp. 276, 277.

10. *Prose Idylls*, pp. 291–297.

11. In Mrs. Kingsley's life of her husband, Charles Kingsley's headmaster at the school in Clifton, Bristol is given as the Rev. John Knight. However, records in the Bristol City Library show that he was much more probably the Rev. William Knight, who kept a school at that locality at that time and who, local legend has it, was Kingsley's headmaster.

12. *Charles Kingsley, Christian Socialist and Social Reformer*, M. Kaufmann (Methuen, London, 1892) pp. 13–14.

13. Ibid., Kaufmann quotes from 'The Working-man's Way in the World, being the Autobiography of a Journeyman Printer', pub. 1844.

14. *Sanitary and Social Lectures and Essays*. 'Great Cities and their Influence for Good and Evil,' Charles Kingsley (Macmillan, London, 1889) pp. 188–190.

15. *John Martineau, Pupil of Kingsley*, Violet Martineau (Edward Arnold, London, 1921) p. 12.

16. *Life of J. A. Froude*, Herbert Paul (Pitman, London, 1905) pp. 10–11.

17. In 1841 Derwent Coleridge left Helston to become principal of St. Mark's College, Chelsea, and Johns became head of Helston. Later on, Johns opened his own preparatory school, Winton House, Winchester, where Charles Kingsley's younger son, Grenville went. Kingsley's simple geology book, *Madam How and Lady Why*, was dedicated to Grenville and the boys at Winton House. Johns also wrote popular botany books. His best known book was *Flowers of the Field*, pub. 1856.

18. *Charles Kingsley. Life and Letters*, Mrs. Kingsley, Vol. I, pp. 25–26.

19. Ibid., pp. 36–37.
20. Ibid., Vol. I, p. 149.
21. Ibid., Vol. I, p. 40.

Chapter 3

1. *The Revolution of the Dons*, Sheldon Rothblatt (Faber, London, 1968) p. 43.
2. *Biographical Sketches*, C. Kegan Paul (Kegan Paul Trench & Co., London, 1883) p. 119.
3. *Charles Kingsley. Life and Letters*, Mrs. Kingsley, Vol. I, p. 82.
4. *A Discourse in the Studies of the University*, Adam Sedgwick (Deighton, Cambridge, 1834) p. 8.
5. Ibid., p. 27.
6. *Alton Locke*, 1st edition (Chapman & Hall, London, 1850) pp. 226–228.
7. Ibid., pp. 196–199.
8. *Charles Kingsley. Life and Letters*, Vol. I, p. 58.
9. Ibid., Vol. I, pp. 44–45.
10. The doctrine of the Christian Church which insists on the Trinity: God revealing Himself in Christ and in the Holy Spirit as well as in Himself.
11. The English translator was George Eliot. She received a fee of £20. The translation appeared in 1846.
12. *Charles Kingsley. Life and Letters*, Mrs. Kingsley, Vol. I, pp. 51–52.
13. *From Coleridge to Gore*. B. M. G. Reardon. (Longman, London, 1971) p. 89.
14. *Charles Kingsley, Life and Letters*, Mrs. Kingsley, Vol. I, p. 61.
15. *Yeast*, Charles Kingsley, Chapter I.
16. Ibid., Chapter VI.

Chapter 4

1. *Charles Kingsley. Life and Letters*, Mrs. Kingsley, Vol. I, p. 61.
2. Wellesley was related to the Duke of Wellington, whose family seat was at Strathfieldsaye, near Eversley. Wellesley had been rector at Chelsea previous to Charles Kingsley's father; at this time was rector at Strathfieldsaye; later became Dean of Windsor.

3. Excavations in the early 1970s showed that the church had almost certainly been used for pagan worship before the advent of Christianity to England. Kingsley would have revelled in such a discovery.
4. *Charles Kingsley. Life and Letters*, Mrs. Kingsley, Vol. I, p. 67.
5. Michael Maurice, father of Frederick Denison Maurice, was a Unitarian who had been an assistant to Dr. Joseph Priestley, the Unitarian chemist. Priestley was an enthusiastic supporter of the ideals of the early French revolutionaries, and for this political support Priestley's laboratory was sacked and burned by a reactionary Birmingham mob. Michael Maurice (who became a minister) passed on to his children and to F. D. Maurice in particular, a detestation of sects and parties which in extreme cases could carry out acts of violence. F. D. Maurice left the Unitarians to join the Church of England. He valued harmony and co-operation above all things, and welcomed everyone who was prepared to work with him, irrespective of background or political or religious dogma.
6. *Charles Kingsley. Life and Letters*, Mrs. Kingsley, Vol. I, p. 69.
7. Ibid., Vol. I, p. 71.
8. *Life of Daniel Macmillan*, Thomas Hughes (Macmillan, London) Letter to Rev. D. Watt, August 31, 1842.
9. *Charles Kingsley. Life and Letters*, Mrs. Kingsley, Vol. I, p. 86.
10. *Charles Kingsley. Life and Letters*, Mrs. Kingsley, Vol. I, p. 190.
11. When Kingsley became rector at Eversley he refused to become a magistrate, and refused to go shooting, because of the risk that he might come up against some of his parishioners.
12. *Swing Unmasked: or The Causes of Rural Incendiarism*, E. G. Wakefield, 1831, pp. 9–10.
13. *Yeast*, Charles Kingsley, Chapter XIII.
14. *The Condition of the Working Class in England*, Friedrich Engels, 1844. Quoted pp. 303–304.

Chapter 5

1. *Charles Kingsley. Life and Letters*, Mrs. Kingsley, Vol. I, p. 118.
2. Ibid., Vol. I, pp. 120–121.
3. The 'Tolpuddle martyrs', convicted ten years earlier for trade union activity, had been Dorset men.

4. His brother inherited the title of Duke of Leeds.

5. This simile of the 'bold horseman' was a favourite among Victorians. J. H. Newman used it to describe Hurrell Froude.

6. *Letters of S.G.O.,* ed. Arnold White Griffith (Farran, Okeden & Walsh, London, no date) Introduction p. xx.

7. It is said that the term 'muscular Christian' was first used by T. C. Sandars in the *Saturday Review.* See *Life and Letters of Leslie Stephen,* F. W. Maitland.

8. Kingsley used Sir John Cope as a model to help him with the characterisation of Squire Lavington in *Yeast,* published in 1849.

9. Bramshill remained in the Cope family until the 1930s. Today it is a police training institution run by the Home Office, and the 'fir forest' which Kingsley so admired is exploited by timber and property interests.

10. *Sanitary and Social Lectures and Essays.* Lecture given in 1855. 'Woman's Work in a Country Parish.' Charles Kingsley (Macmillan, London, 1889) p. 5.

11. *Alton Locke,* Charles Kingsley, Chapter I.

12. *Two Years Ago,* Charles Kingsley, Chapter XVII.

13. Maurice followed Coleridge in the view that the Bible was not a book of divinely dictated material but was full of moral enlightenment which seemed to speak directly to a man's moral and emotional being. This was what Coleridge took to be the Holy Spirit. See *From Coleridge to Gore. A Century of Religious Thought in Britain.* Bernard M. G. Reardon (Longman, London, 1971) p. 89.

14. *Charles Kingsley. Life and Letters,* Mrs. Kingsley, Vol. I, p. 133.

15. *John Martineau, Pupil of Kingsley,* Violet Martineau (Edward Arnold, London, 1921) pp. 4–5.

16. *Charles Kingsley. Life and Letters,* Mrs. Kingsley, Vol. I, p. 135.

17. *Miscellanies.* 'Chalk Stream Studies.' Charles Kingsley, Vol. I. (John W. Parker & Son, London, 1859) p. 197.

18. John Pyke Hullah, 1812–1884, became famous as the composer of music for Dickens' opera, *The Village Coquettes.* Hullah was professor of singing at King's College, and became inspector of training schools. He wrote a *History of Modern Music,* and a *Grammar of Vocal Music.* Kingsley's 'Three Fishers' and 'Oh, that we two were Maying' were his most famous songs.

19. *John Keble,* Georgina Battiscombe (Constable, London, 1963) p. 140.

20. *Charles Kingsley. Life and Letters*, Mrs. Kingsley, Vol. I, p. 137.
21. Ibid., Vol. I, pp. 140–141. F. D. Maurice was to take exactly the same point of view after the revolutionary activities of 1848.
22. See letters with T. H. Huxley on occasion of death of Huxley's young son.
23. Maurice had the endearing habit of inviting young friends to breakfast with him. It was the only time of day when he could be free to discuss personal problems, or simply enjoy conversations.
24. *Charles Kingsley. Life and Letters*, Mrs. Kingsley, Vol. I, pp. 153–154. The Education Act of 1870 set up elementary schools throughout the country.
25. Ibid., Vol. I, p. 153.

Chapter 6

1. Maurice's house has since been pulled down. Its site is part of a garden near the President Hotel, Guildford Street.
2. Adult manhood suffrage. Secret ballot. Salaried M.P.s. No property qualification for M.P.s. Equal electoral districts. Annual elections.
3. *Alton Locke*, Charles Kingsley, Chapter X.
4. 'Will you let me introduce you to my friend, Mr. Kingsley. He is deeply in earnest and seems to be obsessed with the idea of doing something with handbills. I think there is hope for this. Will you talk to him about it? He was exceedingly interested in your plans.' *J. M. Ludlow*, N. C. Masterman (Cambridge University Press, 1963) p. 66.
5. In later life Ludlow said he made a distinction between the material aims of Communism and the human aims of socialism.
6. *Charles Kingsley*, Mrs. Kingsley. One-volume edition (Macmillan, London, 1908) p. 62.
7. Julius Hare had been Maurice's tutor at Cambridge. He was a Platonist, and deeply read in German philosophy. Maurice's second wife was Archdeacon Hare's half-sister.
8. *Charles Kingsley*, Mrs. Kingsley, p. 69.
9. Kingsley strongly disapproved of Voltaire, although he thought that Rabelais was a liberating influence.
10. *Charles Kingsley*, Mrs. Kingsley, p. 66.
11. *Charles Kingsley*, Mrs. Kingsley, Vol. I, p. 201.

12. *Charles Kingsley*, Mrs. Kingsley, Vol. I, p. 179.
13. *Charles Kingsley*, Mrs. Kingsley, Vol. I, p. 325.
14. *Alton Locke*, Charles Kingsley, Chapter VI.
15. *Charles Kingsley*, Mrs. Kingsley, Vol. I, p. 182.
16. *Charles Kingsley*, Mrs. Kingsley, Vol. I, pp. 184–185.
17. *Yeast*, Charles Kingsley, Chapter I.
18. *Yeast*, Charles Kingsley, Chapter III.
19. *Yeast*, Charles Kingsley, Chapter VI.
20. *Yeast*, Charles Kingsley, Chapter XVI.
21. *Charles Kingsley*, Mrs. Kingsley, Vol. I, p. 185.

Chapter 7

1. Mansfield would make mesmeric passes at Kingsley's head and send him to sleep. *Dust of Combat*, R. B. Martin, pp. 99–100.
2. Letter to Ludlow about *Alton Locke*. *Charles Kingsley*, Mrs. Kingsley, Vol. I, p. 197.
3. J. A. Froude also thought Kingsley should stick to poetry, where he was so musical. Matthew Arnold acknowledged that Kingsley had talent as a poet, but thought he was 'too coarse a workman' for that medium.
4. When Froude had turned to journalism for a living, and made a name for himself, Exeter College asked his permission to reinstate his name on the college rolls.
5. *Life of Froude*, W. H. Dunn, Vol I (Oxford, 1961–3) p. 77.
6. *Victorian Minds*, Gertrude Himmelfarb (Weidenfeld & Nicolson, London) p. 241.
7. Mrs. Scott's husband was the Rev. A. J. Scott, who became principal of Owens College, Manchester.
8. *Charles Kingsley*, Mrs. Kingsley, Vol. I, p. 355.
9. Preface to *Alton Locke*, Thomas Hughes. Hughes made a mistake. He meant Highgate, not Hampstead. In addition, Hughes sets this meeting down as occurring in 1848, which Mrs. Kingsley copies in her book, but the evidence is very clear that it took place early in 1849.
10. *Biographical Sketches*, C. Kegan Paul, p. 118.
11. Francis Newman, brother to J. H. Newman. Frank Newman was a university professor and a member of the Maurice circle of friends.

12. Mary T. was an Eversley girl.
13. *Charles Kingsley*, Mrs. Kingsley, Vol. I, pp. 205–206.
14. *Charles Kingsley*, C. W. Stubbs (Blackie, London, 1899) pp. 129–131.
15. *Charles Kingsley*, Mrs. Kingsley, Vol. I, p. 207.
16. Maurice insisted upon the name 'Christian Socialist'. It would commit their supporters to the conflict ahead with the unsocial Christians and the unchristian socialists. Ludlow also saw the coming struggle in military metaphor—'I seem to see the skeleton of a great army, the battleground of a holy warfare.'
17. Octavia Hill was to take a similar line with John Ruskin, and succeeded in persuading him to invest money on model dwelling-houses for the poor.
18. *Charles Kingsley*, Mrs. Kingsley, Vol. I, p. 122.
19. *John Martineau, The Pupil of Kingsley*, Violet Martineau, p. 4.
20. Percy Smith, a Balliol man, was at that time Kingsley's curate. He lived in rooms in the village. Kingsley was sometimes driven to engage a curate temporarily when pressure of work or poor health made it advisable.
21. *John Martineau*, etc., Viola Martineau, pp. 5–6.
22. *Charles Kingsley*, Mrs. Kingsley, Vol. I, pp. 226–227.
23. *Charles Kingsley*, Mrs. Kingsley, Vol. I, p. 242.
24. *Alton Locke*, Charles Kingsley, Chapter VIII.
25. *Alton Locke*, Charles Kingsley, Chapter XXI.
26. *Alton Locke*, Charles Kingsley, Chapter XXXV.
27. R. B. Martin in *Dust of Combat* says that Mrs. Kingsley afterwards identified the reviewer as Lord Coleridge. The article accused Kingsley of encouraging profligacy and heresy and Kingsley departed from his usual practice of pretending such reviews did not exist and at once wrote a hot but dignified rebuttal.
28. Karl Marx remarked that Christian Socialism arose from the guilty conscience of the upper classes: 'Christian Socialism is but the holy water with which the priest consecrates the heart-bearning of the aristocrat.' This comment would have more weight if the leading members of the Christian Socialists *had* been aristocrats. Not all were priests.
29. 'Manly' was one of the highest terms of praise that Victorians, whether Christian, atheist, Liberal, Radical or Tory, could use.
30. *Charles Kingsley*, Mrs. Kingsley, Vol. I, pp. 287–288.
31. *The Dust of Combat*, R. B. Martin, p. 129.

Chapter 8

1. R. B. Martin says that Henry Kingsley was prepared for his university entrance by the Rev. Thomas Drosier, rector of Colebrook, Devon. Drosier had also tutored Charles Kingsley at Cambridge. *The Dust of Combat*, R. B. Martin, p. 110.
2. Henry Kingsley was a heavy and compulsive smoker. He died at the age of forty-six of cancer of the tongue.
3. The nunnery at which Kingsley gazed so sentimentally was not the original building, but an eighteenth-century re-erection of the medieval foundation.
4. *The Dust of Combat*, R. B. Martin, p. 132.
5. *Two Years Ago*, Charles Kingsley, Chapter XXIII.
6. *Charles Kingsley*, Mrs. Kingsley, Vol. I, pp. 296–297.
7. The Froudes lived there.
8. *Charles Kingsley*, Mrs. Kingsley. One-volume edition, p. 135.
9. F. D. Maurice was godfather to one of the Tennyson children.
10. Kingsley's 'little sketch' ran to about 140,000 words.
11. *Charles Kingsley*, Mrs. Kingsley, Vol. I, p. 372.
12. This Biblical expression was one of Kingsley's favourites, and he used it often.
13. In 1862 McDougal became a colonial bishop—Bishop of Labuan.
14. Herbert Spencer met Kingsley about this period. He wrote of him: 'He is a capital fellow: I might with propriety say a *jolly* fellow. We met at a picnic. No one would suspect him of being a clergyman. . . . He is evidently a man of immense energy. He seems to have so much steam that he can scarcely sit still. He said that if he could do something whilst asleep, it would be a great gratification.'
15. *Charles Kingsley*, Mrs. Kingsley, Vol. I, pp. 302–303.
16. *Henry Kingsley*, S. M. Ellis (Grant Richards, London, 1931) pp. 33–34.

Chapter 9

1. *Charles Kingsley*, Mrs. Kingsley, Vol. I, p. 404.
2. *A History of the Working Men's College*, J. F. C. Harrison (Routledge & Kegan Paul, London, 1954) p. 18.
3. The father in *Father and Son* by Edmund Gosse. He was a well-known naturalist, whose books were some of the first to popularise

this study. He was also a minister of the fundamentalist sect of the Plymouth Brethren, and he later found it quite impossible to accept any of Darwin's or Lyell's scientific theories about evolution and geology.

4. *Two Years Ago*, Charles Kingsley, Chapter X.
5. *Edinburgh Institution Jubilee Yearbook*. MDCCCXCVII, p. 17.
6. *Notes on Bideford*, W. H. Rogers, Vol. 3. Typescript. Exeter City Library, pp. 78–79.
7. It is now a girls' school run by a Roman Catholic convent.
8. We are reminded of Bernard Shaw's Saint Joan.
9. *John Martineau*, etc., Viola Martineau, p. 22.
10. *John Martineau*, Viola Martineau, p. 27.
11. *Charles Kingsley*, Mrs. Kingsley, Vol. I, p. 444.
12. *John Malcom Ludlow*, N. C. Masterman, p. 153.
13. *Essays*, George Brimley (Macmillan, 1882) p. 299.
14. *The House of Macmillan*, Charles Morgan (Macmillan, 1943) p. 41.
15. *Westward Ho!*, Charles Kingsley, Chapter II.
16. *Westward Ho!*, Chapter IX. Perhaps Kingsley was recalling a one-eyed Chartist called J. J. Bezer, originally a coster-monger, who published the *Christian Socialist* at 183 Fleet Street. His friends called him 'Monops'.
17. *Westward Ho!*, Chapter XIX.
18. *Westward Ho!*, Chapter XX.
19. *Westward Ho!*, Chapter XXVI.
20. *Westward Ho!*, Chapter XXVIII.
21. Both Kingsley and Karl Marx supported the same side in the Crimean war. Kingsley said that the Turks were 'fighting on God's side'. Marx said that the forces of history made the British and French ruling class fight on the side of the enemies of the Tsar.

Chapter 10

1. He was well advised to insert this apology, since his academic critics were always quick to seize upon points which a layman might disregard. Kingsley's lectures on early German history given at Cambridge later were assailed by opponents who went to quite extraordinary lengths to pick holes in the spelling of names.
2. *Charles Kingsley*, Mrs. Kingsley, Vol. I, p. 459.
3. *Charles Kingsley, Christian Socialist and Social Reformer*. M. Kaufmann, pp. 7–8.

4. In *Chartism*, 1840, Carlyle had advised emigration as a remedy for over-crowded cities to a world where 'Canadian Forests stand unfelled, boundless Plains and Prairies unbroken with the plough'.

5. This was a favourite phrase of Macmillan authors, usually applied to those sessions where authors and publishers met in the London office, seated at the famous 'Round Table', to discuss all manner of subjects.

6. *Charles Kingsley*, Mrs Kingsley, Vol. I, p. 475.

7. *Two Years Ago*, Charles Kingsley, Chapter XXI.

8. Quoted in *The Dust of Combat*, R. B. Martin, p. 202.

9. Lord Goderich was a Christian Socialist, and a good deal further to the Left than Maurice or Kingsley. His title embarrassed him, and he begged to be called plain Jack Robinson, by his friends at least. Kingsley, who was made uneasy by certain forms of un-conventionality in dress and manners, insisted on calling him 'My lord'.

10. It had been part of three verses written for Kingsley's niece. The Major, either deliberately or inadvertently, changed the verb from the first version—'Let who can be clever.' It was probably carelessness on Kingsley's part. He was also so rushed that he frequently misquoted, even himself. A chapter heading in *Westward Ho!* misquotes Shakespeare, and of course his carelessness in misquoting Dr. Newman in 1864 led him woefully astray.

11. *Two Years Ago*, Charles Kingsley, Chapter XI.

12. *Charles Kingsley*, Mrs. Kingsley, Vol. II, p. 75.

13. *Richard Buckley Litchfield*, By his Wife (Cambridge, 1910) pp. 247–248.

14. *Charles Kingsley, Novelist*, J. A. Marriott (Preface, Judge Hughes) (Blackwell, Oxford, 1892).

15. *Mary Hughes*, Rosa Hobhouse (Rockcliffe, London, 1949) pp. 60–61.

16. Tom Hughes wrote that only Ludlow, besides his wife, had seen a word of the manuscript, which seems to contradict his daughter's recollection—unless Kingsley saw the book in such an embryonic state that Hughes did not consider this worth mentioning.

17. *House of Macmillan*, Charles Morgan, p. 47.

18. *John Martineau*, etc., Viola Martineau, p. 46.

19. *Charles Kingsley and the Christian Socialist Movement*, C. W. Stubbs (Blackie, London, 1899) p. 30.

20. *Charles Kingsley*, Mrs. Kingsley, Vol. II, p. 60.

21. W. E. Forster was to become education minister in Gladstone's first government.

Chapter 11

1. *Henry Kingsley*, S. M. Ellis (Grant Richards, London, 1931) pp. 47–48.
2. *Charles Kingsley, Novelist*, J. A. Marriot.
3. *Charles Kingsley*, Mrs. Kingsley, Vol. II, p. 112.
4. *Charles Kingsley*, Mrs. Kingsley, Vol. II, p. 171. In 1870, writing to John Stuart Mill about women's rights, Kingsley used Huxley to support his case: 'I quote my dear friend Huxley's words, with full agreement, though giving them a broader sense than he would as yet—"to reconstruct society according to science"....'
5. *John Martineau*, etc., Violet Martineau, pp. 53–54.
6. *Charles Kingsley*, Mrs. Kingsley, Vol. II, p. 105.
7. *Charles Kingsley*, Mrs. Kingsley, Vol. II, p. 107.
8. *Charles Kingsley*, Mrs Kingsley. One-volume edition, p. 241.
9. Quoted in *The Theory of the Novel in England, 1850–1870*, Richard Stang (Routledge and Kegan Paul, London, 1959) pp. 55–56.
10. *Charles Kingsley*, Mrs. Kingsley, Vol. II, p. 120.
11. Goldwin Smith was a highly respected professor with an international reputation. Queen Victoria called him 'a great democrat'.
12. Some men who refused to join a trade union in Sheffield were murdered by union officials, as an example. Kingsley did not condone acts of illegality and violence, and so blamed the union officials for these murders, but in fairness he could understand how the unions felt pushed into increasingly violent measures by the repressive attitude of the government. 'I and others have been seeing with dread the growing inclination of the governing classes to put down these trades unions, &, by strong measures. What am I to say when I see the working men themselves, in the face of this danger, justifying the measures of those who wish to be hard on them?' (1862).
13. *Water of Life, and other Sermons*, Macmillan.
14. *House of Macmillan*, Charles Morgan, p. 65.

Chapter 12

1. *Charles Kingsley*, Mrs. Kingsley, Vol. II, p. 155.
2. *Charles Kingsley*, Mrs. Kingsley, Vol. II, p. 157.
3. Sir John Lubbock was well-known as an amateur scientist. One of the Maurice group, he later became Lord Avebury. He was the prime mover in getting Bank Holidays instituted.
4. Passage in Sir Charles Fox Bunbury's diary, dated November 1859.
5. *The Life of Sir Charles J. E. Bunbury*, Mrs. Henry Lyell, Vol. II. (John Murray, London, 1906) pp. 150–151.
6. Lord Chelsea became the fourth Earl Cadogan. Lady Chelsea was the daughter of the Hon. and Rev. Gerald Wellesley, a rector of Chelsea before Mr. Kingsley was appointed to that living, and a relative of the Duke of Wellington. The Kingsleys were distantly related to the Cadogans.
7. *Henry Kingsley*, S. M. Ellis, pp. 121–122.
8. *John Malcolm Ludlow*, N. C. Masterman, p. 159.
9. The parent of a prospective student at Wellington College, seeing Kingsley officiating in the chapel but not knowing who he was, almost withdrew his son's application because, he complained, the unknown clergyman was 'too High'.
10. Newman's Latin inscription for his tomb, translated, reads, 'From shadows and images into truth.'
11. Kingsley knew Francis Newman through the Maurice circle of friends. Kingsley and Dr. Newman never met.
12. *Charles Kingsley*, Mrs. Kingsley, Vol. II, p. 193.
13. *Charles Kingsley*, Mrs. Kingsley, Vol. II, p. 199.
14. *Cardinal Newman*, Richard H. Hutton (Methuen, London, 1891) p. 226.
15. *Charles Kingsley and his Ideas*, Guy Kendall (Hutchinson, London) p. 157. Footnote reference to *Life of F. J. A. Hort*, ii. p. 424.
16. *Short Studies on Great Subjects. IV.*, A. J. Froude (London, 1899) pp. 326–328.
   An interesting account is given in *Apologia pro Charles Kingsley*, G. Egner (Sheed & Ward, London, 1969). Egner agreed with Kingsley's point that to let conclusions be determined even slightly by reasons of piety is to undermine the principles upon which historical truth rests.
17. *The Recollections of Geoffry Hamlyn*, Henry Kingsley (Ward Lock & Co., London, no date) pp. 248–249.

Chapter 13

1. Martineau had recently married a Miss Mabel Adeane, a cousin of Dean A. P. Stanley, to the pleasure of all the Kingsleys except young Mary, who had hoped John Martineau would wait for her to grow up.
2. *Life of Martineau, etc.*, Viola Martineau, p. 104.
3. F. W. Maitland says it was almost certainly Leslie Stephen who originated the phrase which said that the creed of the 'muscular Christians' was that they should 'fear God and walk a thousand miles in a thousand hours'. *Life of Leslie Stephen*, F. W. Maitland (Duckworth, London, 1906) p. 138.
4. *Life of Sir Charles Bunbury*, Mrs. Henry Lyell, Vol. II, p. 196.
5. Today's Hawaian Islands.
6. Quoted in *The Life of John Stuart Mill*, M. St. J. Packe (Secker & Warburg, London, 1954) p. 469.
7. *Letters of Queen Victoria, 2nd series*, ed. G. E. Buckle, Vol. I (John Murray, London, 1926) pp. 285–286.
8. *Letters of Queen Victoria, 2nd series*, ed. G. E. Buckle, Vol. I, p. 289.
9. *Henry Kingsley*, S. M. Ellis, pp. 139–140.
10. Lord Palmerston, Whig, 1862. Lord Derby, Tory, 1866. W. E. Gladstone, Liberal, 1868. Benjamin Disraeli, Tory, 1875.
11. He lived in virtual obscurity until his death in 1901.
12. For old times' sake, however, Ludlow still kept a portrait of Kingsley on the wall of his study.
13. The 'dead lad' in the quotation was a brother of Hereward's, killed by the Normans.
14. *Hereward the Wake*, Charles Kingsley (Macmillan, London, 1907 ed.) pp. 182–183.
15. *Hereward the Wake*, Charles Kingsley, pp. 316–317.
16. On the whole, Freeman's friends were in the opposite camp to the Christian Socialists. Ludlow and Ruskin especially were frequently victims of Freeman's sarcasm.
17. *Madam How and Lady Why*, Charles Kingsley (Macmillan, 1902 ed.) pp. 83–85.
18. *Charles Kingsley*, Mrs. Kingsley, Vol. II, pp. 323–324.

Chapter 14

1. *At Last*, Charles Kingsley (Macmillan, London, 1871) pp. 26–27.
2. *At Last*, Charles Kingsley, pp. 96–97.
3. *Charles Kingsley*, Mrs. Kingsley, Vol. II, p. 312.
4. *The Formation of The Chester Society of Natural Science, Literature and Art, and an Epitome of its subsequent history*, J. D. Siddall (printed privately, Chester, 1911) p. 11.
5. *Formation of the Chester Society etc.*, J. D. Siddall, p. 20.
6. *Town Geology*, Charles Kingsley (Strahan & Co., London, 1872) pp. 147–148 and 159–160.
7. An echo perhaps of Milton: 'This is true liberty when freeborn men, having to advise the public, may speak free.'
8. *Charles Kingsley and His Ideas*, Guy Kendall, p. 100.
9. *Charles Kingsley*, Mrs. Kingsley. One-volume edition, p. 319.
10. *Life of Octavia Hill*, Edmund Maurice (Macmillan, London, 1913) pp. 284–285.
11. *Charles Kingsley*, Mrs. Kingsley. One-volume edition, pp. 319–320.

Chapter 15

1. *Formation of Chester Society*, J. D. Siddall, pp. 28–29.
   Dean Wellesley had contributed greatly to seeing that his friend Charles Kingsley obtained the Westminster stall, and of course he had the steadfast support of Queen Victoria in this aim. On March 19, 1873 Wellesley wrote to the Queen: 'The Dean of Windsor's humble duty to your Majesty. He has seen Mr. Gladstone. He has given up Dr. Miller, and will recommend Kingsley to your Majesty for the stall at Westminster. He behaved very well about it.' *The Letters of Queen Victoria*, ed. G. E. Buckle, Vol. II (John Murray, London, 1926) p. 248.
2. *Charles Kingsley*, Mrs. Kingsley. One-volume edition, p. 326.
3. *Charles Kingsley*, Mrs. Kingsley, Vol. II, pp. 415–416.
4. *Henry Kingsley*, S. M. Ellis (Grant Richards, London, 1931) p. 106.
5. Charles and Fanny Kingsley spell this Lotus. According to R. B. Martin, the Lotos Club, a short-lived society, was established as a more liberal literary rival to the older, more conservative Century Association. It was to the members of the Lotos Club that Kingsley said, 'Long life is the last thing I desire.'

6. *Charles Kingsley's American Notes*. Letters from a lecture tour 1874. Ed. R. B. Martin (Princeton, 1958) pp. 10–11.

7. His old school friend had taken a house in Eversley. He set up a preparatory school, and saw a good deal of the Kingsleys. George Curzon, the future Viceroy, was a pupil at Cowley Powles' school, and reported favourably on the fruit cake provided by Fanny Kingsley when some of the pupils took Sunday afternoon tea at Eversley Rectory.

   The purpose of this loan was not disclosed by either of the Kingsleys, but it might well have been to cover the steamship fares. Kingsley of course hoped to recoup all his expenses through lecture fees.

8. Nothing suggests that these fond paternal hopes were realised. Grenville eventually emigrated to Australia, became a sheep-farmer and died at the age of forty.

9. Harrison became rector of Clovelly, so Mrs. Mary Harrison lived in the house where her father, uncles and aunt had grown up. She became a well-known author and literary figure under the pen-name of Lucas Malet.

10. *Charles Kingsley*, Mrs. Kingsley, Vol. II, p. 446.

11. *Charles Kingsley's American Notes*, ed. R. B. Martin, p. 39.

12. This is an interesting selection which reveals Kingsley's personal judgments.

13. *Lectures delivered in America*, Charles Kingsley (Longmans Green & Co., London, 1875) pp. 25–27. This book was compiled by Mrs. Kingsley and dedicated to Cyrus Field and J. A. C. Gray and all the other 'valued American friends who welcomed my husband to their great country'.

14. This is the last letter which has survived from the American tour. The wish to see his grandchildren was never fulfilled. A child was born to Maurice and Marie Kingsley in the United States at the time when Kingsley was ill. The child did not live and Kingsley was not even told about it.

15. A mighty start to this would be made in the following year by Disraeli's government, but Kingsley died before he saw this legislation go through.

16. He stayed with Lord John Thynne in Bedfordshire. Dr. George Kingsley had undertaken literary work for this family.

17. Mrs. Kingsley's account of their last meeting.

18. A similar spontaneous wave of sympathy and appreciation had followed Maurice's death in 1872.

Chapter 16

1. She outlived Henry Kingsley, who died in 1876. Both Dr. George Kingsley and his wife also died in 1892.
2. Scott Holland's career was a witness to his respect for the Maurician tradition. He founded Maurice Hostel, in Hoxton, named after Maurice.
3. *Cosmo Gordon Lang*, J. A. Lockhart (Hodder & Stoughton, London, 1949) p. 74.
4. *The Christian Socialist Revival 1877–1914*, Peter d'A. Jones (Princeton University Press, 1968) p. 458.
5. *Kingsley Martin*, C. H. Rolph (Victor Gollancz, London, 1973) p. 32.
6. *Mrs. Gaskell and Her Friends*, Elizabeth Haldane (Hodder & Stoughton, London, 1930) p. 75.
7. *Mary Russell Mitford*, Vera Watson (Evans, London) p. 288.
8. *T. H. Huxley*, C. Bibby (Watts, London, 1959) p. 78.
9. 'In 1848 itself, a group of Englishmen, including Charles Kingsley, proclaimed themselves "Christian Socialists", with economic cooperation rather than competition as their basic idea.' *Socialism in the New Society*, Douglas Jay (Longmans, London, 1962) p. 4.
10. *Human Dignity and the Great Victorians*, Bernard N. Schilling (Archon Books, New York, 1972) p. 121.
11. *Daylight and Champaign*, G. M. Young (Jonathan Cape, London, 1937) p. 171.
12. In the August 1896 number of *The Commonwealth*, replying to a German comment that '*Alton Locke* was a wonderful book, but was anybody the better for it, or for Kingsley's movement?' the editor retorted: 'We should have thought that of all the Englishmen of our era, no one has had a greater influence than Kingsley; and that the new spirit of the younger generation is mainly due to the fact that they have unconsciously imbibed the spirit of Kingsley and Tom Hughes from the days of their impressionable boyhood.'

13

Authorities consulted

The two books about Charles Kingsley, compiled by his widow, remain the main source of printed information about the rector. There are various collections of letters, notably in Cambridge University Library and in Princeton University Library. The four most interesting modern volumes dealing with Kingsley are those by Mrs. Margaret Thorp, Guy Kendall, Dame Una Pope-Hennessy and R. B. Martin. I should like to acknowledge an especial debt to all these authors. In addition, I have drawn greatly upon material in the Working Men's College, London, to illustrate Kingsley's close connection with the Christian Socialist movement in all its aspects. In writing the book I discovered that it is impossible to read too widely for the literary and historical background, and that luck and an obsessive interest in one's subject may also strangely guide one's steps. Apart from the usual standard reference books, the following are those which I have chiefly consulted:

BIBBY, C., *T. H. Huxley* (Watts, London, 1959)

BRIMLEY, GEORGE, *Essays* (Macmillan, London, 1882)

BROSE, O. J., *Frederick Denison Maurice. Rebellious Conformist* (Ohio University Press, 1971)

BROWN, W. HENRY, *Charles Kingsley. The Work and Influence of Parson Lot* (Fisher Unwin, London, 1924)

BUCKLE, G. E. ed., *The Letters of Queen Victoria* (John Murray, London, 1926)

CARLYLE, THOMAS & OTHERS, *From a Victorian Post-Bag* (Peter Davies, London, 1921)

CLARK, R. W., *The Huxleys* (Heinemann, London, 1968)

COURTENAY, JANET E., *Freethinkers of the Nineteenth Century* (Chapman & Hall, London, 1920)

DUNN, W. H., *James Anthony Froude 1857–1894* (Clarendon Press, Oxford, 1963)

EGNER, G., *Apologia pro Charles Kingsley* (Sheed and Ward, London, 1969)

ELLIS, S. M., *Henry Kingsley, 1830–1876. Towards a Vindication* (Grant Richards, London, 1931)

FABER, GEOFFREY, *Oxford Apostles. A Character Study of the Oxford Movement* (Faber & Faber, London, 1933)

GOSSE, EDMUND, *Father and Son* (Heinemann, London, 1907)

GRAVES, CHARLES L., *Life and Letters of Alexander Macmillan* (Macmillan, London, 1910)

GREG, W. R., *Literary and Social Judgments* (N. Trubner & Co., London, 1869)

HALDANE, ELIZABETH, *Mrs. Gaskell and her Friends* (Hodder & Stoughton, London, 1930)

HARRISON, J. F. C., *A History of the Working Men's College* (Routledge & Kegan Paul, London, 1954)

HIGHAM, FLORENCE, *Frederick Denison Maurice* (S.C.M. Press, London, 1947)

HIMMELFARB, GERTRUDE, *Victorian Minds* (Weidenfeld & Nicolson, London, 1968)

HOBHOUSE, ROSA, *Mary Hughes* (Rockcliffe, London, 1949)

HUDSON, D., *Munby, Man of Two Worlds* (John Murray, London, 1972)

HUGHES, THOMAS, *Charles Kingsley* (*Macmillan's Magazine*, March, 1877)

HUGHES, THOMAS, *Memoir of Daniel Macmillan* (Macmillan, London, 1882)

HUTTON, RICHARD H., *Cardinal Newman* (Methuen, London, 1891)

JONES, PETER D'A., *The Christian Socialist Revival. 1877–1914* (Princeton University Press, 1968)

LITCHFIELD, RICHARD BUCKLEY. By his Wife. Cambridge 1910

LOCKHART, J. A., *Cosmo Gordon Lang* (Hodder & Stoughton, London, 1949)

LYELL, MRS. HENRY, *Life and Diary of Sir Charles J. Fox Bunbury* (John Murray, London, 1906)

KAUFMAN, M., *Charles Kingsley. Christian Socialist and Social Reformer* (Methuen, London, 1892)

KENDALL, GUY, *Charles Kingsley and His Ideas* (Hutchinson, London, 1947)

KINGSLEY, MRS. FANNY, *Charles Kingsley. Lectures delivered in America* (Longman Green & Co, London, 1875)

KINGSLEY, MRS. FANNY. ed., *Charles Kingsley. His Letters and Memories of his Life* (C. Kegan Paul, London, 1878)

MACK, E. C. and ARMYTAGE, W. H. G., *Thomas Hughes* (Ernest Benn, London, 1952)

MAITLAND, F. W., *The Life and Letters of Leslie Stephen* (Duckworth, London, 1906)

MARRIOT, J. A., *Charles Kingsley, novelist* (Blackwell, Oxford, 1892)

MARTIN, R. B., *The Dust of Combat* (Faber & Faber, London, 1959)

MARTIN, R. B. ed., *Charles Kingsley's Notes: from a Lecture Tour. 1874* (Princeton University Press, 1958)

MASTERMAN, C. F. G., *Leaders of the Church. Frederick Denison Maurice* (Mowbray & Co, London, 1907)

MASTERMAN, N. C., *John Malcolm Ludlow* (Cambridge University Press, 1963)

MARTINEAU, VIOLET, *John Martineau: the Pupil of Kingsley* (Edward Arnold, London, 1921)

MAURICE, EDMUND, *The Life of Octavia Hill* (Macmillan, London, 1913)

MAYOR, STEPHEN, *The Churches and the Labour Movement* (Independent Press, London, 1967)

MORGAN, CHARLES, *The House of Macmillan* (Macmillan, London, 1943)

MORRIS, W. D., *The Christian Origins of Social Revolt* (Allen & Unwin, London, 1949)

MURRAY, R. H., *Studies in the English Social and Political Thinkers of the 19th Century.* Vol. I (Heffer, Cambridge, 1929)

NEWMAN, JOHN HENRY, *Apologia pro Vita Sua*, with an introduction by Maisie Ward (Sheed and Ward, London, 1946)

NEWSOME, DAVID, *Godliness and Good Learning* (John Murray, London, 1961)

NEWSOME, DAVID, *The Parting of Friends* (John Murray, London, 1966)

PACKE, M. ST. J., *The Life of John Stuart Mill* (Secker & Warburg, London, 1954)

PAUL, C. KEGAN, *Biographical Sketches* (Kegan Paul Trench & Co., London, 1883)

PAUL, HERBERT, *The Life of Froude* (Sir Isaac Pitman & Son, London, 1905)

POPE-HENNESSY, UNA, *Canon Charles Kingsley* (Chatto and Windus, London, 1948)

RAVEN, CHARLES E., *Christian Socialism. 1848–1854* (Macmillan, London, 1920)

REARDON, B. M. G., *From Coleridge to Gore. A Century of Religious Thought in Britain* (Longman, London, 1971)

ROGERS, W. H., *Notes on Bideford*. Vol. 3. Exeter City Library

ROLPH, C. H., *Kingsley Martin* (Gollancz, London, 1973)

ROTHBLATT, SHELDON, *The Revolution of the Dons* (Faber & Faber, London, 1968)

SCHILLING, BERNARD N., *Human Dignity and the Great Victorians* (Archon Books, New York, 1972)

SEDGWICK, ADAM, *A Discourse in the Studies of the University* (Deighton, Cambridge, 1834)

SIDDALL, J. D., *The Formation of The Chester Society of Natural Science, Literature and Art, and an Epitome of its subsequent history* (Printed privately, Chester, 1911)

STANG, R., *The Theory of the Novel in England, 1850–1870* (Routledge & Kegan Paul, London, 1965)

STUBBS, C. W., *Charles Kingsley and the Christian Social Movement* (Blackie & Son, London, 1899)

THORP, MARGARET FARRAND, *Charles Kingsley, 1819–1875* (Princeton University Press, 1937)

WARD, WILFRED, *The Life of John Henry, Cardinal Newman* (Longmans Green, London, 1912)

WHITE, ARNOLD., ed., *Letters of S.G.O.* (Griffiths, Farrar, Okeden & Walsh, London, no date)

YOUNG, G. M., *Daylight and Champaign* (Jonathan Cape, London, 1937)

Index

DATE DUE

GAYLORD   PRINTED IN U.S.A.